PLATO AND PLATONISM

STUDIES IN PHILOSOPHY
AND THE HISTORY OF PHILOSOPHY

General Editor: Jude P. Dougherty

Studies in Philosophy
and the History of Philosophy Volume 33

Plato and Platonism

edited by Johannes M. Van Ophuijsen

THE CATHOLIC UNIVERSITY OF AMERICA PRESS
Washington, D.C.

Printed in the United States of America

The paper used in this publication meets the minimum requirements of American National Standards for Information Science—Permanence of Paper for Printed Library Materials, ANSI Z39.48-1984.

∞

LIBRARY OF CONGRESS CATALOGING-IN-PUBLICATION DATA
Plato and Platonism / edited by Johannes M. van Ophuijsen.
p. cm. — (Studies in philosophy and the history of philosophy ; v. 33)
"Closely based on lectures given at the Catholic University of America in the fall semester of 1993-94 in the Frank J. Matchette Foundation lecture series under the common tilte 'Plato and Platonism'"—Pref.
Includes bibliographical references and indexes.
1. Plato. I. Ophuijsen, Johannes M. van 1953– . II. Series B21.S78 vol.33.
[B395]
184—dc21
98-5597
ISBN: 978-0-8132-0910-2 (cloth : alk. paper) ISBN: 978-0-8132-2757-3 (Paperback)

Contents

Preface

The following essays are all more or less closely based on lectures given at The Catholic University of America in the Fall semester of 1993–1994 in the Frank J. Matchette Foundation Lecture Series under the common title "Plato and Platonism." I take pleasure in thanking the dean of the School of Philosophy at The Catholic University of America, Dr. Jude P. Dougherty, for his invitation to edit them for publication in the series of *Studies in Philosophy and the History of Philosophy* of which he is the editor; the director of The Catholic University of America Press, Dr. David J. McGonagle, for undertaking to produce the volume; and Dr. Charles J. Griswold, Jr. for his sound advice and friendly interest in the project.

American University of Beirut
May 1996

PLATO AND PLATONISM

Introduction

JOHANNES M. VAN OPHUIJSEN

I

The following chapters form a series of self-contained investigations; they were not originally conceived so as to add up to a whole that is more than the sum of its parts. They have been written from different positions and perspectives, and their collection here into one volume expresses a conviction that interpreting Plato is not the preserve of one school—but, then, this shared conviction in itself is a unifying factor. It presupposes that to shop around widely for philosophical illumination is not necessarily to be less than rigorous in method. Plato's text itself, more than any modern party line, has to provide the tests and measures for validity in what is a common pursuit.

One qualification for this pursuit is an awareness of the limits of formalization, of the dangers of reducing selected ingredients in these texts to a spuriously definite system. This might be expressed positively as a sensitiveness to the "literary" dimension, if we guard against misunderstanding that overworked epithet. We should understand it in the preromantic, wide sense in which Augustine, Montaigne, or Hume are part of literature, and not accept a false dichotomy between Plato the literary author and Plato the philosophical author, as if he sometimes indulged in verbal flourishes that do not serve his purposes as a philosopher. The required sensitivity shows itself rather in the application to one particularly rich and complex author, of the rules of all interpretation: a sustained effort to extract coherent sense from the sum of all the features of the text, to attribute the highest historically plausible degree of intentionality to the author's every move.[1]

1. Ideally, according to Gadamer (1980, p. 159), "We must establish the philosophical significance of the scene, the setting of the dialogues, of the relationship of the speaker to what is spoken, of evolving meaning as it unfolds in live discussion. And we must apply what we can learn thereby to understanding the philosophical questions which Plato puts to us." Unfortunately there is a danger, if not of circularity, then of explaining *obscurum per obscurius*: it is even less clear how we can arrive at an agreement over such imponderables than it is with the more narrowly argumentative ingredients of the dialogues.

A related qualification is respect for the evidence of Plato's Greek. In a recent volume on Plato in an authoritative series, the Greek for 'thinking' is given as *dianoein*.[2] It might seem niggling to remark that the standard form of the verb is the middle voice *dianoeisthai* (διανοεῖσθαι), but the remark is seen to have a point in light of a general difference in Greek between active and middle forms concerning their relation to an object. The active form of the simple verb *noein* implies a distinct external object[3] in a way that *dianoeisthai* does not; it is by no means an accident that what we translate as "the intelligible" is called *noêton* (νοητόν), not *dianoêton* (διανοητόν).[4] Fidelity to such apparent details is not just a matter of historical accuracy—which should of course be motive enough by itself. More important from a philosophical point of view, we should not take it for granted that reading Plato in translation, with no more Greek than is required for spotting the odd technical term in a parallel text, involves no greater risks of distortion than reading Aquinas without Latin or Kant without German.[5]

From the age of Boethius's translations of Aristotle's Organon into Latin and of the translations into Syriac it is possible to trace, if not one continuous tradition, then at least a system of confluences and diffusions through which the philosophical vocabulary of the modern vernaculars derives from its Greek origin; its terms relate to each other so as to constitute structures in semantic fields, and they present family resemblances that would put a heavy burden of proof on any upholder of radical intranslatability. Now it is true that Boethius lived and died before the Academy was closed, and that those of his contemporaries whom we now characterize as Neoplatonists considered themselves to be Platonists, and shared a Greek idiom that, while not identical with Plato's, enabled all to read his oeuvre (and some spurious accretions) and communicate their interpretation of it. It might be argued that this is enough to extend the continuity of our tradition back to Plato himself. Certainly, the Platonic tradition in antiquity, and well beyond it, is distinguished by a remarkable *sense* of continuity; indeed, it is constituted as much by this sense of continuity as by its actually enduring distinctive

2. Kraut (1992); Mueller (1992, p. 184).

3. And a distinct subject in the form of an active mind or intellect (νοῦς) as well? One context from which one might try to extract grammatical information relevant to such a momentous question is Aristotle *De an.* 1. 4 408 b 24–27.

4. A rather different instance of the significance of the distinction between active and middle "voice" is provided by (διαλέγεσθαι), the verb underlying the noun *'dialectic'*. See Stenzel (1931, pp. 189–90) and cf. Stenzel (1921, pp. 152ff.), quoted by Cassirer (1955, p. 258n 170).

5. For examples of connotations of Plato's wording which tend to get lost in translation, see, e.g., Pritzl at 69–73 below.

features. But it would be begging the question to assume that the Platonists of later antiquity had better access to Plato than we do. This tacit assumption for many centuries sustained the monolithic Neoplatonic interpretation of Plato, discredited only in the nineteenth century to be replaced with histories of a development from disciple of Socrates via dogmatic realist into a later Plato who is harder to pin down and even more variously assessed. More recently there seems to be an increasing willingness to acknowledge a considerable amount of continuity[6] both within Plato's thought and between his own thought and that of his followers under the Roman Empire. Few would now resuscitate a Plato who spent half a century teasing his readers by partially unveiling without ever changing his mind;[7] but a Plato who goes through an organic evolution[8] is beginning to seem more convincing, because philosophically more interesting, than one conveniently divided into phases for moderns to choose between according to their own philosophical allegiance.[9] At the same time, those ancient Platonists who were unaware of any major change in Plato's basic views are being taken more seriously as philosophers, and this by itself suggests that justice should be done to the ancient reception of Plato in a way that is philosophically coherent as well as historically plausible. From this perspective, the middle way of a story of gradual unfolding is not so much a credible result as the most promising working hypothesis with a view to making maximum sense both of Plato's own words and of the mass of secondary evidence for his doctrines that has survived from antiquity. From the same point of view, it is natural to include in one volume, under the label "Platonism," studies of the Platonists of later antiquity as well as of their intellectual ancestor: the two subjects can illuminate and even overlap with each other.

6. For the notion of continuity within an "evolutionist" perspective here invoked, see Robinson (1953, pp. 3–4): "There is a continuity and also an identity between the Law of Contradiction as it appears in *Republic* IV and as it appears in *Principia Mathematica*; there is also a difference." The concept of identity seems to me less promising here than that of family resemblance, but the recognition of an intertwining (συμπλοκή) between sameness and difference remains basic.

7. Those who do so tend to make much of Plato's alleged "unwritten doctrine." For a powerful exposition of how the reported doctrine is implicit within the written works from the early period on, see Gadamer (1980, pp. 124–55, 157–58). Cf. M. Miller, below.

8. An evolution that is part of the larger "evolution of ideas, transcending the lives of individuals" that furnishes the "guiding assumption about the history of human thought" of Robinson (1953, pp. vi, 6), who extends the metaphor to include "sudden leaps or 'mutations'" and "very gradual 'variations.'" On such a hypothesis developments in Plato's thought may suggest a tentative relative chronology rather than the other way round. For an example, see F. Miller below.

9. Cf. De Rijk (1986, p. 184); as quoted p. 311, n. 102 below; Meinwald (1992, pp. 389–91).

Even if it is justified to use the ancient Platonist tradition discriminatingly in interpreting Plato, and if our modern philosophical vocabulary is directly connected with this tradition, still Plato's intentions cannot be appreciated on the basis of a method that consists of projecting this vocabulary back upon him and translating it into his Greek. The disturbing question involved in our communication with Plato is that of what was won, what was lost, and what was radically changed when, and by the fact that, within the span of two generations, Plato and Aristotle defined philosophy as their intellectual posterity in the West and the Middle East has known it. This problem in its wider philosophical implications may be associated with the name of Heidegger, but it enters into any approach to Plato's thought that recognizes the challenge to come to terms with its strangeness and newness, not to reduce it to the familiar and common. For this purpose it is less useful to know how Plato anticipates later thought than how he differs from earlier thought. For instance, what Plato meant to convey about the notion that is given in translation as 'the fine', 'the fair', 'the beautiful', or 'beauty' (τὸ καλόν) clearly has a bearing on subsequent discussions of value, but to do justice to his meaning we need to know how the Greek notion differs from our modern conceptions of beauty even before Plato begins to reform it.[10] The risk of misunderstanding him is no smaller in cases where we are not, as here, alerted to it by discrepancies between the modern term and the Greek one as reinterpreted by Plato. The loss of all but fragments of the works of his predecessors and contemporaries should make us reluctant to pronounce on Plato's stature in comparison with these forebears and fellows as a matter of historiographical justice.[11] But what we have shows him, against a background of pre-Socratic speculation and sophistic intellectual acrobatics, and in the context of other claimants to the heritage of Socrates and the title of philosopher, as part of a fervent activity of *donner un sens plus pur aux mots de la tribu*: of redefining the conceptual apparatus embedded in the ordinary language of the day—the only language that he knew. A disproportionate exposure of those of his accomplishments that have been adopted by posterity is unavoidable, but we have no right to increase the evil beyond what is necessary by assimilating protophilosophical Greek concepts to philosophical modern ones. Not only

10. Cf. M. Frede (1987, p. 3): "What [Plato] has to say about perception has to be understood against the background of the ordinary use of the verb 'aisthanesthai' and against the background of the philosophical intentions with which Plato narrows down this common use." Also see Frede (1987, p. 8).

11. As distinct from an assessment of his greatness as a philosopher—an assessment that might aspire to transcend the contingencies of history, though it must be relative to a philosophical standard which in turn is not outside space and time.

we, but the philosopher-scholars of later antiquity, were already, in Oscar Wilde's phrase, "divided by a common language" from an *auctor intellectualis* whose achievement is obscured precisely by its overwhelming impact.

In order to counter the "lumping" tendency to understand Plato in the terms in which he has been posthumously assimilated and appropriated, it is hardly enough to relate him to his predecessors and contemporaries as represented by translations whose reliability as bridges across a conceptual divide is equally uncertain. An indispensable check is analysis of Plato's Greek vocabulary in its internal semantic relationships as well as its ramifications into medical, scientific, historiographical, legal, and other idioms, as well as the more traditional vocabulary of reflective and moralizing verse and wisdom literature.[12] This involves more than exploiting a few more-or-less well-supported ancient or modern etymologies of isolated words, such as those for *knowledge* (ἐπιστήμη) or *truth* (ἀλήθεια). It calls for contributions from lexicographers, linguists, and philologists who between them, as in other disciplines dealing with objects that are historical, human, and individual, apply tools ranging from the very concrete to a fairly abstract level, in this case represented by traditional exegesis and by semantic analysis,[13] respectively.

To insist on such a collaborative effort is to question the opposition between what are called "philosophical" and "philolological" interpretation. In a popular introduction to Plato, a style of interpretation is described that consists in proposing statements in a modern language as possible meanings of a passage in Plato that is not entirely clear and drawing consequences from these.[14] If these consequences are absurd or inconsistent, the choice is between dismissing Plato or concluding that the statement did not represent his meaning. We are warned that this method of interpreting is unsound as a way to get at what Plato meant:

> It is far safer not to attribute to Plato any proposition which cannot be translated into Greek, the language in which he did his thinking. If it cannot be, he cannot have thought that. . . . [T]o be on secure ground, if his own words are unclear or ambiguous, the most we can do is to imagine that we have him with us, put to him questions in Greek, and then speculate as to how he might answer them in Greek. If this method is followed, it will be found that many of the distinctions on which, as modern philosophers, we rightly want to insist, pass him by.[15]

12. Not to mention ordinary language; cf. 312 below.

13. E.g., Lyons (1962).

14. Hare (1982, p. 30). The description, down to the "seed'" metaphor (at 31), recalls the second and third ways of misinterpretation, by abstraction and by inference respectively, distinguished (at 2–3) in Robinson (1953, pp. 1–7), an "Introduction" on "the interpretation of Plato" that still deserves a wide readership—as the book as a whole does.

15. Hare (1982, p. 31). Hare's recommendation is not incompatible with the task of the interpreter as Robinson (1953, p. 5) described it, of "elucidating Plato's meaning

Hare's call for restraint would please many historians and philologists: around the turn of the century a classical scholar of crushing authority, Von Wilamowitz-Moellendorf, recommended and exemplified the technique of explaining Greek authors in their own Greek, and ultimately the method advocated by Hare can be traced back to the Alexandrian grammarians' technique of "explaining Homer out of Homer."[16] One alternative, that of a philosophical interpretation of Plato that is indifferent to results of textual scholarship or to any other historical expertise that may apply to Plato, runs a risk, however exciting it might be as philosophy, of ceasing to be an interpretation *of Plato*.

Yet many would retort that if it is granted, as Hare takes it to be, that we "rightly" insist on these distinctions, then confronting Plato with them and measuring him by standards suggested by them is just more worthwhile and fertile philosophically: if the historical Plato fails to measure up, then so much the worse for him. Against this it may be argued that the rightness of our distinctions should not be taken as final, and that with a past philosopher worth confronting at all the *philosophically* more illuminating and productive confrontation will be with the more historical reading of him, precisely because it defamiliarizes, stresses distance and difference of perspective.[17]

This is not to deny modern philosophers the right to treat Plato as high-handedly as Aristotle did, or as he himself did Parmenides or Protagoras; nor does it imply that interpretation is a single and simple game with a fixed set of rules distinguishing it from whatever other response a text may elicit. It may well seem that for philosophical as for literary texts there is no such thing as "pure" interpretation, as being "only" interpreters, not even in translating or in textual criticism, the laborious

---

where we nowadays, even when reading him in Greek, are liable to get the wrong meaning or no meaning from his words, owing to the differences between us and the audience he had in mind; of restoring the impression Plato meant to give, where the passage of time has caused his words, on first reading, to give another." The continuation, for which Robinson cites Bergson, is singularly appropriate to Plato: more specifically "The interpreter must try . . . to restore by a long and roundabout process the single direct impression that Plato intended." This procedure, which "can only be an endless approximation," mirrors the dialectical path by which Plato leads us through and beyond his dialogues. cf. M. Miller, below. Thus philology becomes "love of λόγοι'", "following the λόγος where it leads," and what a founding father of *Altertumswissenschaft* August Boeckh called "understanding of what has been understood" (*Erkenntnis des Erkannten*). Cf. Robinson (1953, pp. 4–5): "Interpretation . . . is the re-creation of [that] thought" at a level which goes beyond the merely historical.

16. Or 'solving': σαφηνίζειν and λύειν, respectively.

17. "[W]ithout the broader perspectives to be gained from the study of philosophies other than the most familiar we can never acquire the critical range and cross cultural distance that are needed for triangulation and objectification in situating ourselves among the philosophically live options" (Goodman [1992, p. xii]).

reconstruction of what Plato supposedly wrote from manuscripts copied a millennium and a half later.[18] Rather, joint efforts toward interpretation exert contrary strains and pressures on a text; the limits to what the text may reasonably be allowed to bear vary with the object of the interpretative exercise, and the success or failure of each of these exercises has to be decided on balance in relation to its object. In this connection a methodologically informed familiarity with the nuances of the (closest to) original wording obviously is not a sufficient condition for a philosophically adequate interpretation, but is a necessary condition for any serious interpretation of a text as part of the history of philosophy rather than of its mythology. In history of philosophy, as in philosophy of mind or of language, the autonomy of philosophy does not imply autarky or isolation.[19]

II

Three of the following essays deal with what may be called "Socratic" dialogues in a stronger sense than just that of featuring Socrates as a speaker: the *Protagoras* has long, though not unanimously, been appreciated as a particularly vivid recollection of the setting in which a historical Socrates used to cross swords with many of those Sophists with whom the Athenian public came to confuse him—as it turned out, to his bane, or perhaps—as he himself was ready to consider—more to theirs. And both the *Euthyphro* and the *Crito* not only evoke episodes in the drama of Socrates' accusation, trial, and execution but also touch, the one more lightly and allusively than the other, on several of the moral issues that give to all that can be known of his life and death its lasting relevance.

In "Two Arguments in Plato's *Protagoras*" Reginald Allen offers analyses of the arguments concluding the dialogue on the question of whether courage is detachable from wisdom. The question is seen to involve the distinctively Socratic search for essence (ἴδιος οὐσία) as a necessary condition for the basic aim of each of us: to "live well." Allen's discussion contributes to thinking through hedonism—and, in passing, utilitarianism—by sorting out relations between ends and means, between knowledge, "true wish" (βούλησις), and what it is that constitutes the self; but in the process light is also thrown upon such technical matters as the relation

18. Pace Robinson (1953, p. 4).

19. "What the great philosophers have to teach us . . . has yet to be fully appropriated; and it will not be appropriated until it is studied with all the resources we have, both philosophical and historical" (Donagan [1994, p. 13]). The collaborative effort involves other expertise, e.g., on the origins of science, and in anthropology. The chapter on Plato in Dodds's *The Greeks and the Irrational* (1951) remains as relevant as his *Gorgias* (1959).

between part and whole. The first of the two arguments is a dialectical refutation of Protagoras on the basis of his own premises, which with some difficulty reduces him to silence, but the second one brings in the wider knowledge of good and evil, that is, the correct discrimination between pleasures and pains. Socrates' way of handling it is still dialectical, but now in the Aristotelian sense of exploiting the opinions of the majority as well as Protagoras's own claims. In addition to these well-established varieties of dialectic, Allen intriguingly finds in the *Protagoras* a "dialectical analogue" of geometrical synthesis, a mathematical form of inquiry and proof.

Allen takes account of recent interpretations of the two arguments under review with an eye to their underlying assumptions. He warns us against taking it for granted that modern methods of conceptual analysis are philosophically neutral; in fact, the assumption in quantification theory that assertions of existence reduce to assertions that predicates are sometimes true is a "broadly neo-Kantian assumption." He identifies a species of necessarily intensional (whether or not intentional) propositions that cannot be captured in terms of extensional or truth-functional relations, and he offers a timely reminder of a heuristic assumption that it is fatal to lose sight of: that Plato's text makes sense. Throughout his discussion, which contains incisive comments on a number of other dialogues, we get sure-footed guidance to the dialogue's exquisite and effectual humor and irony.

"Making New Gods," the title of Ronna Burger's essay, thematizes the charge on which Socrates has been indicted by his own admission early in the *Euthyphro*, the opening dialogue of a group set in the dramatic context of his trial and death. In the dialogue's discussion of the question "What is the holy?" it is natural to look for reflections not just of this main charge—in fact one possible source of confusion, Socrates' divine sign, is mentioned by Euthyphro explicitly—but also of the subsidiary one of corrupting the young, presumably by making them like himself. It is relevant to note that Euthyphro is a young man whom Socrates is trying to dissuade from an extreme remedy for what he perceives as an evil. The first half of the dialogue, in which Socrates develops his notion of an "Idea" of the Holy that carries authority even with the gods, might on the face of it seem to lend substance to the charge; Socrates' change of direction in the second half would thus be highly significant. Actually, it turns out that his strategy is not straightforwardly to make the gods subordinate to the Ideas even in the first half: whereas looking to the Idea as a paradigm is Euthyphro's way of likening himself to a god, for Socrates the Ideas provide a surprising tool for dragging Euthyphro down from his Olympian heights. And the subsequent shift is partly a change of manipulative tactics: if Socrates cannot motivate Euthyphro to desire knowledge of the Idea, he hopes that fear of the gods and shame before humans will make him abandon his unrelenting pursuit of the law, human and divine, demanding that the impious should be punished. In the process of disentangling these strains, Burger lets Socrates bring out how Euthyphro's version of the way the gods find something dear falls short of full-fledged *eros*.

"The Significance of Some Structural Features of Plato's *Crito*" by Kurt Pritzl starts with the apparent contrast between Socrates' disdain for the opinions of the many as expressed in this dialogue, and Aristotle's inclusion of them among things "of high repute" (*endoxa*) in the *Topics*. One of the wider implications of his detailed analysis of the *Crito* turns out to be that the distance between Plato and Aristotle on this point is much smaller than it seems, since we can identify a foundational set of opinions that are in place prior to reflection and any giving of accounts; that are shared between the many and the expert; and that are needed to make a fully human life within a political society possible. To arrive at this result we have to be attentive to the difference between dialogue and dialectic in a stricter sense, and to different uses of the expression "the many" with different references. This in turn requires an understanding of the dramatic representation of different parties, including "the very Truth itself" and, famously, the Laws of the city and in Hades, by the two directly speaking characters, Crito and Socrates, as well as an ear for some vitally important overtones and associations of the word for what is shared in common (*to koinon*) itself. We come away with a sharpened awareness of the danger of sophistry cutting at the very roots of our civil society in pretheoretical agreement.

Socrates' approaching end provides one occasion for Platonic reflection on the human soul: implicitly in *Crito*, as an explicit theme in *Phaedo*. Another main context for this topic is the design of a city in speech in the *Republic*. In "Plato on the Parts of the Soul" Fred Miller offers intrinsic reasons for taking the *Republic* account to be the more advanced of the two, reasons independent not only of preconceptions about chronology but equally of Plato's political agenda in this work. His point of departure is the observation that these two major discussions of the soul offer substantially different interpretations of the same Homeric passage describing Odysseus torn between contrary courses of action. Against recent attempts to play down some previously exaggerated complexities in the epic representation, he defends Plato's good sense in taking Homer's extended metaphors to reveal a genuine problem: In what sense is Odysseus one, in what sense is he many? He goes on to show that Plato's efforts to solve the problem are not irredeemably vitiated by a confusion of psychological with ethical categories. *Phaedo* makes the soul a thing that brings the form of life with it, and so a cause, but falls short of explaining the connection between life and soul, whereas the account of the soul in the *Republic* seems designed to fit in with those of *Phaedrus*—another tripartite specimen—and *Laws* Book 10 defining soul as self-motion or a self-moving principle. A close analysis of the argument for a tripartite soul in *Republic* 4 clears away some logical puzzles before leading into an underlying theory of human motivations as analogous to bodily actions and affections that again squares with the "kinetic" view of the soul. The description of desire in particular is shown to be carefully phrased so as to escape the "Socratic Paradoxes," by making distinctions, anticipating the Aristotelian insight into desires as relational, which should not be dismissed as merely verbal but are capable of empirical verification. There are reasons, then, for describing some conflicts as conflicts between desire and reason, and others as conflicts between different desires, and similarly for introducing a third "part," "kind," or "form" of the soul; but it is not clear that there are equally good reasons for stopping at three such parts.

Seven of the essays in this volume focus on various dialogues of average length or slightly more that have traditionally been inserted somewhere between the *Republic* and the *Laws* in a suppositious Platonic chronology. Charles Griswold in his provocatively titled "Platonic Liberalism: Self-Perfection as a Foundation of Political Theory" rests his argument more on the *Statesman* and the *Phaedrus* than on either of the political mammoth conversations, while offering fresh and illuminating juxtapositions with Epicurus and Aristotle among others. He challenges a long and distinguished line, stretching from Aristotle to Rawls, of explicit and implicit critics of Plato as a political philosopher, without delivering him into the hands of his most sinister early-twentieth-century would-be allies; and he brings out Plato's deep-seated ambivalence toward democracy, including his appreciation of the liberty "to wander outside the city's walls . . . in the company of some politically doubtful souls." Griswold himself does not evade what he at the same time calls a "disturbing" and a "pressing" thought, that "political liberty and equality seem incompatible with 'absolute' standards of excellence," and shows that one need not ride a hobbyhorse or toe a party line at either extreme of the political spectrum to find some, though not all, of Plato's suggestions in this field to be as valuable and as relevant as in any other: particularly in these two dialogues, more often quarried for quite different riches, in which Plato abandons the hope of finding or raising kings in possession of wisdom as opposed to loving wisdom, and so creates both the need and the space for an "imitation" of the ideal. How this imitation relates to self-perfection, the goal to which self-knowledge is the means, is next to be defined. In this defining process at the one end the value is brought into relief of political institutions informed by that part of self-knowledge that is knowledge of ignorance; at the other end new light is thrown on *erôs*: long-cherished oppositions go by the wayside and we see the requirement anticipated, however different the context, of treating others, regardless of their vocation or social status, as ends rather than reifying them, reducing them to bodies.

The next two chapters are devoted to the *Timaeus.* Daryl Tress in "Relations and Intermediates in Plato's *Timaeus*" addresses what is perhaps the problem most vital to any understanding of Platonism, that of "relating together what is different," in particular of the relation between the intelligible realm of unique Forms and the visible or at least sensible realm of the manifold which is the object of opinion; more specifically this problem concerns the factors of "contact" that mitigate the *khôrismos,* that is, prevent the two realms or domains from drifting apart into two separate worlds. Her close reading concentrates on the dialogue containing the longest sustained cosmogony and cosmology in Plato's oeuvre; the results are surely relevant to the metaphysics of several other dialogues. By a reading that is sensitive to context it can be established that statements that have been taken to imply a high degree of disjunction between Forms and particulars are not meant to be taken as definitive but on the contrary serve as points of departure for a linkage system. A wide range of factors are reviewed from this perspective, some familiar from other dialogues, some peculiar to this one: *psukhê,* the *Demiourgos,* the Receptacle, the mathematicals, marrow, *eros,* and *epithumia.* Each of these is seen to represent a partial aspect of the relation of Being and Becoming; between them they serve, according to Timaeus's proposal, as the means for the generation of composite particulars. The author distinguishes carefully between the often neglected purport of these factors and their adequacy to the task: she frankly takes the upshot to be an aporia that calls for rethinking the original dichotomy between Being and Becoming with all the polarities that ensue. She goes on to indicate boldly though briefly along what lines it might eventually be solved: the barrier to understanding is in our confusion of *distinction* with its image, spatial *separation*; precisely because Being lacks the limitations of space and time and so is utterly different from the material, it is permitted to be present to and intimate with what is other than it—anywhere, everywhere. Her invocation of the all-important distinctions "same" and "other," also found in the *Sophist,* helps us to see how the intermediates contribute to the "deep analyzability of reality."

In "The *Timaeus* Revisited" Thérèse-Anne Druart connects the Demiurge who is shown in action in this dialogue with the injunction in the

Theaetetus to philosophers to become as much as possible like god. She argues that the Demiurge is the god envisaged in this assimilation: he fills the need for a model of rational and responsible action. It follows that the *Timaeus* is highly important for its ethical and broadly educational content: not only the distinction between pleasure and delight, but also those between reason, thought, and forethought, between "thinking along with an account" and "opinion along with sensation of which no account can be given," here function in a predominantly moral context, and so do distinctions in the fields of causation and motivation, and of harmony, measure and proportion. An ancient insight, long lost, into the priorities of the dialogue is thus elegantly retrieved.

Druart, like Tress, hints at ways to locate the *Timaeus*, ostensibly a continuation of the conversation related in the *Republic*, on the same philosophical map with some dialogues apparently very different in atmosphere, on versions of dialectic that seem at odds with the conception of Forms presented in the *Republic*, and whose most conspicuous feature is the method of division. In "Forms and Predication in the Later Dialogues" Anne Wiles demonstrates to what extent Plato anticipates Aristotle in his treatment of predication in the *Parmenides* and in the *Sophist*; she also comments on principles of interpretation currently applied to Plato, distinguishing between a broadly analytic approach that is more often than not "genetic-historical," and a continental European one that she calls "synoptic," since it denies the autonomy of Plato's writings: the self-sufficiency of each and the sufficiency of all collectively as a literal, face-value expression of Plato's thought about the principles of reality. Although her own primary commitment to the analytic approach is clear, she shows by instance that we may learn from the other one, for example, how better to appreciate the irony of the more doctrinal, traditionally "later" dialogues. After a synopsis of the theory of Forms that brings into relief what is constant and common to or at least compatible with all its occurrences in Plato's oeuvre, Wiles outlines the relationship of participation and, briefly, of definition to predication, referring to other dialogues than the two under review and elucidating them with the help of Aristotelian terminology, before embarking on a close reading of parts of the *Parmenides*. She points out how the technique illustrated in this dialogue differs from the dialectical method of the historical Zeno in a way that marks a direction away from refutation and toward discovery of truth and that relies on making careful distinctions—to establish, for example, that contrariety does not entail contradiction—in both respects anticipating Aristotle, whose discussion of the relation between being and unity and whose ten categories are also here prefigured. A discussion of the *Sophist* follows which can be more succinct because several of its distinctions have already been seen to be operative in the *Parmenides*. Again, we find many Aristotelian seeds, although the flower in this dialogue is still a thoroughly Platonic evocation of the philosopher as a dialectician.

Kenneth Dorter's "The Clash of Methodologies in Plato's *Statesman*" deals with the relationship between the method of hypothesis put forward in the *Phaedo* and the *Republic* and the method of division referred to in the *Phaedrus* and deployed in the *Sophist* and the *Statesman*. He focuses on the *Statesman* because among dialogues featuring division it is exceptional in that the method is here applied to the domain of values, which explains why this dialogue has been relatively neglected. Observing that it features the method of hypothesis as well, he begins by exploring a conflict within the method of division as employed in it. Close scrutiny reveals that the division that would turn us into leg-challenged pigs is not as accurate as the one that identifies us as bald birds. To understand why this is so reminds us of the importance of the essence as the true differentia and prepares us for the distinction between the principles of relative measure and of the mean. But the wider implications of Dorter's analysis are far-reaching and provoking, perhaps even disturbing: there is no "single hierarchy of precedence and subordination." Like the tangles of the "longer way," the circularity of the dialogue's overall argument "illustrates that for Plato there is no possibility of a definitive mapping of reality," and any attempt at a definitive map "leads to arbitrariness, inconsistency, or both." However, together with the *Theaetetus* and the *Sophist*, the *Statesman* "can be read as an extended application of the method of hypothesis in defense of the theory of Forms." The *Sophist* reviews the status of Forms as universals in an inquiry into the difference between Sophist and philosopher that neglects intentions and goals; the *Statesman* takes account of the Forms as values: fortunately for us, it provides an antidote to the "value-sterile" longer way in a doctrine, indeed a science, of the mean, that is, of applied goodness, which may do for others what the divine sign did for Socrates. At the same time the problems in the theory of Forms brought out in the *Parmenides* remain intact; the limitations of our ability to eliminate them only become more evident.

In "Dialectical Education and Unwritten Teachings in Plato's *Statesman*" Mitchell Miller takes as his point of departure the enumeration of arts occurring toward the end of the dialogue, and relates it to Aristotle's report of Plato's unwritten teachings in *Metaphysics* A6; the theses attributed to Plato are in turn one by one elucidated with the help of the *Parmenides* and the *Philebus*. Close reading here establishes correspondences that ask to be studied with the same attention to detail:

thus a distinction that Miller has elsewhere elaborated between a Form's nature and its causal power saves the "unwritten teachings" from "a damaging obscurity" and contributes to an impressively precise and definite interpretation of the claim that the One and the Dyad of the Great and Small are conjointly the causes of the Forms.

It remains to bring these findings to bear on the *Statesman*. Like Dorter, Miller calls attention to hints within the dialogue that the method of division (especially bifurcatory division) is only a preparation for a form of analysis directed in a less mechanical way by "the subject itself, in its own proper being"; the *Statesman* is thus "a microscopic exhibition of the long-term process of philosophical education." More particularly, the distinctions at its close offer "a specific exhibition of the general structure" and "ontological order that Plato articulates in the 'unwritten teachings.'" The pages in which this is shown yield a rich harvest, as an elucidation of Plato's maturest reflections both on philosophical method and on the fundamentals of ontology, and as an object lesson in the methodology of Platonic studies.

In "The Problem of Sense Perception in Plato's *Philebus*" Stanley Rosen analyzes a passage in that dialogue and, more briefly, one in the *Theaetetus*, both of which raise the issue of how to distinguish between true and false perceptual judgments. He goes on to relate the Platonic accounts to Kant's doctrine of sense perception and to show how the difference between them is present in a contemporary discussion of this fundamental problem that "takes its bearings by psychology and physiology."

The *Theaetetus* passage (starting from 185c4) seems to turn Plato into a Kantian in a broad sense or at least into a proto-Kantian, a finding that would not have surprised Hegel. Neither from this passage nor from the one in the *Philebus* (38c5–39c6) is it "at all clear that Plato is a Platonist"—a warning that we do well to remember in other contexts. To define a viable distinctively Platonist position we have to be able to distinguish between perception of a given, and judgment as a constructive activity; to distinguish the Form as Idea from the *morphê* or physical Gestalt, the shape of the perceptible entity as construed by the sensory apparatus. From Rosen's perspective, this is not primarily a matter of setting a historical record straight: he is convinced that unless Platonism can be sustained against Kantianism, not just philosophy but the coherence and value of science are in mortal danger. His criticism of Kant focuses on the issue of objective identification: on the adequacy of the Kantian doctrine to account for the identity of a perceived object to serve as a foundation for predicative judgments. His charge is that it fails to explain perceptual identification and to provide a basis for distinguishing between true and false perceptual judgments. If we take this to disqualify the hypothesis of the transcendental ego, then it is a short step from the triumph of Kantianism over Platonism to the current depreciation of the given and the "dissolution of ordinary experience"; and "if the given is a myth, then so is science." The loss is ours, since any "recourse to logically possible alternatives is always motivated by the need to explain the nature of our own given experience," to offer "a plausible account of the given."

Further analysis of the *Philebus* passage shows that the crucial distinction for Plato is that between identifying and predicating; between, on the one hand, *both* the existential "judgments" of sense perception *and* the essential "judgments" of simple, unstructured apprehension of a Form (*noêsis*), and on the other hand predicational or predicative "judgments" in a more familiar sense of the noun. Rosen exploits analogies from recent neurophysiology to throw light on Socrates' metaphor of a set of craftsmen (writer, painter) working to integrate our remembered perceptions into a comprehensive system of beliefs or judgments about the external world, an interpretation of our experience: the discursive demiurge has to write down his sentence on the basis neither of a true perception nor of the vision of an Idea but of his memory of a fantasm. Next the painter draws an accurate copy of the writer's asserted opinion, his interpretation. On the decisive first act of identification, the proto-judgment, Socrates is tantalizingly inexplicit. What we can infer is that we need veridical perceptions to arrive at true perceptual judgments; that in order to perceive we need already to have perceived, that is, already to be ensconced within the perceptual field. Circularity here is inevitable; the circle is inescapable but it is not therefore necessarily vicious. We can affirm the myth of the given and ground *logos* in it, we can affirm the noble lie of modern science and so escape nihilism.

Two chapters follow that are devoted to Platonism in later antiquity. John M. Rist begins his "Moral Motivation in Plato, Plotinus, Augustine, and Ourselves" with an assessment of the value to philosophy of studying ancient philosophy. He questions the assumption that in philosophy we have never forgotten what we once knew; notes that antiquarianism may adopt the guise of analytic philosophy; and warns against the danger of "poisoning the wells" by taking it for granted that ancient philosophers were asking what are at bottom the same questions as their modern counterparts simply because the modern questions are the right ones. One of the first victims of this approach is Plato as an ethical thinker. Rist proposes to retrieve certain features of the Platonic account of human behavior, including its reflections in Plotinus and Augustine, and to show that correcting their ultimately unsuccesful enquiry is not only philosophically worthwhile but is "perhaps the only future for a grounded ethical theory." He reviews a number of distinctions operative in Plato's ethical theory and warns against the dangers that neither Plato nor Aristotle managed to avoid of slipping into dualist ways of speaking, while acquitting Plato of a Cartesian antithesis between reason and the passions. For Plato, the means of unifying the self is an *eros* directed, according to the *Republic*, to Philosophy: not, in the terms of the *Phaedrus*, an exploitative love but a love for Beauty, one that seeks to better the beloved. But here and in the *Laws* we see Plato resigned to the presence of an irremediably perverse element in our human state. So if we are not yet fully ourselves, who or what is to motivate us to escape a downward path? Plato would not have found the answer to his question in Aristotle, nor for different reasons in the Stoics, although these as Rist argues retained more Platonic assumptions than they cared to acknowledge.

As an alternative "pearl-in-the-oyster" theory of the soul, Plotinus introduces the distinction between an empirical self and one that is at once ideal and real, an "upper soul" or "soul above" untainted by sin. Our perverse streak is now represented by a *tolma* or pride that is hard to reconcile with the dependence of the entire world on the One: the generation of plurality and imperfection is logically accountable, but it is not clear why precisely at the level of the human soul *eros* should be corrupted, confused, or diverted from our source to our self and so give rise to moral evil and guilt; nor, what is worse, how we can ever hope to deal with our moral ambivalence. The unfallen soul was abandoned by Plotinus's successors: divine dispensation and aid seemed required for a return of the soul to its origin. It was a short step for Augustine to specify that this was not to be obtained through theurgy, by attempting to be God, but through the gratuitous help of God, by seeking not ourselves but God within us. Platonist ethics and psychology could not be made consistent without a particular form of theism. The solution to Plato's question is that "[f]or the present, we are . . . a set of potential selves"; "we have . . . an identity only in hope." Augustine's challenge still remains.

Dominic J. O'Meara, too, in "Neoplatonist Conceptions of the Philosopher-King," considers developments of Platonic ethics in late antiquity in connection with metaphysics, but now in their bearing on politics. Again part of the problem is latent in Plato's own work as a tension between its otherworldly leanings and the demand that the philosopher should redescend into the cave; in the context of later Platonism one contrast is between a theoretical requirement to renounce the world, and the actual engagement of Neoplatonist circles in practical politics. So why, on a Neoplatonic interpretation, should philosophers renounce contemplative bliss and assume office? In Plotinus this path is recommended as one option rather than made obligatory; accordingly, no grounds for such an obligation are specified. Later authors, however, do provide such grounds, which throw retrospective light on Plotinus's recommendation. According to Proclus, pure souls desire to confer benefit on what is inferior to them and so make it like them, as an instance of the good diffusing itself, *bonum diffusivum sui*. This recalls Plotinus's argument that the world emerges as a by-product of the contemplative life of the higher realities, Soul and Intellect, in the way that human action and production follow from and express theory, that is, contemplation. For Plotinus too we escape the world to achieve union with the One, but we may then desire to return to the world and express and communicate the Good to it: down to the sixth century philosophy as the assimilation of the human to god will be taken to aim at both divine knowledge and providential care for what is inferior. This picture is confirmed and developed in texts from the fourth to the sixth century. A separation of the legislative from the executive comes into view with the Emperor Julian's distinction between a ruler exercising power on a daily basis and his advisers who can maintain their contemplative existence while exerting a far-reaching moral and pedagogic influence. We can trace to Hierocles an identification of the *Phaedrus*'s philosopher and the lover, respectively, with the contemplative and the philosopher-king who communicates intelligible goods to others as an activity whose "philanthropy" makes it positively valuable, indeed equal in value to the contemplative pursuit of self-interested enlightenment. An anonymous Greek dialogue *On Political Science* dated to the earlier sixth century makes explicit the presence in reality of a hierarchical structure of causation and rule; once his intellect has traced this to its transcendent first cause the philosopher-king will govern humans in intimation of it. His political science is a divine method to help them return to the heavenly metropolis and the dignity of the immortal state. The general picture that emerges is that whereas in Plato's *Republic* the philosopher seems to become a ruler because he is a part of the city and has an obligation to serve its common good as integrating the private good, in the Neoplatonic version his return to the cave is an expression of "universal metaphysical principles of the production, ordering, and amelioration of all things."

In "The Continuity of Plato's Dialectic" philosophers of later antiquity are quoted not for their development of Platonic themes but for their testimony to a sense of the unity of Plato's achievement and of the tradition deriving from him. The theme is dialectic, which is described by Plato in terms that sometimes suggest a method and sometimes rather a subject to which different methods are appropriate. In the ancient tradition it is perceived, like the rest of Plato's method and doctrine, as all of one piece, but in the heyday of the genetic approach it too was understood as very much in process, with some of its features at one stage almost contrary to its features at another stage of Plato's development. In my Afterword the notion of a more organic evolution which I have outlined in Section I of this introduction is applied to Plato's conception of dialectic. This conception is contrasted with two competing ones developed in the Peripatos and the Stoa. These, as well as modern views of Plato's dialectic, differ in the extent to which they represent dialectic as a formal discipline and to which they trust it to lead to truth. The first question as applied to Plato may be anachronistic. On the second one we should not play down Plato's claims: dialectic, including the methods of both hypothesis and division, continues to serve the purpose of real definition. Contextual, that is, circumstantial, evidence suggests that it also continues to be aimed at a realm of or charged with values. For any understanding of the relationships between and the order among these values that Plato intends to establish with the help of these methods, we need to distance ourselves from the much more familiar Aristotelian perspective and pay attention to the connotations of Plato's terminology prior to Aristotle's usurpation of it. Doing so may confirm the assessment that much of Aristotle's criticism of Plato either rests on a tendentious interpretation[20] or is anticipated by Plato himself; and more positively, that there are things in Plato that were neither superseded by Aristotle nor fully exploited in a philosophical tradition in which Aristotle gradually ousted Plato.

20. For strictures on Aristotle's reliability as reporter or interpreter, cf. Rosen below.

1 Two Arguments in Plato's *Protagoras*

R. E. ALLEN

My aim is to provide some account of the two concluding arguments in Plato's *Protagoras*, which deal with the question of whether courage is detachable from wisdom. I shall also examine certain recent misunderstandings of those arguments, not eristically for purposes of refutation, but to identify some of the assumptions on which they rest, and in order to help clear the ground.

I

The *Protagoras*, like its companion dialogue the *Meno*, ends in a dialectical tangle. In the *Meno*, Socrates assumes as a hypothesis that if virtue is knowledge, then virtue is teachable; argues that virtue is knowledge; further argues that virtue is not teachable; and ends in skepticism: virtue is present in men by divine apportionment, without intelligence. The reason for failure is clearly and repeatedly stated: Socrates and Meno have tried to find out whether virtue is teachable without first determining what virtue is. The *Meno* emphasizes the priority of the search for essence, for what a thing is in and of itself, the account of which is a definition.

This is also the conclusion of the *Protagoras*. Socrates and Protagoras become so tangled that the argument itself intervenes to mock them. Socrates begins by asserting that virtue cannot be taught, and ends by assuming that virtue is knowledge, which therefore suggests that it can be taught; Protagoras maintains all along that virtue can be taught, but ends by denying that it is knowledge, which therefore suggests that it cannot be taught. The moral is explicitly drawn: Socrates and Protagoras must first find out what virtue is, and then go back to inquire whether or not it is teachable. The "What is it?" question, the question of essence, is prior to all other questions about virtue.

The *Protagoras* by its structure makes clear that the search for essence bears directly on the good of the soul. The connection is not far to seek. The aim of each of us—our primary and fundamental aim—is to live well. We can live well only if we care for our own souls; we can care for our own souls only by living virtuously; and we can live virtuously only if we know what virtue is. So the search for essence is a condition for living well. Wisdom, conceived as knowledge of the true aims of life and the means necessary to attain them, is a necessary condition for virtue.

This is a simple claim, but it constitutes what may be described, without apology either to Copernicus or Kant, as the Socratic Revolution: a turning from outer concerns to inner concerns, from goods such as wealth and political power to goods such as justice and virtue, which involve self-knowledge. In the *Protagoras*, the Socratic Revolution is brought into contrast with a group of professional teachers who expounded the conventional wisdom by telling their audience what their audience wanted to hear—with the Sophists and the chief of the Sophists, Protagoras, with Hippias and Prodicus in his train. The *Protagoras* offers a contrast between two cultures: the sophistical culture or *paideia* that was the dominant element in the intellectual climate of Athens, and that through speech directly or indirectly swayed the history of a great people; and Socratic culture, centered on virtue and the inner life of reason, defended by a man whom the Athenians would eventually put to death.

There is in this, if you accept the Socratic premise, a contrast between appearance and reality, and that contrast accounts for the complex humor that lights the *Protagoras* and provides much of its surface charm. The *Protagoras* is a very funny dialogue. There is the scene of Hippocrates coming at dawn in great excitement to tell Socrates that Protagoras—a Sophist whose teachings he knows nothing about—is in town, and to beg an introduction. There is the scene when they reach Callias's house where Protagoras is staying, and are met by a butler who grunts "Sophists!" and slams the door in their faces—he evidently holds an opinion on the subject of Sophists somewhat at variance with that of Hippocrates. There is the wonderful description of Protagoras talking as he walks back and forth in the portico of the house, with his audience hanging on the words of the great man and wheeling and turning in perfect order behind him. Then there is the touch of epic dignity used to describe Prodicus lying in bed. And there is the wonderful speech of Protagoras, a sales talk for his own rhetorical wares that involves invoking Zeus and other gods, though the audience for whom the *Protagoras* was originally written knew that Protagoras was agnostic and believed in no gods. In this dialogue appearance and reality often conflict.

Socrates himself catches the spirit. After almost breaking up the meeting by his insistence on short answers to questions, not speeches, he proceeds to imitate the Sophists by giving a speech himself on a poem by Simonides, and parodies not only sophistical method but his own doctrine that wrongdoing is involuntary. The speech goes on and on, to the point of tedium—which we are clearly meant to feel—and when it is at last done, Socrates remarks that it is useless to try to interpret poets anyway. Here we have another appearance and reality conflict. Humor, having become parody, turns to satire.

But the search for essence continues. Are the parts of virtue parts like the parts of gold, which differ from themselves and from the whole only in size? Or are they like the parts of the face, eyes, ears, nose, and so on, which differ both in themselves and in their function or power. Protagoras, who is in fact dealing with a genus/species relation, thinks they are parts like the parts of the face.

This is a material analysis of a logical relation, and it leads to a further question: Are the different parts of virtue detachable? Protagoras thinks that they are—and this, let it be observed, goes against the analogy he has just accepted, since eyes and ears and nose, if different, need each other to form a whole face. Socrates, after offering various arguments that cast doubt on Protagoras's claim of detachability—arguments that suggest the equivalence of justice and holiness, wisdom and temperance, temperance and justice—restates the issue with precision: whether wisdom, temperance, courage, justice, and piety are five names for one thing (ἐπὶ ἑνὶ πράγματί ἐστιν), or whether each of these names has its own proper and peculiar nature and reality (τις ἴδιος οὐσία) and is each a thing possessed of its own function (πρᾶγμα ἔχον ἑαυτοῦ δύναμιν ἕκαστον), one not being of such sort as another of them (349b). Protagoras replies that while the others are very much alike, courage is detachable: it is possible to be courageous, and yet be unjust, unholy, intemperate, and unwise.

The two arguments here under consideration follow. In the first, Socrates uses Protagoras's own denial that courage implies wisdom or knowledge as a premise to show that courage does imply wisdom and knowledge, and indeed, without any great forcing of the argument, that wisdom or knowledge implies courage. The second argument offers a clear and eminently sophisticated (in both senses of that word) statement of hedonism, and a denial of akrasia, incontinence or intemperance.

II

Let us examine the first argument first. Protagoras has claimed that courage is detachable from other virtues, and not unreasonably. One thinks of Laches as an embezzler: Aristophanes, *Wasps* 836–38, 894 following Thudydides.

So Protagoras assumes (*i*) that courage does not imply wisdom or knowledge (349d.2–8). Socrates also leads him to agree (*ii*) that the courageous are daring (θαρραλέος) or bold or confident (350c.7–8), and further *(iii)* that those who are daring or bold or confident and do not have knowledge are not courageous (350c.1–2). But if *(ii)* and *(iii)* are taken in conjunction, then courage implies wisdom or knowledge, and this contradicts *(i)*. Furthermore, if *(i)* and *(iii)* are taken in conjunction, then wisdom or knowledge implies courage. Dialectically, if Protagoras denies that courage implies knowledge or wisdom, he must affirm that knowledge implies courage; whether or not he denies that knowledge implies courage, he must affirm that courage implies knowledge.[1] In either case, his detachability thesis collapses: the agreements Protagoras has made are vicious, as internally incompatible. He has suffered the dialectical equivalent of being hit by a truck.

Faced with a result that follows from premises he has himself admitted, Protagoras attacks the truth of the conclusion instead of reexamining the agreements that imply it.[2] His response is irrelevant, and Socrates rightly ignores it. But the task of dialectic is to proceed according to

1. The reader may perhaps forgive a lapse into symbolism as a crutch for those of us less able in reasoning than Socrates himself; the account sacrifices some degree of elegance for greater perspicuousness. Let C = those who are courageous, D = those who are daring or bold or confident, and K = those who have knowledge or wisdom. Then, eschewing quantifiers, if:

(ii) $C \supset D$
(iii) $(D \& {\sim}K) \supset {\sim}C$
Then: $C \supset K$.

This contradicts (i).

On the other hand, (i) and (iii) in conjunction imply that those who have knowledge are courageous: that knowledge is a sufficient condition for courage. If:

(i) ${\sim}(C \supset K)$
(iii) $(D \& {\sim}K) \supset {\sim}C$
Then: $K \supset C$

It may be urged that $K \supset C$ follows from ${\sim}(C \supset K)$ as one of the paradoxes of material implication; so (iii) is compatible with but adjunctive to (i) and the conclusion. But the argument may in fact be made stronger. For if we assume, as is reasonable, that 350c.1–4 states not only that $(D \& {\sim}K) \supset {\sim}C$, but also that $(D \& K) \supset C$, then, given ${\sim}(D \supset C)$ (350b.1–6), it follows without more ado that $K \supset C$, and $C \equiv K$. That is, if daring and knowledge imply courage, and it is not the case that daring implies courage, then knowledge implies courage, and courage implies knowledge. The proof may be checked by a simple truth table.

For those who prefer their quantifiers chewed: if ${\sim}(x)(Cx \supset Kx)$ and $(x)(Cx \supset Dx)$ and $(x)((Dx \& {\sim}Kx) \supset {\sim}Cx)$, then $(x)(Cx \supset Kx)$. Given the additional premise $(x)((Dx \& Kx) \supset Cx)$, then $(x)(Kx \supset Cx)$, and therefore, $(x)(Cx \equiv Kx)$. The conclusion may be derived by natural deduction and subordinate proof.

2. To anticipate the history of logic a little, Protagoras realizes that universal affirmative propositions cannot be converted *simpliciter*. He has granted, he says, that courageous men are daring, but not that daring men are courageous: $C \supset D$ does not imply $D \supset C$. But Socrates' argument does not require $D \supset C$ for its validity, and in fact requires that it be false. Protagoras has flatly misunderstood the argument.

what the respondent admits to be true, and it is by a different argument, involving the identity of pleasure and goodness, that Socrates will lead Portagoras to agree, or, more accurately, to cease denying, that courage implies wisdom, that one cannot be courageous and foolish (360e), on the ground that intemperance[3] is ignorance and courage is knowledge of what is and is not to be feared.

III

We live in an age that talks much of logic—as well it should, if philosophy consists in the study of statements and the relations between them—and that talk has affected talk about Plato, including talk about the *Protagoras.* It is not quite twenty-five years since Gregory Vlastos announced the value of "more sophisticated methods of conceptual analysis in Platonic exegesis,"[4] and suggested that because of those methods we can now understand Plato better than he understood himself; indeed, it seemed to Vlastos that Plato often misunderstood himself. Still, "Only a puerile critic would make immunity to logical error the measure of a philosopher's greatness." Vlastos praised the new methods because they are fecund: their use much increased the volume of articles and books on Plato, which Vlastos thought a good thing.

Certainly, the production of books and articles has proceeded apace. And if the "techniques of logical and semantic analysis" are philosophically neutral and do not involve broadly neo-Kantian philosophical assumptions of their own, then what results from using those techniques may be free of anachronism. On the other hand, if those techniques involve debatable philosophical assumptions—for example, the neo-Kantian assumption in quantification theory that assertions of existence reduce to assertions that predicates are sometimes true—then this style of exegesis is not neutral: it transposes into "Nobody here but us chickens." The use of "more sophisticated techniques of conceptual analysis" then suggests anachronism, and its fecundity gives us cause to consider whether Gresham's Law may not apply to scholarship. Indeed, one might see the reduction of existence to truth as a neo-Kantian attack on the possibility of metaphysics, one carried forward by historians who "interpret" metaphysicians into nonsense. "Nobody here but us chickens" would then transpose into "The Trojan Horse."

The argument of *Protagoras* 349d–50c is of philosophical importance.

3. Because it is a form of folly, or incompatible with wisdom; cf. 332a–33b, with VI below, p. 28.

4. Gregory Vlastos, *Plato* (New York, 1971), Vol. 1, P. 2.

The issue is whether a man can be courageous but unwise. Most people believe that to be true, but Socrates provides cogent reason to believe that it is not true. The results of applying the techniques of "conceptual analysis" to his argument have been something less than encouraging.

Vlastos himself, in an introduction to Ostwald's revision of Jowett's translation of the *Protagoras*, discussed Socrates' argument in a section entitled "How Good Is His Logic?" He did not accurately identify the premises of the argument, seemed unaware of enthymeme, and appeared to suggest that allowing letters to stand for propositions was by itself revelatory of "logical form." At no point did he lift his eyes to consider the philosophical significance of the argument, or whether the conclusion—that courage implies wisdom and is therefore more than animal spirits—just might be true.

The passage subsequently has had a curious history. Despite its intrinsic interest and its importance to the argument of the *Protagoras*, Professor Irwin does not deal with it, though he touches on some of its premises.[5] Professor Nussbaum, in her discussion of the *Protagoras*,[6] ignores it. C. C. W. Taylor devotes eleven pages of logical analysis to the argument, concluding—if I have followed him—that the argument is invalid and Socrates himself is confused. The argument is of course valid, a fact that Taylor might have admitted had he embraced the assumption, which is also a heuristic principle, that Plato's text makes sense. Taylor's account of the argument labors under other difficulties: it analyzes meaningful statements into logical formulae that are not well formed,[7] and there is a question whether the symbolism is not itself meaningless, for instead of the horseshoe of material implication, which despite its paradoxes can be precisely defined, an arrow is used without defining what the arrow stands for. Taylor notes the mote in Plato's argument, but misses the beam in his own.

IV

The concluding argument of the *Protagoras* is perhaps the most remarkable in all this remarkable dialogue. Socrates will prove, by assuming the hedonic equation of pleasure and goodness, that courage is not detachable from knowledge or wisdom. This follows as a corollary of a

5. Terence Irwin, *Plato's Moral Theory* (Oxford, 1977), chap. 4, sect. 5.

6. Martha C. Nussbaum, *The Fragility of Goodness* (Cambridge, 1986), chap. 4.

7. E.g., "Since they are most daring (and also wisest) they are therefore most courageous," is symbolized as (x) (Dx & Wx → Cx) (p. 155; cf. pp. 151, 159, 160). The English is clear. The putative logical expression of it is ambiguous between (x) ((Dx & Wx)→ Cx) and (x) (Dx & (Wx → Cx)).

far more powerful argument, that knowledge is a sufficient condition for temperance. The knowledge in question is knowledge of good and evil, which is to say, knowledge of the relative weight of pleasures and pains.

Socrates here inquires by what Aristotle in the *Topics* (1.11.104b.7.17) calls a dialectical problem, that is, a proposition that is of help in the solution of other problems, including practical problems: "For some problems it is useful to know with a view to choice or avoidance, e.g., whether pleasure is to be chosen or not." Socrates assumes as given that pleasure and goodness are equivalent. He further assumes that knowledge is a sufficient condition for temperance or continence. Instead of deducing consequences as from a hypothesis, Socrates elicits from Protagoras and the many, the majority of men, denial of the first proposition, and from the many, but not Protagoras, denial of the second, and shows in both cases that by their denial they assume what they deny. That is, there are two analyses, which issue in a sequence of dialectical reductiones ad absurdum.[8] These stand as lemmata for the final proof that courage is not detachable from knowledge. Because the argument is dialectical, that is, having to do with what the parties to it believe and what they mean, certain of its propositions are both intentional and intensional—of the form "You said *P* but you meant *Q*." So the argument cannot be reduced to extensional or truth-functional relations.

The results of the analysis of the proposition that knowledge is a sufficient condition for temperance or continence are used in a synthesis, that is, a proof, of that same proposition (358b–d), a proof in which the equivalence of pleasure and goodness is an essential premise. No synthesis, however, is provided for the equivalence of pleasure and goodness, the hedonic equation. That is, there is no proof beyond a reduction to the opinion of the many, who find it impossible to state an alternative.

It may be that the first readers of the *Protagoras* were meant to recognize, and indeed would have recognized, that Socrates is using a dialectical variant of a mathematical form of inquiry and proof. If so, his argument as directed toward Protagoras is not without irony, and even sarcasm. For Protagoras published a refutation of the geometers, denying

8. The argument appears to be a dialectical analogue of geometrical analysis, which proceeds by reducing a theorem or problem to a theorem or problem whose truth-value is known; reductio ad absurdum is a particular kind of analysis that reduces a proposition to a conclusion known to be false. See T. L. Heath, *History of Greek Mathematics* (Oxford, 1921), vol. 1, pp. 371, 2, 291; vol. 2, p. 400. Synthesis, on the other hand, was deductive, providing direct proof; we shall find Socrates using a dialectical analogue of synthesis too, assuming the hedonic equation of pleasure and goodness to prove that virtue is knowledge, or, more precisely, that knowledge is a sufficient condition for temperance. Significantly, there is no synthesis for the hedonic equation itself.

that their reasoning, with its lengthless points and breadthless lines, dealt with reality;[9] this coheres with the contempt for mathematics he expresses at 318.d–e.

But this is perhaps the least important aspect of the argument, which moves on several different levels at once. It is, in the first place, a brilliant exposition of hedonism, which greatly influenced the ancient schools; in the nineteenth century it was embraced by George Grote and (with some misunderstanding of the relation of hedonism to utilitarianism) John Stuart Mill. Second, the argument provides an account of popular or demotic morality, the morality of common sense, which reduces it to hedonism; it further suggests that sophistry reduces to popular morality, and thereby to hedonism too. Third, the argument suggests but does not state that the hedonism of popular and sophistic morality is an εἴδωλον, a deficient likeness, of living well, that is, of living justly, by reason of which Socrates himself died. The humor of the *Protagoras* culminates in an argument whose essence is incongruity, the contrast between appearance and reality. The humor of incongruity is not always funny, however; sometimes it would be funny if it weren't so sad.

V

Socrates undertakes to elicit Protagoras's agreement that some men live well (εὖ ζῆν), others badly; that no man lives well if he lives in misery and pain; and that if a man lives out his life pleasantly, he has lived well. Protagoras agrees only on a condition: "Yes, if he lives pleasantly with beautiful, or noble, or good things" (351c). Socrates questions this. Does Protagoras agree with οἱ πολλοί, the many, the majority of men, who call some pleasant things bad and some painful things good (351d)? Socrates suggests that things that either partake of pleasure[10] or that cause pleasure are pleasant; he is asking whether those things just insofar as they are pleasant are not good. Protagoras restates this as the claim that the pleasant and the good are the same. That is, minimally, they are equivalent, as introducing each other. We might call this the hedonic equation: Whatever is good is pleasant, and whatever is pleasant is good. Since equivalence is one sense of sameness, Protagoras is entitled to his inference.

Hedonism is the doctrine that pleasure is the ultimate human good and the chief aim of human striving. In short, hedonism is teleological: it

9. Aristotle, *Meta.* 3.2.998a3; cf. Diogenes Laertius 9.55.

10. Socrates is imitating Protagoras's language in his great myth, where μετέχειν δικαιοσύνης (323a.6; cf. 322.2, 5), 'to partake of justice', means 'to be just'.

defines goodness in terms of a goal, and identifies that goal as pleasure. In this it both agrees and disagrees with the chief tenet of Socratic ethics, which defines goodness in terms of a goal, and identifies that goal as justice or virtue. There is no evidence, in dialogues other than the *Protagoras* or in Xenophon, that Socrates ever argued that pleasure and goodness are equivalent. On the contrary, Socrates consistently argues that they are not equivalent, on the ground that there can be bad pleasures and good pains.[11]

The touchstone of Plato's moral theory in the early and early middle dialogues is the *Crito*. In the *Crito*, as in the *Protagoras*, Socrates assumes that life has an aim or purpose, and that the aim is not merely to live but to live well (εὖ ζῆν). But whereas Socrates in the *Protagoras* suggests that to live well is to live pleasantly, in the *Crito* he suggests that to live well is to live justly. The *Crito* does not use the word 'soul', but it does refer to "whatever it is of ours to which justice and injustice pertain" (47d–48a), and it does contrast this "whatever" to the body as of higher worth. Life is not worth living if that of ours which is benefited by justice is harmed by injustice. Socrates' argument in the *Crito* is an example of what may be called the Socratic Proportion: Justice is to the soul as health is to the body. Granting that soul is of greater worth than body, the question of whether to escape reduces to the question of whether it is just or unjust to do so (48b–d; cf. *Apology* 29c–30c). This is equivalent to the question of whether escape will harm or benefit the soul. It was for the good of his soul, not, surely, of his body, that Socrates refused to escape from prison and accepted his own sentence of death.

The account of living well in the *Crito* is not only distinct from but incompatible with the hedonic equation of the *Protagoras*. As a matter of common sense, the aim of pleasant living precludes voluntary acceptance of a death sentence on grounds of justice. To a hedonist, justice is another's good and may well be one's own harm, for what is useful or good is what contributes to one's own pleasure. Justice has only instrumental value in attaining pleasure, and so it is sometimes better to do injustice than to suffer it. In the *Crito*, Socrates argues that one must never do injustice or return injustice for injustice, and therefore one must never work injury or do evil in return for having suffered it. To do injustice is to harm others in respect to their proper excellence, as escape from prison harms the proper excellence of the Laws of Athens; it is thereby to harm one's own soul. So justice is not a means to living well,

11. Goods are not the same as pleasures, nor evils the same as pains: See *Gorgias* 497a, e; cf. *Republic* 329a, 353e–54a, 387d; *Charmides* 172a, 173d; *Alcibiades I* 116b; *Cratylus* 399d–e; *Phaedo* 105d. On this issue, the *Crito* is by itself dispositive.

but constitutive of living well. It is therefore always better to suffer injustice than to do it, a proposition flatly incompatible with hedonism. Hedonism is teleological in that pleasure is the end, and virtue, to the degree that it is good, a means to that end. Socratic moral theory is teleological in that virtue is the end, intrinsically good in and of itself, good for its own sake. It is constitutive of and not merely a means to goodness of soul.

The hedonic equation is not only inconsistent with the moral theory of the *Crito*: it is also inconsistent with Socrates' account of his mission to Athens in the *Apology* (30a–b), which was motivated by care for the souls of his fellows. It is therefore inconsistent with the concern for the soul and the danger to it of sophistry which Socrates expresses to Hippocrates at the beginning (31.2b–4c), where he identifies the soul with the self. Socrates' analysis of living well in terms of hedonism is again a contrast between appearance and reality. It continues the element of parody that marks the interlude at 334a–38e, including the parody that Socrates offers, in his comment on Simonides, of the principle that no one voluntarily does wrong (345d–e, 346a).

VI

Socrates now states a second proposition:

> Most people think that knowledge had neither strength nor authority nor power of command; that though a man may have it, it can be overpowered—by anger, by pleasure and pain, sometimes by love, often by fear—as though it were some poor slave to be dragged about at will by the passions. Is that your view, Protagoras? Or would you rather agree that knowledge is a thing of beauty and power, invincible; that once a man knows good from evil, nothing on earth can compel him to act against that knowledge—wisdom being sufficient to his aid? (352b–c)

Both Socrates and Protagoras agree to this, and their agreement is in some sense compelled: Socrates has already argued the unity of temperance and wisdom (332a–33b), while Protagoras claims to teach virtue. Aristotle took Socrates' argument to amount to a denial of ἀκρασία, lack of continence or self-control.[12] Keeping to Plato's own vocabulary, we might say it is a denial of ἀκολασία, intemperance.

VII

To sum up the agreements so far: Socrates and Protagoras agree against the many that knowledge implies temperance; Protagoras and

12. *E. N.* 7.2.1145b.22 ff.; cf. 1147b.15.

the many agree against Socrates that pleasure and goodness are not equivalent. Socrates will next show that though the many say that knowledge does not imply temperance, they in fact believe that pleasure and goodness are equivalent.

Socrates next interrogates the many in an imaginary dialogue. What do they mean by "being overcome by pleasure"? The many hold that men are mastered by food or drink or sex, which are pleasures, and recognize them as bad (πονηρά) but nevertheless pursue them. Why are they bad? The many would reply that they are not bad because of the immediate pleasure they produce, but because they eventuate in pain and take away other pleasures. Again, the many claim that some good things are painful, for example, physical training, warfare, and medical treatment through cautery and surgery and drugs and starvation, not because these things produce pain, but because they eventuate in pleasure and relieve and avert pain. So the many think pleasure is bad only when it takes away greater pleasures or produces pain greater than the pleasure, and that pain is good only when it gets rid of greater pain, or produces pleasures greater than the pains. In effect, the many's mouth has been stopped: if they call pleasure bad with respect to something else besides pleasure and pain, or if they call pain good looking to some other end, then they could tell what it is: but they can't (354c–d). The many are, in effect, psychological hedonists, and this because they are unaware of the primacy of justice and virtue: psychological hedonism is a deficient image of the soul's longing for its own true good.

The many have now been shown, by an informal reductio ad absurdum, that though they claim to deny the hedonic equation, they in fact accept the hedonic equation: their denial rests merely on the distinction between immediate pleasures and pleasures that are more remote. So the many agree that pleasure and goodness are equivalent. This constitutes the dialectical analysis of Socrates' hedonic equation. It is important to realize that the reduction required by that analysis rests on the inability of the many to state an alternative to hedonism. Socrates stated that alternative in conversation with Hippocrates: it is the good of the soul.

Protagoras had rejected the opinions of the many as not worth considering, on the ground that they say whatever happens to occur to them (353a); but his agreement with the many has at this point been elicited at every step of the way, and he, like they, will end with his mouth stopped.

The hedonism of the many is the foundation of the account of popular virtue—the virtue of the many—offered in the *Phaedo* (68d–69a) in contrast to the philosopher's love of wisdom. Ordinary men are courageous through a kind of cowardice, temperate through a kind of intemperance: "they are afraid of being deprived of other pleasures, and desire them, so they refrain from some because they are mastered by others. Yet they call being ruled by pleasures intemperance." Popular or demotic virtue, in short, is a means to an end, namely, pleasure, good in its consequences but not in itself.[13]

VIII

Having questioned the many, Socrates now proceeds to question himself. The many, unlike Socrates and Protagoras, deny that knowledge implies temperance because they claim that men are overcome by pleasure. What is the experience of being overcome by pleasure? The answer is, ignorance.

The many have agreed to the hedonic equation. They can still take back their agreement, if they can say that the good is something other than pleasure and the evil something other than pain. But if they accept pleasure and the avoidance of pain as sufficient for a human life, the notion that men are overcome by pleasure is absurd. The absurdity follows from the hedonic equation. Let good = pleasant, and let evil = painful: whatever is good is pleasant, and whatever is pleasant is good; whatever is evil is painful, and whatever is painful is evil.[14] Then, by substitution, to say that a man does evil knowing it to be evil because he is overcome by pleasure, is to say that he does what is evil knowing it to be evil because he is overcome by what is good. Or again, that he does what is painful knowing it to be painful, because he is overcome by pleasures that don't weigh enough (ἀναξία) to conquer. This is manifestly absurd.

Given the hedonic equation, pleasures and pains can be compared in value only in respect to excess or defect of pleasures and pains: difference in worth is difference in degree. So if someone objects that what is immediately pleasant or immediately painful differs in value from what is subsequently pleasant or subsequently painful, the reply must be that they differ only in pleasure and pain (356b–c). Like a man skilled in weighing, one must add pleasures and pains both near and far and determine which is greater: if pleasures exceed pains, the action is to be done; if pains exceed pleasures, the action is not to be done.

Protagoras claimed that virtue is an art and that he could teach it. Socrates now explains, on the basis of the hedonic equation, what that

13. But see J. S. Mill, *Utilitarianism*, chap. 4.

14. The identity is one of equivalence, substitutability *salva veritate*, and is also intensional, but not intentional: if whatever is good is pleasant, and good means pleasant, it does not follow that the many believe (without instruction or Socratic questioning) that this is true.

art must be. Given that the salvation of life depends on right choice of pleasures and pains—more and fewer, greater and smaller, nearer and more remote—an art of measurement is required,[15] and specifically, an art of weighing pleasures and pains. Men err and do wrong for lack of knowledge about how to add and subtract pleasures and pains—that is, by the hedonic equation, goods and evils.

IX

Socrates asks Hippias and Prodicus whether they agree that what is pleasant is good and what is painful bad (358a–b). They do—but, then, they've just been told that the many refuse to spend money on Sophists, who are educators, by reason of doubting it. This bit of by-play suggests that rhetoric and sophistry are based on the hedonism of the many, and that Protagoras's cavils indicate a misunderstanding of his own position. That point is made explicitly again in the *Gorgias,* which describes what the *Protagoras* exhibits: sophistry and rhetoric are classed together as (εἴδολα), insubstantial imitations of genuine "arts." They are species of (κολακεία), servile flattery, aiming not at what is good but at what is pleasant. As pastry cooking pretends to be medicine, and as pastry cooks claim to know what foods are good as doctors do, so sophistry and rhetoric pretend to be statesmanship and jurisprudence. But they aim at pleasure, and are indifferent to truth or the good of the soul. If this is so, the whole profession of sophistry, the profession not only of Hippias and Prodicus but of Protagoras himself, presupposes that pleasure is an ultimate end. Their rhetoric is flattery, in contrast to philosophical rhetoric, exhibited by Socrates' speech in the *Apology* and the Speech of the Laws in the *Crito,* which aims at truth and the good of the soul, whether it gives pleasure or pain to the hearers. Protagoras is unaware of this distinction.

X

Socrates next proceeds to drive home his point (358b–d). No one voluntarily (ἑκών) pursues what he believes to be evil, for it is not in human nature to pursue evil instead of good—that is, given the hedonic equation, pain instead of pleasure. And if compelled to choose between evils, no one will choose the greater when he can take the less. To this the company all agree.

15. An art of this sort is discussed by the Eleatic Stranger at *Politicus* 283 ff. It should be remarked, that as his name implies, he speaks as an Eleatic and not as a Platonist.

The doctrine that no one voluntarily chooses evils was maintained not only by the Sophists[16] but by Socrates himself. It has generally been supposed equivalent to the claim that virtue is knowledge, or that to know the good is to do it.[17] As Aristotle remarks, the claim seems obviously false. For the self is sometimes divided in conflict of motives: men do what they ought not to do and they leave undone that which they ought to do—and this in some sense knowingly. In the *Meno* (77b–78b), when Meno claims that some men desire evil knowing it to be evil, he is met with the claim that to desire evil is to desire what is harmful, and to be harmed is to be made unhappy: no one wishes that. It has been claimed that this account confuses harm to another with harm to oneself; but assuming premises made explicit in the *Crito* and the *Republic*, to do harm to another is to act unjustly, and to act unjustly is to harm oneself, that is to say, one's own soul.

If this is so, no one willingly and wittingly does evil. In the *Gorgias* (466b ff.), Polus praises rhetoric because it is powerful: orators are like tyrants, who can kill or exile whom they wish. To which Socrates replies that one can do what seems good without doing what one wishes; but those who lack wisdom to understand what is good for them are to that extent not powerful. The tyrant, who does what seems good to him but not what he wishes, is least of all men free. One may choose to do evil, and intend it, but cannot wish it—cannot, that is, choose it willingly and wittingly. Wrongdoing implies a self inwardly divided between wish and desire, inwardly divided in conflict of motives. The doctrine that wrongdoing is involuntary is compatible with the fact of self-division, and indeed implies it. That all wrongdoing is involuntary is a conclusion Plato continued to accept to the end of his life (*Laws* 9.860d): "The unjust man is surely bad, but the bad man is bad unwillingly." The *Laws* makes clear that if action done in ignorance is involuntary, so too is action done when one is overcome by pleasure or mastered by fear.

The *Gorgias* also argues that the virtues are one, and that the good man is happy (506c–7c). The unity of the virtues implies their coimplication, and all are shown to be equivalent (not to wisdom but) to temperance. The fact that all virtues depend upon proper order of soul implies that the presence of temperance, or any virtue, requires the presence of the rest. To live well is to live justly and temperately, wisely and courageously. The moral arguments of the *Protagoras* are to the moral arguments of the

16. See Guido Calogero, "Gorgias and the Socratic Principle *Nemo Sua Sponte Peccat*," in *Essays in Ancient Greek Philosophy*, ed. John P. Anton and Goerge L. Kustas (New York, 1971), pp. 179–81.

17. *E. N.* 8.2.1145b22 ff. See also Richard Robinson, *Plato's Earlier Dialectic*, 2d ed. (Oxford, 1953), p. 14.

Gorgias as sophistry is to philosophy, as εἴδωλον or image is to οὐσία or reality. The pursuit of pleasure as good is a deficient imitation of living well. An art of measurement of pleasures and pains, if there were such a thing, would be a deficient imitation of wisdom.

XI

The hedonism of the *Protagoras* reduces virtue to an art of measurement of pleasures and pains. But though throughout the early and early middle dialogues Socrates accepts an analogy between virtue and the arts, he did not suppose that virtue is an art. An art is a kind of power or ability. The ability to be virtuous is not virtue, however, any more than the ability to play golf is golfing. The ability to be virtuous is actualized due to the βούλησις, the true wish of the soul for its own good (cf. *Gorgias* 466d ff.). "If a man does something for a purpose, he does not wish the thing he does, but that for the sake of which he does it." βούλησις is the rational wish of the self for its own good, and that wish is constant, a necessity of human nature. If this is a reason for claiming that virtue is analogous to an art, in that knowledge is a necesssary condition for virtue, it is also a reason for denying that virtue is an art. Art involves the capacity to produce opposite effects: to know the good in a given field is to know the bad and be able to produce it. For example, a gifted cobbler can artistically produce a pair of shoes that will not fit. But virtue is not a capacity to produce opposites: the virtuous man cannot be vicious. An art is an instrument, a means to attaining an end. Virtue is not a means to an end, but an end in itself. Because this is so, virtue is not an art. Virtue has to do not only with knowledge and power or ability, but with true wish. Put otherwise, virtue pertains to the rational will.

A consequence of this is put in the *Hippias Minor* (373c–76d; cf. *Crito* 44d). By arguing from analogy with the arts, Socrates concludes that only the good man, if anyone, can voluntarily, willingly and wittingly, do wrong, and that it is better to do wrong intentionally than to do wrong unintentionally. This result is necessary, if virtue is an art, and it is a reductio ad absurdum of that claim,[18] a claim that confuses appearance with reality.

18. Compare Philippa Foot, *Virtues and Vices* (Berkeley and Los Angeles, 1978), pp. 7–8:

Aristotle has sometimes been accused, for instance by von Wright, of failing to see how different virtues are from arts or skills; but in fact one finds, among the many things that Aristotle and Aquinas say about this difference, the observation that seems to go to the heart of the matter. In the matter of arts and skills, they say, voluntary error is preferable to involuntary error, while in the matter of virtues (what we call virtues) it is the reverse. The last part of the thesis is actually rather hard to interpret, because it is not clear what

XII

Hedonism is not utilitarianism, nor utilitarianism hedonism, but both unite in refusing to treat the virtues as the primary moral concern: virtues are mere dispositions to action, and the goodness of such dispositions must be defined by what actions are good: so actions are primary, virtues derivative. Kant, indeed, went further and thought that virtues could be vices: the coolness of the villain deepens the dye of his villainy—temperance and courage evidently being detachable from wisdom and justice.

The Socratic view is otherwise: virtue or justice is good in itself. It is to us as health is to our bodies, which must mean that we are more than our bodies: justice is the health of the soul, and actions are to be judged good derivatively, insofar as they tend to promote or preserve goodness of soul. Handsome does as handsome is. Socrates, who believed that justice and virtue are good in themselves, supposed they are, as Kant supposed the good will to be, a supreme principle of morality and of primary value apart from any consequences. In the *Republic*, Thrasymachus challenges Socrates to show that justice is a good to the just man, and Glaucon and Adeimantus ask him to consider justice apart from consequences of reward and punishment, which foreshadows historical fact, for the primacy of justice is the basis on which Socrates went to his death. The *Crito* shows the ethical necessity of the Socratic doctrine of the soul, for voluntary acceptance of execution was of no benefit whatever to his body.

XIII

Return now to the question of courage (358d–60e). Fear (δέος τε καὶ φόβον) is an expectation of evil. No one pursues what he fears if he can pursue what he does not fear, for what he fears he believes to be evil, and no one pursues or voluntarily accepts what he believes evil. Put in terms of the hedonic equation, if pain = evil, then no one voluntarily pursues evil, because no one voluntarily pursues pain.

---

is meant by the idea of involuntary viciousness. But we can leave this aside and still have all we need in order to distinguish arts or skills from virtues. If we think, for instance, of someone who deliberately makes a spelling mistake (perhaps when writing on the blackboard to explain this particular point), we see that this does not in any way count against his skill as a speller: "I did it deliberately" rebuts an accusation of this kind. And what we can say without running into any difficulties is that there is no comparable rebuttal in the case of an accusation relating to a lack of virtue. If a man acts unjustly or uncharitably, or in a cowardly or intemperate manner, "I did it deliberately" cannot on any interpretation lead to exculpation. So, we may say, a virtue is not, like a skill or an art, a mere capacity: it must actually engage the will.

Protagoras claimed that courage is detachable from the other virtues, that men may be unholy, unjust, intemperate, and ignorant, but still courageous. Can we then say that cowards knowingly (γιγνώσκοντες) refuse to pursue what is more noble and better, and therefore more pleasant?[19] If we do, Protagoras says, we'll destroy our former agreements. So if what makes men cowards is cowardice, cowardice must be ignorance of what is and is not to be feared. And if courage is the opposite of cowardice, and wisdom about what is and is not to be feared is opposite to ignorance of what is and is not to be feared, then wisdom about what is and is not to be feared is courage. In short, wisdom and courage are not detachable.

XIV

The foregoing account may be contrasted with that offered by Professor Irwin in his book *Plato's Moral Theory*.[20] The *Protagoras*, he claims, presents the fundamental premises of Socratic ethics, "Plato's first systematic defense of Socratic ethics," for Socrates there undertakes to show "that virtue can be taught as a craft" (p. 102). 'Craft' is offered as a translation of τέχνη. It is an unfortunate translation, if the *Oxford English Dictionary* is right in identifying the chief modern sense of the word as "skill or art applied to deceive or overreach; guile, fraud, cunning." Or, as Hobbes put it in *Leviathan*, "That crooked wisdom, which is called craft." Again, though Irwin speaks of the Craft Analogy, the assumption that virtue is analogous to a craft, it is clear by his discussion that he does not mean that virtue is merely analogous to a craft, but that it *is* a craft.

To rephrase, then, Irwin thinks that Socratic ethics requires that virtue is an art, and that virtue can be taught. This implies the unity of the virtues, he claims, not in the sense of reciprocal implication but of identity, because if knowledge is a sufficient condition for virtue, "then each of the virtues includes the same knowledge of good and evil, and nothing more—they are all the same virtue" (p. 104).

Knowledge is a sufficient condition for virtue because of Socrates' hedonism: pleasure is the final good, that for the sake of which everything is done. Because this is so, virtue is an art with a definite subject matter and procedure, the measurement of pleasure and pain; because

19. That going to war is, if noble and good, pleasant, amounts to a practical reductio ad absurdum of the hypothesis that goodness and pleasure are equivalent. If cowards are afraid with shameful fears (360b), there is a criterion of good and evil other than pleasure and pain, and one needs to answer the question of the *Laches*: What is courage?

20. *Plato's Moral Theory*, chap. 4. Vlastos thought this book one of the main contributions to Socratic moral theory in this century, and said that to read it was one of the outstanding learning experiences of his life.

it is an art, it is teachable; because it is an art, it is also merely instrumental, a means to happiness. Socrates does not suppose that virtue is good in itself.

Now, this is not in fact a moral theory. For Irwin suggests, borrowing a distinction from Sidgwick, that the hedonism of the *Protagoras* is both psychological and ethical (p. 104). Psychological hedonism is the doctrine that volition *is* always determined by pleasures or pains actual or prospective—the doctrine of the *Protagoras*—whereas ethical hedonism is the doctrine that volition *ought to* be so determined, that the pursuit of pleasure is a precept or moral principle. But that one ought to pursue pleasure can only mean, to a psychological hedonist, that it is good to pursue pleasure; and that it is good to pursue pleasure can only mean that it is pleasant to pursue pleasure. This is clearly not an ethical claim.[21] The hedonism of the *Protagoras* is sophistry: it looks like a moral theory, but it isn't one.

If it is not a moral theory, neither is it Plato's. Elsewhere, Socrates is made to offer powerful reasons for denying that virtue is teachable and that virtue is an art. It was the Sophists, or some of them, who claimed that, and Socrates who challenged them, as he challenges Protagoras. Nor does Socrates, except in the *Protagoras*, assert that knowledge is a sufficient condition for virtue; once again, it was Sophists such as Protagoras who claimed that, in claiming to teach virtue. Socrates, it is true, at the end of the *Protagoras*, affirms that virtue is knowledge and that it is teachable, but he does so assuming the hedonism of the many, while urging that the inquiry continue because he and Protagoras have not discovered what virtue is. As in the *Meno*, he supposes that virtue is teachable while explicitly denying that he knows what virtue is. In both dialogues, the dialectic ends in a tangle.

One need only look to the *Crito* to realize that Socrates did not suppose that virtue is a means to pleasure, and that he did suppose that virtue and more specifically justice—a virtue not discussed in the concluding argument of the *Protagoras*—is good in itself. But if virtue or justice is

21. Cf. Sidgwick, *Methods*, p. 41:

> If, as Bentham affirms, "on the occasion of every act he exercises, every human being is" inevitably "led to pursue that line of conduct which, according to his view of the case, taken by him at the moment, will be in the highest degree contributory to his own greatest happiness," then, to any one who knows this, it must be inconceivable that Reason dictates to him any other line of conduct. But at the same time, as it seems to me, the proposition that he "ought" to pursue that line of conduct becomes no less incapable of being affirmed with any significance. For a psychological law invariably realised in my conduct does not admit of being conceived as "a precept" or "dictate" of reason; this latter must be a rule from which I am conscious that it is possible to deviate.

good in itself, then virtue is not an art, since arts are concerned with choice of means, not with ends. Irwin, assuming in effect that justice is "another's good," criticizes the argument in the *Crito* on the ground that "either justice is a virtue and not all virtues benefit the agent, or virtues do benefit the agent, and justice is not a virtue" (p. 59). He criticizes Socrates' argument that since it is wrong to do injustice, it is wrong to do harm (a variant of the claim that it is better to suffer injustice than to do injustice), by suggesting that "the argument will be plausible only if Socrates explains what the psychic benefit will be, and how intentional infliction of harm on someone else damages my soul. His defence is as weak as his overall defense of justice" (pp. 59–60). Morally, of course, the proposition that it is better to suffer injustice than to do it, which Irwin finds tendentious, is necessarily true. Since Socrates, as a historical matter, almost certainly went to his death on the basis of the argument put in the *Crito*, whose foundation is that there is something in us that is benefited by justice and harmed by injustice, and that it is of greater worth than the body, we must conclude either that Socrates was fatally confused about justice in its relation to the human soul, or that Irwin is confused about Socrates.[22]

If it is not a moral theory, and it is not Plato's, it remains to inquire whether it is a theory. Irwin is an unabashed proponent of "The More Fool" Plato style of exegesis: "Much of what he [Plato] says is false, and much more is confused, vague, inconclusive and badly defended" (p. 4). Plainly, this involves a heuristic assumption: faced with a text we do not understand, we may assume either that we do not understand Plato, or that Plato is confused. It is much easier and quicker to assume the latter, and Irwin supposes it is not he but Plato who is confused. This assumption cannot be refuted, for any appeal to Platonic texts that contradict Irwin's assertions about them may be adduced as evidence of further confusion; so Irwin's exegesis is not only self-congratulatory but self-justifying in that it in principle admits of no denial. That is to say, it is unfalsifiable, which is a good reason to claim that it is also unverifiable, and therefore not a theory.

Plato's moral theory? Holy Roman Empire. Once again, we have the issue of appearance and reality.

22. Irwin says of Socrates in the *Crito*: "His comments on happiness, the good of the soul, and justice are not supported by a clear account of happiness or the soul's good; until a clear argument is found, the large claims about justice cannot reasonably be accepted or finally rejected." As it happens, happiness is not mentioned in the *Crito*, nor the soul except by the periphrasis "that in us to which justice and injustice pertain." And justice is not discussed in the concluding argument of the *Protagoras*.

XV

At the conclusion of the *Protagoras*, the argument itself accuses Socrates and Protagoras of foolishness (361c–62a). Socrates began by doubting that virtue can be taught, and now suggests that justice, temperance, and courage are knowledge, from which it would surely appear that virtue can be taught. Protagoras claimed that virtue is other than knowledge, which suggests that it cannot be taught, and yet puts himself forward as a teacher of virtue. Socrates would therefore like to go on to inquire what virtue is, and afterward return to the question of whether it can be taught. The *Protagoras*, which began with a concern for the good of the soul, ends with a demand for essence, an account of the nature of something that is.

2 Making New Gods

RONNA BURGER

INTRODUCTION

Socrates meets Euthyphro, the "seer" of the Athenian assembly (3c), at the stoa of the king, the Athenian archon in charge of impiety cases and responsible for presiding over the most awesome of the ancient sacrifices of the fatherland (cf. *Statesman* 290e). Just how fitting this backdrop is Socrates indicates at the end of the conversation by the use of a Homeric allusion in which he implicitly compares himself to Menelaus, whose journey homeward after the Trojan War was thwarted by the gods because of his failure to offer a proper sacrifice.[1] The sacrifice required of him, which Socrates discovers or confirms in the course of the *Euthyphro*—on the first day in the dramatic chronology of the dialogues surrounding his trial and death—is, apparently, the one he carries out in the *Phaedo*, which brings that series to an end.[2]

Euthyphro, who is altogether unaware of the sequence of decisions Socrates must already have begun to make, unwittingly indicates its starting point when he opens the conversation by wondering what "new thing" could have led Socrates from his usual haunts; for surely, Euthyphro assumes, despite their likeness in other ways, Socrates has not

1. Socrates implies this parallel by comparing Euthyphro to Proteus, whom Menelaus had to hold fast (*Euthyphro* 15d). See the remarks on this allusion to *Odyssey* 4.351–569 at the end of this essay and in note 35 below.

2. The dramatic time and place of the *Euthyphro* locate the dialogue in the sequence of seven that begins with the *Theaetetus*, leads on to the *Sophist* and the *Statesman*, and ends with the *Apology*, the *Crito*, and the *Phaedo*, but in a rather puzzling position. In its expected place, the *Euthyphro* would stand at the center of the series and introduce the trilogy representing Socrates' public trial, imprisonment, and execution; it is inserted, instead, into the trilogy devoted to the theoretical search for the philosopher, behind the split guises of sophist and statesman. More particularly, it intervenes between Socrates' seemingly unsuccessful practice of midwifery on Theaetetus and his replacement on the following day by the Eleatic Stranger, who may be, Socrates suspects, a refutative god in disguise (*Sophist* 216b). It is in this interval, apparently, that Plato finds the appropriate context for bringing Socrates under scrutiny as a maker of new gods.

come before the king, as he himself has, to initiate a lawsuit. Socrates has indeed been brought to this place by some "new thing," which from this moment changes his relation to the city, and thus, perhaps, his practice of philosophy; it is not, as Euthyphro rightly guessed, a lawsuit (*dikē*) he is initiating, but an indictment (*graphē*) against him he is answering, on the charge, as Socrates puts it uniquely on this occasion, of "making new gods" (2b).[3] This charge has its only explicit echo in the *Euthyphro* at the start of the second half of the dialogue, in Socrates' reference to a poet who composed verses about a fear-inspiring god, more literally, "the maker [*poiētēs*], who in making made: 'Zeus . . .'" (12a). The indictment, this echo suggests, takes Socrates to be another poet or maker, whose new authoritative beings threaten those made by the old poets, and he is to be put on trial for this activity perceived as a cause of corrupting the youth. The *Euthyphro*'s vindication of Socrates' practical intention is accomplished by the deed it portrays: Socrates' effort to hold Euthyphro back from his proposed action of filing suit against his own father shows him to be beyond blame for deliberately corrupting the youth. Far less obvious is the *Euthyphro*'s judgment on the charge of making new gods, which must be gleaned from the argument in pursuit of the question "What is the holy?" That argument unfolds in two phases, which divide the dialogue in two halves: in the first, Socrates undertakes with Euthyphro a search for a form of the holy; in the second, he abandons that effort and replaces it with an appeal to fear and shame.

The first phase of the argument culminates in the postulation of gods who are knowers of, and therefore subordinate to, the "ideas." The "idea" of the holy looks like a sample of the beings Socrates ranks higher than the gods; and if the "idea" were in any sense Socrates' construction, the first half of the *Euthyphro* would be a validation of the charge against him. Of course, Socrates seems to have good reasons for the way he puts this "idea" to work: only by placing a constraint on the willfulness of the gods can he place constraints on the mad Euthyphro, who models himself after those gods. The "idea" is a tool Socrates employs when faced with the corrupt state of a man who, on the one hand, takes the poets' stories of the gods so literally that they are altogether real for him, while, on the other hand, he attempts to derive from them universal principles of justice that defy convention. In contrast to the seer on both accounts,

3. It is in this, undoubtedly too literal, translation that one hears the echo of the charge against Socrates, which in turn raises the question of the relation between Socrates and the poets. Socrates' statement of the charge here seems to be his own anticipation of the indictment before receiving it. As Socrates refers to the indictment at his trial, it has nothing to do with "making": he is charged with not accepting in accordance with convention (*nomizein*) the gods the city accepts and instead accepting other new *daimonia* (*Apology* 24b–c).

Socrates admits to finding the poets' stories incredible, while he expresses shock at Euthyphro's readiness to violate ordinary norms of filial piety. Euthyphro's obvious familiarity with Socrates and with his peculiar habits cannot help but make us wonder whether Socratic philosophy is, however unintentionally, the source of Euthyphro's condition of partial liberation—even if what the dialogue highlights is Socrates' deliberate effort to overcome that condition. In keeping with its partial concealment of the issue of Socratic responsibility, the dialogue suppresses the germ of a tragic plot contained in Euthyphro's situation: it is an altogether comic lack of self-understanding of his own radicalism that Socrates discloses in Euthyphro step by step.

This disclosure reaches a pivotal point when Socrates poses his famous question, whether it is because the gods find something dear that it is holy or, rather, because it is in itself holy that they find it dear. On the first alternative, we would have to rely on revelation, sacred text, or hallowed tradition to communicate what the gods approve of; on the second, we could try to figure out for ourselves what the intrinsic property is that would merit divine approval, and thereby avoid the circuitous route of reliance on how the gods feel. The choice Euthyphro makes, which compels him to give up the definition of the holy he has proposed, sounds so Socratic, and Socrates' lack of endorsement for it sounds so contrary to ordinary expectations, that some contemporary references to the "Euthyphro debate" assign the positions in reverse.[4] Actually, what Socrates does is not exactly to reject Euthyphro's choice and embrace the alternative, but to indicate the inadequacy of the dichotomy separating them. In doing so, he suggests how Euthyphro's proposed definition might be defended, so as to preserve the status of the holy as determined by the response of the gods (or god), while precluding the conflict of their authority with human reason, more specifically, with the philosopher's quest for knowledge of the beautiful, the just, and the good.

Socrates can use the "idea" of the holy to restrain Euthyphro; but, as the central interlude of the dialogue makes especially evident, he cannot implant in him the desire to seek knowledge of it. Consequently, in the second half of the dialogue, Socrates must resort to other passions: his aim is to instill in Euthyphro fear of the same punitive gods Euthyphro

4. Socrates is thus taken to be the spokesman for "realism," Euthyphro the spokesman for "antirealism." It is Socrates who maintains, as Crispin Wright puts it, that the gods possess "a certain ability of detection—an ability to track piety," while Euthyphro's counterclaim "intends to repudiate the thought that piety has sufficient, as it were, constitutive independence from the opinions of the best judges [gods] to feature in the explanation of the direction that those opinions take; rather, such opinions enter in some constitutive sense into the determination of which acts are pious" (see *Truth and Objectivity* [Harvard University Press, 1992], pp. 79–80).

himself called upon and shame in the face of the human conventions associated with them. It is through his reflection on the poet's making of a god, or verses about a god, that Socrates introduces the passions of shame and fear into the account. Once he does so, Socrates turns his own understanding of the relation between those passions into a model for the holy in relation to the more comprehensive class of the just; it is, however, no longer the "idea" of the holy that is at stake, but the social practices that constitute it and the end that it serves in the political community.

In the course of the conversation, Socrates moves Euthyphro from an understanding of the holy that elevates the human to the level of the divine—the "imitation of god"—to one that expresses the greatest distance between them—the ritual of sacrifice. While Socrates invests each of these poles with a meaning altogether different from that which Euthyphro has in mind, the movement from the first to the last is one they undergo together: by this movement of the argument of the dialogue, the holy is dragged down from the heavens and into the cities.[5]

I. THE "IDEA" OF THE HOLY

As soon as he hears Socrates' report of the indictment against him as a maker of new gods, Euthyphro is certain of what lies behind it: the unenlightened many, enslaved by the conventions of the city, have no understanding of a phenomenon like Socrates' *daimonion*, the "prophetic" voice that places him in the same class of extraordinary human beings to which Euthyphro believes he himself belongs. Socrates differentiates himself from Euthyphro at first only on the grounds of the response of the Athenians, who laugh at Euthyphro and his prophecies, whereas they are so full of anger at Socrates—perhaps, as Euthyphro supposes, out of envy of his wisdom[6]—that only a seer could know how things will turn out for him.[7] In the idiosyncratic madness of Euthyphro's literal reading of the poets' stories of the gods, the city can ridicule the beliefs it is supposed to hold sacred; Socrates' making of new gods, on the other hand,

5. See Cicero's description of the Socratic turn (*Tusculan Disputations* 5.4.10–11).

6. Euthyphro ascribes to the Athenians the sort of envy Plato's Socrates ascribes to Aristophanes in regard to himself (see *Philebus* 50a).

7. One sign of the link between the *Euthyphro* and the *Theaetetus*, suggested by dramatic chronology, lies in Socrates' assigning to the prophet Euthyphro the same power as that which he grants to the rhetorician Protagoras, whose implicit claim to expertise in this regard contradicts his thesis of relativism; this, at least, is the admission Socrates obtains from Protagoras's self-contradictory supporter, the mathematician Theodorus (*Theaetetus* 178d–79b). Euthyphro's "soul-type," apart from his "art," reappears conspicuously in Theodorus, the theoretical man who thinks the greatest evil is to be ridiculed by the many (cf. *Theaetetus* 174a–75b and *Euthyphro* 3b–e).

is perceived as a threat to the city insofar as it is believed to be, at the same time, a making of others like himself (3c). Euthyphro, as Socrates already anticipates, proves entirely incapable of reproducing his own wisdom about the divine things in Socrates.[8] Whether Socrates is any more capable of reproducing himself is put into question by the Platonic corpus, where Socrates' successful conversion of another to philosophy is conspicuously absent. Surely the Athenians would not have had in mind the one counterexample indicated by Plato's deed. However that may be, the perceived threat that Socrates poses certainly cannot be due, as Euthyphro believes, to the utterly unique *daimonion.* Although Euthyphro himself reformulates the indictment so as to omit any mention of gods as living beings (3b),[9] and although he is about to accept, without any questions, Socrates' demand for an "idea" of the holy and the unholy, he does not suspect that this replacement of gods as the highest beings by "ideas"constitutes that criminal "innovation about the divine things" by which Socratic philosophy has made its mark on others, including himself.

Socrates does not directly attack Euthyphro's understanding of their kindred spirit. But contrary to both the public perception and the seer's, he immediately positions himself over against Euthyphro on the side of his father, by presenting himself as the victim of Meletus, who has run to the city accusing him, as a boy would run whining to his mother. Meletus, at least through Socrates' image, has turned the city into a family writ large, as much as Euthyphro is trying to dissolve the family into a collection of individuals who would be nothing but independent members of the city. In unwitting antagonism to paternal authority, both of them, from opposite directions, attempt to destroy the boundary separating the private and the public.

When Socrates expresses shock at hearing that Euthyphro's suit is against his own father although the victim is not even another relative, he points to the archetypal tragic situation that hovers behind the present comedy. The victim, who is in fact Euthyphro's laborer, was himself a

8. Socrates repeatedly begs Euthyphro, with no satisfaction, to teach him what he must surely know if he is so confident about punishing his father (*Euthyphro* 3d, 6d, 6e, 9a, 9c, 9d, 11e, 12e, 14c).

9. For Euthyphro, as Jan Blits observes, such "innovation" does not indicate impiety, or disrespect for the ancient gods (see "The Holy and the Human: An Interpretation of Plato's *Euthyphro*," *Apeiron* 14 [1980]: 20–23). In adopting Euthyphro's reformulation of the charge (5a), Socrates may be accepting responsibility for the ideas as "innovative" divine things, but not as living beings, nor as something made, in which case it would be their makers who are the gods (cf. *Republic* 10.597b vs. 601d, and see Leo Strauss's discussion in "On the *Euthyphron*," in *The Rebirth of Classical Political Rationalism: Essays and Lectures by Leo Strauss*, ed. Thomas Pangle [University of Chicago Press, 1989], p. 200).

murderer, and his father's intention to await word from the official "exegete," while neglectful, was apparently respectful of the law; his one act, moreover, of binding the man, happens to be the deed of Zeus to which Euthyphro is about to appeal on his own behalf. Of course, what Euthyphro emulates is Zeus's binding of his father, whereas, if Euthyphro's laborer could be said to stand in for himself, the roles would be reversed and the laborer's suffering, while bound and neglected by Euthyphro's father, would sound like the suffering of Oedipus at the hands of his father, in anticipation of the prophesied attack by his son against himself. To locate this theme on a sufficiently elevated level, Euthyphro has turned to the stories of divine fathers and sons.[10] Zeus's deed against his father, however, stands in Euthyphro's eyes as the instantiation of a universal law: the *nomos*—mentioned here for the only time in the dialogue—demands that the impious one should be punished, whoever he may be (5d–e). Euthyphro cannot believe that Socrates would be so conventional as to care what his relation is to the alleged criminal: whatever it may happen to be, to share hearth and home with him—the situation, presumably, of family members only—brings the same pollution (*miasma*), unless purified by prosecuting. In Euthyphro's mind a dark notion of pollution by contagion is tangled up with a universal standard of justice, which barely covers over an angry desire to punish his own father in particular.

Euthyphro must have quite precise knowledge about the divine things, Socrates infers, to violate tradition so boldly; and if he did have it, Socrates implies, he would be justified in doing so. Euthyphro himself, in any case, is well assured of his knowledge and so eager to demonstrate it that he does not stop to wonder why Socrates gives him no chance to answer what sort he says the pious and impious are (*to eusebes* and *to asebes*; 5c). Instead, he accepts immediately Socrates' substitute question, what he says the holy and the unholy are (*to hosion* and *to anhosion;* 5d),[11] hav-

10. It is the crimes of Cronos against his children that Zeus punishes, just as Cronos had taken vengence against his father, Uranus, for the crimes he had committed against his children (see Hesiod's *Theogony* 137–210, 456–508).

11. The two pairs of terms are never explicitly distinguished in the dialogue. The term "*eusebes*," Thomas and Grace West note, "emphasizes the reverence and respect, even fear, which one feels or ought to feel toward the gods" (see their translation of the *Euthyphro*, in *Four Texts on Socrates* [Cornell University Press, 1984], p. 46, n. 18, along with n. 17, p. 45, on "*hosion*"). Euthyphro first speaks about the *hosion* and its opposite, as something the many do not understand (4d9, e2), while Socrates introduces *asebeia* as the crime for which he is being charged (5c7). In the second half of the dialogue, when Socrates has abandoned the search for an *idea* of the *hosion*, it is the set of "the pious and holy things" (*ta eusebē kai hosia*, 12e) that is being sought as some part of the just. The impious things (*ta asebē*) are contrasted with the holy things (*ta hosia*) in the end (14b), as if they were contraries belonging to the same sphere. Plato's use of the two terms raises the question, as Marlo Lewis sees, of whether civic piety (*eusebeia*), or belief in the city's gods, is true piety or "holiness" (*hosiotēs*) (see "An Interpretation of Plato's *Euthyphro*, Part 1," *Interpretation* 12, nos. 2–3 [1984]: 247, n. 8).

ing in the meantime assented, without a moment's hesitation, to the premise that the holy is in every action itself the same as itself, the unholy the opposite of everything holy, itself like itself, everything which is to be unholy having one *idea* in accordance with unholiness (5d).[12] Since Euthyphro proves altogether ignorant of what this standard entails, what makes him ripe for it would seem to be the passion he has just displayed for a universal principle of punishment—itself the transparent veil over a very particular anger, the prototype for which is supplied by the highest god; this, at least, is what his most immediate response to Socrates' question suggests.

The holy, Euthyphro announces confidently, is "the very thing I am now doing," namely, prosecuting the one who is unjust, while not prosecuting would be unholy (5d–e). Socrates will soon criticize Euthyphro for offering a member of the class to be defined, rather than the characteristic shared by all members. If the holy is not something separate, however, but always "in" some action, though somehow the same in all, picking out one paradigmatic action seems to be the most reasonable way to identify it. The action Euthyphro has chosen to play this role is, moreover, a most fitting one. For what Euthyphro claims to be doing—literally what "I am now making" (*poiō*)—is an imitation of Zeus's punishment of his father, and this is just what entitles it to serve as a standard: "likening oneself to a god" seems to be the original version of looking to the *idea* as a paradigm (cf. 6e). The conventionally pious, who would assume an unbridgeable gap between behavior appropriate for gods and that appropriate for humans, are guilty, in Euthyphro's eyes, of holding—at least in the case of an extraordinary human being like himself—an indefensible double standard.

Before criticizing Euthyphro's response on purely formal grounds, Socrates, swearing "by the god of friendship"—Zeus, apparently, in some other mood—expresses dismay about its content. Having no leisure to hear all the startling tales Euthyphro knows, Socrates asks only what he thinks about stories like that of the battle between the Olympian gods and the Titans, which is a public extension of the private quarrel between Zeus and his father.[13] Its representation on the robe of Athena, used in the Great Panathenaea (6c), shows how the poets' narrations

12. Curiously, the holy is assigned self-identity, despite being inseparable from the plurality of holy actions in which it is, while the unholy has only likeness to itself, despite there being one *idea* as the measure of all unholy things (5d–e). It is when Socrates returns to the question to criticize Euthyphro's first response that he introduces, for the only time in the dialogue, "the *eidos* itself" by which all the holy things are holy, without clarifying why it is necessary if, as he claims Euthyphro already acknowledged, there is one *idea* by which both the unholy things are unholy and the holy things holy (6d).

13. See Hesiod's *Theogony* 621–890.

have been transformed by the city into public rituals, which only the mad Euthyphro infuses with the realism of their most literal reading. Why, then, does Socrates not share with Euthyphro the suggestion he slips into the second book of the *Republic* (378d) and try to find the *hyponoia*, or underlying meaning, with respect to which the truth of the poets' writings could be judged?

Socrates' reference in that context is precisely to the terrible deeds of Uranus, Cronos, and Zeus, which may lead young men to believe that in punishing their fathers' acts of injustice, they would only be doing what the greatest of the gods are said to have done; such tales are to be censored, therefore, in the name of the "beautiful lie" that no citizen ever quarreled with fellow citizen (*Republic*, 2.377e–78e)—which, in Socrates' best city, would be the only protection against sons fighting with their fathers. Carrying out his responsibility as the founder of this city, Socrates proceeds to lay down the molds of a theology to serve as law for the poets: the gods must be represented as utterly simple—the cause of good only and completely unchanging in form or appearance (378a–83a). Socrates is unafraid to practice on the gods just that artful care of the defective (*therapeia*) that Euthyphro will eventually reject as impious (cf. 13c–d): his theological canons turn the anthropomorphic gods of the poets before our eyes into "ideas," and Socrates only hints at what is lost in this transformation. What the poets represent are human passions that the city's moral education is designed to cover over; interpreted hyponoetically, then, the poets' representations have the potential of letting one sort of ray of light into the darkness of the cave.

Hesiod's Zeus, Socrates might have suggested to Euthyphro, is not a real being of superior status who is to be emulated, but a mirror in which one could learn something about the antagonism between fathers and sons, which Euthyphro is now, with no self-awareness, in the midst of enacting. Leading Euthyphro to some self-understanding, however, by exploring the *hyponoia* of the poets' stories of the gods, is an effort Socrates apparently finds either undesirable or impossible. His aim, rather, is to pull Euthyphro down from his Olympian heights. The initial device to effect this descent is provided by the "ideas." Euthyphro, who envisions himself among the gods who do whatever is dear to them, must be reined in by being compelled, in the first place, to imagine the gods themselves subjected to some sort of contraints. Hence Socrates puts off—indefinitely—Euthyphro's more esoteric tales to focus on the logical deficiency of his answer.

Euthyphro has failed to furnish the form itself (*auto to eidos*) by which all the holy things are holy (6d), Socrates charges, although he is posing this demand now for the first—and the only—time. For, Socrates goes on as if to explain, Euthyphro surely must remember saying that there is one *idea* by which the unholy things are unholy and the holy holy (6d). Euthyphro assures Socrates he remembers: he is not bothered, apparently, by the fact that the one *idea* belonging to all the unholy things, which he originally acknowledged (5d), has now become one *idea* determining the two opposites, nor is he bothered by the question of how it is related to the *eidos* by which the holy things are holy. Socrates certainly does not address that problem when he restates his request: what he wants to be taught is the one *idea* that can be used as a paradigm for judging any action as holy or not. For any action to serve that paradigmatic function, it would have to be under a description, presumably, specifying the characteristic that action is supposed to embody. Such a description in the case of Euthyphro's own action—although he does not supply it—should be "doing what the gods do."[14] In its rejection of the competing principle, well known to all parents—"Do what I say, not what I do"—Euthyphro's aggression against his father would again be made manifest. Of course, if there were such a thing as philosophic piety, and if it had to be understood more as an "imitation of god" than as submission to divine authority, Euthyphro's notion of himself belonging to the same class as Socrates would not be entirely unjustified.[15]

Euthyphro, in his attempt to meet Socrates' demand for a formally adequate definition, bypasses the problem of the tension between doing what the gods do and doing what they say by proposing a formula neutral to that difference: "what is dear to the gods" (*prosphiles tois theois*) is holy, and what is not is unholy (7a). Socrates praises Euthyphro's answer as an altogether beautiful one, although he replaces it, to begin with, by a compound word (*theophiles*), which might refer to a single god as the measure. The formula Euthyphro proposes, or its Socratic replacement, to which the discussion returns in the end (15b–c), seems in fact to be the only candidate in the dialogue for an "idea." It meets the formal requirement, more specifically, for one *idea* by which anything could be determined to be holy or not. Actually, Euthyphro goes further and makes whatever is

14. Leo Strauss contrasts this implied definition with the orthodox view, that piety is doing what the gods tell us to do, which consists in worshipping the ancestral gods according to ancestral custom ("On the *Euthyphron*," p. 197). Strauss's understanding of Euthyphro's deviation from orthodoxy is an important corrective of a view like that of P. T. Geach: "Euthyphro is an earnest and simple believer in the old tragic religion of the Hellenes" ("Plato's *Euthyphro*: An Analysis and Commentary," *Monist* 50 [1966]: 370).

15. "Likening oneself to god as far as possible" takes on a special meaning in the context of the central interlude of the *Theaetetus*—the conversation immediately preceding this one. When Socrates appeals to it as the only escape from the necessary evils hovering around "mortal nature and this place" (176b), he seems to be speaking aloud his own thoughts about responding to the indictment against him while at the same time presenting to the mathematician Theodorus an image of the one he called the "philosopher."

not dear to the gods unholy, so that everything must fall under one contrary or the other and nothing remain unaffected by the gods' response. Socrates pulls back from this consequence by means of yet another unacknowledged revision: if being dear to god is holy, to be the contrary, unholy, something must be hated by god. Socrates in this way allows for the possibility of cases that are neither holy nor unholy, and thus for a whole sphere of actions undetermined by the gods' response. The limited range of applicability of the definition is not, apparently, a fatal flaw; the only thing that would be is a self-contradiction resulting from its application, so that the same thing would turn out to be holy and unholy at once. Euthyphro's innocent affirmation of his belief in the fabled wars among the gods (6b–c) generates just that fatal flaw. The action he is contemplating, Euthyphro must admit, is bound to be dear to Zeus but hateful to Cronos, hence holy and unholy at once, which is reason enough, he grants, to reject the proposed definition.

If, as Socrates explains, it is precisely those hostile disputes for which no agreed-upon measure is available that motivate us in the first place to turn to a higher authority, gods who dispute these same matters can furnish no standard for us. The disputes in question, Socrates makes clear, are those concerning the just and the unjust, the beautiful and the ugly, or the good and the bad. The gods, as depicted by the poets, each recognize different things as beautiful and good and just; but whatever each recognizes as such, Socrates assumes, he finds dear, while hating the opposite (7d–e). Before making the issue explicit, Socrates implies an account according to which there is an intrinsic property, or a set of properties, to which a god's approval is a response; however much this response might bestow on something the characteristic of being holy, the response is itself determined by the god's recognition of that thing as beautiful, just, or good in itself. If there were many gods, some kind of contract among them might constitute an agreed-upon measure, equivalent to the standard unit of length or weight. But such unanimity could be guaranteed only if the disputed opinions about the beautiful, the just, and the good were transformed into shared knowledge of these "ideas" and recognition of their instantiations. And even a single god, if his response were not determined by such knowledge, could always be in conflict with himself.

Euthyphro, in contrast, stakes his last-ditch effort to avoid the problem of disputing gods on the same principle by which he justified his own action (cf. 5e): no god would disagree that one who kills unjustly must be punished (8b).[16] For this, though, the gods are hardly necessary

16. Actually, according to the *nomos* Euthyphro originally formulated, it is one acting impiously who is not to go unpunished, although he wants to prosecute his father for act-

as a standard; at least Socrates is pretty confident that Euthyphro has never heard the claim from any human being that one who has killed or done anything unjust should not be punished. What the gods must dispute, then, no less than human beings, is whether a particular action is just or unjust; "for certainly, wondrous one," Socrates addresses Euthyphro, "no one either among gods or humans dares to say that one doing injustice ought not be punished" (8d–e). Euthyphro, who assents wholeheartedly, has no idea how wide a gulf separates Socrates from gods and humans on the question of the legitimacy of punishment.[17] If he and Socrates share in the principle that piety is a matter of "likening oneself to god," the punitive gods Euthyphro emulates and the rational one Socrates posits have nothing in common.

For present purposes, Socrates is willing to grant to Euthyphro that all the gods think that the death of Euthyphro's laborer is unjust and hate it (9d)—he is silent about the gods' unanimous approval of Euthyphro's proposed action against his father[18]—because he is eager to get on with examining what could now be laid down as an emended "hypothesis": the holy is that which all the gods love, the unholy that which they all hate, while those matters that some love and some hate would be neither or both together (9d). Euthyphro is pleased with this proposal; he does not seem to be bothered by the thought that his own action remains a possible member of this last, indeterminate, or even self-contradictory class, despite the fact that Socrates had just rejected the original version of the definition of the holy on the grounds that it led to this consequence. Perhaps, being satisfied with Socrates' concession that all the gods hate his father's deed, he has become less interested in defending his intended action than in defining the holy itself.

---

ing, not impiously, but unjustly (6a). By now (8b), however, all unjust action has become a concern to the punitive gods.

17. The personified laws in the *Crito*, which seem to be equivalent in that dialogue to the poets' gods in the *Euthyphro*, conclude the speech Socrates imagines with a threat of vengeance against any disobedience to them, to be carried out by their brother laws in Hades (54c). Before the voice of the laws fills his ears, however, Socrates seeks Crito's agreement on the principle that it is never right to requite injustice or, when suffering bad, to respond by doing bad in return (49d): if, as Socrates insists, this principle is so fundamental that those who disagree on it have no common ground for discussion at all, it must mark an unbridgeable divide between him and the city that punishes him.

18. Socrates begins with a promise to praise Euthyphro's wisdom unceasingly if he can demonstrate sufficiently that all the gods believe his action to be correct (9a); but he changes the test when something occurs to him that makes him doubt that he would learn anything about the holy and the unholy even if Euthyphro could demonstrate that all the gods believe a death like that of his laborer to be unjust. For that would make this act hateful to god; but since there could always be another case where disagreement was possible, and contradiction the consequence, the required unanimity must be incorporated into a revision of the definition itself.

Should the proposed definition be examined, Socrates asks casually, or just accepted because someone says it is correct? Despite having no doubts that the definition is "beautifully spoken," Euthyphro acknowledges the need to investigate: he seems ashamed to accept by a mere appeal to authority the holy as defined by appeal to the gods' authority. Either out of genuine ignorance, however, or anticipated self-defense, Euthyphro claims to have no idea what distinction Socrates is after when he subjects the definition to the standard of a causal account: Is something holy because it is found dear by the gods or, rather, is it found dear by the gods because it is in itself holy (10a)? Socrates offers to clarify the point by a series of examples meant to establish that, if anything becomes or undergoes something—being carried, being led, being seen—it is only because of a corresponding action on it by an agent—carrying, leading, or seeing. If, as Euthyphro immediately grants, being found dear is like these cases, something would be a thing found dear only because someone finds it dear. Socrates artificially stops the account from proceeding to the question of whether there is something intrinsic in the object that arouses the response of one who finds it dear. He stacks the deck in just the opposite way when he returns to the holy and asks whether it is found dear by all the gods because it is holy, or for some other reason, to which Euthyphro understandably replies, "because of this" (10d).

Socrates prevents, or at least discourages, Euthyphro from maintaining, on the one hand, that there may be no reason for what the gods find dear—or if there is, that it is something other than the holy—but on the other hand, when anything else is concerned, that there may be some intrinsic property of something that leads someone to find it dear. He splits the specific case, involving the gods, from the general account of finding something dear; he treats them in opposite ways—the latter is only a cause, the former only an effect; and, with no protest from Euthyphro, he refutes his definition of the holy as that which is dear to the gods. What Socrates has split is a whole constituted by the double direction that characterizes the experience of *eros*: while the lover perceives and responds to something in the beloved, his love in turn magnifies or enhances its object in such a way that it becomes more than what it was in itself (cf. *Phaedrus* 251a–53c).[19] The gods Euthyphro takes over from Socrates here are not erotic; in finding dear (*philon*) that which is intrinsically holy, they

19. On the one hand, as Seth Benardete describes it, "Each soul-type seeks out a soul-type in conformity with its own paradigmatic god," on the other, "Each type deliberately sets out to construct and fashion a kindred nature into a statue and a god" (see *The Rhetoric of Morality and Philosophy: Plato's "Gorgias" and "Phaedrus"* [University of Chicago Press, 1991], p. 148).

are not like the lover who worships his beloved like a god.[20] Euthyphro's choice does reflect some effect of Socrates' effort—the gods are now constrained by an *idea*; only this *idea* is left unintelligible and the gods who contribute nothing to it are superfluous.

Euthyphro had already in effect abandoned an appeal to what the gods find dear as an irreducible determinant of the holy when he granted, in the prior stage of the argument, the necessary unanimity of the gods; for if the shared response of all the gods, indeed the consistency of one god with himself, were necessary and universal, it would be because it is grounded in knowledge. Euthyphro chooses the alternative that leads to the rejection of his definition, perhaps, because he wants the gods to be the objects of a knowledge he can claim to possess, which will distinguish him from the many. He does not see the clues Socrates has furnished for a way of defending the definition of the holy as that which is dear to all the gods without sacrificing the intelligibility of the holy and therefore the rationality of the gods: while nothing is holy, he could have argued, apart from the gods' approval, or unholy apart from their disapproval, such a response is the product of the gods' knowledge of the just, the beautiful, and the good, or their contraries, as recognized in particular cases. Of course, it might still look, in that case, as if the gods and the sacred communication of what they hate or find dear could be dispensed with while we figure out for ourselves what the grounds would be for such responses.

That Socrates does not advocate such an attempt to bypass the gods[21] — at least not in the case of the rational gods he has imagined—seems to be the result of a complex set of reasons. In the first place, not everyone devotes himself to seeking out the grounds on which the wise gods, if they existed, would condone and prohibit what the tradition of a community

20. All the terms for the gods' loving have been related to *philon*, while *erōs* and cognate terms are absent—unless at 14c the manuscript reading "the lover must follow the beloved" (*ton erōnta tō erōmenō*), rather than "the questioner must follow the questioned" (*ton erōtōnta tō erōtōmenō*), were adopted. Socrates, in that case, would be claiming to follow Euthyphro as beloved—while of course in fact leading him—just before concluding that the holy is gratifying to the gods (*kekharismenon*; 15b).

21. On Laszlo Versenyi's reading of the *Euthyphro*, this is just what Socrates does. The assumption that piety is knowable and a virtue, which he takes Socrates and Euthyphro to share, entails the acceptance of holiness as a "concept logically separate from and prior to the concept of what is god-loved." Although this rejection of a "god-centered definition" brings the first half of the dialogue to a negative conclusion, it "points dialectically to a humanistic, man-centered definition of even this supposedly 'religious' virtue." But the consequence, which Versenyi finds supported by the second half of the dialogue, is that piety or holiness has no special domain apart from virtue as an indivisible whole (see *Holiness and Justice: An Interpretation of Plato's "Euthyphro"* [University Press of America, 1982], pp. 131–32).

claims they do; even if it were true that all human beings have a natural desire to know, it is far from true that all are willing and able to do everything necessary to act on such a desire. The philosopher might be defined as someone who is so willing. If he sets out to ask, Why would a wise god find this action just, or beautiful, or good?, he is led to the questions: What is the just? What is the beautiful? What is the good? It is precisely on the basis of his claim to have knowledge of his ignorance of the answers to these questions that Socrates separates his own "human wisdom" from divine wisdom (cf. *Apology* 23a–b). In such a condition, positing a god who knows provides a standard by which to judge one's own falling short of knowing and at which to aim—as long as this is not a jealous god, who sets willful limits on the human striving for knowledge.[22]

The assumption of divine wisdom plays a role, that is, for the philosopher as well as for the nonphilosopher—for the latter because of his lack of autonomy; for the former because realizing his autonomy requires positing a standard of knowledge that he does not believe himself to have already attained. This seems to be the sort of piety Socrates displayed when confronted with the riddling speech of the Delphic oracle, who pronounced him the wisest of men—or at least no one wiser: Socrates' awareness, on the one hand, of his own lack of wisdom, together with his assumption, on the other hand, that the word of a god could not simply be a lie, produced a state of perplexity that propelled him into a lifelong investigation of what the oracular message must mean (cf. *Apology* 21a–b). This paradoxical Socratic piety is, perhaps, not an inappropriate model for the reader confronted with the riddling text of a Platonic dialogue: proceeding on the assumption that its author possesses a divine wisdom, particularly when it is hidden, motivates the interpreter to figure out its meaning for himself.

Socrates' hint of how to save Euthyphro's proposed definition has fallen, however, on deaf ears: being dear to all the gods may be an attribute of anything holy, but, Euthyphro accepts in conclusion, it has not shown itself to be what makes something holy, and hence is not the "beingness"

22. Aristotle admits, in the *Metaphysics*, that the "divine" wisdom being sought might justly be thought beyond human power to acquire; but he is careful to reject the poet's explanation of this—a jealous god withholds it—in favor of his own—human nature is in many ways slavish (1.2, 982b29–93a4; cf. Seth Benardete, "On Wisdom and Philosophy: The First Two Chapters of Aristotle's *Metaphysics* A," *Review of Metaphysics* 32, no. 2 [1978]: 215). Maimonides, similarly, addressing the potential philosopher in the *Guide of the Perplexed*, stresses his agreement with "our sages" on the principle that there are reasons for all the commandments even when not obvious to us; but in place of their explanation—God hid them from us so they would not be held in little esteem—he refers only to the deficiency of our intellect (3.26).

(*ousia*) of the holy (11a). Socrates regards this as a temporary defeat and is ready to begin again from the beginning, but Euthyphro has started to despair: whatever they put forward so enthusiastically somehow moves around and is unwilling to abide where they set it up (11b). Euthyphro does not at first assign any blame for this predicament—not until Socrates presents an image that denies his own responsibility. If only, Socrates grants, the "works in speeches" were his own, Euthyphro could have laughed at him for taking after his ancestor, the sculptor Daedalus, whose statues were said to be so lifelike they would get up and run away.[23] But given Euthyphro's understandable protest—the speeches would have remained perfectly still if it had been up to him—Socrates must admit to being an even more clever artist than Daedalus, able to set in motion not only his own things, but, apparently, alien ones as well, albeit by a strange artistry operating against his will, since he wants nothing more than to have the speeches abide. Socrates is not a maker of artifacts, that is, of opinions; he only breathes the life of thought into opinions that would otherwise be calcified by complacency. But it is another form of fixity—that which Socrates posits as the *idea*—that is the source of motion, paradoxically, in the opinions that fail to live up to it. The motion of the speeches is a dim adumbration of the motion of Socrates' desire to know; but this is a desire that Euthyphro does not share, and that cannot be acknowledged in a conversation where "*eros*" is as absent from mention as "soul" or "philosophy."[24]

II. SHAME AND FEAR

If, as Socrates surmises, it is Euthyphro's assumed wealth of wisdom that has made him lazy, it must be Socrates' awareness of his own poverty in this regard that enables him to offer a contribution, still in the hope of being instructed by Euthyphro (11e). What Socrates knows he does not know is the class characteristic that constitutes the "beingness" of the holy; in that state of ignorance he now proposes to identify the members of the class of the holy by determining the relation of that class to the

23. Socrates puts the same image to work at the end of his conversation with Meno to answer the question why true opinion and knowledge should be other, and one more honorable than the other: true opinions are beautiful works and bear good results—as long as they are true—but they run away as easily as the statues of Daedalus unless tied down by "figuring out the cause," which would transform them into knowledge (*Meno* 97d–98a).

24. Jan Blits notes the absence of "soul," "philosophy," and "nature" ("The Holy and the Human," p. 21), to which "*eros*" could be added. It is striking that Socrates concludes his reflections on the decisions he has made in both the *Apology* and the *Crito* with a reference to "god" in the singular, which never appears in the *Euthyphro*.

just.[25] The just, according to the account Socrates implied in the first half of the dialogue, makes itself manifest as an intrinsic property of something that elicits the gods' approval, that in turn conferring the relational property of being holy. Anything holy, in that case, would necessarily be just, but not the other way around. Socrates now begins from that relation of class inclusion, without tracing it back to the causal account he implied, according to which the holy was derivative from the just.

The genus Socrates seems to have in mind now, of which the holy would be a subset, is punitive justice; at least the model he constructs is that of fear as the comprehensive class of which shame would be a species, and these passions seem intended to disclose something about the just and the holy beyond a merely formal analogy. It is on the grounds of this model that Socrates separates himself from the poet, whose composition of verses he describes as a matter of "making: 'Zeus. . . .'"[26] Whatever it is exactly that the poet has made—the god, or his name, or a claim about him—it hardly gives rise to a sense of control; on the contrary, the specter of the angry superior being it conjures up seems to arouse shame or awe rooted in trepidation: "where fear is, there is shame" (12a). Socrates claims to hold just the opposite. What he is rejecting at the moment is not the poet's punitive god—for that may prove useful (cf. 15d); it is, rather, the poet's genetic account of the passions inspired by such a god (fear as a source of shame) that Socrates wants to replace with an eidetic account (shame as a kind of fear), in order to model on it a relation in which the holy will occupy a restricted sphere within the territory of the just, while necessarily conforming to the standard of the just.

Before giving Euthyphro a chance to apply the model, however, Socrates alters it by adding another, seemingly unnecessary, example. The odd is a part of number, he explains, just as shame is a part of fear; but it is one part codefined by another within a neutral genus, as Socrates indicates when he goes on to illustrate the form of the answer he is looking for by declaring what he would say if asked what part of number the even is. If odd and even number were the fitting model, the just and the holy would be two mutually exclusive and jointly exhaustive species of some comprehensive genus and no single action could be holy and just at the

25. That part of the just that constitutes the holy is no longer referred to as an eidos or as something that has an idea, and nothing is said about its self-sameness, its relation to a contrary, or to the particulars characterized by it. The class of holy things might be a subset of the class of just ones without, in fact, precluding the possibility that being dear to the gods is the class characteristic of the holy.

26. Given the controversial manuscript for these lines, it is difficult to determine with any confidence precisely what it is, according to the poet, that arouses fear, and with that shame.

same time, in contrast with the original model of shame and fear, where everything holy would necessarily be just. Euthyphro does not notice the difference. If, as it seems, he is relying on the model of odd and even number when he divides in two the genus he should call "*therapeia*," care of the gods and care of humans would be two mutually exclusive species. But while he identifies care of the gods as the holy, he leaves care of humans unnamed; for he retains "the just," from the model of fear and shame, as the name for the comprehensive genus. If Euthyphro has in this way mixed Socrates' two models, the result would entail that something holy could be called "just" in a broad sense, but no single action could count as caring for gods and at the same time caring for human beings. The action Euthyphro is contemplating against his father makes his own commitment clear.

Socrates, who has obviously led Euthyphro to this problem, finds him to have spoken beautifully; the one small point still uncertain is just what Euthyphro means by "*therapeia*." If it is an art analogous to that which horsemen practice on horses, huntsmen on dogs, or oxherders on oxen, our *therapeia* of the gods would be another case in which the superior artisan aims at some good or benefit for the needy inferior it treats. The holy, which was in the first half of the dialogue doing what the gods like, has now become doing what is good for them: the alternatives are either gratification or artful care aiming at the best.[27] But gratification turns out, according to Socrates' implicit account in the first half of the dialogue, to be of beings who find dear not what they experience as pleasant, but only what they take to be just, beautiful, or good; artful care, on the other hand, is driven back finally to gratification, since the gods, as Socrates gets Euthyphro to admit now, should have no need or defect that we could make better. Euthyphro, apparently already affected by Socrates' model of fear and shame, swears by Zeus that he had no such hubristic intention in defining the holy as a kind of *therapeia*. He certainly does not understand the *therapeia* Socrates practiced in the first half of the dialogue, with the rational reconstruction that transformed the gods of the poets into knowers of the just, the beautiful, and the good.[28]

What he had in mind, Euthyphro now explains humbly, is the kind of care slaves pay to their masters; Socrates proposes the label "artful service"

27. It is on the basis of these fundamental alternatives—either the arts engaged in "care" (*therapeia*) or the practice of flattery—that Socrates precludes Gorgianic rhetoric from being an art, given its ignorance of the causes of its power and its lack of concern with the good (*Gorgias* 464b–65b).

28. This insight—which seems crucial to understanding the argument of the whole—I owe to Robert Berman.

(*hypēretikē*)—the term by which he will describe to the jurors his own relation to the god, only in his case without the suffix indicative of an art (*hypēresia; Apology* 30a). Euthyphro has so much at stake in the claim to expertise, Socrates must realize, that as long as he does not have to give that up, he can be led to assume his proper position. If service to the gods, though, is one art among others, there should be some special deed (*ergon*) it accomplishes. Socrates does not spell out what exactly he has in mind when he offers as a model artful service to or for doctors, which produces health (13d). He is thinking, presumably, of some subordinate, say the nurse, who ministers to the master artisan, not for his benefit, essentially—that comes to him indirectly, in the form of payment—but for the good of the patient whose defect is to be treated. Whatever that subordinate service is by which we minister to the gods, it must be, according to this model, for the satisfaction of human needs. Service to the gods, though, hardly seems to constitute one particular art among others, directed to one particular defect of nature; if piety has a more universal end, however, it would be in competition with the city of arts as a whole, which aims at self-sufficiency and mastery over nature. It would indeed be superfluous if, as Socrates' two further pairs of examples suggest, all the arts had the same kind of control as shipbuilding and housebuilding have over their material (13d–e), and none were as vulnerable to the vicissitudes of chance as generalship and agriculture (14a):[29] there would be no place in the city of arts, under these conditions, for such pious practices as prayer and sacrifice before planting and battle. The dialogue that began with the role of piety in relation to passions in the family ends with its role in relation to the arts in the city: if it is a desire for autonomy that underlies Euthyphro's resentment of his father, its echo in the city would seem to be the quest for self-sufficiency through the arts[30]—and one may need as much as the other the external constraint provided by recognition of the gods.

Whatever the benefit that results from our service to the gods, it could follow simply from our attitude of subordination to superior beings, even if they did not exist. But Socrates allows his original formulation to slide, unnoticed by Euthyphro, into the question of what the gods accomplish by using us as servants, and in the end, simply, what the many

29. If, as Socrates' examples indicate, chance marks the limits of control by human art, and such limitation is the condition for recognizing dependence on the gods, that would be manifest above all, as Strauss observes, in the case of the architectonic art, that of legislation ("On the *Euthyphron*," p. 203).

30. The beginning and end of the *Euthyphro* would thus suggest the link Michael Davis brings to light in juxtaposing the aims of the tragic hero in Sophocles' *Ajax* and of modern science in Descartes's *Discourse on Method* (see *Ancient Tragedy and the Origins of Modern Science* [Southern Illinois University Press, 1988], esp. pp. 1–5).

beautiful things are, in sum, that the gods accomplish (13e–14a).[31] The end of the holy becomes unrestricted at the moment we are no longer the practioners of artful service, but the gods themselves have become the agents. Exasperated at this point by Socrates' inability to grasp what a lengthy task it is to learn precisely about such matters, Euthyphro is ready to answer "simply": knowing how to say and to do what is gratifying to the gods, in praying and sacrificing, constitutes the holy things, which save private families and the city in common, while the things not gratifying to the gods, which are impious, overturn and destroy everything (14b). The impious things destroy private families and the city, for one thing, as Euthyphro's case indicates, by violating the boundary between them; practice of the holy things, on the other hand, serves the city by affirming the limits of the city—of its arts and of its principles of justice.

Socrates rebukes Euthyphro for veering off from this answer, as if he made it impossible to examine the end of piety by stipulating the practices that constitute it, which, moreover, seems to be precisely the point toward which Socrates has been dragging Euthyphro all along: the formula "prayer and sacrifice"—into which Socrates must read his own distinctive meaning—brings about Euthyphro's acknowledgment of the holy as it is "first for us," that is, the conventional behavioral rituals prescribed by civic religion. Of course, Euthyphro may be willing to accept it only because Socrates speaks of it as an *"episteme"* (14c)—the science of asking from the gods what we need and giving them what we think they need. Holiness as an art of barter, which hardly strikes awe in the heart, leaves unsolved, in any case, the problem of what the gods get out of the deal. The only possibility would seem to be recognition of their status as superior beings, through honor, praise, and gratitude; but this, Euthyphro grants, is certainly dear to the gods, and the argument thus appears to fall prey to Socrates' attack against it, for having been led right back to its central moment of defeat. To Socrates' observation that either they did not agree beautifully before or they are now positing something incorrect, Euthyphro responds only "It seems so" (15c): he may suspect, but he cannot articulate, that being dear to the gods was rejected as the cause of anything being holy, but not as a possible attribute of the holy thing, which is all that is being claimed at present. Socrates used the *idea* in the beginning to shake Euthyphro's perfect confidence

31. Socrates first asks not about the *ergon* of the gods (cf. Mark McPherran, "Socratic Piety in the *Euthyphro*," *Journal of the History of Philosophy* 23, no. 3 [1985]: 298–309), but about the *ergon* accomplished by our service to the gods, like that accomplished by service to shipbuilders or housebuilders or service to doctors. It is only after reminding Euthyphro of his extraordinary knowledge of these matters that Socrates, unnoticed, changes the question to what the gods accomplish by using us as servants, analogous to what generals or farmers accomplish (13d–14a).

in the extraordinary knowledge of the divine things he claims to have; he exploits Euthyphro's lack of understanding of that standard in the end to prevent his conventional description of the holy things from being presumed sufficient.

If, as Socrates charges in the end, Euthyphro were responsible for making the speeches go round in a circle, he could hardly do so "more artfully than Daedalus" (15b–c): that could only be Plato's accomplishment. "Statues in motion" sounds, in fact, like a fitting description of the Platonic dialogue,[32] whose fixed speeches seem to be self-moving when our act of interpretation awakens them. Socrates had introduced this image at the center of the conversation to deny his own production of anything but motion. He seems to confirm that self-assessment by the Homeric tale to which he alludes in conclusion.

In his unsuccessful attempt to fix on anything stable in the ever-flowing motion of Euthyphro's speeches, Socrates compares himself to Menelaus, who finally managed to get hold of the sea god Proteus, as he constantly wriggled out of one shape into another. Menelaus is describing to Telemachus, in the passage alluded to (*Odyssey* 4.351–569), his attempt to return home at the end of the war. Unaware of a sacrifice he owed to the gods, he was held back in Egypt, until one of the higher beings, the goddess Eidotheia—whose name means something like "divine in form"—took pity on him and informed him how he could wrest from her father Proteus the secret of the sacrifice required. Only through the mediation of form (Eidotheia), to paraphrase Homer, is it possible to arrest the unintelligible flux of the first things (Proteus);[33] but that activity, according to Homer's story, far from leading to neglect of the gods, is that without which we live in ignorance of what higher beings would expect of us. What Menelaus learned led him back to the river Egyptus, to offer holy hecatombs that made possible the continuation of his way homeward. The sacrifice Socrates is contemplating is presumably that of his own life, and his journey homeward leads to Hades, the invisible.[34]

32. That the statues of Daedalus are the Platonic dialogues is the striking suggestion of Seth Benardete.

33. With the goddess Eidotheia, Homer himself provides a fitting image, as Marlo Lewis notes, of the Socratic–Platonic "transvaluation of values" that carves out of the Homeric world of flux a place for investigation of "forms"; it is hard to believe, though, that this is merely "by a strange coincidence" (see "An Interpretation of Plato's *Euthyphro*, Part 2," *Interpretation* 13, no. 1 [1985]: 63).

34. To convince Crito that his death will not take place on the following day, Socrates reports the dream he just had in which he was told "on the third day you would come to fertile Phthia" (*Crito* 44a–b). While the speech is assigned to a beautiful woman in white—Achilles' mother who warns him of his impending death if he enters the war (*Iliad* 18.96), its words are those of Achilles, threatening to set sail for his homeland (9.363), as Leo Strauss notes (see "On Plato's *Apology of Socrates* and *Crito*," in *Studies in Platonic Political Phi-*

Socrates does not indicate whether this sacrifice is an expiation for past neglect or an offering for future benefit.[35] There is one other possibility: the sacrifice itself is to be condemned, and Plato's writing up of Socrates' decision to make it an "indictment" (*graphē*) against him, for his failure to protect philosophy from the harshness of the city except through the most extreme measure. Such an indictment would be a paradoxical one. For Plato's protection of philosophy without the need for self-sacrifice is accomplished through the fabricated image—the moving statue—of Socrates in conversation. Meletus's indictment seems to be misdirected against Socrates: the maker of new gods is Plato.[36]

---

losophy [University of Chicago Press, 1983], p. 55). The two alternatives for Achilles—either a long life at home after abandoning the war or a heroic death in it—are incompatible; Socrates can conflate them insofar as the philosopher's homeland is Hades, "the invisible place" (cf. *Phaedo* 80d).

35. Socrates' sacrifice of his life is, apparently, incomplete: he dies still owing a cock to the god of healing and must rely on Crito to pay the debt (*Phaedo* 118a).

36. This study began with the support of a National Endowment for the Humanities Research Fellowship in 1993. My reflections on the *Euthyphro* were stimulated by discussion with graduate students and faculty at The Catholic University of America when I spoke on the dialogue in the fall of 1993. A summer grant from the Tulane University Committee on Research in 1996 enabled me to complete revisions of the paper for publication.

3 The Significance of Some Structural Features of Plato's *Crito*

KURT PRITZL, O.P.

Plato and Aristotle agree that some opinions and not others are to be esteemed. Plato has Socrates explain in the *Crito* that he honors (πρεσβεύω καὶ τιμῶ; 46c1) and hearkens to (προσέχειν τὸν νοῦν; 46d1) the opinions of the expert few, and not to the opinions of the many. Aristotle in the *Topics* distinguishes a class of opinions that he calls ἔνδοξα, that is, opinions "held in esteem or honor," opinions "of high repute."[1] This class consists of the opinions held by everyone, by the majority of people, and by the wise.[2] Aristotle's inclusion of the opinions of the many among ἔνδοξα seems explicitly and directly to disagree with the *Crito.*

Aristotle's advocacy of the opinions of the many in the *Topics* is remarkable in itself as a philosophical position, and all the more so for the fact that he shares with Plato a low regard for the many as a social class.[3] The contempt for the many and their opinions that Plato exhibits throughout his writings is less surprising, but it reaches an extreme in the *Crito.*[4] In fact, the opposition that Socrates develops in the *Crito* between the standpoint and views of the vulgar many and those of the wise few is so extreme that one wonders on these terms how cities, possessed of the

1. *LSJ*, s. v., ἔνδοξος, 1.1. J. Barnes, in "Aristotle and the Methods of Ethics," *Revue internationale de philosophie* 34 (1980): 490–511, retrieves this sense against the previously accepted renderings of "resting on opinion, probable, generally admitted."

2. *Top.* 1.1.100b21–23: "those opinions are reputable which are accepted by everyone or by the majority or by the wise—i.e. by all, or by the majority, or by the most notable and reputable of them." The Revised Oxford Translation of Aristotle's works is used throughout unless otherwise noted.

3. *E.N.* 1.4.1095b19–20; *Pol.* 2.7.1267a41–b9 and 5.8.1308a9–10; *Rh.* 2.5.1382b4–5. See J. E. Garrett, "The Moral Status of 'the Many' in Aristotle," *Journal of the History of Philosophy* 31 (1993): 171–89, for a good discussion with references and some important distinctions; and H.-D. Voigtländer, *Der Philosoph und die Vielen* (Wiesbaden, 1980), for a full-scale comparative study.

4. N. A. Greenberg, "Socrates' Choice in the *Crito,*" *Harvard Studies in Classical Philology* 70 (1965): 56, 60.

many and needing the expert few to do well at all, hold together, and more fundamentally, how humans communicate in human ways across the divide of the vulgar and the wise.[5]

The thesis of this essay is that Plato's *Crito,* despite its contempt for the many and their views (in fact, in tandem with it), affirms the existence of a foundational set of opinions held in common by the many and the expert few. These opinions are foundational in at least three ways. First, they are views held by all or most people, and thus they constitute a common outlook in a society or community, however obscure and inarticulate. Second, these common opinions express basic views with respect to human life and conduct that properly serve as starting points for reflection and discussion on these fundamental matters. To the extent that shared discussion and common deliberation are necessary for social and political life, this foundational set of opinions conditions the possibility for the many and the few of a common life as citizens and as humans. Third, this set of opinions functions in the thought of the *Crito* much in the way that the ἔνδοξα of all or most people function in the account of revered opinions in Aristotle's writings. Such opinions express basic views insofar as these views are pretheoretic or prescientific and can be considered independent of a λόγος, account, or explication. Views implied in our use of language are often foundational and common in this sense. Aristotle gives this example: Everyone agrees that the final good achievable by action is happiness. People disagree, however, about what happiness means or what constitutes happiness, that is, about what the λόγος or account of happiness is (*EN* 1.4.1095a17–28).

I argue for these claims about Plato's *Crito* through the structural analysis of the text that follows. The comparative claims about Plato's *Crito* and Aristotle's account of ἔνδοξα can be described here but not established, since they require more discussion of Aristotle's account than can be managed in this space.[6]

5. L. Strauss, in "On Plato's *Apology of Socrates* and *Crito,*" *Studies in Platonic Political Philosophy,* with an introduction by T. L. Pangle (Chicago and London, 1983), states: "The cleavage among men is no longer that between knowers and ignoramuses, or between the philosophers and the non-philosophers ['philosopher' does not occur in the *Crito*], i.e., between the few who hold and the many who do not hold that the unexamined life is not worth living, but that between those who hold that one may not requite evil with evil and those who hold that one may, or even ought to, do it. One may wonder how there can be a city if there is no common deliberation between those few and these many" (p. 59). Cf. T. Payne, "The *Crito* as a Mythological Mime," *Interpretation* 11 (1983): 6.

6. Regarding the background in Aristotle for this comparative claim, see my "Opinions as Appearances: *Endoxa* in Aristotle," *Ancient Philosophy* 14 (1994): 41–50, and my "Ways of Truth and Ways of Opinion in Aristotle," in *The Importance of Truth: Proceedings of the American Catholic Philosophical Association* 67 (1993): 241–52.

STRUCTURE

The text of the *Crito* divides in an obvious and uncontroversial way into five sections: (1) an introduction in which Socrates awakens to find Crito at his side and where a conversation ensues about the imminent return of the sacred ship from Delos and Socrates' dream of a beautiful woman clothed in white (43a1–44b5); (2) Crito's speech to Socrates in which he urges Socrates to agree to his friends' plans for his escape from prison and rescue from execution (44b5–46a8); (3) the dialogical middle portion of the *Crito* where Socrates and Crito consider the value of majority opinion and the power of the many, and agree upon two tenets central to the issue of escape, namely, (i) that injustice should not be repaid by injustice, and (ii) that just agreements must be kept (46b1–49a3); (4) the speech of the personified Laws and constitution of the city where the Laws urge Socrates to remain in prison and be executed (50a6–54d1); and (5) the closing where Socrates with the speech of the Laws in his ears says he is enraptured as by Corybants (54d2–e2).

These five sections constitute a symmetrical plan, built about the central third section. When the *Crito* is folded along the crease of this center, the other parts align with each other and display their own mutual structural similarities. The first introductory section parallels the fifth closing section. Both these sections feature religous themes, either civic or personal, and make Crito silent while Socrates is entranced by prophetic dream or religious rite. The second section, Crito's speech, parallels the fourth section, the speech of the Laws and the constitution.[7] Both these sections make Socrates silent or nearly silent and subject him to the impassioned rhetoric of Crito or the Laws. Both these speeches, as I argue below, represent the views of "the many," though a different majority in each instance.[8] At the fold is the third section, the center of the *Crito*, which stands between the parallel halves it both separates and binds together.[9]

7. K. Quandt, "Socratic Consolation: Rhetoric and Philosophy in Plato's *Crito*," *Philosophy and Rhetoric* 15 (1982): 248 and n. 25, n. 26. Quandt fails to see a "measured" character of the speech of the Laws; see below.

8. The many (οἱ πολλοί) can be considered quantitatively or qualitatively. From a quantitative standpoint, a given community has without equivocation one "the many" (different majorities arising in a given community under different formalities [political party affiliation, religious affiliation, ethnic identity, etc.] would mostly overlap in membership). In my argument Plato's introduction of a second majority in the fourth section does represent an expansion of the given community by the introduction of the personified Laws and constitution of Athens with their brothers in Hades. From a qualitative standpoint "the many" in the most basis sense represents those incapable of philosophy. Both majorities displayed in the *Crito* are nonphilosophical (though in importantly different ways) and thus accurately designated qualitatively as "the many."

9. This symmetrical plan, which I find apparent in the text and whose significance is at issue, is indicated without prejudice to a recognition of the Platonic dialogue as an ascent. I

This structural center is indeed the true center of the dialogue. It is the only part of the *Crito* where dialogue becomes, more strictly speaking, dialectic.[10] This conversation, in which Socrates asks questions and Crito answers them, holds the key for understanding the meaning of the symmetrical structure of parallel parts and the unity of these parts with the center.

This dialectical middle section of the *Crito* itself has a threefold structure. Two stretches of dialectic between Socrates and Crito (46b1–48b10, 49a4–e4) frame a statement of the true nature of the issue in dispute between them and of the proper way to resolve it (48b11–49a3).

The true nature of the issue in dispute is whether it is just (δίκαιον) for Socrates to escape (48b8–d5). All other considerations regarding circumstances or consequences are irrelevant. The proper way to resolve this issue is through a shared inquiry of the Socratic kind based on questions and answers and relying on mutual agreement at every step (48d8–49a1).

These two points–(i) what is to be examined (τοῦτο σκεπτέον; 48b11) and (ii) how it is to be examined (. . . ὦ Σωκρατες, ὅρα δὲ τί δρῶμεν. Σκοπῶμεν, ὦ ἀγαθέ, κοινῇ . . . ; 48d6–8)—are the center of the center of this work. They are reached by the agreement of Socrates and Crito in the dialectical discussion that opens the third (middle) section (46b1–48b10; see 48b11), and they are immediately followed by the second dialectical discussion that attempts to move from them by mutual agreement and which closes the middle section when Crito can no longer continue in dialectic (49a4–e4; see 49a1–3).

Thus at the fold of the *Crito* stand two characters in a drama of disagreement, who are found to agree about the issue between them and how to resolve it. One of them, Crito, has made an impassioned plea for Socrates to escape. The other, Socrates, has said directly in response that he will only change his mind and abandon his own arguments on the basis of the type of reasoning that yielded those arguments in the first place (46b1–c6).

---

would suggest, however, that in the case of the *Crito* the ascent turns at the middle of the dialogue so that at different heights the same ground is viewed at the correspondings parts of the text. I am grateful to Mitchell Miller for raising this issue. The late Leonard Woodbury liked the image of climbing a martello tower and viewing the same terrain from different heights to describe the ascent of a Platonic dialogue.

The structural considerations I raise here, which emphasize the importance of the center or middle of the text, have affinities with the notion of pedimental structure developed by H. Thesleff, though he denies Platonic authorship of the *Crito* and argues that it has a climactic rather than a pedimental structure. See H. Thesleff, "Looking for Clues: An Interpretation of Some Literary Aspects of Plato's 'Two-Level Model,'" in *Plato's Dialogues: New Studies and Interpretations*, ed. G. Press (Lanham, Md., 1993), pp. 19, 23, 33, and 36.

10. Quandt, "Socratic Consolation," p. 240 and n. 6.

Who are these two characters according to the plan of the text and what do they stand for? They are alone together in Socrates' prison quarters and talk, and yet through them other parties enter into the discussion. Who are these other parties that participate in the text through Socrates and Crito, and what do they stand for?

PARTIES OF THE DIALOGUE

An inventory of the parties of the *Crito* obviously begins with Socrates and Crito. They are alike and bound to one another as affectionate friends of the same age from the same deme.[11] They are also different, indeed opposite. Socrates is poor and Crito is rich; Socrates can sleep sweetly, but Crito is in anxious wakefulness; Socrates is philosophical and Crito is not. Through these two figures in their likeness and opposition other distinct parties enter the drama of the text. The rationale for listing these other parties who appear and even speak through Crito and Socrates is this: Socrates and Crito, despite their differences, stand at the center of the *Crito* in agreement. This agreement takes several forms: there is agreement in their shared background; their friendship betokens an agreement, since friends are other selves; they agree upon the issue at hand; and, to the extent that they engage in dialectic at *Crito* 49a–50a5, they agree step by step in the conversation. The parties who enter the text by likeness to one or the other of them and gather about them according to the symmetrical plan of the text share more or less in this link and agreement. Who are these others?

First, Socrates and Crito have friends in common. Crito alludes to these other companions of Socrates and to their readiness to aid his escape despite its attendant risks to themselves (44e2–45b5). As befits his long-standing attachment to Socrates, Crito enjoys preeminence among them; indeed, the news so grievous to all of Socrates' companions, that the ship from Delos is back, is most grievous to him (43c5–8). Socrates and Crito also have friends in common in the sense of Socrates' children, whose well-being Crito considers his own proper interest (45c8–d8, 54a1–b1).

Second, Crito as different from Socrates brings parties unlike Socrates into the text.[12] For example, Crito has his own foreign friends, including associates in lawless Thessaly, who would honor those friendship ties and

11. *Plato's "Euthyphro," "Apology of Socrates,"* and *"Crito,"* ed. with notes by J. Burnet (Oxford, 1924), pp. 172–74. For the strength of the friendship tie within the deme, see F. R. Earp, *The Way of the Greeks* (Oxford and London, 1929), pp. 32–33.

12. For a nice statement of Crito's speech, see Quandt, "Socratic Consolation," pp. 240–42.

give refuge to a fugitive Socrates (45c2–4, 53d3). More importantly, Crito represents and gives voice to the nonphilosophical many, that is, the πολλοί or the Athenians.[13] This is not to say that Crito is a friend of the many. He is not. The many, as the enemy of Socrates his friend, are an enemy to him too. We might suspect, of course, that were it not for Socrates, Crito could live quite at peace with the many, but the fact is that Crito finds himself at enmity with them for the sake of Socrates. In any case, Crito sees it necessary to care about the opinions of this vulgar enemy and to respect their power. Furthermore, Crito's speech to Socrates shows that in fundamental ways he thinks and feels as the many do.[14] Crito conceives justice as they do and finds shameful what they find shameful. Thus, if not a friend of the many, he is a friend of their outlook. For example, he tells Socrates at the beginning of his speech: "what could be more shameful [αἰσχίων], than the appearance [δόξα] of putting money before friends? People [οἱ πολλοί] won't believe that you refused to escape even though we were eager to help" (44c2–5).[15] Crito would rather try to persuade Socrates now than the many later, not just because he must believe that he has better chances with Socrates than with the many, but because he agrees with the many. It is shameful and ignoble for both Socrates and for Socrates' friends for him to stay in prison and be executed when he has a chance to escape. The highest standard for goodness, nobility, and justice is recognized success at helping and preserving oneself and one's family, friends, and associates, and at harming one's enemies. This traditional moral standpoint is the basis for Crito's speech and the sign of his agreement with the vulgar many.[16]

Third, Socrates as different from Crito brings parties unlike Crito into the text. One such party is the expert, whose opinions alone, according to Socrates, are worthy of attention and respect. Who actually is the one expert in matters pertaining to justice (48a7), to whom Socrates would have recourse in this issue of just action, remains a question.[17] Some

13. J. Adam, ed., *Crito* (Cambridge, 1927), p. xv; Greenberg, "Socrates' Choice," p. 49; Payne, "The *Crito*," p. 1; Quandt, "Socratic Consolation," p. 243 and n. 17; L. Pearson, *Popular Ethics in Ancient Greece* (Stanford, Calif., 1962), pp. 240–42.

14. With the previous note, see also K. J. Dover, *Greek Popular Morality in the Time of Plato and Aristotle* (Berkeley and Los Angeles, 1974), pp. 39–45.

15. Translations of the *Crito* are from R. E. Allen, *Socrates and Legal Obligation* (Minneapolis, 1980). Translations of the other works of Plato are from E. Hamilton and H. Cairns, eds., *The Collected Dialogues of Plato Including the Letters* (Princeton, N.J., 1963).

16. For a good general discussion of traditional Greek morality, see Earp, *Way of the Greeks*, pp. 30–40; more specifically, see Dover, *Greek Popular Morality*, pp. 180–84, 273–78, and 301–6, and Mary Whitlock Blundell, *Helping Friends and Harming Enemies: A Study in Sophocles and Greek Ethics* (Cambridge, 1989) pp. 26–59.

17. At *Laches* 184c9–85a3 Socrates argues for expert opinion over the opinion of the many with Lysimachus, Melesias, Laches, and Nicias, and says that if an expert does not

think that Socrates himself is the expert.[18] In a striking phrase Plato writes that the expert about just and unjust things is "but one man, and the very Truth itself" (ὁ εἷς καὶ αὐτὴ ἡ ἀλήθεια; 48a7). It is of great moment, of course, whether in fact he exists, since, as Crito puts it with regard to the proposed escape, "it isn't time to decide but to have decided" (46a4–5). A decision must be reached, and it must be reached by some standard.[19] The speech of the Laws is important in this regard, for in a limited time it accommodates Crito to a course of action formerly repugnant to him by a measured quasi- or nonphilosophical discourse which, nevertheless, enraptures the philosopher Socrates (see below).

In fact, the Laws and the common constitution of the city (οἱ νόμοι καὶ τὸ κοινὸν τῆς πόλεως; 50a7–8) are a second party that Socrates introduces into the text. Two variations of this phrase also appear, namely, the Laws and the city (πόλις; 50b1–2, 50d1, 51d3–4, 51d7–8, 52b2, 52b8–c1), and the Laws and the country or fatherland (πατρίς; 51a2, 51a5, 51c1).[20] They are friends of Socrates, who appear as persons and present themselves as parents.

This personification of the Laws, constitution, city, and fatherland is unparalleled in the Platonic corpus.[21] Although all are personified, only the Laws speak. Since the time of Solon, a distinction had been made between laws and the constitution.[22] The constitution established offices such as courts and assemblies, while laws specified the rules and procedures by which they functioned. Plato seems to observe this distinction. The Laws speak of "the ways we render judgment and govern the other affairs of the City" (51e2–3), and they imply that finding a city pleasing entails finding its laws pleasing but is not constituted by it (53a4–5). Hence the constitution gives the city a specific shape and the laws implement the constitution in the lives of those who inhabit the city and have it as a fatherland.

---

exist among themselves (εἰ ἔστιν τις ἡμῶν τεχνικὸς περὶ οὗ βουλευόμεθα ἢ οὔ; 185a1), then they will have to seek one somewhere else (ἄλλον τινὰ ζητεῖν; 185a3). See also Strauss, "On Plato's . . . *Crito*," p. 58; and Payne, "The *Crito*," p. 5.

18. G. Grote, *Plato and the Other Companions of Sokrates*, 2d ed. (London, 1867), vol. 1, p. 308.

19. Regarding Socratic conversation, the search for a standard for moral excellence, and the competence of the many, see R. E. Allen, *Plato's "Euthyphro" and the Earlier Theory of Forms* (London, 1970), pp. 22–23, 34–35.

20. Regarding the claims of the πάτριος πολιτεία, see A. Fuks, *The Ancestral Constitution: Four Studies in Athenian Party Politics at the End of the Fifth Century B. C.* (London, 1953).

21. Greenberg, "Socrates' Choice," pp. 61–62; T. B. L. Webster, "Personification as a Mode of Greek Thought," *Journal of the Warburg und Courtauld Institutes* 17 (1954): 12 and passim.

22. G. R. Morrow, *Plato's Cretan City: An Historical Interpretation of the "Laws"* (Princeton, N.J., 1960), pp. 81–82, 196–97; cf. Aristotle, *Pol.* 3.11.1282b10–13, 4.4.1292a32.

The Laws who speak through Socrates constitute a πολλοί or a many, but not the vulgar many represented by Crito. They are presented and speak in the plural. They speak for, just as they implement, the constitution as the κοινόν, as what is shared by all in the city and as what binds all together. Most importantly, as is pointed out by many commentators in different ways, what they say is not fully philosophical in character (or not philosophical at all) and it includes suppositions that the vulgar many hold.[23] Thus when they speak they have means to persuade Crito, who has had to drop out of the philosophical argument of the third section of the text, and others like him.[24]

The Laws, nevertheless, are not the vulgar many. They appear in the fourth part of the *Crito* as the counterpart of the vulgar many presented through Crito in part two, according to the symmetrical plan of the text. Although their arguments include suppositions shared by the vulgar many, they argue for a conclusion opposed by them. Plato's use of the phrase τὸ κοινόν for "constitution" or "government" (instead of, say, πολιτεία) is significant. In the analysis below several interconnected senses of the common emerge and Crito's many appear alienated from the common in various ways. The text also holds out, however, a many not so alienated from the common, namely, the Laws and τὸ κοινόν themselves.

With the Laws another party enters the text, their brothers in Hades. The brother Laws in Hades are the correlate of Crito's friends in Thessaly. The quality of their respective receptions of Socrates would be based solely on Socrates' friendship or enmity with their respective friends, namely, the Laws of the city or Crito.

Finally, Socrates introduces the beautiful woman dressed in white from his dream and the Corybants from his rapturous experience of the speech of the Laws.

All these parties figure in the philosophical significance of the *Crito*. Five of them—the many, Crito, Socrates, the expert, and the Laws—are the parties most important for my argument. I distinguish them and the others for these reasons.

(1) I draw these distinctions in order to unite. The vulgar many, Crito, Socrates, the expert, and that other many, the Laws, are all distinct

23. See, e.g., R. E. Allen, "Law and Justice in Plato's *Crito*," *Journal of Philosophy* 69 (1972): 557–67; Grote, *Plato*, pp. 302, 305; Payne, "The *Crito*," pp. 19–20; G. Vlastos, "Socrates on Political Obedience and Disobedience," *Yale Review* 63 (1973–1974): 519; E. J. M. West, "Socrates in the *Crito*: Patriot or Friend?," in *Essays in Ancient Greek Philosophy, Vol. 3: Plato*, ed. J. P. Anton and A. Preus (Albany, N.Y., 1989), p. 77; G. Young, "Socrates and Obedience," *Phronesis* 19 (1974): 1–29.

24. Pearson, *Popular Ethics*, p. 201.

participants in the text. The structure of the text connects or links them all one to another, however, through the linked pair that is Crito and Socrates. Socrates and Crito, similar and different, stand together in agreement at the center of the text. Through them and their respective standpoints the others arrive on the scene and participate in the agreement binding Socrates and Crito. (2) To explain what this common link or bond consists in is the chief burden of the rest of this essay. (3) The explication of this common link or bond must observe and respect the differences of the various parties. A fundamental issue of the *Crito* is the division and, indeed, the opposition between the senseless many and the philosophical one. My argument that Plato's *Crito* understands them to share common ground at some foundational level requires maintaining their differences as much as showing what binds them as citizens and human beings. The explication of this link of many and one begins with an investigation of the *Crito*'s characterization and critique of the many.

THE RANDOM MANY

The opening section of the *Crito* previews the division between the philosophical one and the nonphilosophical many that becomes the subject of considerable discussion later. Crito remarks concerning how cheerfully and easily Socrates endures his misfortune. Socrates responds that it is inappropriate for a man his age to be vexed at having to die. Crito replies that others the same age in similar misfortune do not behave in a similar way. Socrates simply agrees without further comment (43b6–c4). Both men see the difference.

In Crito's speech one of the first arguments Crito puts to Socrates concerns one's reputation (δόξα; 44c2) among the many. Crito says that it is necessary (ἀνάγκη; 44d1) to care about the opinion (δόξα; 44d2) of the many, even though they do not know the facts (44b9), because the ignorant many can inflict the greatest of evils (44b9–c5, d1–5), including the loss of an irreplaceable friend (44b7–8). Socrates questions why one should be concerned about the many's opinion (δόξα; 44c7) and denies that they are able to accomplish either the greatest evils or the greatest goods. His reason? "[T]hey cannot make a man wise [φρόνιμον] or foolish [ἄφρονα]. They only act at random [ποιοῦσι δὲ τοῦτο ὅ τι ἂν τύχωσι]": 44d9–10. By "random action" Socrates means that on any given occasion the many do whatever it is that they happen to do. There is an indifference to their actions in the sense that they shift heedlessly from one course of action or one opinion to another.[25] Crito concedes the point

25. Adam, *Crito*, p. 32; Burnet, *Plato's . . . "Crito,"* p. 180.

(ταῦτα μὲν δὴ οὕτως ἐχέτω; 44e1), and shortly thereafter he argues for the justice of escaping prison by accusing Socrates of shameful indifference with respect to his children: he begat them and now he proposes to abandon them ("the choice you're making is one of the most heedless indifference"; 45d4–6).

Socrates himself provides a premiere example of this indifference later, at the very middle of the dialogue. When Socrates has established with Crito that the single issue before them is whether or not it is just (δίκαιον) to escape, he adds:

> But as for these other considerations you raise about loss of money and raising children and what people think [δόξης]—Crito, those are really fit topics for people who lightly kill and would raise to life again without a thought if they could—the multitude [τῶν πολλῶν]. (48c2–6)

The phrase "without a thought" renders the Greek οὐδενὶ ξὺν νῷ (48c6) and expresses the inability of the many to hold to one determination in thought over time, an indifference that extends even to matters of life and death. The text gives ξύν instead of σύν. Burnet notes that ξύν was obsolete in Plato's day, but Plato does use it in the corpus and his decision to use it here may be significant.[26]

There are two parallel instances with thematic relevance to consider. The first is from Aristophanes' *Clouds*, the play that hurt Socrates' reputation among the Athenians (*Apol.* 18d1–2). *Clouds* 580 reads μηδενὶ ξὺν νῷ. In this part of the play the chorus leader in accordance with the norms of the traditional friendship ethic accuses the audience, that is, the city, of injustice against the Clouds, represented by the chorus. The Clouds, he complains, bring more blessings to the city than all the other gods, and yet they are not given sacrifices or even libations. As an example of their care, the chorus leader points out that when the city mounts some military expedition μηδενὶ ξὺν νῷ, the Clouds let loose with warning omens of thunder and rain. K. J. Dover comments on this phrase: "The ordinary soldier, whose standpoint Old Comedy adopts, commonly regards his generals and their orders as half-witted."[27] Aristophanes' text, then, applies to the generals, the elite and presumably expert few, the tag that Socrates applies to the many.

When Socrates uses οὐδενὶ ξὺν νῷ at 48c6 to characterize how the many act, he has already in an earlier passage denigrated the opinion of the many by appeal to our common reliance on expert opinion (46c6–48a10). The issue remains what constitutes expert opinion and whether

26. Burnet, *Plato's "Crito,"* p. 196. Cf. J. Kerschensteiner, "Zum Gerbrauch von σύν und ξύν bei Platon," *Münchener Studien zur Sprachwissenschaft* 1 (1952, rev. 1956): 28–41.

27. Aristophanes, *Clouds*, ed. K. J. Dover (Oxford, 1968), p. 174.

true experts actually exist. Socrates does argue in *Republic* 6 that the many correctly hold a negative view of philosophy, given those whom they take to be philosophers (6.489d1–5). This part of the *Republic* combines a description of the genuine philosopher with an account of the many's disdain for those whom they see to be philosophers (5.474b3–6.497a8). Socrates' criticism of the many by recourse to expert opinion must include a specific enough account of genuine expert opinion and reasoning with respect to the δίκαιον to fend off or even appropriate some part of the sentiments of the many regarding purported experts. Aristophanes' use of μηδενὶ ξὺν νῷ at *Clouds* 580, where we get a view of (so-called) expert opinion from the perspective of the many, tallies with this point.

The second, much older, parallel text is fragment 114 of Heraclitus, which reads:

> Those who speak with sense [ξὺν νόῳ] must rely on what is common to all [τῷ ξυνῷ πάντων], as a city must rely on its law, and with much greater reliance. For all the laws of men are nourished by the one [law], the divine [law]; for it has as much power as it wishes and is sufficient for all and is still left over.[28]

Heraclitus is punning here (ξὺν νόῳ, or "with sense," and ξυνῷ, or "what is common") to the effect that to have sense or thought is to have what is common to all things. The common, in turn, is linked to the city through its laws, a link that Plato himself presents by his coupling of the Laws and the constitution (τὸ κοινόν). In fragment 2 Heraclitus makes the further connection between the common and the λόγος, and then uses the notion of the common to describe the relationship of the many to the λόγος. Fragment 2 says:

> Therefore it is necessary to follow the common [τῷ <ξυνῷ>; but although the Logos is common [ξυνοῦ] the many live as though they had a private understanding [ἰδίαν . . . φρόνησιν].

Thus fragments 114 and 2 of Heraclitus lead us from having thought to the common and from the common to the λόγος. The many are oblivious of the common and hence are oblivious of the necessity to follow it. Thus they do not follow the λόγος, which is common. They act, rather, according to a private understanding, even though the λόγος is all around them. As common, the λόγος is the source of their life in the city and, indeed, is given in the very use of language that unites them to each other.[29]

28. Translations of Heraclitus are from G. S. Kirk, J. E. Raven, and M. Schofield, *The Presocratic Philosophers: A Critical History with a Selection of Texts,* 2d ed. (Cambridge, U.K., 1983).

29. See the discussion below of the text from *1 Alcibiades* where Socrates and Alcibiades agree that the many can teach the Greek language.

Oblivious of the common, they are oblivious of the λόγος and are without thought or sense, οὐδενὶ ξὺν νῷ. Plato's use of οὐδενὶ ξὺν νῷ recalls Heraclitus's connection of the λόγος with the common and the common life which the many share, although they are not cognizant of it.

In fact, immediately after Socrates says that the many carry on οὐδενὶ ξὺν νῷ, he uses the word λόγος in a line strikingly translated by Allen: "As for us, the argument [λόγος] has chosen . . ." (ἡμῖν δ', ἐπειδὴ ὁ λόγος οὕτως αἱρεῖ; 48c6–7).[30] Burnet renders the key clause ὁ λόγος . . . αἱρεῖ by "the reckoning proves."[31] What the λόγος has chosen or proves is that the only question worth considering is the rightness of escape from execution (48c7–d5). For Heraclitus, the λόγος ultimately is a cosmic principle of order and direction that is expressed in the things derived from it, such as the laws of the city or the language shared by all. Socrates is not using λόγος in this cosmic sense here. The proximate reference of this instance of λόγος as argument or reckoning is the immediately preceeding passage 46b1–48b10, especially 47a2, where Socrates and Crito consider in common (κοινῇ; 46d5) the worth of Crito's λόγος about the worth of opinions (46c7–8). This passage, like 48c6–8, also leads to the conclusion that only the question of rightness should determine how Socrates acts (48b11–c1). It does so by the type of shared argument or reckoning that is typical of Socrates and indeed which Socrates, Crito, and other interlocutors engaged in often before. Some of these previous discussions are folded into the present instance of reckoning (46b6–8, 46c8–d2, 46d7–e1, 47a13, 48b3–6). Thus λόγος here refers to the ordered and nonarbitrary reckoning exemplified in the previous dialectical section of the text. λόγος or argument in this sense includes all the unchanging demands and requirements that engagement in argument entails for those who give themselves to it. Thus Plato recognizes in what he means by λόγος, a λόγος that chooses, qualities of the Heraclitean λόγος.

The λόγος or argument does choose for Socrates and Crito. The λόγος chooses in the sense that the course of the inquiry is not left to their private determinations or choices but must follow a certain order, proceed by certain rules, and obtain a certain result. The choice of the λόγος is for a conclusion that is common in the sense of valid in all circumstances and over time. Those without λόγος are "without thought," without the common, and as though possessed of a private understanding that shifts according to their random and indifferent sense of things.

30. With respect to an allusion to Heraclitus, J. van Ophuijsen has pointed out to me the relevance of noting ὁ λόγος αἱρει as an idiomatic expression in Ionic. For some details, see Burnet, *Plato's "Crito,"* pp. 196–97.

31. Cf. Burnet, *Plato's "Crito,"* pp. 196–97.

In *Metaphysics* 12.10, where Aristotle discusses the teleological arrangement and order of the universe (what in Heraclitean terms is a consideration of the λόγος of the universe), he draws this analogy:

> For all are ordered together to one end. (But it is as in a house, where the freemen are least at liberty to act as they will [ὅ τι ἔτυχε ποιεῖν], but all things or most things are already ordained for them, while the slaves and the beasts do little for the common good [τὸ κοινόν], and for the most part live at random [ὅ τι ἔτυχεν]; for this is the sort of principle that constitutes the nature of each.)[32]

The freemen are least at liberty in their actions, which are ordered for them according to the κοινόν, whereas slaves and animals have little connection to the κοινόν and act at random. The freeman's nature is thus fixed with respect to the κοινόν; the slave's is not.

This understanding of the ordered nature of the freeman, who does not act at random but for the κοινόν, sheds light in several ways on the *Crito*. For example, the Laws claim later that citizens are the offspring and slaves of the κοινόν (50e3–4). Commentators sometimes construe this notion as one that would have been been highly offensive to Athenian freemen.[33] It occurs in contemporary oratory, however, and must have had some popular appeal.[34] These remarks of Aristotle present the freeman's lack of liberty and subjugation to the κοινόν in positive terms, namely, an ordination to an end that slaves lack. Our present concern is the randomness of the many in their thinking and action. This randomness is found in thoughts and actions that are "without νοῦς." It shows itself as indifference and inconsistency with respect to the κοινόν and to λόγος and its norms. Aristotle's remarks concur with the indications in the *Crito*. The many, to the extent that they think and act at random and have little to do with the κοινόν and λόγος, are inconsiderable slaves. As in action, so in the crafting of λόγοι and the commitment to the beliefs and convictions that result from λόγοι, those are most at liberty who are thoroughly subject to and confined by the necessary rules and standards dictated by a λόγος that is common and not subject to their private understandings and impulses. This is slavery of another order.[35]

32. *Metaph.* 12.10.1075a18–24.

33. A. W. H. Adkins, *Merit and Responsibility: A Study in Greek Values* (Chicago and London, 1960), p. 263; Greenberg, "Socrates' Choise," p. 63.

34. Cf. Morrow, *Plato's Cretan City*, pp. 82–85; L. Noussan-Lettry, "Das Bedeutete und das Gesagte: Zu δοῦλος, δουλεύειν im Platons Kriton," *Wissenschaft und Weltbild* 26 (1973): 147–50; Grote, *Plato*, p. 302; and the sensible remarks of D. F. Dreisbach, "Agreement and Obligation in the *Crito*," *New Scholasticism* 52 (1978): 183: "And we should not push the servant or slave metaphor too far. It is only a metaphor. The citizen's slavery to the law is of an unusual sort, as he can end it at almost any time." Regarding the combination of ἔκγονος καὶ δοῦλος, see *Lysis* 207d–10d.

Socrates honors and reverences some λόγοι and not others. λόγος here means "account," specifically, an account based on some process of reasoning or calculation. For instance, Socrates says that Crito has a λόγος about opinions (46c7–8), a λόγος Crito has articulated more or less precisely in his speech. Thus λόγος as account is connected with λογισμός, "reasoning," "reckoning." Right reasoning is nonarbitrary and has necessary ways to it. When the λόγος as account arises from right reasoning, it is common and linked to the common. When a λόγος is ordered to the common, it abides over time despite changing circumstances, as is Socrates' expectation for any λόγος he regards and honors (46c7–47a2, 48b3–5); it is "with νοῦς" in the sense that it is nonrandom and governed by a rational standpoint available to all inquirers, and so on. Socrates would accept Crito's λόγος about opinions or his λόγος about escape from prison only if it were based on a λογισμός grounded in and ordered by the common. I now turn to an examination of this Socratic reflection or calculation as it relates to the opinions of the many.

THE MANY, λόγος, AND λογισμός

Socrates' response to Crito's speech as the middle section of the *Crito* opens includes a self-description: he is and has always been someone persuaded only by the λόγος which appears best to him upon reflection, reckoning, or calculation (λογιζομένῳ; 46b4–6).

This reflection or calculation alone determines which λόγοι Socrates ranks in the highest place, reverences, and honors (πρεσβεύω καὶ τιμῶ; 46c1). Socrates will not agree with Crito about any λόγος (οὐ μή σοι συγχωρήσω; 46c3) unless the standard set by his notion of reflection or calculation is met.

Socrates goes on to employ his brand of reflection or calculation to consider what he calls Crito's λόγος about opinions (46c7–8). In the course of this examination, which stretches from 46c6 to 48a10, Socrates and Crito agree that opinions fall into two groups, the worthy ones and the unworthy ones. The principle of this division is found in another division, namely, a division with respect to the humans who hold opinions (47a2–4). This division is between the many and the one expert

35. Cf. *Lysis* 207d–10d where the freeborn youth without knowledge is properly subject to domination by others. The attainment of knowledge, such as knowledge of a language, with its different subjugation to elements, principles, rules, and standards, nevertheless enables freedom, power, and friendship.

(48a5–7). The opinions not worthy of attention or honor are identified as the opinions held by the many.

From these agreements Socrates and Crito move on "together," that is, "in common" (κοινῇ; 48d8), to the issue at hand: whether or not it is just to escape from prison. They consider two tenets. The first is the tenet against retaliation of injustice with injustice; the second is the requirement to abide by just agreements (49d7–9; 49e5–7).

The nonretaliation tenet is reached by an a fortiori argument that is plainly and neatly given at 49b8–c1:

SOCRATES: Then one must never do injustice [οὐδαμῶς ἄρα δεῖ ἀδικεῖν].
CRITO: Of course not [οὐ δῆτα].
SOCRATES: Nor return injustice for injustice, as the multitude think, since one must never do injustice [οὐδὲ ἀδικούμενον ἄρα ἀνταδικεῖν, ὡς οἱ πολλοὶ οἴονται, ἐπειδή γε οὐδαμῶς δεῖ ἀδικεῖν].
CRITO: That follows [οὐ φαίνεται].

Socrates continues by developing some implications of this conclusion and then delivers the *Crito*'s most powerful articulation of the decisive and necessary division between the few and the many:

Then one ought not return injustice for injustice or do ill to any man, no matter what one may suffer at their hands. Look to this, Crito. Do not agree [ταῦτα καθομολογῶν; 49d1] against your real opinion, for I know that few men think or will ever think it [ταῦτα] true. Between those who accept it and those who do not, there is no common basis for decision [κοινὴ βουλή]: when they view each other's counsels, they must necessarily [ἀνάγκη] hold each other in contempt. (49c10–d5)

Some commentators write as if this grim assessment of relations between the many and the philosophical few refers to the matter of the entire argument.[36] The many and the few, who will always contemn each other and who will never be able to have common deliberation (κοινὴ βουλή), are divided not only regarding the nonretaliation tenet, but also with respect to the premise that entails it, namely, the assertion of the shamefulness of doing injustice. In fact, *A Greek-English Lexicon* by Liddell, Scott, and Jones cites this passage in its entry for βουλή and writes: "They have no common *ground of argument*."[37]

When Socrates makes this claim at 49c11–d5, however, the reference to the views that Socrates asks Crito to consider carefully according to his actual opinion (the antecendents of ταῦτα at 49d1, d2) is most easily read as the immediately preceding lines expressing only the nonretaliation tenet (49c10–11). The nonretaliation tenet is, in fact, the only part

36. E.g., see Grote, *Plato,* p. 299.
37. *LSJ,* s. v. βουλή, 1.2.

of the argument that is explicitly stated—twice—to be denied by the many (49b10–11, c4–5). In and of itself the premise regarding the shamefulness of injustice is not in dispute between the many and the few. When it is introduced and discussed at 49a4–b6, it is treated as contentious by Socrates rather in view of its implications and under the pressure of shifting circumstances. Thus the deep division between the many and the few, made plain by the nonretaliation tenet reached a fortiori from the premise asserting the shamefulness of doing injustice, does not cut all the way through. The many and the few appear in fundamental agreement *that* it is always shameful to commit injustice. There is this minimal ground of shared conviction and so a common ground of argument.[38] *What* they take to be just or unjust, however, would be another matter.

Recogniton that the shamefulness of injustice is not in dispute between the many and the few fits the text of the *Crito* in two immediately relevant ways. First, the sense we get of the many from Crito's speech, where the views of the many are showcased, is all in the direction of attributing shame whenever someone acts against what is δίκαιον. Their sense of what is δίκαιον, however, worked out in terms of a traditional ethic, is not shared by Socrates. Crito shows this fundamental appeal to justice, for example, when he says that it is δίκαιον for Socrates' friends to risk much to save him (45a2) and the opposite for Socrates to remain in prison and be executed when he is able to escape (45c5). These two basic duties in justice for Socrates and his friends would be supported not only by Crito and Socrates' other friends, but by the many who condemned Socrates in the first place and who would expect him according to this δίκαιον standard to escape with the help of his friends.[39]

Second, when it is recognized that the many as well as the few see injustice always as shameful, the specific nature of the division between the

38. It has been argued that the ἀγαθόν and the καλόν (49a6; the "honorable" and the "good" in our translation) are the original basic and generally accepted norms of moral assessment among the Greeks, and that arguments are required to show that what is δίκαιον is ἀγαθόν and καλόν. If this is true in this text, a more fine-grained argument is needed to get to the one aspect of this portion of the *Crito* that I am trying to show, namely, the existence of common foundational agreement between all. Were I to grant on these grounds that there might be some ambivalence in the many about the initial claim that justice is always to be done, this would add an extra step to what I take this passage to be showing. That is to say, perhaps the common agreement of all is more foundationally to the ἀγαθόν and the καλόν, rather than to the δίκαιον. Then the move to the final conclusion regarding nonretaliation would be logically more complicated than an a fortiori argument. See Adkins, *Merit and Responsibility,* pp. 230–32 and passim.

39. See, e.g., *Crito* 45a1–3: "It is right [δίκαιοι] for us to run that risk to save you, and still greater risk if need be"; and *Crito* 45c5: "Furthermore, Socrates, I think the thing you're doing is wrong [οὐδὲ δίκαιον]." Crito's emphatic objection to the Laws and the city is that the city did Socrates an injustice (50c1–3). Cf. the Laws' replies about what is δίκαιον at places like 51b7, 51c1, 51c7, and the threefold injustice at 51e5.

many and the few becomes more explicit. As Socrates explicitly states, the many and the few disagree about a conclusion, namely, the nonretaliation tenet, which has been drawn a fortiori from a single commonly shared premise.[40] This is the radical example offered in the *Crito* of the random thinking of the many, for at the same time it displays their random thought and also shows its source in the disregard of rules of inference. The many accept the premise of the general shamefulness of practicing injustice, but they refuse to accept a conclusion necessarily drawn from it by one of the simplest of logical inferences. They are not ashamed to violate, nor do they fear, logical necessity, without which no λόγος should be honored, and in this they are unlike Socrates.[41] Rather, they find it shameful to act against their conception of the δίκαιον as given in the traditional ethic based on helping friends and harming foes, however much the simplest forms of logical inference suffer. Common deliberation and mutual regard for the results of particular deliberations have no chance among parties divided in this way, precisely because they cannot move in common from a common starting point.[42]

In this section Socrates and Crito also agree upon a second tenet, namely, that one must keep just agreements (49e5–8, 50a2–3). There is no discussion of this additional claim.[43] One could take it as somehow following from the first claim about the performance of justice, since it is stipulated that the agreements be just.[44] The demand of keeping agreements, however, is also so basic both to the traditional ethic of family and friendship alliances and to the conduct of shared Socratic dialectic that neither Crito nor Socrates would feel the need to establish or argue the case. Here too, then, is a case where at a fundamental level, prior to reflection or calculation, there is a point of shared conviction, now recognized. This is a point of agreement about agreement.[45]

40. Grote, *Plato*, p. 303.

41. See *Gorgias* 457e1–58a1; *Laws* 5.746c8–d2.

42. When Anytus joins the inquiry of Socrates and Meno about who are able to teach, Socrates and Anytus first reach a number of initial agreements (*Meno* 90b–e). Having developed this common base of agreement, Socrates tells Anytus that it is now possible to deliberate in common (νῦν τοίνυν ἔξεστί σε μετ' ἐμοῦ κοινῇ βουλεύεσθαι; 90e10–91a1). Cf. *Meno* 86c4–6; *Laws* 5.746c4–d2; *1 Alc.* 119b1–3; *Theages* 125a6–8; *Minos* 315e1–4.

43. τὸ μετὰ τοῦτο; 49e3, 5; see Adam, *Crito*, p. 60, with its citation of *Apol.* 39c1 as a parallel text.

44. Allen, *Socrates and Legal Obligation*, p. 563; Quandt, "Socratic Consolation," p. 246, n. 19.

45. Regarding the philosophically basic theme of agreement in Platonic writings, see F. Adorno, "Appunti su ὁμολογεῖν e ὁμολογιά nel vocabolario di Platone," *Dialoghi di Archeologia* 2 (1968): 152–72; and G. Bornhamm, "'Ομολογιά: Zur Geschichte eines Politischen Begriffs," *Hermes* 71 (1936): 377–93.

This interpretation of this key passage is faithful to the emphasis Socrates has put on the reflection or calculation that makes a λόγος honorable and that distinguishes those who are philosophical in any degree from the many who act at random and are without thought. Indeed, it intensifies its importance by making the precise point at which the many and the few differ to be subsequent to some shared common ground. This common ground consists of a shared and common unarticulated commitment to the shame of doing injustice and to the nobility of keeping just agreements.

Furthermore, this interpretation shows that the division between the many and the few does not cut all the way through. While it is true that there can be no common deliberation (κοινὴ βουλή) between them because of the many's indifference to the norms of genuine reflection or calculation, it is not asserted, nor in my opinion does the *Crito* hold, that the many and the few are totally or inescapably separated from each other in mind and heart. They do share some basic opinions at a foundational level prior to articulation or explanation about the matters discussed by Socrates and Crito in this section and which Socrates would include in what he calls the "starting point of the inquiry" (τῆς σκέψεως τὴν ἀρχὴν; 48e5), namely, the shamefulness of doing injustice and the nobility of keeping just agreements.[46] These are two key elements present both in the traditional ethic based on alliances to which Crito appeals in order to persuade Socrates to escape and in Socrates' arguments for the opposite conclusion. Thus it is not gratuitous that later the Laws can persuade Crito of a philosophically warrantable proposition even though he is incapable of proceeding with the λόγος philosophically (50a4–5).

This common ground involving shame regarding justice and the keeping of just agreements is a condition for the possibility of human life in common based neither solely on coercive power (a community wholly of masters and slaves) nor on pervasive philosophical insight (a community wholly of philosophers). Hence in the unified good community that comes to birth in λόγος in the *Republic*, justice and agreement based in justice belong to all classes, while philosophy belongs only to a small and golden one.[47]

46. Aristotle, *E. N.* 8.11.1161b5–7, argues that a free man can be a friend of a slave, insofar as the slave is a man "for there seems to be some justice between any man and any other who can share in a system of law or be a party to an agreement."

47. Regarding justice and sharing in the common by all citizens, see E. N. Lee, "Plato's Theory of Social Justice in *Republic* II–IV," in Anton and Preus, eds., *Essays in Ancient Greek Philosophy*, vol. 3, pp. 126–27, 139 n.4.

ADDITIONAL CONSIDERATIONS

There are three considerations that fill out and confirm this picture.

1. When Socrates considers Crito's λόγος about opinions he divides opinions based on who holds them, the many or the one expert. In this argument he fails to consider an ambiguity in the notion of the opinions of the many. On the one hand, an opinion of the many can be a majority opinion, that is, an opinion held by most people. Aristotle considers such an opinion ἔνδοξον. On the other hand, an opinion of the many can be an opinion held by one or some of the many, but not held by others.[48] Aristotle does not consider such opinions ἔνδοξα, but at *Nicomachean Ethics* 1.4.1095a22–25 he indicates their existence.[49]

This distinction is observed in *1 Alcibiades* where Socrates and Alcibiades distinguish between things that the many know and can teach, such as the use of the Greek language, and things that the many do not know and therefore cannot teach. The occasion of the distinction is Socrates' request of Alcibiades to explain how he acquired the sense of justice he already was displaying in childhood when he was cheated at games (110b). The criterion for what the many know and are capable of teaching, such as the Greek language, is that they do not disagree among themselves about the subject at issue. Those who have knowledge never disagree among themselves. Thus the many, who both in private and in public agree among themselves about how to use the Greek language to signify things, can be said to know and to be able to teach Greek (111a1–d5).

When it comes to saying anything about the things signified by the Greek language, however, the situation is different. That is to say, when it comes to giving explications or accounts of things to which they refer linguistically, the many disagree among themselves and have no knowledge. In matters of what is just or unjust, least of all, do the many agree among themselves or have knowledge (111e11–112d3).

Aristotle makes the same point at *Nicomachean Ethics* 1.4.1095a17–26.

> Verbally there is very general agreement [about what the highest of all goods achievable by action is]; for both the general run of men [οἱ πολλοί] and people of superior refinement say that it is happiness, and identify living well and faring

48. Cf. Aristotle, *Pol.* 3.11.1281a39–b21, 4.4.1292a11–15.

49. At this place, quoted more extensively below, Aristotle notes that the many and the wise agree in name (ὀνόματι; 1095a17) that the end of man is happiness, but that when an account is to be given, the many and the wise give different accounts of what happiness is (1095a20–22). Then Aristotle points out that among the many there is disagreement about what happiness is, and even that individuals within the class of the many give different accounts at different times (1095a23–25).

well with being happy; but with regard to what happiness is they differ, and the many [οἱ πολλοί] do not give the same account as the wise. For the former think it is some plain and obvious thing, like pleasure, wealth, or honour; they differ, however, from one another—and often even the same man identifies it with different things, with health when he is ill, with wealth when he is poor; but, conscious of their ignorance, they admire those who proclaim some great thing that is above their comprehension.

This text and *1 Alcibiades* agree in several ways. First, the many share in an agreement that is estimable in some limited way and that is κοινόν and of a public character, such as knowledge of the common language or recognition that the final end of man is happiness. Second, this basic agreement functions prominently in the linguistic order, as communal success at indicating the same realities shows. Finally, when the many attempt to articulate or explain that to which they can refer successfully and about which they share some basic inchoate sense, their success ends. The many are incapable of the kind of reflection or calculation that gives accounts of things, and they are incapable of expert opinion. When they attempt it, they disagree among themselves and often with the expert, unless they are awed and voice assent to what they do not understand.

Plato in the *Crito* does not consider this ambiguity between majority opinion and opinion held by one of the many. They are lumped together as opinions of the many. As I have argued, however, the root of Socrates' contempt for opinions of the vulgar many is their disregard for the kind of reflection or calculation that binds opinions to the common and forbids randomness in the drawing of conclusions. This criticism and contempt is not directed at the prereflective or precalculative opinions that the many hold before they attempt to give accounts and go astray. Thus Socrates' criticism and contempt are not directed against the opinions of the many where they do not disagree at all with each other or with experts, opinions which Aristotle would classify as ἔνδοξα.[50] Such opinions as these, opinions such as those implicit in the use of a language or those expressing basic recognitions of the shamefulness of injustice or of failing to keep just agreements, function at a level prior to reflection, calculation, or explication. They also function as a foundational common ground alike for those who are capable and those who are incapable of dialectic and philosophy.

An obvious objection to this interpretation is that the opinion of the many that is most relevant to the argument of the *Crito*, namely, that it is shameful for Socrates not to escape, appears to be a view on which the many, represented by Crito, agree. Thus it would appear to have the

50. See note 6.

distinctive feature described in *1 Alcibiades*, unanimity of opinion. But this is where the structural analysis outlined above and the recognition of the Laws as a many are significant. There is, in fact, disagreement among the many about whether Socrates should escape. The Laws present the case of the many who disagree that Socrates should escape. Hence the opinion of the many that Socrates should escape prison or be blamed for injustice and cowardly unmanliness is an opinion about which the many disagree. Hence Socrates' criticism and contempt is confined to those opinions of the many that are the outcome of slovenly reflection or calculation on their part. Other, more basic, opinions of the many, such as convictions about the shamefulness of injustice or the rightness of keeping just agreements, escape this net, and the contempt and inability of the many and the philosophical one to have a κοινὴ βουλή are not based on a tear running all the way through the fabric of human life in society.

2. Socrates in plain terms derides the processes of reflection or calculation the vulgar many possess. Indeed, my interpretation depends on this fact to avoid a wholesale Socratic condemnation of the opinions of the many. This interpretation also shows, however, that this denigration of the many and their reckonings needs to be qualified. The Laws, who are a many, offer in their speech a λόγος supporting the conclusion Socrates himself supports to the point of death. There is a mitigation of Socrates' apparently general condemnation of the reasoning of the many, in accord with the distinction within the many between the Laws and ordinary citizens. The speech of the Laws is estimable, holds Socrates to a consistent standard, and yet falls short of the philosophical discourse that is also beyond Crito.

It is important to notice that Socrates' preliminary account of the criterion for accepting or rejecting λόγοι at the beginning of the middle section of the *Crito* favors superlative grammatical forms. Socrates is only persuaded by what he takes to be the best (βέλτιστος) λόγος (46b6). He reverences λόγοι. The Greek word here is πρεσβεύειν, which more literally means "to place as oldest or first, put first in rank."[51] Most importantly, Socrates concludes this preliminary discussion with a question for Crito that Crito never answers: "Now, how might we most fairly [μετριώτατα; 46c6] consider the matter?" The word μετριώτατα is the superlative of μέτριος, whose basic meaning is "within measure, moderate," understood in the positive sense of good or right measure.[52]

There is a measure for the thoughtful crafting of estimable λόγοι.[53] λό-

51. *LSJ*, s.v. πρεσβεύω.

52. *LSJ*, s.v. μέτριος. I am grateful to J. van Ophuijsen for emphasizing this point with me.

53. See *Statesman* 283c3–84e8 for a discussion of the standard with respect to τὸ μέτριον (283e11), which is "a standard by which we can accord praise to what is said or cen-

γοι born of serious inquiry subject to this measure succeed by degrees. Hence Plato indicates with the use of the superlative that the approbation of λόγοι according to this nonarbitrary standard is mostly a relative matter. The best λόγος or the most measured inquiry may not be the λόγος best or most measured *simpliciter*, but relative to the available λόγοι or the circumstances of the specific situation of inquiry. Hence Socrates can find the speech of the Laws of its kind and under the circumstances to be a λόγος most measured and moderate.[54] The Laws know to ask for "what is by nature just" (ᾗ τὸ δίκαιον πέφυκε) and will only be persuaded by that (51c1–3); they analyze and make distinctions: an act of disobedience like escape would be "injustice in three ways" (against birth, against nurture, and against the agreement; 51e5). Compared to a presentation like Crito's, such a discussion is well measured, well measured like the flute playing of the Corybants that brings peace to those who are initiated by them. The circumstances where the speech of the many Laws, who have brothers in Hades, is the most measured by Socratic standards, are not only that Crito is incapable of continuing the dialectic at 50a4–5 (he says, "Socrates, I can't answer what you ask, for I don't understand what you mean"), but also the fact that Socrates, who professes ignorance, does not claim to possess expert knowledge in things just and unjust.[55] He must, nevertheless, both make a decision in a philosophically responsible way and defend that decision to all who have an interest in it. When practical decisions cannot wait for a thoroughly satisfactory outcome through expert philosophical reflection and calculation received and appropriated by the community party to them, the most measured consideration of the matter at hand would be a speech such as that given by the Laws.[56]

3. The *Euthydemus* can be considered a companion piece to the *Crito*. They are the only two dialogues that feature Socrates and Crito together in principal dramatic roles, and they both show obvious structural symmetry.[57] They seem to be foils of one another.[58] The *Euthydemus* is about

---

sure it, either as excessive or as deficient" (283c3–5). I am grateful to Mitchell Miller for directing my attention to this section of the *Statesman*.

54. Allen, *Socrates and Legal Obligation*, pp. 558–59; cf. Vlastos, "Socrates on Political Obedience," p. 519.

55. Quandt, "Socratic Consolation," p. 251–52; cf. Strauss, "On Plato's . . . *Crito*," p. 58.

56. The *Euthyphro* is another Platonic dialogue where an immediate practical decision is called for. Socrates and Euthyphro do not know what piety is. At its end this "dialogue of failure" falls back on the definition of piety given at the middle of the dialogue (9c–11b), namely, piety as what all the gods love. This is recourse to the majority view, albeit an exalted one.

57. R. K. Sprague, in *Plato's Use of Fallacy: A Study of the "Euthydemus" and Some Other Dialogues* (New York, 1962), writes: "From the point of view of pure symmetry, the *Euthydemus* is probably Plato's most beautifully constructed dialogue" (p. 1).

58. Strauss, "On Plato's . . . *Crito*," p. 67. W. K. C. Guthrie, *A History of Greek Philosophy, Vol. 4: Plato: The Man and His Dialogues: Earlier Period* (Cambridge, 1975), notes the careful

sophism. The Sophists are conspicuously absent from the *Crito.* As noted above, a wide range of parties relevant to Socrates' situation enter the text through Socrates or Crito—Athenians and visitors, friends and enemies, the many and the single true expert—and yet one party, the Sophists, so relevant to a consideration of Socrates' practice of philosophy, his reputation in Athens, and his present predicament, receives not a mention. At the end of the *Euthydemus* Socrates, ironically congratulating Euthydemus and Dionysodorus for their victory in argument and the blessedness it connotes, says to them:

> [Y]ou do not concern yourselves with the multitude of men, nor men of solemn looks or great reputation, but only with those like yourselves. For I am quite sure that there are very few men like you who would appreciate these arguments, and all the rest know so little of them that they would feel more ashamed to refute others by such ways of speech than to be refuted themselves. (303c–d)

The arguments of Euthydemus and Dionysodorus depend on undermining language itself and its ability to signify opposite things. Both the many and the more refined of the city would be ashamed to use speech in this way. Sophistic ways as depicted in the *Euthydemus* are inimical to the proper consideration of any determinate opinion in the city, whether by the many or by the few. They destroy even the possibility of the prereflective shared common ground between the many and the few that the *Crito* affirms and that is a necessary condition for life and communication together, despite the fact that they trade on that shared common ground, particularly the linguistic common ground, to insinuate themselves into the life of the city. All the parties of the *Crito,* through the agreement despite difference of Socrates and Crito at the center of the dialogue, share in this basic common ground, a common ground Aristotle explicitly describes as εὔδοξον. The Sophists, who belong to no one city, place themselves outside this circle, and so they are outside the drama of the *Crito.*[59]

CONCLUSION

I have argued that through a recognition of the structure of the *Crito* and the meaning of that structure we see that Plato in the *Crito* acknowledges in humans a fundamental bond of basic opinions or convictions. These opinions are prior to reflection and reckoning, and in their vague

---

structure of the *Euthydemus* (p. 274) and the difference between Socrates, who appears to be a Sophist, and Euthydemus and Dionysodorus, who are Sophists: whereas all proceed by question and answer, Socrates "works by reaching agreement at every step" (p. 272).

59. Strauss, "On Plato's . . . *Crito,*" p. 88, takes a very different view. Socrates and the Sophists are not enemies. Rather "the political multitude (*Republic* 492a5–e6), i.e., the enactor of the Athenian laws," is the greatest Sophist and the greatest enemy of philosophy.

and indeterminate way they provide the possibility of a common life for the vulgar many and the philosophical few. Such convictions have to do with shame at doing injustice and the commitment to honoring just agreements. The division between the many and the few cuts deep in the *Crito* but does not cut through.

The existence of a common and shared lode of basic and authoritative convictions among humans such as the shamefulness of injustice or the rightness of keeping agreements, seen here in the *Crito*, is significant for the most important themes not only in political theory but also for those in psychology and the theory of knowledge. How is it that the condition not only for political life but for human knowledge and communication is planted and functions in this "weak and degenerate race of beings"?[60] Is it identically possessed by the vulgar many and the philosophical few? What is its relation to λόγος and λογισμός? With this account Plato presents a view similar to that of Aristotle in his account of εὔδοξα of all and many. In Aristotle the claim of a shared and authoritative set of convictions is a philosophical position of the first order. How far Plato and Aristotle agree in this matter of a commonly shared pretheoretic or prephilosophical experience in its relation to reckoning and philosophical reflection are issues worth pondering.[61]

60. Edward Gibbon, quoted in J. Pelikan, *The Excellent Empire: The Fall of Rome and the Triumph of the Church* (New York, 1987), p. vii.

61. My best thanks are due to Jean DeGroot, Joan Franks, O.P., William McCarthy, Mitchell Miller, Johannes M. van Ophuijsen, and readers for The Catholic University of America Press for assistance, criticism, and encouragement, and to an audience at The Catholic University of America for a helpful discussion of this essay.

4 Plato on the Parts of the Soul

FRED D. MILLER, JR.

After many years of wandering, Odysseus returned to Ithaca and found his home overrun by the insolent suitors of Penelope. In disguise he visited his own house, where he was abused by the suitors. As he rested in a courtyard and plotted his revenge, he saw Penelope's maidservants entering the house to consort with the suitors. Homer describes the scene as follows:[1]

There, devising evil in his spirit [ἐνὶ θυμῷ] for the suitors,
Odysseus lay awake; and out of the palace issued
those women who in the past had been going to bed with the suitors,
full of cheerful spirits and greeting each other with laughter.
But the spirit [θυμὸς] deep in the breast of Odysseus was stirred by this,
and much he pondered with his mind [κατὰ φρένα] and spirit [κατὰ θυμόν]
whether to spring on them and kill each one, or rather
to let them lie this one more time with the insolent suitors,
for the last and latest time; but the heart [κραδίη] was growling within him.
And as a bitch, facing an unknown man, stands over
her callow puppies, and growls and rages to fight, so Odysseus's
heart was growling inside him as he looked on these wicked actions.
He struck himself on the breast and spoke to his heart [κραδίην] and scolded it:
"Bear up, heart [κραδίη]. You have had worse to endure before this
on that day when the irresistible Cyclops ate up
my strong companions but you endured it until intelligence
got you out of the cave, though you expected to perish."
So he spoke, addressing his own dear heart [ἦτορ] within him;
and the heart [κραδίη] in great obedience endured and stood it
without complaint, but he himself [αὐτὸς] was twisting and turning.
And as a man with a paunch pudding, that has been filled with
blood and fat, tosses it back and forth over a blazing
fire, and the pudding itself strains hard to be cooked quickly;
so he was twisting and turning back and forth, meditating
how, though he was alone against many, he could lay hands on
the shameless suitors.

1. Homer, *Odyssey* 20. 5–30 (Lattimore translation, adapted).

This passage from the *Odyssey* fascinated and perplexed Plato. In Plato's *Phaedo* 94d6–e1 Socrates quotes from the passage in an argument supporting his doctrine that the soul is an immortal entity that is distinct from the body. In Plato's *Republic* 4.441b5–7 Socrates returns to the scene, but this time in support of the quite different thesis that the soul itself contains three distinct parts. It is worthwhile to consider why Plato found this passage intriguing and to speculate about why he offered different interpretations of it in these two dialogues. This inquiry may shed light both on Plato's understanding of the phenomenon described by Homer and on the development of Plato's own theorizing about the soul.

It should first be noted, however, that there is a controversy concerning Homer's descriptions of human thought and action. According to a number of classical scholars active in the mid-twentieth century, Homer belonged to a "primitive" and "irrational" stage of thought in that he could not conceive of human beings as possessing a unified individual consciousness or personality. An influential exponent of this view was Bruno Snell, who argued on philological grounds that "the early Greeks did not, either in their language or in the visual arts, grasp the body as a unit." He observed that Homer's term σῶμα (*sôma*), the word for the living body in later Greek, refers to a corpse, and that Homer has no other single word for the living body as a unified whole. Similarly Snell argues that "Homer has no one word to characterize the mind or the soul. ψυχή (*psuchê*), the word for soul in later Greek, has no original connection with the thinking and feeling soul. For Homer, *psuchê* is the force which keeps the human being alive." The word *psuchê* also refers commonly to the shade or ghost that leaves the body when someone dies and travels to the house of Hades. Snell points to passages like the one describing Odysseus and the maidservants to argue that Homer attributed "mental" functions to particular "organs"; for example, θυμός (*thumos*) denotes an organ of emotion, and νόος (*noos*) an organ of perception, just as *psuchê* refers to an organ of life. However, Snell argues that Homer's view is more primitive than Plato's. "At first it might be suspected that *thumos* and *noos* are nothing more than the parts of the soul, such as we know from Plato's psychology. But these parts presuppose a psychic whole of which Homer has no cognizance." Thus, Snell contends, "What we interpret as the soul, Homeric man splits up into three components each of which he defines by the analogy of physical organs." But it is misleading to call them "organs," because Homer lacks the concept of a unified organism to which they belong. According to Snell, "[T]he distinction between body and soul represents a 'discovery' which so impressed people's minds that it was thereafter accepted as self-evident, in spite of the fact that the relation between body and soul, and the nature of the soul itself, continued to be the topic of lively speculation." He regards Heraclitus as one of the discoverers of "the new concept of the soul," and Plato as a contributor to the further development of this concept, which Snell sees as the ancestor of the modern concept of mind.[2]

Snell's *The Discovery of the Mind* appeared in 1948.[3] The following year E. R. Dodds endorsed Snell's thesis "that Homeric man has no unified concept of what we call 'soul' or 'personality'" and defended related views in his Sather Lectures, which were published in 1951 as *The Greeks and the Irrational* (University of California Press). A similar interpretation of Homer was offered by Robert Onians in *The Origins of European Thought about the Body, the Soul, the World, Time, and Fate* (Cambridge University Press, 1954). An extreme version of this interpretation was promulgated by Julian Jaynes, who alleged that "there is in general no consciousness in the *Iliad*."[4]

Although Snell's thesis was at first very influential, it has since come under increasing criticism. Hugh Lloyd-Jones complained that scholars had gone too far in emphasizing the irrational features of Greek thinking, "believing that or acting as if Homer's world were itself primitive and depriving his human characters of all power of decision and mental independence." Lloyd-Jones argued that although Snell was obviously correct to point out that Homer lacked the modern concept of the will, it does not follow that characters like Odysseus are unable to deliberate, make decisions, or act on the basis of reasons.[5] Two recent books have subjected Snell's argument to intense criticism. Bernard Knox, in *The Oldest Dead White European Males*, objects to Snell's use of the argument from the alleged "gap in the Homeric vocabulary":[6] from the fact that speakers do not have a particular word it does not follow that they lack the idea expressed by it.[7] Knox adds that "there are many passages in the

2. B. Snell, *The Discovery of the Mind: The Greek Origins of European Thought*, trans. T. G. Rosenmeyer (New York, 1960), pp. 5–8, 14, 17. U. von Wilamowitz-Moellendorff previously discussed this and other Homeric passages that anticipated Plato's tripartite psychology, in *Die Heimkehr des Odysseus* (Berlin, 1927), pp. 189–201.

3. The book was first published in Germany as *Die Entdeckung des Geistes* (Claassen und Coverts). It was translated into English by T. G. Rosenmeyer and published by Harvard University Press in 1953. In 1960 it was reprinted in a popular Harper Torchbooks edition, cited in note 2.

4. J. Jaynes, *The Origin of Consciousness in the Breakdown of the Bicameral Mind* (Boston, 1976), p. 69.

5. H. Lloyd-Jones, *The Justice of Zeus* (Berkeley and Los Angeles, 1971), pp. 9–10.

6. Snell, *Discovery of the Mind*, p. 8.

7. B. Knox, *The Oldest Dead White European Males* (New York, 1993), pp. 43–44. As Knox remarks, although English lacks a synonym for the German term *Schadenfreude*, English speakers understand what it means to take pleasure in the misfortunes of others. Against this example, it might be objected that *Schade* and *Freude* have direct counterparts in En-

poems that suggest a Homeric conception of the unified individual personality. There is above all the hero's name, the name he proudly bears and proclaims on all occasions, whether exulting over a fallen enemy or claiming his share of glory, that name Odysseus conceals in the Cyclops' cave and later proudly—and, as it turns out, rashly—announces to his blinded enemy." The name designates "the heroic self." Knox argues that "an individual personality is also suggested in those recurrent passages where a hero addresses some part of himself—his *thumos* or his *kradiê*, his heart; the words used imply the central personality of the speaker, a personality to which the part addressed belongs."[8]

Bernard Williams offers similar arguments in *Shame and Necessity*. In fact, he cites Homer's passage concerning Odysseus and the maidservants as evidence that Homeric characters are capable of self-restraint. Williams objects that Snell ignores the manifest fact that Homer's characters are the "unities" to which thoughts and experiences belong. Snell is mistaken because "[t]he terms *thumos* and *noos* and other terms that Homer uses in relation to psychological functions, such as *phrên*, belong to a vocabulary in which the person himself plays an essential and irreplaceable role. People think and feel with or in their *thumos*; they standardly reflect or deliberate with or in [*kata*] their *phrên* and their *thumos*. If people need a *thumos* to think or feel with, it is equally true that a *thumos* needs a person if any thinking or feeling is to go on." Williams argues that in attributing a primitive prototheory of action to Homer, Snell implausibly claims that Homer uses *thumos* as a technical term for a distinct psychological organ. But in the passage concerning Odysseus and the maidservants, Homer uses the terms for the diaphragm (*phrên or phrenes*) and the heart (*kradiê*) interchangeably with *thumos*. Evidently, Homer selects among such terms for formulaic convenience.[9] Further, although he depicts the gods as intervening in human affairs, Homer also describes human beings as having desires, beliefs, and purposes, and hence as having reasons for action, and as deliberating on the basis of these reasons and as acting as a result of their deliberations. Although Homer's

glish, and the combination of the concepts they express is readily intelligible to an English speaker, whereas Snell's thesis concerns whether Homer had a concept of mind representing a certain level of abstraction. Whether the *Schadenfreude* analogy is fair depends on whether it can be shown that Homer had the linguistic resources to express the psychological concept at issue.

8. Ibid. Snell might reply that although the words imply the personality of the speaker, whether this is "a personality to which the part addressed belongs" is the question under dispute.

9. B. Williams, *Shame and Necessity* (Berkeley and Los Angeles, 1993), pp. 26–27. For more general discussion, Williams cites T. Zahn, *Zum Wortfeld "Seele-Geist" in der Sprache Homers* (Munich, 1987).

vocabulary differs from ours, beneath these different terms "lies a complex net of concepts in terms of which particular actions are explained, and this net was the same for Homer as it is for us." "Indeed, if it were not," sensibly asks Williams, "how could we understand Homer as presenting us with human actions at all?"[10]

These critics are surely correct to criticize Snell's claims as simplistic and exaggerated when he denies that Homer represented Odysseus and other characters as single individuals who are capable of deliberating and acting. The Greeks in Homer's epics knew how to apply the words αὐτός, αὐτή, and αὐτό in a manner analogous to the English 'himself', 'herself', and 'itself'. Nonetheless, it would be a mistake to suppose that Odysseus, as he is depicted in the Homeric epics, is an *unproblematic unity*. For, as we see from the case of Odysseus and the maidservants, the Homeric "self" (*autos*) deliberates by talking to a thing within himself—which is variously called his *thumos*, his *phrên*, or his *kradiê*—and his decision is the result of a struggle between "himself" and this thing within himself. But how can Odysseus's "self" be identified with the whole, if it must persuade a part of itself to obey it or engage in a struggle with a part of itself? It might be suggested that this part is merely an instrument used by the self. But what if the part had *not* obeyed the one speaking to it and had rebelled, so that Odysseus attacked the maidservants in a rage? Might not this so-called self instead be only a part of the whole that is talking to and fighting with another part? Why, then, should we refer to one part, rather than another, as the "self"? Who, or what, is this "self" anyway? It might be objected that we should not be misled by Homer's poetical language: perhaps talking to one's *thumos* or to one's heart is a *façon de parler* that is not to be taken literally. To this it may be replied that Homer's metaphor points to a real psychological phenomenon: we do experience conflicting motivations within ourselves, and we do find ourselves doing things that we do not accept and cannot justify. The poetic metaphor has a real meaning for Homer's audience, just as it does for us. It was not unreasonable for later philosophers such as Plato to take the metaphor to reveal a genuine problem: In what sense is Odysseus a one, and in what sense is he a many?

Williams also criticizes Plato's treatment of these matters. Plato, on his view, did not "discover" any truth about the human soul. Instead, he says, Plato "invented" a new idea not found in Homer, namely, "that the functions of the mind, above all with regard to action, are defined in terms of categories that get their significance from ethics. . . . The tripartite division of the soul in the *Republic* is the earliest full expression of it, and one

10. Williams, *Shame and Necessity*, p. 34.

of the most extreme." According to Williams, "The divisions of the soul are invoked, basically, to describe and explain conflicts between two kinds of motive: rational concerns that aim at the good, and mere desire." To Homer's commonsensical descriptions of human motivation, Plato added only philosophical confusion by attempting "to discover ethically significant categories inside human nature." Rather than being praised for making genuine progress, Plato, Aristotle, and their philosophical heirs are indicted for fabricating "the illusion that the basic powers of the mind are inherently constituted in terms of an ethical order."[11]

This account of Plato's theory of the parts of the soul is harsh and uncharitable. It is true that Plato uses the tripartite psychology in the *Republic* to defend his ethical and political views, and it is also true that his argument has been criticized as inconclusive on a number of counts. However, even though his analysis of psychological conflict may involve difficulties, it should not be dismissed as a muddled attempt to solve a pseudoproblem. In attempting to reconsider Plato's contribution, it is first necessary to compare the passages of the *Phaedo* and the *Republic* in which Plato makes reference to the scene in the *Odyssey* involving Odysseus and the maidservants.

In the *Phaedo*, while Socrates is waiting in prison for the hemlock, he tries to demonstrate to his friends that the soul is immortal. He offers proofs based on the cycle of opposites, founded on the theory of recollection, and arising from the affinity of the soul with the forms. Among other objections, it is pointed out that the soul may be like an attunement or *harmonia*: "Our body is at a certain tension and is held together by hot and cold, and dry and wet, and so on, and our soul is a mixture or attunement [ἁρμονίαν] of these things, when they are combined in just the right proportion. Then, if the soul is really an attunement, obviously as soon as the body is lowered or increased beyond the mean, the soul must be destroyed by diseases or other evils, divine though it is" (86b7–c6). To this objection Socrates replies that the soul is opposed to and therefore distinct from the body. His argument has two premises:

1. A *harmonia* or any other composite thing cannot be in any other condition than that of its constituents (92e4–93a3); it cannot act or be acted upon otherwise than its constituents (93a4–5); and it cannot move or utter in an opposed way to its parts or oppose its parts in any other way (93a6–9, 94c3–8).

2. The soul can oppose the feelings of the body: for example, when one is thirsty the soul drags one the opposite way, not to drink. "It is just

11. Ibid., pp. 42–46.

like Homer's description in the *Odyssey*" (94b4–c2, c9–e1; reference to *Odyssey* 20.17–18).

3. Therefore, the soul cannot be a *harmonia* of bodily parts (94e8–95a1).

The argument of the *Phaedo* has the following notable features: Desires and emotions are attributed to the body. The soul is understood as opposing the undergoings (πάθη) of the body. Reason is attributed to the soul in distinction from the body.

Plato makes very different use of the Odysseus example in Book 4 of the *Republic*. Here the context is an inquiry into justice, and Socrates is attempting to answer the challenge of Glaucon and Adeimantus that Socrates prove that justice is valuable for its own sake as well as for its consequences. Socrates has adopted the method of searching for justice in the city because the city is larger and easier to study, and because a just man does not differ from a just city in respect to the form of justice (2.368d–e, 4.435a–b). Socrates has just distinguished and defined the four cardinal virtues of the city—wisdom, courage, temperance, and justice—and he now turns to the soul. He recalls that the city is called just because the natural kinds in it—the guardians, the warrior-auxiliaries, and the workers—each perform their distinctive function, and he asks whether the soul contains the same three kinds. He proceeds to argue that the soul, like the city, contains these three forms, kinds, or parts[12] because it has opposed motivations.

The analysis of the *Republic* departs from that of the *Phaedo* in two important respects: now desires and emotions are attributed to the soul itself rather than to the body, and the soul has parts. In the *Phaedo* Socrates asserts that "the soul is entirely indivisible or something close to this," presumably on the grounds that divisibility implies destructibility (80b9–10; cf. 78c6–8, 80b1–5). If we may suppose that the *Republic* was written after the *Phaedo*, a question arises: Why did Plato apparently abandon his earlier doctrine of the monadic soul? To this question I offer the conjectural answer that Plato is inclined in the *Republic* to attribute all desires, perceptions, and thoughts to the soul because in this dialogue he is shifting toward the view that such movements or changes must be due to the soul understood as a self-moving principle. The *Phaedrus*, which was evidently written after the *Phaedo*, contains the definition of the soul as self-motion in conjunction with the tripartite psychology represented by the simile of a charioteer and two horses (245e2–4, 253c7–d1). The definition of soul as self-motion recurs in Book 10 of

12. Plato uses εἶδος, 'form', at 435c1, 439e2, and 440e8–10; γένος, 'kind', at 441a1 and 443d3; and μέρος, 'part', at 442b11. The terms are evidently used interchangeably.

the *Laws* where it is used in a proof of the immortality of the soul (895e10–96a4). The *Laws* suggests a related reason why Plato might have revised the theory of the soul as found in the *Phaedo*. The concluding argument of the *Phaedo* has the crucial premise that the soul is a cause (αἰτία) in the sense of a thing that brings the form of life with it and will not admit the opposite form of death (105c9–e7). However, the *Phaedo* leaves the connection between soul and life unexplained. The *Laws* has an explanation for this: we call a thing "living" when it moves itself, and this implies that it has a principle of self-motion within it; hence, if the soul is the cause of life, it must be identified with self-motion (10.895c7–96a4). Because the movements of the soul are prior to those of the body, it follows that moods, habits of mind, wishes, calculations, true judgments, purposes, and memories will all be prior to physical lengths, breadths, and depths, which are conditions of the body (896c9–d3). If we suppose that Plato was moving toward this view of the soul as an ultimate source of motion when he wrote the *Republic*, this may provide a reason why he came to attribute all desires to the soul rather than some to the soul and some to the body.[13]

Let us now examine more closely Plato's argument for the tripartite psychology in *Republic* Book 4. At the beginning of the passage Socrates remarks that each person performs three quite different sorts of acts: "we do these things: . . . we learn . . . , we are angry, . . . we desire the pleasures of eating and reproduction and things of their kind" (436a8–10). He then asks whether we are impelled to do all these acts with the same thing—that is, with our whole soul (ὅλῃ τῇ ψυχῇ)—or do we do each thing with a different thing—that is, with three different things? In posing the question this way, he is assuming that wanting a drink, for example, is an action, something we do (πράττομεν), and that it is in order to ask, "With *what* do we want a drink?" The expression, "with *X*," the instrumental dative in Greek, ordinarily refers to a thing distinct from the agent, whether a tool or a part of the agent's body. "With what did you sip the soup?" is answered by "With a spoon." "With what did you pick up the spoon?" is answered by "With my fingers." "With what did you desire the soup?" also has an answer according to Socrates: either "With my whole soul" or "With a part of my soul." When I do two distinct actions A_1 with X and A_2 with Y, I can ask whether X and Y are the same thing or different things.

Socrates argues that there are three distinct forms, kinds, or parts with

13. A caveat: this discussion is confined to Plato's account of the *embodied* soul and does not consider his view of the immortal soul "as it is in truth" or as "pure," and not as it is "while it is mutilated by its communion with the body and other evils" (see *Republic* 10.611b9–c3).

which we perform actions of the soul. He infers this from the claim that each of the parts can be opposed to the other two parts. Reason (τὸ λογιστικόν) is opposed to appetite (τὸ ἐπιθυμητικόν) in the case of a person with a disease like dropsy who is thirsty but unwilling to drink.[14] Spirit (τὸ θυμοειδές) is opposed to appetite in the case of Leontius who unsuccessfully resists his urge to view the corpses of executed criminals. Spirit is opposed to reason in the case of Odysseus and the maidservants.

The argument for dividing the soul into parts is developed most fully in the case of the first distinction between reason and appetite, although Plato evidently intends the argument to take a similar form in the case of the other two distinctions. The argument contains the following major explicit steps:

1. Principle of Non-Opposition: It is evident that the same thing cannot do (or undergo) opposite things (τἀναντία) in the same respect (κατὰ ταὐτόν) toward, or in relation to, the same thing at the same time (436b8–9; cf. 439b5–6).

1A. Corollary: If these things (doing or undergoing opposite things in the same respect toward, or in relation to, the same thing at the same time) happened in these cases, we would know that there was not the same thing but more than one thing (436b9–c1).[15]

2. Desiring, willing, and wanting (as well as desiring not, wanting not, and being unwilling) are actions (and hence fall within the scope of [1] and [1A]) (437b1–38e9).

3. Some people sometimes, though thirsty, do not want to drink (439c2–3).

4. Therefore, there is more than one thing in these cases, namely, reason and appetite (439d4–e3).

Identifying the logical sinews that are supposed to hold this skeleton together proves to be a difficult task. I shall consider the three main premises in turn.

First, there is what I am calling the Principle of Non-Opposition (also called "the Principle of Opposites"): Scholars disagree over the logical relationship of this principle or *hupothesis* (see 437a6) to the Principle of Non-Contradiction. The fact that "opposite things" (τἀναντία) are

14. The term ἐπιθυμητικόν which I translate as 'appetite', is derived from the noun ἐπιθυμία (9.580e2–4). However, Plato uses the noun ἐπιθυμία in a wider sense that can belong to any of the three parts of the soul (580d7–8). I translate the ἐπιθυμία as 'desire' and the related verb ἐπιθυμέω as 'to desire' when they may have this wider sense.

15. Stalley points out the importance of this corollary in unpacking premise (1), in "Plato's Argument for the Division of the Reasoning and Appetitive Elements within the Soul," *Phronesis* 20 (1975): 117.

mentioned in the principle indicates that it is not "the earliest explicit statement in Greek literature of the maxim of Contradiction."[16] For the Principle of Non-Contradiction is not concerned with opposites; instead, it states that the same thing cannot be *and not be* the same thing (adding all the qualifiers). In the *Sophist* 257b3–7 the Eleatic Stranger distinguishes between negation and opposition. The opposite of the large is the small. The "not large" is the equal as well as the small, both of which are different from the large (cf. *Symposium* 201e10–202b5). Thus, if τἀναντία refers to "opposites" in this sense in (1), this principle is not equivalent to the Principle of Non-Contradiction. However, this is not a serious difficulty. For it is clearly implied by the *Sophist* that opposites are incompatible—for example, the same thing cannot be both small and large in the same respects—so that the opposite of large merits the label "not large." Therefore, the Principle of Non-Opposition follows from the Principle of Non-Contradiction, in that any case that runs afoul of the Principle of Non-Opposition will also violate the Principle of Non-Contradiction.

In the *Republic* Socrates uses the example of a person—whom I shall call "Dipsios"—who is thirsty but does not want to drink. From the premise that his thirst is opposed to his simultaneous unwillingness to drink, it is inferred that "if anything draws [his soul] back when it thirsts, it is something different from that which thirsts and drives it, like a beast, to drink" (439b3–6). I. M. Crombie contends that this reasoning involves "a confusion between two distinct principles":

(NC) A person cannot both have a pro-attitude to a thing and also not have a pro-attitude to the same thing.

(NO) A person cannot both have a pro-attitude to a thing and have an anti-attitude to the same thing.

Following Crombie, principle (NC) is a tautology of the form ~(P&~P), whereas (NO) has the logical form of ~(P&Q) and is not a logical truth but an empirical proposition. Indeed, (NO) apparently admits of counterexamples. For example, a smoker who is trying to break the habit may have a pro-attitude toward a cigarette and an anti-attitude toward it at the same time. There is no necessary incompatibility in this.

It has been replied in Plato's behalf that Crombie's objection is "implausible" because Plato's Principle of Non-Opposition is distinct from the Principle of Non-Contradiction and "although Plato regards a person who is unwilling to drink as being affected in the opposite way to that in which a thirsty person is affected, this is no evidence at all that he took

16. As J. Adam alleged in *The Republic of Plato* (Cambridge, U.K., 1902), vol. 1, p. 246.

'being unwilling to drink' to mean the same as 'not having a desire to drink.'"[17] This is correct, but it does not help Plato very much. For, although Plato does not say explicitly that 'being unwilling to drink' is *equivalent* to 'not being thirsty', he does hold that '*X* is unwilling to drink' *entails* '*X* does not desire to drink'. For he maintains that desiring and being unwilling are opposites and, as we saw, '*X* is opposite to *Y*' entails '*X* is not *Y*'.[18] However, Crombie's objection is, in effect, that Plato is mistaken to hold that desiring and being unwilling are incompatible in this sense, so that Plato is wrong to view (NO) as an implication of the Principle of Non-Contradiction.

Does Plato's argument, then, rest upon a mere confusion about the logic of words used to ascribe attitudes? There is a more plausible interpretation of his argument, which requires a consideration of Plato's underlying theory of human motivation (437b1–d7). A key to this theory is Socrates' description of motivations in the soul as analogous to bodily actions or passions. Bodily actions can belong to pairs of opposites: for example, nodding one's head and throwing back one's head (the Greek ways of showing assent and dissent); also, seeking and avoiding; again, drawing to oneself or thrusting away. These pairs are opposites in the sense that one agent cannot perform both actions in relation to the same object at the same time (437b1–5). Similarly, Socrates asks:

> What, then, of thirst and hunger and the desires generally, and again wanting and willing, would you not put all these in the kinds just now mentioned? Will you not say, for example, that the soul of the person who desires either *strives for* that which he desires or *draws to itself* that which he wills to possess, or again, in so far as it wants that something be presented to him, it *nods assent* to itself like someone being questioned, as it *stretches toward* the possession of it? . . . And shall we not put being unwilling and not wanting and not desiring with cases of *repelling* and *driving away* from it [i.e., the soul] and put them in the opposites of the kinds considered before? (437b7–c10)

Socrates thus analyzes 'Dipsios desires the water' provisionally as 'The soul of Dipsios strives for or draws to itself the water'; and 'Dipsios does not want to drink the water' as 'The soul of Dipsios repels or drives away the water'. Motives are thus viewed as opposites (*enantia*) in the same way as bodily pushings and pullings. It seems most likely that Plato is inclined to this view of desires and aversions because he regards states of the soul

17. I. M. Crombie, *An Examination of Plato's Doctrines* (London, 1962), vol. 1, pp. 355–56. Stalley, "Plato's Argument," p. 120.

18. It is noteworthy that at 437c8–10, ἀβουλεῖν (to be unwilling) as well as μὴ ἐθέλειν (not to want) and μηδ' ἐπιθυμεῖν (not to desire) are placed in the kinds ἀπωθεῖν (to push away) and ἀπελαύνειν (to drive away). This suggests that when one rejects (ἀπωθεῖ), one is unwilling (ἀβουλεῖ), so that it is not the case that one wants (οὐκ ἐθέλει).

generally as motions (*kinêseis*) of some sort. If, as suggested earlier, we suppose that the *Republic* was composed while Plato was shifting from the *Phaedo*'s view of the soul as like an immutable Form to the view of the *Phaedrus* that the soul is a self-moving principle, this would help to account for why he is inclined to view desire and aversion as motion of the soul.[19] This kinetic theory of motivation indicates why Plato regards the phenomenon described in premise (3) as involving opposition, and thus as falling under the Principle of Non-Opposition.

Socrates' provisional analysis yields the following inconsistent tetrad (439a9–c3):

a. If Dipsios drinks, his soul does not will anything other than to drink and yearns for this and is impelled to this.

b. If Dipsios does not want to drink, his soul pulls him back.

c. The same thing at the same time cannot urge (κελεύειν) and hold back (κωλύειν) Dipsios from the same act (from the Principle of Non-Opposition).

d. Dipsios thirsts and yet is unwilling to drink.

These four propositions are inconsistent, and the solution Socrates proposes is to replace the occurrences of 'his soul' in (a) and (b) with references to different parts of the soul, namely, to appetite in (a) and to reason in (b). Given the kinetic theory of motivation, we have a parallel to the archer: "it is not well said of the archer that his hands at the same time thrust away the bow and pull it close, but we should instead say that one hand pushes it away and another pulls it close" (439c5–7). Analogously, Dipsios's reason pulls him back while his appetite pushes him to drink.

However, the argument involves a further complication. Proposition (a) states that the soul of Dipsios "does not will anything other (οὐκ ἄλλο τι) than to drink" (439a9–b1).[20] This qualification reflects another com-

19. *Republic* 9.583e9–10 also describes pleasure and pain which occur in the soul as a sort of motion (κίνησίς τις), as noted by C.D.C. Reeve, in *Philosopher-Kings: The Argument of Plato's "Republic"* (Princeton, N.J., 1988), p. 124. Note also the language of being "impelled" (ὁρμήσωμεν, ὁρμᾷ) at 436b2 and 439b1. *Philebus* 35b1–d3 (a later dialogue) also claims that all impulse (ὁρμή) and desire (ἐπιθυμία) belong to the soul, on the grounds that these things are opposed to the undergoings (παθήματα) of the body. For example, thirst is opposed to the loss of fluid in the body, for through memory the soul apprehends replenishment and desires it.

20. Presumably (b) should also be expanded to say that something holds him back from nothing but drinking, so that both the desire and aversion are focused on the same object. As noted by J. Moline, in "Plato on the Complexity of the Psyche," *Archiv für Geschichte der Philosophie* 60 (1978): 1–26, Plato makes similar statements about the spirited part: it is "wholly set" on ruling, winning, and good reputation (9.581a9–10). See also 5.475a3–c4 on the idea that the desires belonging to the different parts of the soul are for specific sorts of objects (e.g., for wine, for honor, for wisdom).

ponent of Plato's theory of motivation which is developed at some length (437d2–39a7). Socrates indicates that he wants to avoid the objection that since everyone wants the good, Dipsios does not drink because he wants a *good* drink but he realizes that this is not a good drink (438a1–5). Here Plato is evidently rejecting the sort of reasoning that underlies the so-called Socratic Paradoxes of his earlier dialogues:[21] for example, that nobody desires bad things believing that they are harmful, because they believe that harmful things will make them unhappy and nobody wants to be unhappy (*Meno* 77c1–78b2). Against this, Plato makes two interconnected points: First, desires are specified with reference to specific kinds of objects: "Each desire itself is of that thing itself of which it is by nature" (437c7–8). For example, thirst itself is of drink itself, and hunger itself is of food itself. A desire is naturally (πέφυκεν) of a specific kind of thing; or, in Aristotelian language, desires are "essentially relational."[22] Second, the desire for a complex object, such as the desire for a good drink, can be analyzed into two different specific desires. Suppose I am thirsty and want a drink, but it is a hot day so I desire something cold. Then I want a cold drink, but this is a combination of two distinct desires. Similarly, if it were a cold day and I wanted a hot drink, there would be two different desires (437d8–e6). Plato has been criticized for indulging here in empty "semantical analysis," and making statements that have no bearing on the real world.[23] However, this criticism is mistaken. Plato is, to be sure, offering an "analysis" of the language of desire, but his main claim is that certain human activities are essentially relational in that it is part of their nature that they have specific kinds of objects. Desires, he claims, are these sorts of activities. Whether or not Plato's analysis accurately describes human desires as relational is an empirical issue.

Let us return to the case of Dipsios and consider why Socrates concludes, "what hinders such acts intervenes, when it intervenes, from reasoning [ἐκ λογισμοῦ]" (439c9–d1). No clear basis is provided in Plato's text for the sudden introduction of reasoning, but the point seems to be that reasoning must be involved if Dipsios's desire to drink is to be directly

21. See T. Penner, "Thought and Desire in Plato," in G. Vlastos, ed., *Plato: A Collection of Critical Essays* (Garden City, N.Y., 1971), vol. 2, p. 100; and M. Woods, "Plato's Division of the Soul," *Proceedings of the British Academy* 73 (1987): 42.

22. The sense in which desires are "such as to be of something" (438a7–b2) is explained by means of several analogues: the larger is of the smaller; knowledge generally is of the knowable; and a specific kind of knowledge, for example, architecture or medicine, is of some kind of object, for example, housebuilding or health. The latter examples suggest that Plato is thinking of a desire like thirst as for a specific kind of object such as drink. Desire therefore is not merely for a particular object but for the object as a specific kind of thing.

23. R. Robinson, "Plato's Separation of Reason from Desire," *Phronesis* 16 (1971): 42.

opposed by his unwillingness to drink. This case differs from that of an unreasoning beast that is pulled about by its desires. Contrast the case in which a thirsty cat is thoughtlessly given a bowl of hot milk. The cat simultaneously desires the milk but is averse to the hot, and whether it ultimately drinks the milk will depend in part on which of these impulses is stronger. But this is not like the case of Dipsios, because the cat is not pulled toward and pushed away from the same object. Dipsios is, however, attracted and repelled by the same object, namely, drinking, presumably because he has *reasoned* that drinking is detrimental to his health.

It can, however, still be objected that this argument does not show that reason as such is the ultimate source of any desires of its own—of what can be called "rational desires."[24] A theorist like David Hume might object that *all* that is established here is that reasoning contributes in some way to volition, but not that reason as such is the *origin* of such a desire. The Dipsios example seems compatible with Hume's claim that reason never opposes the passions and is, in fact, "the slave of the passions." On Hume's account, reason plays a role in human action, not of originating impulses but of "directing" them toward certain ends.[25] It is noteworthy that Plato himself describes reason as playing such a servile role in the soul of the oligarchic person, who sets appetite and love of money upon the throne of his soul and stations reason and spirit on each side like slaves; "he will permit the former to calculate and inquire into nothing but how many will result from less," and spirit is likewise directed to honor only riches and rich people (8.553b7–d7). Such a person could resist a particular desire through reasoning of the following sort: "I desire wealth most of all, and I reason that the indulgence in sexual pleasures would interfere with the satisfaction of this desire. Hence, I am unwilling to indulge in sexual pleasures." However, the unwillingness to engage in sex is a result of reasoning that might, on occasion, be opposed by a strong sexual urge (554b7–c2). A Humean might agree that the oligarchic person uses his reason to move from a mere set of subjective preferences to a set of considered preferences of the sort Plato describes: namely, that it is through money that desires are especially satisfied (9.580e5–81a1); but this does not show that the rational part of the soul *originates* any desires of its own. Similarly, Dipsios's reason is merely a slave of his passion for health.

24. For rational desires, see Penner, "Thought and Desire," p. 114: "opposition to any standard positive desire of appetite will be from a desire of reason"; and T. H. Irwin, *Plato's Moral Theory* (Oxford, 1977), p. 328, n20: "*to logistikon* consists of rational desires, and not just of reasoning."

25. See Hume, *A Treatise of Human Nature*, 2d ed., ed. L. A. Selby-Bigge and P. H. Nidditch (Oxford, 1978), pp. 414–15.

However, the oligarchic soul is in Plato's view deviant. Plato does not see the proper function of reason as being confined to deliberating about how one might effectively satisfy whatever desires happen to be strongest.[26] Rather, the rational part exercises foresight for the sake of the whole soul (441e4–5) or of the whole soul and body (442b6–7). It possesses "knowledge within itself of what is advantageous for each [part], and for the whole community of these three [parts]" (442c5–8). In a person like Dipsios, then, the reasoning might be of the following sort: "I desire health, which is good for the whole soul and body. I know that drinking in this case is detrimental to health. Therefore, I am unwilling to drink." It would seem, then, that Plato is making another tacit assumption: a subject can be motivated by opposing parts only if these parts are *sources* of different motivations.[27] In the Dipsios case, if (M_1) the desire of the appetite to drink is opposed by (M_2) the unwillingness to drink, the soul must have two different sources of motivations: (S_1) appetite and reason (S_2), respectively.

That this is Plato's meaning is strongly suggested by Socrates' explicit statement in *Republic* 9.580d7–81c4 that each part of the soul has a distinct pleasure, desire, and type of rule. The pleasure and love of appetite is directed to profit (here he is taking the oligarch as a representative of the person devoted to the bodily objects); the pleasure and love of spirit, to honor and victory; and the pleasure and love of reason, to wisdom and learning and truth (cf. 5.485d6–e1, 9.581b5–7, and 9.586e4–87a1). Different parts rule over the souls of different people, so that we find three different sorts of people: the money-loving (again a representative of the wider class of those loving bodily objects), the honor-loving, and the wisdom-loving (see 4.435e1–36a3). Each of these finds his own way of life most pleasant and praiseworthy, that is, the way of life that has profit, honor, or wisdom as its ultimate end.

Let us now turn to Socrates' claim that the soul has *three* parts. We may ask why Socrates is not content with a distinction between a rational and a nonrational part of the soul.[28] Why does he also distinguish between

26. Cf. Cooper, "Plato's Theory of Human Motivation," *History of Philosophy Quarterly* 1 (1984): 19, n9.

27. This is not to say that the parts of themselves are *subjects* of desire, as Woods points out ("Plato's Division," pp. 34–38). Thus, Dipsios can be the subject of both desires—the one doing the desiring—although the desires have different sources in the soul of Dipsios. C. Kahn, in "Plato's Theory of Desire," *Review of Metaphysics* 41 (1977): 81–82, n8, argues that on Plato's account, "There is no room for a person or self over and above the three parts *on the level of explanation*." However, the evidence cited by Kahn is compatible with the interpretation that the parts of the soul are different sources of desire within a single subject or self.

28. See D. A. Rees, "Bipartition of the Soul in the Early Academy," *Journal of Hellenic Studies* 47 (1957): 112–18; and W. W. Fortenbaugh, "On the Antecedents of Aristotle's Bipartite Psychology," *Greek, Roman, and Byzantine Studies* 11 (1970): 233–50.

two nonrational parts, appetite and spirit? It is often charged that Plato's tripartite soul is an ad hoc device used to support his division of the ideal state into three parts. But it could be replied that his division between guardian and auxiliary classes is inspired by the observation that philosophers and warriors have different psychologies.[29] Spirit is concerned with honor, specifically with command, victory, and good reputation (9.581a9–b3). Although it is a natural ally of reason when there is faction in the soul, it is essentially irrational and capable of rebelling against reason (4.440a8–41c2). Plato may well be influenced by Homer's descriptions of warriors like Odysseus who are motivated by anger when they are threatened with dishonor. The spirit is "the part with which we feel anger (θυμούμεθα)" (439e2–4). All of Socrates' examples of spirit involve anger: Leontius's anger at himself for wanting to gaze at corpses, Odysseus's anger at the maidservants, and the rage of children and animals at being dominated or resisted by others. The desire for honor and the aversion to dishonor are thus very different from the desires of the other parts, for example, the love of wisdom or the desire for bodily objects.[30] But this will not suffice to show that spirit is a different part. For this we need the aforementioned tacit premise that the distinct parts involved in opposed desires are sources of different desires.[31] At the same time that Leontius's appetite inclines him to look at the corpses, he is unwilling to look at the corpse because something else in his soul, namely, his spirit, has an aversion to the dishonor of shameful gazing.

However, if this *is* Plato's argument, another problem looms. If the case of Leontius shows that his spirit and his appetite are distinct and

29. Cf. Cooper, "Plato's Theory," p. 4.

30. Although he rejects the tripartite psychology, Aristotle agrees with Plato that there are three forms of desire (ὄρεξις): namely, appetite (ἐπιθυμία), spirit (θυμός), and rational wish (βούλησις) (*DA* 2.3.414b2; *MA* 6.700b22, 7.701a36–b1; *EE* 2.7.1223a26–27). Aristotle also uses the distinction between spirit and appetite to distinguish between two forms of incontinence (*EN* 7.6.1149a25 ff.). This suggests that the distinction between *thumos* and *epithumia* may reflect ancient Greek culture, which placed greater importance on aristocratic values such as honor (τιμή) and nobility (τὸ καλόν) than do modern Western cultures.

31. Irwin, in *Plato's Moral Theory*, p. 192, offers an alternative interpretation, namely, the three parts differ because they have different desires. Reason is distinguished by having good-dependent desires (influenced by beliefs about the overall good), spirit by having partly good-dependent desires (influenced by beliefs about some kinds of goods), and appetite by having good-independent desires (uninfluenced by beliefs about goods). The characterization of spirit is questionable, since whether spirit responds to considerations of the good depends on whether such considerations are relevant to honor, which is the specific end for spirit (cf. Cooper, "Plato's Theory," p. 16). Moreover, Irwin's account is doubtful as an interpretation of the argument of *Republic* 4 because it renders the Principle of Non-Opposition superfluous. Irwin himself complains that the principle is of little use and "Plato would have done better to introduce his argument about desires at once" (p. 327). Irwin also acknowledges that Socrates' way of distinguishing the three parts in Book 9 differs from his own (p. 337, n53).

possibly opposed parts of his soul, why does not the case of the oligarch torn between his sexual urge and his love of money imply a further division within his appetitive part as well (see 7.554b7–e5)? Plato's argument for a tripartite soul thus faces a dilemma: depending on how we understand the argument, either it establishes too little (namely, only two parts of the soul) or too much (a part of the soul corresponding to every desire).[32] Socrates seeks a controlled form of psychic fission, terminating in three parts, but his argument seems to lead to uncontrolled fission, with an unending proliferation of parts.

The source of Plato's difficulty seems to be his tacit assumption that the different parts of the soul implicated in conflict must be the sources of different desires. It is noteworthy that Aristotle in *De anima* rejects this doctrine as "absurd" (ἄτοπον) (3.9.432b4–7), and he defends the opposed view that there is only one source of all human movement, namely, appetite (called ὄρεξις by Aristotle), which is however influenced by reasoning (3.10.433a21–b4). Nonetheless, even if Plato's tripartite psychology is not free of difficulty, it is not a complete failure. Plato should be credited with recognizing the problem of psychological conflict, which was disclosed to him by passages in Homer where characters like Odysseus debate and struggle with something within themselves. Homer suggested, and Plato agreed, that a human being is both a one and a many, a unitary agent capable of internal conflicts. Plato's early theory of the soul was substantially revised in order to explain conflicting motivations. Central to this revision were the conceptions of the soul as a self-moving principle and of desires as motions of the soul. The *Phaedo*'s doctrine of the simplicity of the soul on both counts had to yield to the tripartite psychology.

The tripartite psychology should not, finally, be dismissed—as Bernard Williams suggests—as a mere imposition upon the soul of categories drawn from Plato's ethical or political theory. To make this charge is to misconstrue the basic character of Plato's psychology. It is true that a principal aim of the *Republic* is to support the claim that justice is intrinsically better than injustice. However, the tripartite psychology is a causal theory of action that is distinguishable from the ethical and religious views Plato is seeking to defend. For at the end of *Republic* Book 4 Socrates combines the tripartite theory with another principle, namely, that within wholes certain parts are fitted by nature (φύσει . . . πρέπειν) to rule over other parts (444b1–8). Within the body there is health when

32. 4.443d7, which refers to the three parts as high, low, and mean, adds "and all others there may be between them," suggesting there may be more than three parts of the soul. Also, 9.574a6–10 seemingly describes division within the appetitive part, as unnatural desires rebel against natural ones.

the appropriate parts rule, according to nature (κατὰ φύσιν), and disease when other parts rule, contrary to nature (παρὰ φύσιν) (444d3–6). He further claims that there is an analogous natural condition of the soul when the appropriate part, namely, reason, rules over the other parts (444d8–11, 441e4–6). The basis for this, presumably, is that reason is uniquely able to apprehend the ends of all the parts of the soul and to understand their proper (i.e., natural) interrelationships, so that it is able to "reason about the better and the worse" (441c2). He makes, finally, the crucial claim that this natural condition of the soul is identical with the virtue of justice (443c9–44a2, 444d8–e2). It needs to be emphasized that the tripartite psychology is a distinct theory from the principle of natural rule and the identification of justice with "psychic harmony."[33] Indeed, the long-standing furious debate over whether or not Socrates' attempt to derive his ethical conclusion from his tripartite psychology is "fallacious" has been possible precisely because the tripartite psychology is a causal theory of desire and action that is distinct from Socrates' ethical conclusion.[34] It is also noteworthy that although Aristotle rejected much of the Platonic tripartite psychology—and especially the thesis that reason and appetite are separate sources of opposing desires—he did accept Plato's theses that the soul has parts in some sense, and that the natural condition of the soul involves the rule of reason. Throughout the history of Western thought, Plato's theory of the divided soul has undergone a number of reincarnations, and seems to be continually rediscovered. For it remains difficult to resist Plato's underlying insight suggested by Homer: that although human beings plainly are unitary agents, conflicts of motivation must be explained in terms of different causal factors within human agents.

33. See G. Vlastos, "Justice and Psychic Harmony in the *Republic*," *Journal of Philosophy* 66 (1969): 505–21.

34. See D. Sachs, "A Fallacy in Plato's *Republic*," *Philosophical Review* 72 (1963): 141–58.

5 Platonic Liberalism: Self-Perfection as a Foundation of Political Theory

CHARLES L. GRISWOLD, JR.

> But what is government itself but the greatest of all reflections on human nature? If men were angels, no government would be necessary. If angels were to govern men, neither external nor internal controls on government would be necessary. —*James Madison*[1]

INTRODUCTION

Whitehead famously declared that "the safest general characterization of the European philosophical tradition is that it consists of a series of footnotes to Plato."[2] This statement is true with respect to the history of political philosophy only in the sense that Plato's political theory has continually functioned as a provocation to which almost everyone has felt the need to respond. The footnotes in the history of political philosophy have mostly been negative and critical. The critique of Plato's political philosophy began almost immediately with Aristotle. The third sentence of the *Politics,* in fact, contains an unmistakable, and negative, reference to the equation suggested in Plato's *Statesman* (258e) of statescraft with the art of ruling over slaves, and substantial consideration is given in the *Politics* to attacking various proposals set forth in the *Republic, Laws,* and *Statesman.* Luminaries of the liberal Enlightenment, such as Jefferson, Madison, and Adams, were particularly sharp in their criticism of Plato.[3]

1. *Federalist* no. 51, in *The Federalist Papers,* ed. C. Rossiter (New York: New American Library, 1961), p. 322. (Subsequent reference advert to this edition.)

2. A. N. Whitehead, *Process and Reality: An Essay in Cosmology,* rev. ed., ed. D. R. Griffin and D. W. Sherburne (New York: Free Press, 1978), p. 39.

3. In his semiretirement, Thomas Jefferson turned back to the classics, and after rereading Plato's *Republic* he wrote to John Adams that Plato is "one of the race of genuine

The most famous recent scholarly attack is undoubtedly that of Karl Popper, while I. F. Stone's much discussed book presented the attack at a more popular level.[4] For Popper, Plato's views were "totalitarian" and prepared the way for Nazism and Stalinism (certain Nazi theorists did in fact view themselves as continuing the program of Plato's *Republic*).[5] Even though Popper's interpretation of Plato has been subjected to endless examination and refutation,[6] it remains difficult to free oneself from the long-standing judgment that at least in his political philosophy, Plato's views are deeply flawed.

The specific accusations against Plato's political philosophy are fourfold in nature. First, Plato's schemes are accused of being unfair because not committed to a notion of the moral equality of human beings. Plato's theories seem inegalitarian at their core, and the social and political schemes he sets out are hierarchical. Correspondingly, we hear nothing about "natural rights" in Plato.[7] Second, these schemes seem illiberal to the extreme. Especially as presented in the *Republic*, they seem to leave very little room for political liberties. And this too seems unjust. Third, they are accused of being tied to complex and doubtful metaphysical and psychological doctrines, doctrines that just about nobody wants to

---

Sophists" whose reputation has survived only because it was incorporated into equally doubtful doctrines of Christian theology. Jefferson adds: "It is fortunate for us that Platonic republicanism has not obtained the same favor as Platonic Christianity; or we should now have been all living, men, women, and children, pell mell together, like beasts of the field or forest." See Jefferson to Adams, July 5, 1814, in *The Adams-Jefferson Letters*, ed. L. J. Cappon (Chapel Hill: University of North Carolina Press, 1988), p. 433. On Madison, see below.

4. I refer to his *The Trial of Socrates* (Boston: Little, Brown, 1988). For a critique of Stone's book, see my "Stoning Greek Philosophers: Platonic Political Philosophy and the Trial of Socrates," *Classical Bulletin* 67, no. 1 (1991): 3–15.

5. See Popper's *The Open Society and Its Enemies*, 2 vols. (Princeton, N.J.: Princeton University Press, 1962), vol. 1, p. 87 and passim. On the appropriation of Plato by Nazi theorists, see R. F. A. Hoernlé's "Would Plato Have Approved of the National-Socialist State?," in *Plato, Popper, and Politics*, ed. R. Bambrough (New York: Barnes and Noble, 1967), pp. 32–35.

6. For a sample of the debate, see the essays collected in *Plato, Popper, and Politics*, ed. Bambrough, and those in *Plato: Totalitarian or Democrat?*, ed. T. L. Thorson (Englewood Cliffs, N. J.: Prentice-Hall, 1963); and R. Robinson, "Dr. Popper's Defence of Democracy," in *Essays in Greek Philosophy* (Oxford: Clarendon Press, 1969), pp. 74–99. Further discussion may be found in R. B. Levinson's *In Defense of Plato* (Cambridge, Mass.: Harvard University Press, 1953), and in G. Klosko's *The Development of Plato's Political Theory* (New York: Methuen, 1986).

7. Averroes, an otherwise sympathetic reader of the *Republic*, indicated a related disagreement with Plato. He objects to the *Republic* view that the Greeks are best suited by nature to perfection. See *Averroes on Plato's Republic*, trans. R. Lerner (Ithaca, N.Y.: Cornell University Press, 1974), 27.1–14, pp. 13–14. Averroes implicitly indicates that Islamic universalism is at odds with that sort of particularism (46.10–21, p. 46). On the other hand, Averroes appears to accept Platonic communism, among other aspects of the *Republic* (57.23–58.14, pp. 65–66).

defend and which were immediately rejected, in whole or in part, by his best student: Aristotle.

A fourth set of criticisms alleges that Plato's schemes in the *Republic* and the *Laws* are simply unworkable or fail to produce the results intended. Aristotle's arguments to the effect that abolishing private property does not remove either strife or the desire for accumulating property fall into this class.[8] In early modernity, Madison takes it as a crucial axiom that "a nation of philosophers is as little to be expected as the philosophical race of kings wished for by Plato."[9] Locke's pragmatic criticisms of a civic religion that is coercively implemented,[10] criticisms echoed over and over again in the liberal Enlightenment by thinkers such as Rousseau, Adam Smith, and Voltaire, are implicitly directed against the kind of scheme for a coercive civic religion set out in great detail in Book 10 of Plato's *Laws*.

To these points about the unworkability of Plato's scheme, we may add the objection, articulated by Rawls (among others), that since there exists no popular consensus as to the truth of a single notion of the human good, such a scheme would be politically irrelevant even if its truth could be established philosophically. Large modern commercial republics are characterized by wide, even extreme, disagreement about the human good in the sense that Plato's dialogues speak of that good.[11] This characteristic of modern liberal societies is a cause of lament for some (such as MacIntyre) and of celebration for others. In either case, Rawls takes it to

8. *Politics* 2.1262a37–64b25. Aristotle also implies at *Politics* 2.1265a10–18 that the scheme of the *Laws* is fundamentally impossible. With respect to Phaleas's proposal that the possessions of the citizens should be equal, Aristotle notes that "the nature of desire is without limit, and it is with a view to satisfying this that the many live. To rule such persons, then, [requires] not so much leveling property as providing that those who are respectable by nature will be the sort who have no wish to aggrandize themselves" (2.1267b3–7). Here and below I cite from C. Lord's translation (Chicago: University of Chicago Press, 1984).

9. *Federalist* no. 49, p. 315. For a similar point, see D. Hume's "Idea of a Perfect Commonwealth," in *Essays Moral, Political, and Literary*, rev. ed., ed. E. Miller (Indianapolis, Ind.: Liberty Press, 1987), p. 514.

10. I refer to the arguments in Locke's *A Letter Concerning Toleration*.

11. See John Rawls, *A Theory of Justice* (Cambridge, Mass.: Harvard University Press, 1971), pp. 330–31; "Kantian Constructivism in Moral Theory," *Journal of Philosophy* 77 (1980): 518–19; and "Justice as Fairness: Political not Metaphysical," *Philosophy and Public Affairs* 14 (1985): 223, 245. In this and other articles, Rawls took himself to be working from not an a priori, permanently true set of political principles, but from "intuitions" and "convictions" implicit in a constitutional democracy ("Justice as Fairness," p. 225). See also the *Theory of Justice*, pp. 243–44: "The principles of justice define an appropriate path between dogmatism and intolerance on the one side, and a reductionism which regards religion and morality as mere preferences on the other. And since the theory of justice relies upon weak and widely held presumptions, it may win quite general acceptance." The centrality of disagreement to political life is implicit in Madison's seminal discussion of faction in *Federalist* no. 10.

be a basic fact that must orient any realizable theory of justice. As Rawls put it, a theory of justice must be "political" and based on an overlapping consensus rather than be "metaphysical."[12] Hence, he argues, "Philosophy as the search for truth about an independent metaphysical and moral order cannot, I believe, provide a workable and shared basis for a political conception of justice in a democratic society."[13]

I think that we can put these various criticisms in focus by noting that they (rightly) take Plato's political philosophy to be a version of what we may call, following Rawls, "perfectionism." Rawls characterizes perfectionism as a form of a teleological theory, namely, one in which the realization of human excellence is taken as the good. Utilitarianism is another form of teleological theory, one in which (to put it very roughly) the good is defined as the satisfaction of desires or interests.[14] As Rawls points out, in the various teleological theories, justice—or what Rawls calls "the right"—is taken as that which maximizes the good. Rawls, of course, argued the obverse, that the right precedes the good in political theory.[15]

In a preliminary way, let me parse a bit further the notion of "perfectionism." In classical perfectionist theories, such as those of Plato and Aristotle, we are presented with arguments that run something as follows: As political philosophers we are to orient ourselves by a notion of human nature, and in particular by what it would mean to exhibit some relevant aspect of human nature perfectly, or at least as perfectly as is humanly possible. The best human life is exemplified by the person having that trait in the requisite degree. As Aristotle states in the *Politics*: "Concerning the best regime, one who is going to undertake the investigation appropriate to it must necessarily discuss first what the most choiceworthy way of life is" (1323a13–16). Further, the best polity is that in which this best life is attained as much as possible by all those who are capable of it. Aristotle writes that "a polis is excellent, at any rate, by its citizens'—those sharing in the regime—being excellent; and in our case all the citizens

12. Rawls notes in "Justice as Fairness" (p. 245) that "[t]he absence of commitment to these ideals [comprehensive moral ideals such as autonomy and individuality], and indeed to any particular comprehensive ideal, is essential to liberalism as a political doctrine." Should liberalism assume a set of ideals, it becomes "another sectarian doctrine" (p. 246). And "[i]n such a society [a democratic society] a teleological political conception is out of the question: public agreement on the requisite conception of the good cannot be obtained" (p. 249).

13. Rawls, "Justice as Fairness," p. 230.

14. Rawls, *A Theory of Justice*, pp. 24–25.

15. See, e.g., his "The Priority of Right and Ideas of the Good," *Philosophy and Public Affairs* 17 (1988): 251–76; and his "Justice as Fairness: Political not Metaphysical." Since mine is an essay on Plato and not on Rawls, in citing Rawls here I have not taken into account any variations of his ideas offered in his most recent work, *Political Liberalism*.

share in the regime" (1332a32–35; cf. *Laws* 707d).[16] Statescraft is the art of bringing about the best life for as many as are capable of it.[17] For perfectionism, political theory is really an extension of ethics. A theory is thus perfectionist in (a) orienting itself by an account of human perfection, and (b) taking the task of statescraft to be that of bringing about human perfection in the polis, either directly or indirectly. A direct perfectionist scheme attempts to bring about excellence in human beings by perfecting human nature, by involving itself intimately in the improvement of the citizenry. An indirect perfectionist scheme attempts to make perfection of human beings possible by supplying the conditions under which individuals can improve themselves.

As noted, perfectionism and utilitarianism share a common teleological orientation, and revolve around what one might loosely sum up under the title of "interests." Both versions of teleological theory insist that various goods are to be judged relative to what they accomplish for human interests.[18] In this sense both are what Joseph Raz calls "humanistic"; they explain and justify the goodness or badness of things relative to their actual or possible contribution to human life and its quality.[19] I interpret Plato's political philosophy as "humanistic" in this broad sense. But perfectionists and utilitarians take "interests" in different ways. First, perfectionist theory views human beings in terms of their potentialities rather than in terms of their *given* interests, wants, or properties. Utilitarians tend to take "interests" as givens rather than as potentialities (though, to be sure, Mill's deliberations about this point complicate the distinction). Perfectionists orient themselves not by interests as agents understand them (not by "subjective preferences"), but by interests as agents would understand them had they full self-knowledge.

Second, utilitarians and perfectionists are likely to disagree about the nature of the human good. While utilitarians take happiness to be the

16. At *Politics* 6.1324a23 we read "Now that the best regime must necessarily be that arrangement under which anyone might act in the best manner and live blessedly is evident."

17. Toward the conclusion of the *E.N.* Aristotle tells us that to be a good man is to be properly trained and educated, and that good laws are crucial to that process (1180a14 ff.). The science of legislation has a pedagogical intent and so is oriented by a notion of human flourishing (cf. also *E.N.* 1103b3–25). Cf. *Euthyd.* 292b4–c1: statecraft is aimed to make the citizens happy; and *Laws* 683b.

18. As Mill says in *On Liberty*, "I regard utility as the ultimate appeal on all ethical questions; but it must be utility in the largest sense, grounded on the permanent interests of man as a progressive being" (C. V. Shields edition [Indianapolis, Ind.: Bobbs-Merrill, 1976], p. 14.) On p. 77 of the same text Mill rhetorically asks: "[f]or what more or better can be said of any condition of human affairs than that it brings human beings themselves nearer to the best thing they can be?"

19. Raz, "Right-Based Moralities," in *Theories of Rights*, ed. J. Waldron (Oxford: Oxford University Press, 1984), p. 183.

human good, and evaluate interests relative to that standard, perfectionists take the development of "human nature" to be the good, and see happiness as a consequence of the realization of human nature.[20] The import of the perfectionists' commitment to some form of naturalism is perhaps visible in terms of their description of happiness in contrast to the description that utilitarians are likely to give. While the one will talk about virtues understood as excellences of self, the other will talk about pleasure, satisfaction, tranquillity.

There exists wide latitude among perfectionists, of course, in the specification of that which constitutes excellence, as well as in the degree of excellence required for a certain level of moral approbation. At the one extreme, Nietzsche posits so high a standard for excellence that only a few can reach it; he tells us that all those who fail to reach it are, in effect, natural slaves.[21] Toward the other end of the spectrum, Aristotle thinks that a basic capacity for deliberative rationality is (putting aside the thorny question of theoretical virtue) the standard for moral excellence and is a capacity whose realization is available to most human beings. Nonetheless, whether in their milder or harsher versions, perfectionist theories tend to be nonegalitarian, for it is felt that human beings do not share equally in the requisite aspect of human nature. That is, stated simply, political liberty and equality seem incompatible with "absolute" standards of excellence. This is a disturbing thought, and one as pressing now as it ever was.

Given what I said earlier, it might seem that any attempt to defend Platonic perfectionism against its critics is wasted time in that it entails a defense of an illiberal, unfair, unworkable, and metaphysically cumbersome political theory. But if the defense is that Plato's political philosophy does not entail these undesirable features, the effort would seem more worthwhile. In the present essay I shall take a few steps up that road, with the aim of showing that, at least according to some dialogues, Plato's political philosophy, while perfectionist, is neither simply illiberal nor inegalitarian. Hence the first part of the title of this essay. I want to suggest that the "Socratic" virtues of toleration and open-minded inquiry can be seen as founded on "Platonic" metaphysics.[22] Interpreters as diverse as Popper and Mill have agreed that these virtues are liberal ones, and have

20. See H. Sidgwick's *The Methods of Ethics*, 7th ed., rpt. (Indianapolis, Ind.: Hackett, 1981), pp. 1–11 (and notes), 114–15.

21. Nietzsche, *Untimely Meditations*, Third Essay ("Schopenhauer as Educator"), section 1, and passim. Nietzsche's comments in section 8 about Plato, philosophy, and politics are also germane to my discussion here.

22. I note that by "Socrates" I shall mean, in this essay, the Socrates of the dialogues, not the historical figure.

thus seen Socrates as a champion of political liberty.[23] Yet our portrait of Socrates comes in good part from Plato, and in Plato's dialogues some of the objectionable propositions mentioned above are put in Socrates' mouth. It seems, furthermore, an extraordinary provocation that the philosopher who wrote so movingly about love, with such sensitivity about our imperfections, and with such praise of the striving for the good, should have thought that a totalitarian, soul-crushing political regime did justice to the human condition. These tensions within Plato's dialogues are worth resolving.

The general line of argument here offered is not without precedent.[24] The project of rehabilitating ancient perfectionism along the lines I have indicated has its adherents, as the work of neo-Aristotelians such as Doug Den Uyl, Douglass B. Rasmussen, Fred Miller, Stephen Salkever, Henry Veatch, Bernard Williams, and Martha Nussbaum shows. Their approach comes to something like placing a theory of rights within the frame of what is now called "virtue ethics." Nussbaum has recently argued for what one might call "Aristotelian liberalism," thus developing a tradition that includes earlier neo-Aristotelians such as T. H. Green.[25] A return to the ancient vocabulary of "virtue" might be motivated by the perception that terms such as "moral ought," "moral obligation," "end in

23. Mill, *On Liberty*, p. 30. Popper, *The Open Society*, vol. 1, pp. 128–31 and passim.

24. I have in mind R. Kraut's work in particular. See his *Socrates and the State* (Princeton, N.J.: Princeton University Press, 1984), chap. 7. For discussion of Kraut's "liberalized" Plato, see his exchange with C. Orwin in *Platonic Writings, Platonic Readings*, ed. C. Griswold (New York: Routledge, Chapman, and Hall, 1988), pp. 171–82. See also C. D. C. Reeve, *Philosopher-Kings* (Princeton, N.J.: Princeton University Press, 1988), chap. 4 (esp. pp. 213–34); and D. Clay, "Reading the *Republic*," in *Platonic Writings, Platonic Readings*, pp. 19–33. Other efforts along the same general lines may be found in G. M. Mara's "Socrates and Liberal Toleration," *Political Theory* 16 (1988): 468–95; A. de Lattre, "La liberté Socratique et le dialogue platonicien," *Kant Studien* 61 (1970): 467–95; L. G. Versenyi, "Plato and His Liberal Opponents," *Philosophy* 46 (1971): 222–37; S. Salkever, "'Lopp'd and Bound': How Liberal Theory Obscures the Goods of Liberal Practices," in *Liberalism and the Good*, ed. R. B. Douglass, G. M. Mara, and H. S. Richardson (New York: Routledge, Chapman, and Hall, 1990), pp. 167–202; and my "*Politike Episteme* in Plato's *Statesman*," in *Essays in Ancient Greek Philosophy*, ed. J. Anton and A. Preus (New York: State University of New York Press, 1989), vol. 3, pp. 141–67.

25. See Nussbaum's "Nature, Function, and Capability: Aristotle on Political Distribution," *Oxford Studies in Ancient Philosophy*, suppl. vol. (1988): 145–84. See also her exchange with D. Charles in the same journal, pp. 185–214; and her "Aristotelian Social Democracy," in *Liberalism and the Good*, pp. 203–52. Some of T. H. Green's reflections on the matter may be found in *Lectures on the Principles of Political Obligation* (London: Longmans, Green, and Co., 1895), pp. 47–48 and passim (Green refers to Aristotle on p. 47). See also H. Veatch, *Human Rights: Fact or Fancy?* (Baton Rouge: Louisiana State University Press, 1985); B. Williams, *Ethics and the Limits of Philosophy* (Cambridge, Mass.: Harvard University Press, 1985); F. Miller, *Nature, Justice, and Rights in Aristotle's "Politics"* (Oxford: Clarendon Press, 1995); S. Salkever, *Finding the Mean: Theory and Practice in Aristotelian Political Philosophy* (Princeton, N.J.: Princeton University Press, 1990); and D. Den Uyl and D. Rasmussen, *Liberty and Nature: An Aristotelian Defense of Liberal Order* (La Salle, Ill.: Open Court, 1991).

itself," and so forth, have lost (as E. Anscombe argued[26]) the original theological context that gave them sense. The question Plato's Socrates insists on is not "What ought I to do?" (this is Kant's question; *CPR* A805 = B833) but "What sort of person should I be?" (e.g., *Rep.* 443d–e). The return to classical virtue ethics also seems motivated by the view that pre-Christian ethics offers valuable insights about the centrality of dialogue, knowledge of ignorance, friendship, love, and the virtues to our thinking about politics and ethics.

The effort to argue for a liberalism on perfectionist principles has found its supporters as well. That effort invariably begins with a critique of Rawls's view to the effect that the right is "prior" to the good and that a theory of justice should be "political" and not "metaphysical."[27] Victor Haksar, for example, argues that perfectionist theory is unavoidable if the liberal intuitions to which Rawls appeals to are to be defended.[28] Joseph Raz argues for a conception of rights that explicitly bases itself on a conception of human well-being. Raz refers to this as the "beneficiary view of rights,"[29] and characterizes his theory as "perfectionist moral pluralism."[30]

In section 1 of this essay I shall begin by developing further the definition of perfectionism. I shall then turn briefly to the *Republic,* as that dialogue is clearly problematic for the line of interpretation I am advancing. I shall say just enough to show how I would disarm the objections the *Republic* seems to pose. I will then offer, in section 2, a more detailed consideration of the *Statesman* (supported by references to the *Laws*). I shall attempt to show that the *Statesman* not only supports my comments about the *Republic,* but also points us in the direction of a constitutional democracy as the best available *politeia.* In order to move the argument closer to that destination, I shall turn, in section 3, to the

26. Anscombe, "Modern Moral Philosophy," *Philosophy* 33 (1958): 1–19. The argument is elaborated in A. MacIntyre's writings, most recently *Three Rival Versions of Moral Enquiry* (South Bend, Ind.: University of Notre Dame Press, 1990), chaps. 7–8.

27. The list of these critics is a long one. M. J. Sandel's *Justice and the Limits of Liberalism* (Cambridge, Mass.: Harvard University Press, 1982) is no doubt among the most influential discussions. Rawls's claim that he is articulating widespread intuitions of a democratic culture is questioned in W. Galston's "Pluralism and Social Unity," in *Liberal Purposes: Goods, Virtues, and Diversity in the Liberal State* (New York: Cambridge University Press, 1991), pp. 140–62 (see esp. p. 158).

28. Haksar, *Equality, Liberty, and Perfectionism* (Oxford: Oxford University Press, 1979).

29. Raz, "Right-Based Moralities," p. 183. Raz there remarks that "'X has a right' means that, other things being equal, an aspect of x's well-being (his interest) is a sufficient reason for holding some other person(s) to be under a duty." This view "would fit well with a view which regards the interests of people as the only ultimate value." For fuller discussion, see Raz's *The Morality of Freedom,* part 3, chap. 7. W. A. Galston argues along similar lines in *Justice and the Human Good* (Chicago: University of Chicago Press, 1980).

30. Raz, *The Morality of Freedom,* p. 133.

Phaedrus (with brief reference to the *Symposium*). Along the way, I shall discuss why, for Plato (in contrast with Epicurus), the pursuit of perfection of self involves concern for political association, and indeed political association of a certain general type. The story line of the essay is that polities compatible with Platonic perfectionism would be considerably more liberal than traditional readings of Plato suggest. Political liberty and equality need not be at odds with the assertion of the highest standards of human excellence.

The essay is programmatic both in the intentional brevity of the comments on the *Republic* and in leaving for another occasion discussion of connections between Plato's political philosophy and the contemporary debate about liberalism and perfectionism. My argument is compatible with the proposition that there are tendencies in Plato's political philosophy contrary to those I have elicited, and compatible with any of a number of hypotheses to explain any inconsistency of this sort. This observation is especially important with respect to the *Statesman* and the *Laws*; passages in the former about punishing all those who corrupt the youth (299b–c), or in the latter about the Noctural Council (909a), will correctly be cited as illiberal to the extreme. I do not overlook or deny the existence of these passages. I am asserting that there are also other passages with contrary implications. To reconcile these various passages, comprehensive interpretations of the dialogues in question would be required. I cannot supply these here, but merely offer, as a sort of promissory note, my belief that these passages can be reconciled, and in a way that is consistent with the thesis advanced in the present essay.

I

Let me begin by distinguishing between two species of perfectionism. I shall call them "communitarian" and "individualist" perfectionism. I take Aristotle to belong to the first species. As already noted, for Aristotle excellence in the city is determined relative to excellence in the soul of the individual. The purpose of the political association is not just to bring out excellence in a few lucky souls, but in all the citizens. Hence the polis exists not for the sake of living, but for the sake of living well, in accordance with excellence. Further, Aristotle argues that excellence in the individual's soul cannot be brought out fully except through rightly structured civic association, and that participation in a rightly ordered polis is not just a means to moral excellence but is partially constitutive of it.[31]

31. The difference between a polis and other sorts of association is not just numerical but qualitative; it has a form of unity particular to its nature and distinct purpose, and Aris-

Correspondingly, there is room for the notion of the public good in Aristotle's theory.[32] In committing himself to the views that the polis is natural (1253a25), that humans are by nature political animals (1253a2–3), that the polis is a type of association distinct from (among others) the household and family, and that the polis provides a collective good, Aristotle falls into the camp of what I am calling communitarian perfectionists.

I take it that a moral theory is individualistic if it assigns only instrumental value to any collective or public good.[33] Individualistic perfectionism will also hold that the individual's chief ethical end is self-perfection. This is very different from understanding individualism as that doctrine according to which subjective preferences are good reasons for action. Epicurus may be taken as an extreme example of what I am calling individualist perfectionism. Epicurus sees the individual's *autarkeia* not just in self-origination but more importantly in the correctness of beliefs about his or her own ends. For Epicurus, the *summum bonum* is the agent's happiness, understood, roughly, as pleasurable tranquillity of mind (*ataraxia*), freedom from pain, and invulnerability to fortune.[34] The emphasis on stability of happiness and imperviousness to luck makes it difficult for Epicurus to explain consistently why even friendship could have an important place in the life of the self-perfected individual.[35] Further, Epicurus understands self-perfection in such a way that all political involvements are judged solely for their instrumental value.

---

totle criticizes Plato at length for failing to appreciate that fact. For Aristotle, Plato insists on the wrong kind of unity in the polis, and fails to see that the hierarchical relationship of master and slave is not of the essence of the polis. These criticisms suggest that Plato does not see the polis as a precondition for the expression of moral excellence. By contrast, the polis is, for Aristotle, a "sort of multitude" consisting of persons of different kind (1261a17–24); and political rule properly speaking is rule of those free by nature and equal, while household management is monarchy (1255b16–20).

32. The public good would be that good (a) which is made available by the polis, (b) the distribution of the whole of which is not subject to the voluntary control of individuals, and (c) which is constitutive of the individual's realization of his or her own excellence and is not merely instrumental toward that end. This definition of the public good follows, in rough form, Raz, "Right-Based Moralities," p. 187.

33. In this definition of individualistic moralities I again follow Raz, "Right-Based Moralities," p. 186.

34. See the *Letter to Menoeceus* 128–29, 132–35, in *Epicurus: The Extant Remains,* trans. and ed. C. Bailey (Oxford: Clarendon Press, 1926), pp. 87, 91–93; *Sententiae Vaticanae* 77, p. 117; *Kuriai Doxai* n. 16, p. 99; and Diogenes *Lives* 10.118, in Bailey, p. 165. (Page references to Epicurus's writings refer to the Bailey edition.) This can be interpreted along perfectionist rather than utilitarian lines, for Epicurus seems to see this summum bonum as a fulfillment of the way in which our material natures are constituted; and he assigns no place to a principle of the equal value of individuals (hence he nowhere points to the happiness of the aggregate of individuals as the summum bonum).

35. See *Sent. Vat.* 23, p. 109; and for discussion, P. Mitsis's *Epicurus' Ethical Theory,* chap. 3, esp. pp. 117–28.

Correspondingly, prudence (*phronēsis*) functions as the chief virtue for Epicurus; its task is primarily to deliberate about the means best suited to self-interest rightly understood. Justice, Epicurus says, is nothing but a contract; the agent is obligated to be just only insofar as it is in his interest (rightly understood) to be such.[36] What substantive commitments a just contract makes (putting aside the agent's commitment to his own perfection) will depend. For example, an Epicurean might accept slavery as a just institution in some cases, and in other cases not.[37]

In sum, Epicurus's teaching seems at its core apolitical; it leaves no room for anything like the view that the polis is natural (in Aristotle's sense), that human beings are political animals by nature, or that political association is intrinsic to the realization of self.[38]

There is only partial overlap between Plato's and Epicurus's views. On the one hand, the *Phaedrus* shows, as I shall argue, that part of the individual's self-perfection must include care not just for other individuals but for communities. Plato has significantly different notions of "self" and "happiness" than does Epicurus. On the other hand, nowhere is it argued in Plato that the polis is natural (in Aristotle's sense), or that human beings are by nature political animals. Like Epicurus, Plato takes self-perfection to be the overriding *telos* of the human being. It seems that, for Plato, what is due to others is extrapolated from what we owe ourselves once we have rightly understood ourselves (hence the subtitle of the present essay). Where does this way of looking at political theory lead Plato?

Let us turn briefly to the *Republic*. In Book 2, Socrates is pushed to prove that we are motivated to be just not because justice is instrumentally good, but because it is an intrinsic good. In Book 4 (433a–b, 443d–e) Plato has Socrates offer what is surely a counterintuitive definition of justice as the right ordering of the individual's soul, such that the individual minds his own business ("ta eautou prattein," "doing one's

36. *Kuriai Doxai* n. 31, p. 103. See also P. Mitsis's *Epicurus' Ethical Theory* (Ithaca, N.Y.: Cornell University Press, 1988), p. 80.

37. Diogenes Laertius notes that Epicurus owned slaves, and that he both treated them well and manumitted several on his death (Diogenes interprets all this as indicative of the kind of person an Epicurean would want to be) (*Lives* 10.10 [p. 147], 10.21 [p. 155], 10.118 [p. 165]). In a manner reminiscent of Plato's Socrates, Epicurus does maintain that the pursuit of self-perfection removes motivations at the root of actions commonly labeled unjust. The Epicurean will care little about wealth or power, for example, and so will take no steps to acquiring any.

38. Correspondingly, Epicurus was accused of shirking his civic duty. See Epictetus's *Discourses* 3.7.19–23. On a purely prudential basis it would be possible to spell out a politics most likely to be conducive to the Epicurean's pursuit of self-perfection. For example, in light of Epicurus's emphasis on the role of scientific investigation in clearing the mind of superstition, one would expect that a society that encouraged such investigation would be useful.

own thing"). Justice is a quality of a perfected soul in that each of its "parts"—the rational, the spirited, and the desiring—does its proper job. The connection between justice as a virtue of self, and justice as conventionally understood (in connection with equality, law, duties toward others, etc.), is the subject of a now-well-established debate.[39] At least within the *Republic*'s "city in speech," however, the argument is that the structure of the polis is isomorphic with that of the soul; justice in the polis is justice of the soul writ large (435a–b, 368c–69a). The political and the psychological are to parallel each other. This "holistic" model, to the effect that a political arrangement is good or virtuous insofar as it has the same structure of goodness or virtue that belongs to the soul of an individual, leads to illiberal and inegalitarian measures.[40] The idea is that meaningful choice of a way of life cannot be had without an understanding of better and worse ways of life, an understanding reached through philosophical reason. The higher parts of the soul or city should rule over the lower; the lower parts lack the rationality requisite for meaningful self-rule and should therefore be ruled by the higher. Just as knowledge rules in a healthy self, so the philosophers, those persons knowledgeable about the Forms, rightly rule the polis, for the polis's own good.

This scheme runs into difficulties quickly, as many readers have noticed.[41] It leads to the paradoxical result that the majority of the citizens of the just polis are not just. The largest class of citizens seems to be that dominated by the "lower" desires; but by definition those individuals are not just, because they lack proper ordering of the parts of their soul. It is tempting to modify the thrust of the city/soul analogy and say that only the philosopher-rulers in the just city are just. But the just polis seems unjust in its treatment of them by forcing them to rule (a similar problem arises with respect to the guardians, who are forced to do their job whether or not they are happy doing it). In Book 7 of the *Republic* we are told that, even in the ideal state, philosophers—here taken to be those ultimately perfected human beings—must be "compelled" to rule, and will rule only because it is a necessary thing, not a good one (519c, 519e,

39. The discussion was inaugurated by David Sachs's "A Fallacy in Plato's *Republic*," rpt. in *Plato*, ed. G. Vlastos (South Bend, Ind.: University of Notre Dame Press, 1978), vol. 2, pp. 35–51. The same volume contains a useful response to Sachs by R. Demos.

40. I take the term "holistic" from Nussbaum, "Nature, Function, and Capability," pp. 155–56. As Nussbaum points out, other models also operate in Plato's text.

41. The paradoxes to which the holistic conception leads are examined in B. Williams's "The Analogy of City and Soul in Plato's *Republic*," in *Phronesis*, suppl. vol. 1 (1973): 196–206. In short, Williams points out that the just city must be divided into parts as the soul is, and so that the lowest (and largest) class of the just city is composed of epithymetic people; but these people are not just because they are not ruled by reason. Therefore the just city must have a majority of citizens who are not just. This contradicts the principle (implied in 433–34) that the city is just if and only if its citizens are just.

520e). Even in the ideal state, there seems to be great difficulty in harmonizing self-perfection and care by the self-perfected for the polis. Socrates is explicit that such harmony is not to be hoped for in any nonideal state.[42]

Even if these difficulties were solved, we might want to voice three objections against the *Republic*'s scheme. First, Socrates assumes that every person's nature is suited to a particular sort of job (370a, 395a–b). But this is nowhere demonstrated, and much doubt is cast upon it in the *Phaedrus.* Second, he assumes that the rulers of the city can, for a time at least, discern the natures and so the appropriate occupations of individuals (415b). But this would require omniscience on the part of the rulers. Third, it is assumed that philosopher-kings could exist. These individuals are not just philosophers in the sense of the term used in the *Phaedrus* and the *Symposium* (204a), that is, of persons who, as *lovers* of wisdom, are lacking the thing they love. The *Republic*'s philosophers *are* wise; they have gazed directly upon the Forms. Even if it is just to compel wise philosophers to rule, and even if the just city need not be composed only of just persons, the just city cannot be just unless wise philosophers rule it. But the *Statesman* and the *Phaedrus* will show us that there are no philosophers so understood, and this has crucial political consequences.

Further, the preconditions for setting up the *Republic*'s third city (which Socrates refers to as "Kallipolis") virtually ensure that it will never come to pass, as is indicated not just by the requirement that the rulers be perfectly wise, but also by the proviso at the end of Book 7 to the effect that everyone over the age of ten be expelled. At the start of Book 8 we learn that this polis-in-speech would not last long anyhow; Socrates throws out an elaborate mathematical joke to "explain" how the polis's inevitable decay comes about (and given that the passage is a joke, the implication is that there is no formula for the right breeding of the guardians and hence no way to sustain the regime past the first generation). As Diskin Clay has argued, the dialogue is structured in ways that indicate Plato's intention that the closed regime of the middle books of the *Republic* be read as open to question. As he and Charles Kahn have insisted, we ought not in any case read off Plato's intentions from the utterances of his dramatis personae without further ado. The dialogue form entails a lack of transparency with respect to authorial intention. Plato can have

42. E.g., at *Rep.* 497b we hear that "not one city today is in a condition of worthy of the philosophic nature." (Here and below I shall be citing from A. Bloom's translation [New York: Basic Books, 1968]). The reasons for which that is true very probably would still hold, in Socrates' view. One reason is stated as a permanent truth: "it's impossible that a multitude be philosophic" (494a; cf. *Stsm.* 292e). This generates the alienation of philosopher from city graphically described at 496b–e. Still, there may be degrees to which *poleis* are unsuitable to the philosophers.

his characters assert all sorts of things without his wishing either to affirm those assertions or to persuade the reader to accept them uncritically.[43] Indeed, his use of the dialogue form positively warns the reader against any such uncritical acceptance.

Let us distinguish between two questions. Granted that the Kallipolis is inegalitarian and illiberal: Did Plato (a) intend the *Republic* as a blueprint for social action? and (b) does he intend the "story" (*Rep.* 501e) he tells to be a description of the perfectly just community or, as I will argue is true of the *Statesman* (below), did he intend the reader to see that even a supposedly "ideal" state of affairs suffers from grave defects? For my present purposes, it suffices to focus on the first of these questions. Socrates explicitly gives us the answer at the end of Book 9 of the *Republic.* He there concedes that the "city in speech" will come to be only by divine chance and adds "but in heaven, perhaps, a paradeigma is laid up for the man who wants to see and found a city within himself on the basis of what he sees" (592b2–3).[44] The city/soul analogy, and the sense in which the city is the soul writ large, must therefore be completely recast. The whole of the *Republic*'s effort to define justice seems of value, that is, because of the role of this effort and of the definition in the individual's self-perfection. The emphasis at the end of the *Republic* is on the individual's choice of a way of life; this is a major theme, in fact, of the myth with which the dialogue concludes.

Let me restate the thrust of the preceding paragraph. We learn at the end of Book 7 (as we shall also learn in the *Statesman* and the *Laws*), that the first best regime is unavailable. We have in effect seen the need to reflect on what such a polity would look like; we are provided with opportunities to reflect on how desirable such a regime would be for us; and we are led to reflect on the consequences of the fact that we cannot plan on its coming into being. Theory and practice cannot be straightforwardly reconciled, and the "practical" question about what follows is itself a matter for theoretical speculation. Thus this third reflection is crucial: it

43. I refer to Clay's "Reading the *Republic.*" Kahn's point is worked out in a number of places, beginning with "Did Plato Write Socratic Dialogues?," *Classical Quarterly* 31 (1981): 305–20. For extended discussion of Kahn's interpretive assumptions, see my "Unifying Plato: Charles Kahn on Platonic *Prolepsis,*" *Ancient Philosophy* 10 (1990): 243–62. On the general question of the intentions of the *Rep.*, see also D. Hyland, "Plato's Three Waves and the Question of Utopia," *Interpretation* 18 (1990): 91–109. The reading of the *Republic*'s Kallipolis as an (almost certainly) unrealizable polis is argued by Clay, Hyland, and also Klosko (*The Development of Plato's Political Theory,* p. 179 and context).

44. This passage echoes a much earlier description in Book 6 of the philosopher's passion for and absorption in "things that are set in a regular arrangement and are always in the same condition—things that neither do injustice to one another nor suffer it at one another's hands, but remain all in order according to reason—he imitates them and, as much as possible, makes himself like them" (500c2–5).

leaves us with several pressing questions, such as: What is the *second* best regime? Or in different terms, what is that polity that best "imitates" the ideal? What would it mean to "imitate" an unobtainable ideal? The answer to these questions must take into account a whole range of factors, including facts about human nature and its imperfections; views about how much knowledge is accessible to humans and how we are to "recollect" more of the truth; theories about the different types of regimes and their (perhaps genealogical) relationship; arguments about how we might best "pattern" our souls so as to perfect them in the midst of an irremediably imperfect world; and of course, views about what regime here and now best serves the means for the self-perfection Socrates praises at the end of Book 7. The political need not and cannot express our personal ideal; what then follows for the politics of self-perfection? What polis does justice to us as erotic and therefore perpetually incomplete beings? Book 8 takes up some of the just mentioned questions, and similar discussions occur in the *Statesman* and the *Laws.*

It is within the space of this question about "imitation," opened up by the necessity for deciding what might be the second best (that is, the best practicable) polity, that the case for a relatively "liberal" regime would be made. Plato follows up the remarkable passage at the end of Book 7 with a discussion of various regimes, and the analysis of democracy is striking. Democracy is portrayed as degenerate and yet, as Socrates remarks in a frequently ignored passage, it is also a convenient place to look for a polity: "thanks to its license, it contains all species of regimes, and it is probably necessary for the man who wishes to organize a city, as we were just doing, to go to a city under a democracy" (557d). In other words, the sort of philosophical discussion that is the *Republic* can best be undertaken in a democracy. This regime is "sweet" because it is many colored, dispenses a certain equality (558c), and also provides significant political liberty, thereby providing a context for a Socrates. In this polis one is not compelled to rule (557e), and this is crucial; in the *Apology* Socrates tells us that he remained alive by staying out of politics (31d). A democracy is permissive enough to allow him both to stay alive and to philosophize, at least for a longer time than would other regimes. A democracy allows one to live the life of the private man laudably chosen by Odysseus (620c–d), and by Socrates. Paradoxically, a democracy is in theory to be rejected by philosophy, while in practice it is hospitable even to philosophy's rejection of it in theory. And we live, Socrates told us at the end of Books 7 and 9, in the realm of practice, not of theory. How the philosopher would rejoin the two is at the heart of the problem of "imitation" here, and I will say more about it in sections 2 and 3 below.

If the interpretation I am sketching is accurate, it may seem not merely that the *Republic* is not a blueprint for political action, but that the activities of actually founding a city, of taking part in politics, or of specifying what sort of polity is best in practice, are matters whose value is purely instrumental. We seem returned to Book 1 of the *Republic,* where Socrates asserts that the philosopher would want to hold office only in order to prevent being ruled by a worse person (347c).[45] Taken in isolation, such passages suggest little place in the well-ordered philosophical life for care for a polis. As in Epicurus, Platonic self-perfection seems to offer us little more than prudence and self-interest rightly understood as a basis for political theory. It seems that while the philosopher may not be compelled to espouse an illiberal and inegalitarian polity such as that of the *Republic,* he or she might do so for prudential reasons.

But that conclusion does not follow, as I shall now try to show with respect to the *Phaedrus.* We shall see that Plato does provide us with an argument showing that love of wisdom does include attachment to others in their collective capacity. But first, let me show how at least parts of the *Statesman* cohere with the interpretation of the *Republic* just sketched.

II

If the comments in the preceding section are well directed, then for Plato political philosophy will orient itself by a distinction between ideal and nonideal regimes. The "second best" polis theme is explicit in the *Statesman* (below) and the *Laws* (712a ff. and context; 807b, 875a–d).[46] It is also to be found in Aristotle's political theory. Plutarch tells us that when Solon was asked if he had left the Athenians the best laws that could be given, he replied "The best they could receive"; and Hesiod's account of the successively degenerating "ages of man" suggests, indirectly, a difference between best and relatively best conditions. The distinction between ideal and nonideal regimes, and its political importance, is scarcely unique to Plato. The view that the best *practicable* form of political association will be imperfect or, in a Platonic phrase, be second best, complicates in interesting ways Platonic perfectionism. It decisively tempers perfectionist social engineering, and turns moderation into a central political virtue.

45. Cf. also *Rep..* 496b–d, where we are told that philosophers despise the business of the city and look beyond it, and that they mind their own business.

46. The distinction between best and inferior regimes is also explicit in Aristotle. But Aristotle does not draw out, in the ways that the Platonic dialogues do, the paradeigmatic status of the best regime, the reasons for which that regime is unavailable, and the ways in which the realization that the best is unattainable should condition our reception of nonideal regimes.

The *Statesman* is part of a trilogy.[47] It is immediately preceded by the *Sophist,* and was to have been followed by the *Philosopher.* At the start of the *Sophist* Socrates turns to the newly arrived Eleatic Stranger and asks him the question that leads to, and provides the main topics for, the ensuing two dialogues: do people from the Eleatic Stranger's region divide the genera "sophist," "statesman," and "philosopher" into three, just as the names indicate? The Eleatic Stranger answers affirmatively, and accepts both Socrates' invitation to define each of these types and Socrates' selection of an interlocutor. Having thus given shape to the ensuing conversations, Socrates sits back and listens. A similar scene occurs at the start of the *Statesman,* where Socrates picks a new interlocutor for the Eleatic Stranger, a young mathematician named "Young Socrates."

The *Statesman* attempts to define the genus "statesman" by defining the science he possesses.[48] The Eleatic Stranger's rationale is evidently the belief that possession of political science is a sufficient condition for someone's being a statesman (259b). The Eleatic Stranger proceeds by using the method of diairesis. The first definition of political science is arrived at as a result of a long series of divisions that occupy the first third of the dialogue. Each step of the division is woven together such that the definition of political science is the sum of its genealogical parts. The Eleatic Stranger begins by dividing "epistēmē" (knowledge or science) into "praktikē epistēmē" (as in the art of carpentry) and "gnostikē epistēmē" (as in arithmetic and kindred arts). The ensuing series of divisions yield a startling definition: the statesman is he who possesses the cognitive science of giving his own orders for the nurturing and grazing of the two-footed, pedestrial, hornless, noninterbreeding herd of animals (267b–c). In other words, political science is the art of ruling featherless bipeds. This reductive definition omits what is essential about human beings: the soul, the interiority of self, rationality. But Young Socrates accepts this definition as satisfactory without qualification.[49]

47. For a much fuller discussion of the *Statesman,* see my "*Politike Episteme* in Plato's *Statesman,*" from which these remarks are drawn. A recent study of the *Statesman,* one in substantial harmony with my own interpretation, is S. Rosen's *Plato's Statesman: The Web of Politics* (New Haven, Conn.: Yale University Press, 1995).

48. Since in the *Statesman* the possessor of statescraft is referred to with masculine pronouns, it seems pointless to do otherwise when commenting on that text.

49. Three brief comments about this initial definition. First, Young Socrates is a mathematician; thus the opening definition of political science as a theoretical branch of *epistēmē* expresses his own proclivities. Second, the final definition is also Young Socrates'; not only did he assent to each step as well as the conclusion, but the definition expresses his traditionalist notion that the ruler of a polis is a "shepherd of the people," to use Homer's characterization of Agamemnon. If the ruler is a shepherd, we are sheep. Third, the definition is tidy in a way that a politically inexperienced mathematician might be expected to appreciate: there is one ruler; the ruled are treated as units to be manipulated as the ruler sees fit;

Many commentators stop here, assuming that Young Socrates speaks for Plato. Popper alludes to this opening section of the dialogue when he accuses Plato of advocating totalitarianism.[50] This definition is of a piece with the initial definition of the political art (258e) according to which, as the Eleatic Stranger asserts, the art of political rule and the art of ruling over slaves are effectively the same. But in fact Plato has the Eleatic Stranger proceed immediately to reject the definition. In a very Socratic way, the Eleatic Stranger has led Young Socrates down the garden path. Young Socrates is thrown into a state of *aporia.* The Eleatic Stranger's initial objection is that the definition does not isolate the statesman's art, for "thousands" of other types of people will claim to be "statesmen" in the sense specified so far (267e–68c). That is, the Eleatic Stranger focuses on a crucial aspect of political life, namely, the existence of widespread and deep disagreement about who should rule, and so about what just rule is. Title to legitimate rule is in doubt, and a successful political arrangement must take into account the liberty of thinking that the phenomenon of disagreement signals. Each person thinks he or she ought to rule. Thus civil strife and dissolution constantly threaten our lives (cf. 273d, 302a, 308a). The *Laws* puts this even more strongly: every person is an enemy of every other person, and each person is also his own enemy (626d; cf. 744d). The problem with the *Statesman*'s opening definition of political science, that is, is that it is strangely apolitical. It has little to do with real-world politics.

The Eleatic Stranger develops his point in a surprising way. He proceeds to recount a long, complicated, and quite bizarre cosmological myth. I think that this myth is the pivot of the dialogue, that on which the competing definitions of statescraft turn. We can read it as a sort of thought experiment whose central point is that the initial definition of the *Statesman* assumes a state of things that does not exist in the sort of world we presently occupy. Among other things, the myth attacks the definition's assumption that an all-knowing shepherd-of-the-people presently exists. We are given to infer that a person who thinks he possesses political science in that sense, who sees himself as different in kind from the ruled, and who takes the ruled to be comparable to sheep, is nothing other than a tyrant. Let me fill out this account with a very brief summary of the myth.

---

they are inert, things to be manipulated, having no potentiality or freedom; the ruler is the measure of the whole.

50. Popper, *The Open Society*, vol. 1, pp. 86–87; I refer to section (A) on p. 86 in particular (no doubt Popper there thinks of the *Rep.* too). I note that Aristotle's *Pol.* discussion of Plato's political philosophy is carefully stated; Aristotle repeatedly refers to "Socrates" rather than to "Plato" as the author of the various views he rejects.

The Eleatic Stranger says that current stories about a distant golden age are dim recollections of a truth. The cosmos turns in two cycles. The cycle contrary to that in which we now live—let us call it the divine cycle—is governed by the god Kronos. In the divine cycle the god guided and reenergized the cosmos, taking it and winding it up like a spindle hanging from a thread. Kronos regulated everything along with helper gods, among whom care of the herds of living creatures is divided. Just as now men graze the inferior species, so then the god grazed humans (271e5–7). It was a beautiful era. Everything operated with extreme efficiency and mathematical precision. In those days there was no disagreement or competition among people. Indeed, humans and animals could converse with one another and got along perfectly (272c). There was no private property, no family, no work, no sexuality (people are generated out of the earth), and no war (271e–72a). There was no reason to develop any of the arts, not even the arts of agriculture or of clothes making; people in those times went about naked and found food without effort. They possessed no sense of shame. I think it safe to infer that there existed no politics in the ordinary sense of the term, and this because there existed no human beings.[51]

This picture of things supplies the background for the *Statesman*'s initial definition of statescraft as the rule of the all-knowing person over featherless bipeds. The myth suggests that such a scheme would be appropriate to the golden ages and so, first of all, that it is impossible in practice. The first definition holds only for the cosmos's countercycle (274e–75a). As the Eleatic Stranger goes on to say, things are radically different in our cycle of the cosmos. At a preordained time, god let go of the tiller of the cosmos. There was a gigantic quake, and a near-total destruction of all living things. God retired to his "observation tower" (*periope*, 272e5; a sort of "ivory tower") along with his helper gods. The cosmos began to unwind, and in the ensuing cycle—our cycle, the human one—the cosmos and all things in it are left to care for themselves. Disagreement, war, and competition arise. So do the arts, customs, communities, religion, philosophy, sexuality, and procreation; all are forms of autotherapy. We live in the best of times and the worst of times. For a while things go well. But unfortunately the universe is ineluctably entropic. It degenerates into chaos, and god once again grabs hold of the tiller and winds up the universe.

51. Another strange aspect of life at that time is as follows: people were born full grown and then became younger. It would thus seem that there was no learning in the countercycle, only forgetting. As the Eleatic Stranger says, no one possessed any memory of preceding generations (271e8–72a2); there thus existed no sense of history or continuity with the past, no traditions.

The Eleatic Stranger pauses to ask Young Socrates which cycle is happier. Young Socrates is unsure. The Eleatic Stranger prompts him with this criterion: if the residents of the countercycle (that which Kronos ruled) had philosophy, then they were happier. It seems clear, as I have said, that in the golden age there was no philosophy. The model of statescraft appropriate to the golden age is neither possible nor ultimately desirable, for utopia was not unequivocally good. This is a point that, as I suggested earlier (section 1), might be read in the *Republic* as well. It follows that, among other things, our conception of politics must be conditioned by a deep sense of our neediness and a recognition of our fallibility; of the inevitability of self-reliance thanks to god's absence (the art of politics cannot claim divine guidance as the source of its knowledge); by a deep sense of the constant pressure of decay and the tendency to entropy; of the omnipresence of disagreement and of the ever present danger of war; by the development of *technai* that will save us from the destructive hand of nature; and finally by—to use a Socratic phrase—knowledge of ignorance, by our recognition that no human can or ought to rule as god would. Indeed, the Eleatic Stranger defines the tyrant as someone who rules without established law in the belief that he possesses the true political *epistēmē* (300b10–c4). The tyrant exhibits ignorance of ignorance in the highest degree. That crucial point is a strongly Socratic one. In sum, the *Statesman* points us to a deeply fallibilistic teaching about the human condition and the world, and draws the appropriate political consequences.[52]

These consequences include a recognition of the importance of written law. In a now famous discussion, the Eleatic Stranger argues that while in a perfect world the ruler could dispense with written law and instead legislate for each and every case, in a world of imperfections and fallible knowledge written law is best. Since a god cannot rule, it is best for the laws—the result of trial and error, experience, prudence—to rule (294a6–8).[53] The laws ought to rule as justly and impartially as possible, but always with an awareness as to why they, and not a fallible person, rule.

52. The Eleatic Stranger has told a story that illustrates why the choice of theoretical knowledge as the branch under which to seek political science was a mistake. It abstracted from our fallibility, our limits, from the world's unwinding. Now we infer that statesmanship is a branch of practical science. The Eleatic Stranger puts this metaphorically: political science is like the art of weaving woolen cloaks, i.e., the art of uniting the citizens through mores and laws protecting all from hostile nature.

53. As the Eleatic Stranger says, "[T]here is no king that comes to be in the cities, as we in point of fact assert, who's of the sort that naturally arises in hives—one who's right from the start exceptional in his body and his soul—they [the citizens] must, it seems, once they've come together, write up writings while they run after the traces of the truest regime" (301d8–e4). I quote here and below from the S. Bernadete translation in *The Being of the Beautiful: Plato's "Theatetus," "Sophist," and "Statesman"* (Chicago: University of Chicago Press, 1984).

With this in mind, the Eleatic Stranger sets out a hierarchy of imperfect polities relative to the perfect one that they "imitate." The imitative polities may be governed according to law or lawlessly (i.e., without laws, contrary to laws). The question is this: Given the cosmological conditions outlined, which polity is the "mean," the timely or appropriate one, for the times?

After a discussion about measure and the rule of law, the Eleatic Stranger sets out the types of polities. He remarks that while a monarchy is best *if* it is governed by *good* writings or laws, in a situation tending to lawlessness and intemperance democracy is best, for while it is not capable of the greatest goods, neither is it capable of the worst evils (303a–b). If we order the six regimes he names from best to worst, we get this sequence: monarchy, aristocracy, democracy according to law, lawless democracy (mob rule), oligarchy, and tyranny. In the light of the cosmological myth, it seems clear that our times make democracy according to law appropriate, for we surely live in a time tending to lawlessness and intemperance. "Precision"—a favorite word in these passages of the *Statesman*—simply does not characterize our lives as political beings or individuals, in sharp contrast to the world governed by Kronos. Further, we are told that people refer to anyone claiming the title of monarch as "tyrant."[54] Even well-intentioned rulers are corruptible by the usual temptations. Plato makes this point explicit in a remarkable passage in the *Laws*, and with a familiar-sounding formulation: absolute power corrupts and is not to be entrusted to a mortal, corruptible being (*Laws* 713c, 714a, 691c–d, 875a–d). The point is there made with reference to the same Kronos myth that plays such a large role in the *Statesman*. And as in the *Statesman*, the conclusion is that the laws must rule in such a way as to provide constitutional restraints on absolute power lest the situation devolve into that which plagued Persia (*Laws* 697d–98a). So monarchic rule is not desirable in a nonideal situation.

The same objection that the Eleatic Stranger articulates against the claim by one person to absolute rule would a fortiori hold against the claims of a few such persons. And that leaves us with the third best alternative, namely, a lawful or constitutional democracy. As ruled by law and structured by institutions that prevent the (corrupting) concentration of power in one or a few hands, a polity of this sort would differ fundamentally from the "democracy" criticized in Book 9 of the *Republic*.

A constitutional democracy might satisfy the demand of each person

54. As the Eleatic Stranger says, people simply "don't trust that anyone would ever prove to be worthy of a ruler of that [kingly] sort, so as to be willing and able as ruler with virtue and science to distribute correctly the just and holy things to all" (301c8–d2). In a comprehensive interpretation of the *Statesman*, I would seek to show that the section on law recapitulates the whole course of the dialogue, and is a highly dialectical section.

to rule. A polity of this sort might encourage development of the arts and sciences in that each person is left at liberty to create under competitive conditions. If knowledge is fallible, then the opportunity to improve it must be encouraged (at 299e the Eleatic Stranger notes that a system of laws excluding progress in the arts eventually destroys the polis). Those arts and sciences are essential for self-preservation in an entropic age. Since civil war is forbidden and all are equal before the rule of written law, politics is to be carried on by persuasion rather than by force. That and the diffusion of power that a properly structured democracy ensures should check the lust for power so evident in the political life of an unravelling world. Finally, I note that at 276e the tyrannical art is characterized as "care of those who submit to force," while the political art is characterized as voluntary care of voluntarily participating citizens. The distinction between political rule and rule over slaves, demanded by Aristotle at the start of the *Politics,* is now granted. In sum, the *Statesman* points us to constitutional democracy composed of free citizens as the "best" regime for the current cycle of the cosmos.[55] This might be interpreted broadly enough to include elements of other polities, as in the *Laws'* mix of democratic, aristocratic, and monarchic models (756e–57a and passim).[56] And as the Athenian Stranger stresses in the *Laws,* the lawgiver's aim must be to secure for the polis not just internal harmony but freedom and wisdom (701d).[57]

55. We can connect the Eleatic Stranger's account with Socrates' view of things. The Eleatic Stranger tells us that it is extremely difficult to separate the true statesman from the "Sophists of Sophists," the "greatest imitators and greatest enchanters" who falsely claim to be legitimate rulers (291c, 303c). The problem of images and originals is central to our understanding of political life. Now, this is a favorite Socratic theme. And Socrates responds to the problem by cross-examining claimants to wisdom in order to see which of them really possesses wisdom and which only seems to. In the *Apol.,* he recounts that he concluded from his dialogues that no one is perfectly wise; the best one can do is human wisdom or knowledge of ignorance. That sort of self-knowledge entails recognition of one's limitations as human—a pervasive point in the Platonic dialogues. The famous Socratic and Platonic emphasis on dialogue, that is, supports the *Stsm.*'s fallibilistic critique of despotic rule.

56. But how exactly is this polity to be structured? Will it mix in, say, other forms of *poleis*—artistocratic and monarchic elements, as in the *Laws* (756e–57a and passim)? At this point, I think Plato has no a priori answer. The answers will be, to borrow a phrase from a founder of American liberalism, "inventions of prudence" (J. Madison, *Federalist* no. 51, p. 322). It will depend on everything from the social and political history of the people in question to the geography of the place. Trial and error will be one of our teachers (300b). This is unsatisfying if one thinks of political philosophy as capable of answering a priori detailed questions of constitutional structure or social policy. But one could also argue that a strength of the approach is precisely that it leaves a great deal of room for deliberations about empirical and contingent affairs. The large role that Plato and Aristotle assign "phronesis" in political theory is connected with their conviction that particularities must be given their due in both ethics and political theory.

57. As the *Laws* indicates, Platonic perfectionism would grant significant space to liberty of speech, liberty to trade, to travel, to gather with other citizens, to participate in politics,

The *Statesman* confirms, I am arguing, my reading of the *Republic.* Yet both dialogues seem to leave us with the impression that the public realm is not a context within which excellence is to be pursued by individuals. The value of the polis, once again, seems merely instrumental. To revert to the Eleatic Stranger's question as to where happiness is to be found, we seem led to answer that it is to be found in the individual's private life. This is puzzling within the context of a perfectionist theory, as the point seems now to be that there is little perfection to be gotten by means of the state's direct intervention in the lives of individuals. It also seems that individuals have little reason, other than an instrumental one, to care about a polis. To see that this is not the end of the story, we need to turn to the *Phaedrus.* If some connection between self-interest and the interest of others can be established at the heart of the nonpolitical, perfecting pursuit of self-knowledge, then we may be able to see in a general way the connection between that pursuit and politics.[58]

III

Close to the start of the *Phaedrus,* Socrates declares that he cares only about self-knowledge.[59] With this striking declaration Socrates presents us in the strongest form with the assertion of the primacy of self-perfection, for that is the goal to which self-knowledge is the means. This emphasis on self-knowledge and self-perfection is, as we know, repeated

---

to the right to own private property. The glaring exceptions concern the public expression of atheism, public disagreement with the civic religion, or the creation of private religions. All are strictly forbidden in Book 10 of the *Laws.* I would want to argue that with regard to freedom of religion, Plato either erred, or thought the threat of civil war so great (*Laws* 744d) as to require him to put aside the "liberal" consequences of his own theories.

58. Sections of the following discussion of the *Phr.* are adapted, with many changes, from Parts A and B of my "The Politics of Self-knowledge: Liberal Variations on the *Phaedrus,*" in *Understanding the "Phaedrus,"* ed. L. Rossetti (Sankt Augustin: Academia Verlag, 1992), pp. 173–90. I am grateful to the press for permission to adapt that article to my present purposes. I refer the reader to the original article for a fuller discussion of the *Phr.* and liberalism. The general strategy of turning to the "discourses on love" for insight into the foundations of Plato's political philosophy has not been followed through, so far as I know, in the detail I have attempted. But moves in that direction are made by R. Kraut in "Egoism, Love, and Political Office in Plato," *Philosophical Review* 82 (1973): 330–44 (Kraut refers to the *Symp.*).

59. "I am not yet capable," he says, "in accordance with the Delphic inscription, of 'knowing myself'; it therefore seems absurd to me that while I am still ignorant of this subject I should inquire into things which do not belong to me. So then saying goodbye to these things [the question as to the truth of various myths], and believing what is commonly thought about them, I inquire—as I said just now—not into these but into myself" (229e5–30a3). Translation by C. J. Rowe, in *Plato: "Phaedrus," with Translation and Commentary* (Warminster: Aris and Phillips, 1986). I shall use this translation throughout.

many times in the Platonic dialogues.[60] In the *Apology*, for example, Socrates characterizes his life as a divinely provoked pursuit of self-knowledge (21a ff.). Yet in the very same dialogue he describes his purpose in a very different way when he portrays himself as dedicated to the moral improvement of his fellow citizens, thereby manifesting (so he claims) great civic concern for Athens as well (29d–30b). How do these two sides of Socrates' moral life cohere? If the philosopher cares only about knowing himself, is there any room for his caring for others?[61]

I think we can make some progress here by recalling some of the metaphysical propositions of Socrates' second speech—often referred to as the "recantation" or "palinode"—in the *Phaedrus*. In the palinode we learn that the Forms are not directly visible to embodied souls; that privilege is reserved to the gods and to the disembodied souls that accompany them. For us, the Forms are visible only through their images and so through sense perception; we know the Forms only through recollection, through "memory" (*mnēmē;* 254b5). This theme of recollection (*anamnēsis*), which is absent from the *Republic*, accents the partiality and indirectness of our understanding of the Forms. The *Phaedrus* insists much more strongly than does the *Republic* that the philosopher cannot escape the cave altogether. In the *Phaedrus*'s universe there could be no "philosopher-kings" since there could be no "philosophers" in the requisite sense.[62]

The palinode concentrates on Beauty, but also mentions Justice. If Socrates had chosen Justice rather than Beauty as the Form with which to illustrate the workings of Eros, how would the account have proceeded? Where would the images of Justice present themselves? Presumably they would do so in the words and deeds of other persons individually and collectively considered. Just as the directedness of the soul toward the Forms, and the availability of the Forms through images in "this" world,

60. E.g., *Rep.* 578c ("for, you know, the consideration is about the greatest thing, a good life and a bad one"); *Gorg.* 487e11–88a1: the key issue is what qualities a person should have and what his pursuits should be.

61. I shall usually refer to the philosopher using the masculine pronoun because Plato does so in the *Phr.*, and to avoid cumbersome switching back and forth. I do not, however, believe that Plato's story here about soul, perfection, and love *has* to be gender-specific.

62. The cycle of departure from and return to the cave, narrated so briefly in the *Rep.*, consumes much of the *Phr.*'s palinode. The palinode tells not only about a heavenly scene above the earth, but about the fate of earthbound, fallen souls—a fate that entails forgetfulness of what was seen above, and a struggle to remember. Down here, our intelligence is bound to sense perception, and in different ways. Beauty is the "clearest" of all the Forms, accessible as it is to the sense of sight; Wisdom ("phronesis"), by contrast, is invisible to sight, and very hard to recollect and to love (250d3–e1). The earthly likenesses of Justice and Sophrosyne also lack luster; they are hard to see (250b1–3).

ties the philosopher to a beloved in the case of Beauty, so we can envision that a similar connection would hold in the case of Justice. A philosophical attraction to that Form would tie the philosopher to persons in this world; perfection of self would seem in this event to include attachment to others in their collective capacity—to one or more communities, in effect.[63]

The pursuit of Justice cannot be a merely "otherworldly" one, particularly if another aspect of the story Socrates tells about lover and beloved holds by analogy with respect to the philosopher and his or her beloved polis. An old debate surrounds the issue of whether the lover cares for the beloved for the latter's own sake, or merely as a means to his (the lover's) own perfection. This debate, initiated by an article by Vlastos, lies at the heart of the problem I mentioned earlier as to whether or not the polis is merely of instrumental value to the philosopher.[64] I wish to propose that the dilemma is a false one. I shall suggest that the relationship between philosopher and polis parallels that between lover and beloved, such that the polis too may be of more than merely instrumental value. While the lover cares about the beloved because he sees in the other an image of both his own perfection and of the Form, he does genuinely care for the beloved's welfare as measured by the latter's potential for perfection (cf. *Rep.* 401d–2d, 518b). The lover does not better himself at the expense of the beloved, but in such a way as to better the beloved as well. The lover does not throw the beloved away at the end of it all; rather, if things go successfully, they become lifelong friends (256a–b). The beloved's potential is not a mere means to the realization thereof, as though once perfected he is a different self. That potential is itself treated, in the *Phaedrus* and in the *Symposium*, as a source of wonderment and respect. It is true that a self is held to be worthy of love in virtue of the lovable qualities immanent in it; but I take Plato's point to be that the "separable" nature of these qualities rescues value for soul rather than deprives it of value.[65] A universe in which a self could not be seen

63. Since at 250b and passim Socrates indicates that our attraction to Justice is not as passionate as that for Beauty (at least not initially?), I use the word 'attraction' rather than 'passion' here. That is, the justice that the organization of the laws of a body politic and of the characters of its citizens may exhibit will lack the brilliance present in a particular, potentially philosophical beloved.

64. I refer to G. Vlastos's "The Individual as Object of Love in Plato," reprinted in *Platonic Studies*, 2d ed. (Princeton, N.J.: Princeton University Press, 1981), pp. 3–34.

65. Cf. G. Vlastos's "The Theory of Social Justice in the *Polis* in Plato's *Republic*," in *Interpretations of Plato*, ed. H. F. North (Leiden: E. J. Brill, 1977), p. 33. As Vlastos rightly points out there, if Plato were to ask "what is excellence [of soul] for?," we might answer "for humanity." But Plato would want to take the reverse tack, asking "What is humanity for?" and answering with reference to excellence or perfection. And this answer might seem to lead (and does lead in some Platonic dialogues) to a view of justice that is compatible with-

as reflecting these eternally perfect and complete qualities would, on this view, leave us with little motivation for valuing a soul deeply.[66] Love and friendship, in turn, are indispensable components of the good life precisely because of, rather than in spite of, their being intrinsic to the philosophic activity of *anamnēsis*, to being the kind of self that is perfected.

A similar picture may hold with respect to Justice. The philosopher will see images of Justice in *poleis*, and therefore take an interest in these *poleis* in the course of trying to understand what Justice itself is. A polis that embodies or, in its institutions, "images" Justice in a high degree would be particularly promising in his eyes. Should he discern in a polis the reflection of the Form Justice, the philosopher would want to bring out a polis's justice in something like the way that the philosophical lover wants to bring out the best in his beloved.[67] As an overflow of his own desire for self-perfection (for justice in his own soul, say), the philosopher will want to perfect his polis. But just as the lover tries to select a beloved whom he divines is of the same type, so the philosopher would grant his attentions to a community in which he or she divined the potential for

---

substantive inequality. But the *Phr.*, as I shall suggest, at least points in another direction. For a very fine response to Vlastos on this point, see A. Kosman's "Platonic Love," in *Phronesis*, suppl. vol. 2 (1976), ed. W. H. Werkmeister, pp. 53–69.

66. My purpose here is neither to defend the just stated point as an exegesis of the *Phr.* nor as a philosophical position in its own right. The former task I undertook in *Self-Knowledge in Plato's "Phaedrus"* (New Haven, Conn.: Yale University Press, 1986), pp. 124–33 (for the debate about the possible "egoism" of this portrayal of love, see pp. 128–29). A difficult problem about the relationship between Beauty and Justice lurks here. One might ask, for example, what makes Justice (or an instance thereof) attractive to the philosopher, if not its Beauty, whose motivational property Socrates makes so much of. Perhaps it is the rational order that might partly define what it is to be just that attracts the philosophical soul, an order or symmetry that might qualify as "beautiful." In this event, the correlate to justice in the city would be justice in the soul, that of beauty in the city would be beauty in the soul. Perhaps justice could be seen as exhibiting harmony and unity that are marks of beauty; and this would account for the philosopher's attraction to justice in the city. Beauty would here function almost as the Good does in the *Republic.*

67. For a discussion of the *Rep.* that leads to similar conclusions (though from quite different premises) see J. Cooper, "The Psychology of Justice in Plato," *American Philosophical Quarterly* 14 (1977): 155: "it does not follow that they [philosophers] would always choose to live a contemplative life. . . . a just person is a devotee of *the* good, not *his own* good; and these are very different things. Knowing the good, what he [the philosopher] wants is to advance the reign of rational order in the world as a whole." A similar point is made with reference to the *Symp.* by R. Demos in "A Fallacy in Plato's *Republic*?," in *Plato II*, p. 55: "To aim at the good is also to aim at the *production* of good things; thus for an individual to aim at justice means that he cares not only for justice in the abstract, but also that justice should be embodied in human beings in general. . . . The health of the soul includes, above all, the fulfillment of its reason: and the concern of reason is that the good should be exemplified everywhere." See also M. Miller's "Platonic Provocations: Reflections on the Soul and the Good in the *Republic*," in *Platonic Investigations*, ed. D. O'Meara (Washington, D.C.: The Catholic University of America Press, 1985), 163–93. Miller stresses the element of "generosity" on the philosopher's part that results from his vision of the Good.

justice.[68] As the choice of a correct beloved initiates the love affair, and ultimately the friendship, that provides the lover with the context for self-perfection, so a friendship with the right polis may provide the lover with the context for self-perfection as a just human being.[69] And as not just any beloved will help the lover accomplish these ends, so not just any polis will help the philosopher accomplish analogous ends. Perhaps there is a hierarchy of *poleis*—the most potentially just to the most tyrannical and unjust—as there are of soul types (248c2–e3). Indeed, in Book 9 of the *Republic* Socrates matches up a hierarchy of polities with a hierarchy of soul types.[70] No more than the beloved, then, is a polis a dispensable feature of the philosophers' love of Forms.[71] This I think is the thrust of Socrates' comments about laws and customs in the *Symposium*'s ascent passages. There we are told that the ordering of cities and households with moderation and justice is the most beautiful part of wisdom; a

68. Recall that there are two kinds of "recollection" in the palinode, and that they are connected: e.g., (a) to recognize oneself as a follower of Zeus—i.e., as a philosopher—is to see oneself as the type of soul passionate about (b) tracking down or recollecting the Forms present in their images. One cannot apprehend one's own nature directly, without the mediation of the other who serves, in Socrates' word, as a "mirror" (255d6). I am suggesting that, at least in the case of justice, the polis serves as the philosopher's mirror. What dimension of the soul is mirrored and brought to consciousness by the polis? Presumably, the aspect of soul that would be engaged as dialectician and (in a suitably defined sense) pedagogue in the polis (that engagement described in the *Apol.* as being both beneficial to Socrates and to the citizens). Further, in the palinode's account, the beloved is portrayed as confused by the lover, unclear as to what he (the beloved) is loving and as to what he sees reflected in the lover (255d). If the present analogy holds, we would expect the polis to undergo a similar experience when facing the philosopher. The relationship is asymmetrical in each case. Finally, as Socrates shifts between the language of making (252d7, e4) and of discovering (252e1–4) in describing the lover's stance toward the beloved, so too, perhaps, with respect to the philosopher's stance toward the polis: the given polis, as potentially just, is both discovered to be an image of Justice and made into a more perfect image thereof.

69. This is compatible with the *Rep.* view that ruling is drudgery (*Rep.*, 540a–b); but there are other forms of political activity, such as that described by Socrates in the *Apol.* as an alternative to direct participation in ruling. Aristotle points out that (Plato's) Socrates "praises above all the city's being one, which is held to be, and which he asserts to be, the work of affection," and goes on to allude to the *Symp.* Aristotle rightly points out that the *Rep.*'s scheme dilutes the possibilities for affection by dissolving the family; the implication being that the *Symp.* is inconsistent with the *Rep.* (*Pol.* 2.1262b8 ff).

70. I note that at *Phr.* 246e6–47a1 we hear of a multitude of communities in heaven, varying as soul types do.

71. The general point of the preceding paragraphs could be taken much further, of course. For one could argue that (like other Forms) Justice is not an entity that can be defined in and of itself, that in isolation from contexts and examples in which it is (even if imperfectly) instantiated, there is relatively little to *say* about it (except by negation, as at *Symp.* 211d8–e4), however much it may be something one can "see" (*Symp.* 211e1 and passim). In the *Phr.* Socrates in fact says nothing about the substantial meaning of any Form, except that vision of it is deeply fulfilling. I note in passing that not even the gods care solely about the Forms: they are portrayed, rather, as "caring" for the cosmos (246e5–6), contemplating the Forms only intermittently. *Imitatio dei* thus involves more than contemplation.

lover of beauty will want to give birth to admirable regimes, and will admire them too as instances of beauty (209a, d, 210c, 211c).

This way of looking at the relationship between self-perfection and community entails giving up the holistic model of the city/soul analogy, according to which a philosophical polis is one ruled by philosophers just as a philosophical soul is one ruled by reason. In light of the *Phaedrus* and the *Symposium*, we might rather say that while neither a city nor a soul is admirable if ruled by passion, a city is admirable if it enables each of its members to pursue whatever excellence their natures may hold.[72]

The first two speeches of the *Phaedrus*, which portray the beloved as an object to be manipulated, gives us an idea as to how persons may be mistreated. Particularly in Lysias's speech, the "other" is reified, reduced to a body, unsouled, having value only in the sexual gratification it can yield. The burden of the palinode, and so of the "ascent" from Lysias's speech, is to show why that conception of the person is inadequate, why it is that someone possessing self-knowledge would not be disposed to demean others in that way. Socrates introduces the notion of "soul" to denote a core function without which we would not be human. He implies that to treat persons as though this were not true of them would be to act ignorantly.[73]

Socrates' palinode take us some ways toward a critique of the reification or objectification of others so prominent in the first speech (that attributed to Lysias) of the dialogue. That speech implies a denial that persons have internality, that they are "subjects of a life" in a way that things and other animals seem not to be.[74] By contrast, the whole description, in the palinode, of the experience of falling in love portrays vividly the self as having "inner" experiences, an inwardness articulated

72. A promising community need not, on this view, be seen as an individual—here the disanalogy between Socrates' account of the love of Beauty and my analogous account of the love of Justice is important. I note that individuals who are in love with a particular city are not praised by Plato. For they seem to be according the wrong kind of affection to the city, treating it as though it were an individual. Cf. Pericles' funeral speech where we are urged to become the "lovers" of Athens, inspired by the vision of her greatness (Thucydides 2.43).

73. For some discussion, see *Self-Knowledge*, chaps. 2–3. In the *Phr.*, souls have a fixed upper limit, at least within cycles of embodiment; a Hera-like soul cannot in principle become a Zeus-like soul. But the lower limit is not fixed in the same way, and souls can act in ways that are, as it were, beneath themselves. They can fail to reach their full potential. They can also come to see, and attempt to realize, their full potential. As self-directing in that sense, persons possess an inner freedom that permits them to become objects of praise and blame, to be held responsible for failing to live up to themselves.

74. I take it to be part of Plato's purpose to show that the speech is internally inconsistent. For the nonlover gives a speech precisely to persuade the beloved, i.e., he assumes the beloved is capable of choice (231d6–7; cf. 233a4–5). In Socrates' first speech we are presented with a demand for definition of terms, a tactic designed in part to make us see that how we value others makes assumptions about what kinds of beings they are, assumptions that if thought through would require that we treat these beings differently.

here with remarkable subtlety and sensitivity. The "inner/outer" self distinction keeps reappearing in the *Phaedrus* (245e4–6, 275a2–6, 279b9–c1; cf. 235c4–d1), pointing to the presence in each of us of interiority, one might even say of individuality or of subjectivity, the possibility of a first-person perspective.[75] Plato's version of Kant's imperative will be "hypothetical": treat others with respect (*aidōs*) for the selves they truly would be, if you would become a happy, perfected self. This is part of the story as to how Plato will get from "justice" conceived as an excellence of self (i.e., as "virtue") to "justice" conceived of in terms of what is due to others.[76] Conversely, as Socrates says in the *Republic* (443a) as well, the just person lacks the motivations that commonly lead to injustice in the conventional sense—regardless of the presence or absence of incentives conventionally understood. Socrates wants us to see that selfhood should be understood not as "individuality" cut off from others, not as an entity to which other persons are mere means, but as having a kind of being (*ousia*; *Phr.* 245e3) whose good includes the good of others and, indirectly, of suitable communities. A polity that founded itself on a misunderstanding about this nature of the self will not qualify as just; and Socrates would, I think, hold that many conventional regimes fail to pass muster on precisely this ground.[77]

Let me briefly indicate what sort of communities would pass muster.

75. "Individuality" and "subjectivity" are obviously controverted notions, especially in the context of Greek ethics; hence my tentative use of it. I would only note here that they should not be confused with uniqueness.

76. Worked out in the way suggested in the present essay, this way of bridging the gap between justice understood as a quality of self, and conventional justice, leads to rejection of the "holistic" model of justice.

77. The view of soul as self-moved, of learning as recollection, and the critique of motivation that assumes faulty notions of the human good (and so of what it means to be human) at the very least exclude much conventional politics and *poleis* on the grounds of injustice or some other vice. For example, any regime that claims wealth as a title to rule can claim no legitimacy, and Socrates is very harsh on oligarchs and their regime in the *Rep.* 8. Rule based on brute force is obviously illegitimate as well, for Socrates; it amounts to tyranny in one form or another. Any regime that claims virtue is inherited is based for Socrates on a falsehood. And, more subtly, any regime that fails to promote the development of moral excellence rightly understood will be, in various degrees, less than perfect and so less than worthy of approbation. I would expect that in criticizing such regimes Socrates would follow his usual practice of searching for internal contradictions, unsupported assertions, and false beliefs. Ultimately he will argue that a person who advocates, say, a tyrannical regime, manifests a tyrannical soul, one that is enslaved to its own fears and desires (*Rep.* 579d–e). This elenchus would narrow considerably the political options Socrates would consider acceptable, and would point, as I have argued, to an important place for political liberties. In the *Phr*'s. account, the tyrant lies at the very bottom of the hierarchy of soul types.(248e3) because he is most ignorant of the Forms and is motivated solely by the basest of desires, a motivation that stems from an impoverished conception of his own "self" and, by extension, of what it means to be a "self." He reifies others because he has reified himself. The tyrant is, as it were, Lysias's nonlover armed with ambition and political power.

I note, first, that knowledge and self-knowledge are both, for Socrates, types of remembering. Whatever else this may mean, it strongly suggests that the requisite knowledge is to be found "within" and that it has value as appropriated through one's own dialectical or erotic labors. Socrates contrasts to this process knowledge that is poured in from the "outside," as he thinks book-learning to be (275a). The process of Socratic dialectic famously embodies the view that while souls can be helped to learn, they cannot be taught philosophy directly. The application of political compulsion would presumably transform *anamnēsis* into rote memorization, perhaps hypocritically performed. The type of perfectionism compatible with Socratic dialectic and *anamnēsis* would be indirect, and would recognize the key role of the agent's effort and choice in self-perfection.

Second, recollection is to be undertaken dialectically, for Socrates, and this requires suitable interlocutors.[78] Correspondingly, the question of the polity is not a matter of indifference for the *Phaedrus*'s philosopher. The liberties to discuss, to question, to have students of one's choice, to wander outside the city's walls, and to do so in the company of some politically doubtful souls, seem essential.[79] As we have already noted, Socrates points out in the *Republic* (557d) that anyone wishing to set out a regime, as he and his companions have been doing in that very dialogue, would prefer to do so in a democracy.[80]

Finally, while the *Phaedrus* sets out a hierarchy of soul types on the basis of how much each soul "saw" of the Forms (248d–e), it does not follow that the distribution of liberties among the citizens should be very restricted, such that the best practical polity must be substantively

78. The philosopher must live within the walls of the city and—again, precisely in order to pursue his own perfection—want to live among interlocutors of the requisite soul types (say, types ranging from Phaedrus to Protagoras to Plato).

79. It is significant that at the end of the *Phr.*, a conversation that takes place in the countryside, Plato makes a point of Socrates' and Phaedrus's return to Athens. Plato has them vote for that polis with their feet. Socrates and Phaedrus have wandered out of the embracing walls of the city, but just for this day. At the end of the dialogue, they return to Athens. As the gods return "home" (*oikade* 247e4) after feasting on the eternal verities, so when finished with their feast of speeches Socrates and Phaedrus return to the home suitable for embodied souls—a polis, indeed a specific polis. That polis is not just a *faute de mieux*, life outside the walls of which would be infinitely preferable. Socrates leaves uncorrected Phaedrus's assertion that he (Socrates) never leaves Athens "at all" (230d2), and provides an interesting explanation: "Forgive me, my good man. You see, I'm a lover of learning, and the country places and the trees won't teach me anything, as the people in the city will" (230d3–5). Of course, Socrates *has* been outside the walls—and significantly, for my present purposes, in order to fight on behalf of Athens. And when he and Phaedrus reenter, they do so armed with a lengthy discussion of rhetoric, a theme to which the polis is relevant.

80. The reason Socrates cites is that a democracy contains many different models of polities. But it does so because, as Socrates says at 557b, it is a city full of freedom and free speech. These goods would also be required to discuss publicly which of the models is best.

inegalitarian.[81] For accurate institution of the various soul types as social classes would depend on accurate discernment of the soul types. And the palinode leaves us—deliberately, in my view—utterly unclear as to how a list of vocations, a list of character types, and various quantities of knowledge-of-Forms, are to be coordinated.[82] Indeed, the palinode may be taken to claim that the relative weighing of these factors cannot be rationally understood.[83] Given the inherent fallibility of that procedure, the ever present possibility of error on the part of the dialectician, and the limited number of persons one can examine, it seems to follow that any effort to institute an illiberal hierarchy of social classes is deprived of rational justification from the outset.[84]

In sum, the *Phaedrus* suggests that the best practicable polity will be committed to institutions that encourage persuasion rather than coercion, development of self rather than debasement thereof, philosophy

81. Presumably those at the top have a better claim to know justice and to be just than those lower down. After the seeker for wisdom and beauty Socrates ranks the law-abiding king, and so on down the ladder. This scheme seems to lead directly to a nonegalitarian political polity, for one could argue that those persons who are by nature incapable of recollecting much, and who "forget" even that of which they were capable, thanks to their way of life (248e3–5, 250a3–4), occupy a lower moral rank than the philosophers and ought to be treated accordingly. So the most "philosophical" polity, the one most beautiful in a philosopher's eyes, would seem to be hopelessly far from anything like a regime that recognized basic principles of fairness and equality.

82. At 253b Socrates says that each follower of a given god strives to make his beloved resemble that god. Hera-types look for royal natures, and so forth. One might ask how followers of Ares will "love" their polis, and what Forms (or what understanding of Form[s]) they seek to have reflected in their own soul and their polis. Part of the answer may lie at 252c, where we learn that followers of Ares are possessive to the extreme; if they think their beloved is doing them some injury, they will shed their own and their beloved's blood. Something like this may fit the description of Alcibiades at *Symp.* 213d, and correspondingly the ways in which Alcibiades repaid his "beloved" Athens for perceived injustice toward him (on Alcibiades as a lover of the demos, see *Symp.* 216b). It remains unclear how that sort of account meshes with the "degree of knowledge of the Forms" issue. Things become still murkier if there exists a Form of Injustice (as suggested at *Rep.* 476a), a possibility that risks seriously disrupting the *Phr.*'s account of things. For then the tyrant would be not a person forgetful of Forms who treats the polis as he would treat himself—e.g., as a thing to be reified and manipulated—but a person who remembers a Form (e.g., Injustice) and passionately seeks to have that Form realized. Presumably, that Form exists in the antipode to the hyperuranian place, somewhere "under the earth" (256d6).

83. For substantiation, see *Self-Knowledge*, pp. 102–3.

84. Whether this interpretation can be reconciled with the *Rep.* is a fascinating question far too complex to broach here. If I am right, the *Phr.* suggests that we abandon the *Rep.* view that the city is good if its parts are related in a way analogous to the way in which the parts of a well-ordered soul are related. Nor, on the present account, does the *Phr.* suggest that the good polis is that all of whose parts are actually (rather than just potentially) good (those would be very few in number). The palinode's teaching is much more fallibilistic than that of the *Rep.*, as already indicated. The *Rep.*'s argument for an inegalitarian regime depends on the premise that moral experts are to rule over nonexperts; but there are no moral experts in the requisite sense.

and the love of knowledge rather than tyranny and the love of power or wealth, the treatment of others as potentially perfectible in some degree (a degree not inferable from the person's vocation or social status), and whatever liberties conduce to the above. It will recognize its own limits; in particular, the fallibility of our knowledge, and the necessity that true knowledge be appropriated by the individual. We would thus expect the philosopher to admire a polis whose institutions are shaped by a knowledge of ignorance parallel to his own. For all practical purposes, we may infer, a polis would do better to proceed along egalitarian lines in its organization of political participation (this is of course compatible with a meritocracy in other spheres of social life). The duty to respect liberties could well be expressed in terms of rights (where a right to something is understood as the legitimate claim to be protected in doing that thing.)[85] In a Platonic context, talk about rights would serve as a proxy for the sorts of moral reasons clustered around the notion of self-perfection that I have discussed. When at the end of *Republic* 9 Socrates bids us to order our souls by contemplating the "paradigm" of the "city in speech," I think he means us to adopt just this stance toward politics.

IV

Let me close. I distinguished earlier between individualist and communitarian perfectionism. I characterized Epicurus as an extreme representative of the former camp, and Aristotle as a representative of the latter. To which camp should Plato be assigned? As in the case of the characterization of the lover/beloved relationship, I want to claim that neither alternative alone does justice to Plato's theory. In that friendship for individuals and care for an appropriately defined polis are intrinsic to a person's development of self—and I have argued that they are such, for Plato—

85. Even if this answer is accepted, though, it may seem that we have been furnished with no principled way of defining the liberties, or if you like, the rights, of the citizens in Plato's second best polis. Further, these liberties—whatever they may be, exactly—seem placed on a highly insecure basis; and this has been a reason for rejecting perfectionism as a political theory, as noted at the start of the essay. I take it that Plato would want to reply to the second point that the basis is as philosophically firm as it ever gets; no theory is so obviously sound that discussion about its merits ends among philosophers. He might continue to say that political liberties would be as soundly embedded institutionally in a scheme he would devise as in one we might devise. But if one wants something still more specific, something comparable to the American Bill of Rights, one will find Plato of limited help. I expect that he would see precise enumeration of rights as a task for a legislator in a specific situation. I also expect that worries (as expressed in the *Phr.*) about the inherent weaknesses of the written word might make him reluctant to sanction in any real-world situation an enumeration of rights in a constitution. Of course, this is a worry expressed in the American tradition itself. See Madison's comments in *Federalist* no. 84.

then Plato is in the "communitarian" camp. In that the qualities by virtue of which we admire persons and *poleis* are separable—and the Forms are characterized as such in the *Republic* and the *Phaedrus*—and insofar as the Forms are apprehensible in and of themselves—the great prize Plato promises those who have perfected themselves—then the good is realized in an activity of contemplation of which community is not constitutive. In a perfect world, Platonic perfectionism would be individualist rather than communitarian. In this world, among us, it would be both.[86]

86. I thank Aryeh Kosman, Mitchell Miller, David Roochnik, Amelie Rorty, and David Schmidtz for their very helpful comments on various drafts of this essay. I am also grateful to the Earhart Foundation and the Woodrow Wilson Center for Scholars (Washington, D.C.) for the support of work leading to this essay. Drafts of this essay were delivered at Scripps College (Claremont, Calif.), Rutgers University, Loyola College (Baltimore), George Mason University, the Graduate Center of the City University of New York, Yale University, the Université de Paris (XII), and The Catholic University of America. I am indebted to audiences at all these institutions for useful discussion and suggestions. Another version of this essay was published as "Le libéralisme platonicien: De la perfection individuelle comme fondement d'une théorie politique," in *Contre Platon: Le platonisme renversé*, ed. M. Dixsaut (Paris: Vrin, 1995), vol. 2, pp. 155–95.

6 Relations and Intermediates in Plato's *Timaeus*

DARYL McGOWAN TRESS

I. INTRODUCTION

Early in the *Timaeus*, Socrates tells his hosts, Timaeus, Critias, and Hermocrates, that based on what he has heard from them so far he is expecting a complete and brilliant (*teleos te kai lampros*) feast of words to come (27b). This may well be Plato's way of alerting us that we, too, might expect this of the dialogue: a complete and brilliant account of the cosmos. And certainly, in reading the *Timaeus* for the first time or even after many times, one has—in a way—the undeniably satisfying experience of having encountered something full and whole and indeed magnificently beautiful. And it is not long after Socrates' statement about his expectations concerning the upcoming talk that Timaeus establishes wholeness (*teleon*; 33a), beauty, and goodness as chief attributes of the world. In a most skillful way, then, Plato suggests a coordinated series: a whole, beautiful world; a complete, brilliant discourse about that world; a thoroughly satifying experience of both the discourse and the world about which it tells.

But perhaps, like the ordinary world in which we live, puzzles and problems abound in the *Timaeus* and interfere with the neat coordination of this perfect series. Plato himself is the first to draw attention to such difficulties. The world, we are told, is moved not only by Reason but by Necessity, the wandering cause. Regarding the discourse, there is, for example, the often-noted fact that Plato repeatedly has Timaeus remind his listeners that he is offering a likely account, not the certain truth; the account, it seems, is somehow uncertain. Furthermore, on close inspection, the structure of the *Timaeus* appears awkward: the format switches from dialogue to lengthy monologue, the topic switches from politics to cosmology to physics to medicine, and the presentation contains numerous "regressions, corrections, repetitions, and abrupt new beginnings."[1]

1. Hans-Georg Gadamer, "Idea and Reality in Plato's *Timaeus*," in *Dialogue and Dialectic:*

Simply judging by Platonic standards of composition, this is not what we would regard as "brilliant."

Indeed, Plato scholars during the twentieth century have hardly come away from the *Timaeus* with a simple sense of its satisfying completeness.[2] Based on his observations about the peculiarities of the *Timaeus*, A. E. Taylor proposed—radically—in *A Commentary on Plato's Timaeus* (1928) that the *Timaeus* represented above all the views of Pythagorean science, thus challenging the very idea that the *Timaeus* presents positive Platonic meaning.[3] Cornford answered Taylor's claim, arguing that the dialogue's conceptual consistency with other dialogues showed that the *Timaeus* was indeed *Plato*'s cosmology (1937).[4] More recently, the issue that has perplexed many commentators concerns the correct place of the *Timaeus* within the corpus, particularly its dating relative to the *Parmenides*. The *Timaeus* plainly appeals to a theory of Forms and particulars that are like those Forms, but the *Parmenides*, by traditional dating an earlier dialogue than the *Timaeus*, is widely held to signify a crisis in Plato's theory of Forms. Harold Cherniss and G. E. L. Owen have strenuously debated the sequence of these parts of the ouevre and its implications, and the debate continues.[5]

Eight Hermeneutical Studies on Plato (New Haven, Conn.: Yale University Press, 1980), p. 160. Jacob Klein, in *A Commentary on Plato's "Meno"* (Chapel Hill: University of North Carolina Press, 1965), pp. 192–95, notes the "advance/withdrawal" movement in the *Republic*'s discussion of stereometry and aludes to a similar pattern in the *Timaeus*'s Timaeus's telling of the ordering of world body and world soul. On the dialogue's many peculiarities, see Seth Benardete, "On Plato's *Timaeus* and Timaeus' Science Fiction," *Interpretation* 2 (1971): 21–63. Kenneth M. Sayre writes simply, "The *Timaeus* is a highly controversial dialogue"; See *Plato's Late Ontology* (Princeton, N.J.: Princeton University Press, 1983), p. 238.

2. Controversy about the *Timaeus* hardly began in the twentieth century, of course. As Guthrie remarks, "Plato's younger contemporaries were already debating its meaning" (p. 241). Guthrie offers a brief history of the dialogue's reception in *A History of Greek Philosophy* (New York: Cambridge University Press, 1978), vol. 5, pp. 241–42.

3. "Radical" because it has been held since antiquity, e.g. by Diogenes Laertius that Timaeus is one of the figures in the dialogues who speaks for Plato. (Diogenes Laertius, *Lives of Eminent Philosophers*. "Plato" III, 52. Cambridge: Harvard University Press, 1938.) It remains a common assumption that Timaeus voices Plato's own views.

4. Glenn Morrow also takes Timaeus "as a spokesman for Plato himself," i.e., he takes Cornford's side against Taylor's thesis. See "Plato's Theory of the Primary Bodies in the *Timaeus* and the Later Doctrine of Forms," *Archiv für Geschichte der Philosophie* 50 (1968):12–28.

5. See discussion by Henry Teloh, *The Development of Plato's Metaphysics* (University Park: Pennsylvania University Press, 1981), pp. 209–18; and Sayre, *Plato's Late Ontology*, pp. 256–67. Also see G. E. L. Owen, "The Place of the *Timaeus* in Plato's Dialogues" and H. F. Cherniss, "The Relation of the *Timaeus* to Plato's Later Dialogues," both in *Studies in Plato's Metaphysics*, ed. R. E. Allen (New York: Routledge & Kegan Paul, 1965). Numerous contributions to the *Timaeus* literature have appeared on the dialogue's particular concepts as well. It should also be noted that the two debates about the *Timaeus* identified here, i.e., Taylor vs. Cornford and Owen vs. Cherniss, are the major ones in the recent English-language scholarship. Other themes have received more attention in European scholar-

The contended issues in the scholarly literature on the *Timaeus* reflect, in their form, some of the various complexities and difficulties Plato himself tried to face in composing the dialogue: questions of philosophical origins and genealogy (central to the Taylor–Cornford debate), and of sequence and the kinds of changes that occur over time (central to the highly influential Owen–Cherniss debate). And it can be added that the *chorismos* or discontinuity between these two sets of scholarly debates and the difficulty of unifying them (debates that we may take as models for two differing styles of modern Plato scholarship: one of which emphasizes the structure and integrity of the dialogue as a whole, often with special attention to the drama and personalities portrayed; the other of which emphasizes the corpus as a whole and the problems basic to Plato's work, often with attention to the solutions or lack of solutions to those problems) exemplifies the difficulty of relating together what is different, an issue I take to be basic to the *Timaeus* itself.

It would seem, then, that the dialogue is still very much with us. The *Timaeus* remains, like the world it presents, dazzling, the work of an enormously powerful intellect. But, as Plato himself also indicates, and as the scholarship and our own experience testifies, there are difficulties—of incompleteness and imperfection and ungainliness—with this world, with our experience of it, and with the "feast of words" (in the *Timaeus* and elsewhere) that might explain it all.

I would like to examine this double character of the cosmos as it is presented in the *Timaeus*. Here as elsewhere in Plato's work, to attend to what is perfect and ideal, on the one hand, and to what is ordinary and incomplete, on the other, is to be led to the Forms and to the question of the relation of particulars to them. For Plato posits the Forms to explain both that which we find to be perfect and beautiful and that which fails to meet our needs and expectations. According to Plato, neither completeness nor incompleteness can be recognized without the Forms as absolute and stable realities.[6] It is really the presence of the Forms in the *Timaeus* that argues against Taylor's thesis, and convincingly in favor of the dialogue's containing a Platonic teaching. The presence of the Forms also indicates that the dialogue is something more than Plato's

ship, especially the contributions that the *Timaeus* makes to revealing Plato's unwritten doctrines and "esoteric" philosophy. See, e.g., Giovanni Reale, *Plato and Aristotle* (Albany: State University of New York Press, 1990), and H.-G. Krämer, *Plato and the Foundation of Metaphysics* (Albany: State University of New York Press, 1990). Krämer offers a history of recent European Plato scholarship and a comparison with some English-language scholarship.

6. A short and economical review of Plato's ontological, epistemological, and ethical reasons for positing the Forms can be found in H. F. Cherniss, "The Philosophical Economy of the Theory of Ideas," in *Studies in Plato's Metaphysics.* Paul Friedlander's, "Eidos," in *Plato: An Introduction* (New York: Harper, 1958), is a fine treatment of this topic.

cosmology, as in Cornford's translation and commentary.[7] The approach I will take, in keeping with much recent scholarship, is that the *Timaeus* is a significant ontological dialogue, attempting to deal with the interrelation of Forms and particulars—that is, for Plato, the relation of perfection and imperfection, completeness and incompleteness, brilliance and obscurity.[8] The ontological problem of relationality in the *Timaeus* is perhaps most easily exposed by looking at the dialogue in its relation with other dialogues. Recent commentators, in taking this approach, see Forms and particulars as more distantly separated in the *Timaeus* than elsewhere. I intend to show however, that the structure of the dialogue reveals that Plato investigates the separation and, without eliminating the basic distinguishability and hierarchy of Being and Becoming, that he provides the opportunity for reconceiving their relation as one of closer contact.[9]

What would be the point of the close conjoining of Forms and particulars? Plato's account faces a problem: the problem of relationality. When a transcendent, perfect, and complete domain of Being comprised of perfect and complete Forms is first posited, and along with it a world of Becoming comprised of things that are fundamentally changeable and unfinished, the question posed for a Platonic ontology is: What is the relation between these two and how, or "in virtue of what," does the relation work? Because, according to the *Timaeus* as well as other dialogues, the two are indeed connected.[10] Plato has elsewhere named the general relation between Forms and particulars "participation"; particu-

7. This is not at all to suggest that Cornford did not recognize the proper ontological ordering that underlies the cosmology set forth in the dialogue.

An additional argument against reading the *Timaeus* just as a cosmology is that it is then hard to explain the presence of the exchange about politics that begins the dialogue; Cornford makes very little of it. The odd structure of the dialogue and its range of topics, wider than the usual cosmology, also remain obscure on this interpretation. The relation of *Republic* 5 to the *Timaeus* merits further attention.

8. Kenneth M. Sayre (in *Plato's Late Ontology*) regards it as a serious but ultimately failed attempt to make the theory of participation satisfactory. R. E. Allen, in *Plato's Parmenides* (Minneapolis: University of Minnesota Press, 1983), sees the *Timaeus* making adjustments in the world of sense perception that become necessary, after the *Parmenides*, in order to save the Forms.

9. While my thesis that the separation of Forms and particulars is reconceived in this dialogue may appear at first to be part of the family of scholarship that takes a revisionist view of Plato's work, it is not my intention here to argue for or against "revisionism" or its counterpart "unitarianism," or the related chronology question. These complicated issues require detailed consideration of their own.

10. See the *Sophist* 251c–52e on the relations of Forms to one another. There are three logical possibilities: (1) no *koinonia* or relation among them; (2) complete mutual relationality; or (3) some relationality. The first two are impossible, and only the third option remains. Applying this scheme to the relation of Forms to particulars produces similar results: it is impossible both that there be no relation between them and that they be indis-

lars participate in Forms (*Phaedo* 100b–101c). Forms are sometimes said to be the causes of particulars (*Euthyphro* 6d–10e); they are models of which particulars are copies (*Timaeus* 28c ff.) and from which particulars derive their names (*Phaedo* 103e; *Timaeus* 52a). But how can Being and Becoming, Forms and particulars, resemble one another, and how can they interact when their natures are fundamentally different? As Aristotle commented, the participation relation remains obscure and largely unexplained (*Metaphysics* 987b12). This, in brief, is the difficulty Plato confronts in the *Timaeus*. Given these two very different ontological domains, what is the nature of their interrelation?[11]

My thesis is that in the *Timaeus* Plato addresses some of the issues regarding the separation of Forms and particular things—raised forcefully in the *Parmenides*—and that he does so on two levels: First, Plato has Timaeus present an account that assumes at the start separate Forms and things and then proceeds to join these by means of a series of intermediates (namely, the Demiourgos, the *psyche*, the Receptacle, and the mathematicals, along with the marrow, *eros*, and *epithumia*). These intermediates are meant to span the gap between Being and Becoming, thus narrowing the *chorismos* between them and transforming their apparent remoteness to proximity. (It should be observed that they also maintain the boundary between Being and Becoming, preventing their collapse and thus preserving their crucial distinguishability.) In Timaeus's proposal, the linking capacity of the intermediate entities allows them to serve as the means for the generation of composite particulars. The intermediates are stationed throughout his talk, and it is only by examination of the dialogue in its entirety that their bonding pattern becomes plain and the intended propinquity of Forms and particular things emerges. In other words, Plato uses Timaeus to make the best case relating Being and Becoming by means of intermediates. Second, however, Plato makes available in the dialogue a further reflection *on* Timaeus's account. This reflection arises out of the detectable incompleteness of the intermediates and the inadequacy of the initial characterizations of Being and Becoming. This second means is, shall we say, sotto voce, and it is indicated by Plato's structuring of the dialogue. It is an invitation to a level

---

tinguishable. The third option remains, that there is some relation between the two—a relation that remains to be understood.

Jacob Klein discusses this passage in the *Sophist* in *Greek Mathematical Thought and the Origin of Algebra* (Cambridge, Mass.: M.I.T. Press, 1968) pp. 88–89.

11. See the presentation of the problem in Mitchell H. Miller Jr., *Plato's "Parmenides": The Conversion of the Soul* (Princeton, N.J.: Princeton University Press, 1986), p. 130 and chap. 4, for Mitchell's analysis of the issue in the *Parmenides*. A concise statement of the problem of the relation between Forms and particulars can be found in Sayre, *Plato's Late Ontology*, pp. 245–46.

of critical reflection addressed to those attentive students who are prepared to engage philosophically with ideas at this advanced level.[12] I suggest that Plato intends the shortcomings in Timaeus's account to be noticed and lead to a better conceptualization of the initial relation between Being and Becoming. A less-than-perfect account can still be instructive, as I believe Timaeus's is meant to be, particularly in its efforts to minimize the *chorismos* between Being and Becoming. The dialogue thus encourages its readers to discover what is right about Timaeus's presentation no less than what is wrong.

Plato indicates the close relation of Forms and particular things in a number of ways throughout the dialogue's course. I propose to begin with a brief recapitulation of the dialogue, emphasizing its clearly demarcated sections. This will be followed by a highlighting of Timaeus's key statements that often serve as grounds for other scholars asserting that a high degree, indeed, the highest degree of disjunction of Forms and particulars is found in the *Timaeus.* I will then show that those statements, when read according to their place in the dialogue's structure, represent not conclusions but rather points of departure in the presentation which then "generate" different outcomes. That is, that Plato modifies those initial statements of separation, exploring the possibility of establishing the propinquity of Forms and particulars through a linkage system of generative intermediates. Finally, I will discuss the provocative inadequacy of Timaeus's attempts to explicate the relation of Forms and particulars by way of intermediate things. The insufficiency of the intermediates for explaining the relation of Being and Becoming is meant by Plato to encourage reconsideration of their basic natures and the initial distinction between them which, in Timaeus's account, misleadingly incorporated the imagery of spatial separation.

12. A word is in order about my general approach to reading Plato, an approach that takes into consideration what the dialogue does as well as what it says. I do not assume, for example, that characters speak for Plato or that Plato intends, in a straightforward way, to present doctrines in the dialogues. Rather, the dialogues present views, some of which Plato has Socrates (or others) object to strongly, others of which he may find congenial in a number of ways, others of which Plato himself may be actively investigating. The range of views offered in the dialogues serves their pedagogic and philosophic purpose, both historically in the Academy and more generally for any reader: to encourage the deep inquiry into various accounts by way of this carefully structured whole (the dialogue), while inviting the listener or reader to notice the effects of these accounts on the persons involved in the conversations. Students of philosophy are meant to listen carefully to the arguments and principles expressed and to critically examine them, especially with a view to their context. This active philosophical scrutiny is meant to move the *psyche* and help in its own proper ordering. Thus, I believe the appropriate critical response to the *Timaeus* is to examine Timaeus's account and consider whether it is adequate, and if not, in what ways.

II. SUMMARY OF THE *Timaeus*

The following is a brief review of the *Timaeus*, indicating its four major sections.

1. 17a–27c: In this opening section, Socrates meets with Timaeus, Critias, and Hermocrates for a feast of words promised by the three men to Socrates in return for his talk to them yesterday. Socrates reviews the themes of yesterday's talk having to do with a way of life for men and women, and the generation of children. (These plans are strongly reminiscent of *Republic* 5.) Socrates wishes he could see such plans as his "come alive," "in motion" (19b), and at war, but says that he himself is incapable of the task. Critias answers Socrates' wish by telling of a very ancient and noble *genos* of Greeks who for the most part are forgotten but who are the true progenitors of the Greeks of the present day. Socrates approves of what he hears about them, and Critias promises to provide all the details later, after Timaeus speaks first, beginning as planned with the origin of the world and ending with the appearance of humankind.

2. 27c–47e: Timaeus begins his presentation by first naming "Being" as distinct from "Becoming" and asking about the nature of each. He speaks of the conditions involved in the world's coming to be, especially the Same and the Different. He explains the living nature of the universe as a whole (*tou pantos*): it is a visible copy or image produced by the divine Demiourgos of the Intelligible Living Creature (i.e., Becoming comes to be as a copy or image of a Form of living entity within Being). Timaeus details the formation of the world body and the world soul and their joining together to form a living world in accordance with *nous* and the god's goodness. World body and soul share the same three-dimensional spherical shape (they have the same depth), and so are relatable. Timaeus also explains that it was the task of the lesser gods, not the Demiourgos, to fashion humankind. He ends this section with talk of causes subsidiary to intellect.

3. 47e–69a: Having given an account of the working of *nous* in the genesis of the world, Timaeus makes what he emphasizes is a "new beginning" and turns next to the work of the *planōmenē* aitia, the wandering cause or "Necessity." He tells in full detail how the material elements arose, and discusses the sensible qualities associated with material bodies.

4. 69a–91c: Timaeus now declares that the remainder of his *logos* must weave together (*sunuphanthēnai*) the causes he previously expounded. He recapitulates his earlier points, and then elaborates on the composition of the living human body and soul and its healthy and sick conditions.

After urging special attention to the *psyche* and its needs, Timaeus closes the dialogue by speaking about the sexual generation of human beings and mentioning the subhuman forms in which they might be regenerated absent the practice of virtue. Timaeus ends his presentation—and the dialogue—with an encomium to the universe.

III. EVIDENCE FREQUENTLY CITED FOR THE RADICAL SEPARATION OF FORMS AND PARTICULARS IN THE *Timaeus*

As we just saw, Timaeus begins his presentation by distinguishing Being and Becoming. The distinction appears to serve as the foundation for all that follows, in that Becoming is different from Being but nonetheless like it and must be understood in relation to Being. But Timaeus puts the primary distinction quite strongly, and the idea that Being and Becoming, Forms and particulars, as Henry Teloh says, are radically separated in the *Timaeus*, indeed perhaps here more so than in any other Plato dialogue, has played a significant part in modern Plato scholarship. For example, it forms the basis of G. E. L. Owen's famous challenge to the accepted sequence of Plato's writings and the scholarly activity that followed.[13] Owen puts the matter unequivocally:

> The *Timaeus* distinguishes absolutely between *to on aei, genesin de ouk echon* and *to gignomenon men aei, on de oudepote* (27d–28a); that is [and here he is quoting from Taylor's *Commentary*, p. 32], "it treats *genesis* and *ousia* as simple incompatibles."[14]

As I noted earlier, once separation is absolute it becomes difficult indeed to see how to retrieve Becoming so that it can be related to Being. In this direct statement of his position, Owen identifies the premier passage (27d–28a) in the dialogue that serves as the basis for this position. Let us examine that passage.

13. Henry Teloh interprets the separation this way in *The Development of Plato's Metaphysics*, pp. 209–18. He says: "[T]here is a more radical separation between Forms and phenomena in the *Timaeus* than in any other dialogue, and . . . Plato desubstantializes phenomena more in the *Timaeus* than elsewhere. . . . the position of the *Timaeus* is more radical with respect to separation than that of the *Phaedo* and *Republic*" (p. 209). Reginald Allen writes in *Plato's Parmenides* that "[t]he ultimate problem arises from the assumption of the separate existence of sensibles and Ideas. . . . Plato's own solution, offered in the *Timaeus*, is the mirror image of Aristotle's: it is that sensibles have no independent reality of their own" (p. 180).

14. G. E. L. Owen, in "The Place of the *Timaeus* in Plato's Dialogues," asserts that "absolute distinction," indeed "incompatibility," characterizes the relations of Forms and particulars in the *Timaeus* (p. 322). This assertion of separation forms the basis for his argument in favor of revising the place of this dialogue in the Platonic corpus.

After invoking the gods and goddesses (and adding that "ourselves we must also invoke so as to proceed"; (27c–d), Timaeus immediately begins his analysis. He starts with two questions: "What is that which is always and has no becoming? And what is that which is becoming always and never is?" (27d–28a). The juxtaposition of the two questions emphasizes the difference between the two "kinds" of things: one always is, the other never is but is always becoming. Timaeus also specifies the different means of knowing them: one is grasped with the intellect, the other is a matter of opinion based on sensation. This brief but clear statement of fundamental ontological and epistemic difference between *ousia* and *genesis* is often regarded as sufficient in itself to establish the case. We might note, too, that there is further evidence to be found when Timaeus next speaks of causality. Everything which becomes must, of course, have a cause of its coming to be, he says. He does not say, although it is implied, that whatever always *is* neither needs a cause nor admits of one, so that causality constitutes another difference between them. Becoming needs a cause, but Timaeus does not say that Being is its cause but rather that it is the Demiourgos who is the "maker and father" (28c) of the whole.

Further evidence for the complete disjunction of Forms and particulars can be found at the start of the second major section of his presentation, Timaeus's "new beginning." Here he tells of the role of Necessity in the formation of the world, in the function of the elementary triangles and the five solids, and in body generally. Early in this clearly defined new portion of his talk, Timaeus describes the nature of what the early naturalists had taken to be the four material elements: earth, air, fire, and water. In contrast to the naturalists, Timaeus says that the four are not stable, definite objects (49e) but rather are constantly changing. In fact, they are so indefinite that they do not even deserve the definition lent to them by the names "earth," "air," and the like; instead, material objects should properly only be called "earthlike," "airlike," and so forth. Such a characterization, clearly in contrast—even in opposition—to the stability of the self-subsisting realities (51c), presses the difference between them. Timaeus states that "these two Kinds must be declared to be two, because they have come into existence separately and are unlike in condition" (51e). In the discussion that immediately follows, the ontological and epistemic differences between the two are listed (51e–52d). The passage as a whole, then, repeats and thus might seem to secure the position Timaeus apparently takes at the start of his presentation, that is, that Being and Becoming, Forms and particulars are completely different and radically separate.

We might note briefly, too, that this position would itself repeat and amplify that apparently taken within other dialogues, such as the *Phaedrus* and the *Parmenides.* In the *Phaedrus,* Socrates' mythic palinode provides an image of the long distance between Forms and particulars. We hear of the upward journey that divine and human souls make to feast on the vision of the Formal realities beyond the rim of the heavens; those humans with underdeveloped wings plunge far below to earth and earthly particulars. In the *Parmenides,* Parmenides asks the young Socrates:

> Have you yourself drawn this *distinction* you speak of and *separated apart on the one side* Forms themselves and on the other the things that share in them [*autos su outō dierēisai hos legeis, chōris men eidē auta atta, chōris de ta toutōn au metechonta*]? (130b; Cornford translation; my emphases)

Socrates answers that he does make this distinction, and that he holds there to be likeness itself apart from the likeness we possess.[15] These passages, then, along with indications from yet other dialogues,[16] provide a background some scholars have used for viewing the statements in the *Timaeus* as an intensification of the position on the *chorismos* between Forms and particular things.

IV. EVIDENCE IN THE *Timaeus* FOR THE NARROWING OF THE SEPARATION OF THE FORMS AND THE PARTICULARS BY WAY OF THE INTERMEDIATES

Despite these quotations and their agreement with various moments elsewhere in the dialogues, there is ample evidence in this dialogue that Timaeus is in the process of conjoining Forms and particular things, Being and Becoming, and narrowing their separation. We will observe that the dialogue is structured in sections and that within this structure is a system of intermediates, most notably the Demiourgos, the *psyche,* the Receptacle, and the mathematicals, along with the marrow, *eros,* and *epithumia.* The intermediates are bonds that bridge the *chorismos* and modify what can be seen to be Timaeus's *initial* statements of it in each section. Timaeus prepares us for this approach to the relation of Being and Becoming by way of intermediates early in his presentation when, speaking of the formation of the world body, he says:

> But it is not possible that two things alone should be conjoined without a third; for there must needs be some intermediary bond to connect the two. (31b–c)

15. See *Parmenides* 130a–d for the repetition of *choris,* 'separately'.

16. Also on the differences between Forms and particulars, see *Cratylus* 439–40; *Republic* 476 (cited by Vlastos in "The Third Man Argument in the *Parmenides,*" in *Studies in Plato's Metaphysics,* p. 245 n2). For a discussion, also see Harold Cherniss, *Aristotle's Criticism of Plato and the Academy* (Baltimore: Johns Hopkins Press, 1944), pp. 206–11.

Plato clearly structures the *Timaeus* in four distinct sections.[17] Let us leave aside for now the beginning section in which the four men talk about what they had talked about and will talk about,[18] and concentrate on Timaeus's presentation, the second through fourth sections that comprise the rest of the dialogue (referred to here as Sections II, III, and IV). Each of these sections begins with an announcement of basic bipolarity. In Section II the bipolarity is that of Being and Becoming. In Section III the bipolarity is that of Reason and Necessity. In Section IV the primary bipolarity is that of human soul and body; a secondary one is male and female.[19] These announcements, particularly the ones regarding Being and Becoming in Section II and Reason and Necessity in Section III, often have served as the grounds for positing radical separation, as we noted above. But it is apparent in each case that these constitute *initial* statements in each section and that Timaeus attempts their rapprochement almost immediately. While he never collapses or identifies the two, he provides for intermediates in each case so that the two categories or causes are linked and generative action can occur:

In Section II, Timaeus posits the Demiourgos as the first and the *psyche*

17. Section I, differing from the others in format and topic, begins at the beginning—which is not, in fact, a new, independent start but rather has its origins in what we are told began yesterday. It ends with Socrates' hosts being assigned a topic and a place in the sequence of speakers. (That is, Timaeus and Critias take assignments; somehow Hermocrates is left out.) Section II is described at its outset as a beginning, a *horme*, by Timaeus (27c). It ends at 47e with Timaeus referring to the foregoing part of his discourse, and calling for another sort of account to be given. Section III is repeatedly and emphatically referred to at its start as a "new beginning"(48a–e). At its close, Timaeus remarks that we now have the causes (namely, *nous* and Necessity) lying before us, ready to be joined in the weaving together of the rest of the account. Section IV begins by calling for a recapitulation from the starting point (*archē*) and by promising, now, to finish and place a head (*kephalēn*) on what has gone before (69a–b). With the matter of human sexual generation at the close of the dialogue, Timaeus's presentation as a whole can be seen to move from the beginning of the universe up to the generation of humankind, as promised, and thus to be complete.

These divisions have been observed by many Plato scholars. See, for example, Ross, *Plato's Theory of Ideas* (Oxford: Oxford University Press, 1951), p. 120, and Cornford's analysis of the dialogue into a prelude and the three prime sections of Timaeus's presentation; note his Table of Contents in *Plato's Cosmology* (London: Routledge & Kegan Paul, 1948), pp. xv–xviii, and pp. 32–33).

18. Vlastos speaks of the "irrelevant" introduction; see "The Disorderly Motion in the *Timaeus*," in *Studies in Plato's Metaphysics*, p. 381. Cornford does not make much of it either; see *Plato's Cosmology*, p. 20.

19. These are coordinated, of course, and form a pattern of their own. The emphasis in Section II, the start of Timaeus's presentation, is on Being, gradually arriving at Becoming. Then, Section III begins with its emphasis on the role of Necessity in Becoming and then gradually arrives at the production of body. This discussion in turn, then, must be woven with the one at the start, so Section IV tells of the conjoining of body and *psyche*. Note the braided process at work. The discussion is filled out in depth along its major thematic axes.

as the second major intermediates between Being and Becoming. The generated outcome is the composite living world.

In Section III, Timaeus posits the Receptacle as the first and the mathematical figures (elementary triangles and five solids) as the second major intermediates between Reason and Necessity. The generated composite outcome is body having depth.

In Section IV, Timaeus posits marrow (*muelos*) as the intermediate between human body and soul. He further posits *eros* and *epithumia* as intermediates between male and female. The generated outcome is the composite human being.[20] Let us examine each of the intermediates and how each serves to link an initially opposed pair.

Demiourgos

We have already examined Timaeus's significant opening questions at 27d–28a about the distinction between *ousia* and *genesis*, Being and Becoming. Making this distinction, Timaeus says, is the first thing to do (27d). This invites consideration of what might be the next thing to do. In fact, there is a synthesis to follow this initial division, by means of an intermediate. Timaeus directly sets down in this passage, as we noted, that Becoming needs a cause and the cause of this visible, bodily cosmos is not Being but rather the "maker and father" (28c), the Demiourgos. Timaeus soon speaks of him as a god (e.g., at 30a, 30c, 32b) who fashions the world by copying the Forms using preexistent material, thus relating Forms and world as "like."[21] Note that the Demiourgos does not

20. The need for *two* intermediates in each section is explained at 32a–b, as a requirement of the depth of the world: "Now if the body of the All had had to come into existence as a plane surface, having no depth, one middle term would have sufficed to bind together both itself and its fellow-terms; but now it is otherwise: for it behoved it to be solid of shape, and what brings solids into unison is never one middle term alone but always two." See Jacob Klein's comments on *bathos*, "depth dimension," in *A Commentary on Plato's Meno*, pp. 190, 198–99.

That each of the three sections of Timaeus's talk displays a similar structure should not surprise us. In fact, *each* of the sections, along with his talk as a whole, fulfills the same conditions announced at the beginning by Critias (27a) and repeated by Timaeus himself at the close (90e), i.e., to speak beginning with the origin of the cosmos and ending with the generation of mankind.

21. On the question of the mythic status of Plato's Demiourgos, see, e.g., Vlastos "The Disorderly Motion in the *Timaeus*," pp. 380–83. He holds that these passages should not be treated lightly as myth. Gadamer, in *Dialogue and Dialectic*, pp. 190–92, holds that they should be demythologized. Cornford, in *Plato's Cosmology*, pp. 26 ff., 280, sees the Demiourgos and the lesser gods as mythic.

Beyond the status Plato intends for the Demiourgos is the broader question of the dialogue itself as a *muthos* and/or a *logos*. See T. M. Robinson's discussion of the seriousness of the dialogue in "Understanding the *Timaeus*," in *Proceedings of the Boston Area Colloquium in Ancient Philosophy*, ed. John J. Cleary (New York: University Press of America, 1987). Follow-

create the world from nothing but instead brings it about by an ordering process that delivers material from the extreme pole of *genesis*, described at the start as verging very close to Not-Being, into a better, ordered district of *genesis*, "closer" to *ousia*. While the Demiourgos resembles Being in that he is a model of goodness (e.g., he wishes to make everything as much like himself as possible), and while he resembles Becoming in that he has the capacity to change and to be affected (e.g., he is joyful at the sight of the newly ordered world; 37c), still the Demiourgos is neither Being nor Becoming, but rather a third kind of nature or reality intermediate between the other two. He is easily imagined as positioned between the Formal patterns of Being on the one hand and the generated world of Becoming on the other.

Both the method Timaeus employs and the content of his teaching in this passage reveal the intended relation of Being and Becoming and the joining function of the intermediate. First, let us examine his method. He posits two apparently fundamental principles of the universe. In doing so and in setting this pair in polar opposition to one another he follows the method common in much early Greek thought of establishing opposites as principles that "provide a simple and apparently comprehensive framework by reference to which other things may be described or classified."[22] The Pythagorean Table of Opposites is a good example of such a procedure.[23] As a comprehensive framework, Being and Becoming together would make up the totality of reality and divide everything in the world as one or the other (like other such *genē*, e.g., Limited and Unlimited). Being and Becoming are the realities that are most fundamental, that is, the first, and the most comprehensive, that is, having the most fully extensive reach. Indeed, if the reader has in mind the method of division discussed in other Plato dialogues such as the *Sophist* and the *Statesman*, the reader might well expect Timaeus to carry out a division here, successively subdividing Becoming, or perhaps both Becoming and Being. He does not engage in division, however, but rather after a brief initial characterization claims a distinct third thing, the Demiourgos who is the maker and father of the universe. In this way he disturbs our likely expectations regarding the character of the distinction between Being and Becoming: (1) the dichotomy between the two is not fundamental,

the thesis of this essay that mediation is an (intermediate) key to understanding the relation of apparent polarities, *muthos* functions as an intermediate between *logos* and opinion, offering useful but limited imagery of reality.

22. G. E. R. Lloyd, *Polarity and Analogy* (Cambridge: Cambridge University Press, 1966), p. 86. Lloyd's first chapter discusses the many ways polarity was employed in Greek literary, religious, medical, and philosophical thinking.

23. Aristotle, *Metaphysics* 986a22 ff. See Lloyd, *Polarity and Analogy*, pp. 48–49.

since the Demiourgos precedes it, at least in the sense that he is responsible for constructing Becoming; (2) the dichotomy is not completely comprehensive, since the Demiourgos is beyond it and cannot be classified simply as one or the other; and (3) it is not exclusively disjunctive, since Being and Becoming are not a contradictory pair in which any given item must necessarily be one or the other, but appears instead to admit of intermediates.

Not only Timaeus's method but the nature of the principles he chooses avoids an exclusive disjunction. The passage is a reminder, by way of contrast, of Parmenides' fundamental distinction between what is and what in no way is. For Parmenides, the alternatives are absolutely exclusive so that mediation between them is impossible. The initial distinction in the *Timaeus*, however, is between what is and what is coming-to-be and hence in some way is. Thus, in addition to the crucial differences between them, from the start Timaeus asserts some ontological relation between Being and Becoming.

This passage, especially in evoking Pythagorean and Parmenidean procedures and doctrines of opposition, highlights the unexpectedness of Timaeus's introduction of a third kind in his scheme. This surprise can be an invitation to consider the *prōton diaireteon*, Being and Becoming (27d). Again, what is the meaning of the initial dichotomy and the discussion of the Demiourgos? We noted above that Being and Becoming are not contradictories (such as Being and Not-Being). Might they however be contraries that are incompatible but admit of intermediates (e.g., black and white, sweet and bitter, wisdom and confusion)? One argument against characterizing Being and Becoming as contraries is that contraries that have intermediates are continuous in some sense, and their intermediates lie on the continuum between the two (such as gray between black and white). But Timaeus does not present Being and Becoming as continuous (rather, we recall, Becoming is a copy of Being), nor is the Demiourgos continuous with them. Indeed, intermediates of contraries do not have the power to join contraries but instead *presuppose* continuity between the initially opposed pair.

Thus, although characterized as opposed, Being and Becoming are neither contradictories nor contraries. Timaeus declares that they are primarily distinct in nature but are related in some way by the Demiourgos who fashions and orders some basic stuff of Becoming according to the perfect model of Being. That is, in beautifully fashioning Becoming, the Maker and Father creates resemblance between the two and "he leads it [Becoming] into order out of disorder (*eis taxin auto ēgagen ek tēs ataxias*)" (30a5). In this he seems to draw Becoming "closer" to Being. Cosmic spatial imagery abounds here at the start of Timaeus's presentation;

among other things, Timaeus's listeners evidently are encouraged to visualize the Demiourgos as spatially located between Being and Becoming, as he moves his gaze from Being down to Becoming.

Psyche

In this section of his talk, Timaeus also notes that the first entity produced by the Demiourgos is *psyche*, and the *psyche* is clearly identified as intermediate.[24] The Demiourgos makes *psyche* by the measured joining of Being, Same, and Different. Timaeus says this about *psyche*'s generation:

> Midway between [*en mesōi*] the Being which is indivisible and remains always the same and the Being which is transient and divisible in bodies, He blended a third form of Being compounded out of the twain. (35a)

While *psyche* resembles its components of Being and Becoming and partakes of them, *psyche* itself is neither of these.[25] Timaeus repeats and emphasizes its in-between status (35a).[26]

The discussion of *psyche* reveals not only that it takes up a position between Being and Becoming, but that it is itself internally composed of intermediates (35b–36d). Timaeus elaborately details the numerical proportions of Being, Same, and Different that the Demiourgos measures from his blend, and the smaller numerical proportions of these components then inserted in the intervals of the first proportions to serve as bonds (*desmoi*).[27] Once again, intermediates serve as linkages,

24. Regarding the proportionate linkage of separate entities, notice how Timaeus's discussion proceeds and what is placed between the generation of body and *psyche*. He first talks about the proportionate organization of the material "elements" to form body (31b–32c). Afterward, he describes the measured generation of *psyche* (remarking that, in fact, *psyche*, not body, is first in age and excellence; 34b–36e). The interstice between the discussion of body and *psyche* at 32c–34b is where Timaeus tells of the Demiourgos' intentions for what he is generating: that it be living, perfect, and a single whole. The composition shows that the divine intentions serve as the *desmos*.

25. Nor, it might be added, is it simply divine like its maker and father, the Demiourgos. It appears to be a second sort of intermediate.

On *psyche's* intermediate status, Cornford (*Plato's Cosmology*, p. 63) quotes Proclus who interpreted Plato as positing three orders of existence.

26. Even in his composition of the passage at 35a, Plato presses the intermediacy of the *psyche*. Note the way in which the *psyche* is "sandwiched" between two highly similar lines: (a) "midway between the being which is indivisible and remains always the same and the Being which is transient and divisible in bodies; (b) He blended a third form of Being [i.e., *psyche*]; (c) and in like manner He compounded it midway between that one of them which is indivisible and that one which is divisible in bodies."

27. Timaeus says that the process of inserting the binding smaller proportions in the intervals between the larger ones continues until the original mixture from which he had been cutting all of them was spent (36b). Clearly, since proportions necessarily possess intervals, no matter how small, intervals or gaps remain even at the end of the process.

successively narrowing the numeric "spaces" between components on smaller and smaller scales.

In this case, the intermediate fulfills its joining function mathematically. The Demiourgos constructs/generates *psyche* and its internal differentiation through the mathematization of the Being, Same, and Other blend. He employs a complex process of mathematically determined divisions to bring about the *psyche;* the relations comprising *psyche* are a series of mathematical proportions. In its mathematical character, Timaeus's discussion of *psyche*'s generation in general is abstract and less spatially imagistic than the previous discussion of Being, Becoming, and the Demiourgos, and so depends less on visualization.[28]

Receptacle

At 47e Timaeus makes his "new beginning" to explain how things come to be, not by the work of Reason, as in Section II of the dialogue, but by the operation of Necessity, the wandering cause. After some preliminaries, his explanation begins in earnest this way:

> We must, however, in beginning our fresh account of the universe make more distinctions than we did before; for whereas then we distinguished two forms, we must now declare another third kind. (48e)

In coming to terms with Necessity, there is a need to identify a third kind as such, a form that is hard to grasp and articulate (49a). What is the special power of this third, Timaeus asks?[29] "This especially, to be the Receptacle and as it were the nurse of all Becoming"(49a). The Receptacle, understood as eternal place (*aei choras*; 52b), is eternal and indestructible, and thus like Being. But like Becoming it moves and is moved (52e) by the figures that enter it, the copies of the eternal Forms (50c), thus displaying the power to be affected characteristic of Becoming. Timaeus indicates the Receptacle's affinity to the generated world of Becoming in other ways as well: he uses as examples the malleability of gold and the odorlessness of a perfume base to convey its receptivity (50b–c, 50e) and

28. Diagrams and charts of the harmonic and arithmetical means Timaeus describes may have been available at the time so that students could see the series of numbers. On this topic, see Robert S. Brumbaugh, *Plato's Mathematical Imagination* (Bloomington: Indiana University Press, 1954).

29. This echoes the questions raised about the nature of Being and Becoming and their natures at 27d.

Sayre recognizes the intermediate status Timaeus attributes to the Receptacle as a device with which Plato attempts to solve problems of the Form-particular things relationship. But Sayre holds that the device is ultimately unsuccessful. See *Plato's Late Ontology*, pp. 238–55, esp. 247 ff.

he says that parts of the Receptacle become "fiery" or "liquified," and so forth (51b). He makes plain its role as a third and intermediate kind several times.[30] In addition, Timaeus mentions that the figures that form inside the Receptacle do so in the middle (*metaxu*; 50b3), intensifying by this description the image of coming-to-be occuring "between."[31]

The exact nature of the Receptacle has been a vexing question in the long history of commentary on the *Timaeus*: Is it prime matter? Place? Space? I shall not enter into these important disputes at this point, but with our present aims in mind of determining the nature of the relations and intermediates in this dialogue it can be noted that Timaeus's adoption of maternal metaphors for the Receptacle (mother, nurse, and womb) heightens the distinctness of this third kind from the earlier two. At the same time, these metaphors indicate the problem to be solved, although not the solution to it: By what means or medium could Being be brought to bear beyond itself? In his task to describe the coming-to-be of the world, this has been an issue for Timaeus since his positing of the opposition between Being and Becoming (at 27d; the problem is also stated at 51b–52d). In Section II he began a resolution, proposing an agent operating between the two (i.e., the Demiourgos in the domain of Reason). Now in Section III he develops this resolution, "furnish[ing] an account of what comes into existence through Necessity" (47e), via that which is operated on, itself distinct from both but sharing some features in common with each. The parallelism of the accounts in Sections II and III is plain, particularly in setting up distinct kinds at the start and then mediating them by way of metaphors and images of spatial extension. The Receptacle, then, links Being and Becoming with respect to the generation/production of Becoming by its "third" nature which is spatial, partaking of both and "located" between the two. It links passively as a generative/productive conduit between Being and Becoming.[32]

30. Evidence that the Receptacle is to be regarded as a third and intermediate kind: at 48e and 49a, the need for a third kind is mentioned; at 50c, that the Receptacle is a molding-stuff for the things that become, marked by Being; at 50c–d, the need to conceive of three kinds (Becoming, that from which it comes and that in which it comes to be); at 50c, likened to a mother; at 52a–b, a third kind.

31. Questions might be raised about how there could be a middle of that which is shapeless (51a9). Also, "For the present, then, we must conceive of three kinds (*genē*)—the Becoming, the 'Wherein' it becomes, and the source 'Wherefrom' the Becoming is copied and produced." Even in this phrasing, the "Wherefrom" or Receptacle is listed between the two other kinds. But in the next sentence a shift appears: "Moreover, it is proper to liken the Recipient to the Mother, the Source to the Father and what is engendered between (*metaxu*) these two to the Offspring" (50d). Thus, the passage presents several puzzles.

32. Timaeus also emphasizes—perhaps weaning his listeners from dependence on the image of a physical-material "nurse"—that she is invisible and without shape and partakes somehow or other in the intelligible (51a–b).

Mathematical Figures

Having established the Receptacle in this "third" intermediate position between Being and Becoming, and setting it up as a creative factor parallel to the Demiourgos in the previous section, Timaeus is ready to introduce the second major intermediate in the generative process, the mathematical figures. These are the elementary triangles and the five Platonic solids.

Timaeus wishes to present the nature and origin of each of the four material "elements": earth, air, fire, and water. Thus he begins his discussion of them:

> In the first place, then, it is plain I presume to everyone that fire and earth and water and air are solid bodies; and the form [*eidos*] of a body, in every case, possesses depth also. (53c)

The nature of these four is to be regular solid bodies having depth. In Timaeus's account, these are not self-subsisting, eternal elements but rather derive from the Receptacle by way of the two elementary triangles, the isosceles and the scalene. Form and depth are provided by the regular, patterned arrangement of these triangles (into the five "Platonic solids": the tetrahedron—fire; the octahedron—air; the icosahedron—water; the cube—earth; the dodecahedron—used by the god in the decoration of the Whole; 54d–55d). Since earth, air, fire, and water are not eternally existing elements, they themselves cannot serve as principles of generation, as the *physiologoi* had thought. Rather, according to Timaeus, the true elements of bodies and the principles of their generation are the two triangles. The triangular figures are intelligible, and as a consequence the material cosmos has an intelligible foundation. Still, the triangles have only an intermediate ontological status (53b) and their intelligibility is not the full intelligibility of the Forms. Timaeus says that the figures that enter and leave the Receptacle "are *copies* [my emphasis] of those that are always existent"(50c), that is, they are neither Forms nor are they material instances of triangles, but rather they are figures of some third, intermediate kind.[33]

33. Note that this is Aristotle's interpretation of the ontological status of mathematical things in Plato's philosophy. He says in *Metaphysics* A:

> Further, besides sensible things and Forms he [Plato] says there are the objects of mathematics, which occupy an intermediate position, differing from sensible things in being eternal and unchangeable, from Forms in that there are many alike, while the Form itself is in each case unique. (987b16–18; McKeon edition)

There is extensive scholarly debate concerning mathematical intermediates in Plato's thought and Aristotle's understanding of them. For discussion of the problem, see Sayre,

In discussing the mathematical figures and elements, Timaeus proceeds here, as he did in Section II, from a description of the intermediate means to the generative/productive result (in Section II, from the Demiourgos to the *psyche* it constructs, itself an intermediate kind; in Section III, from the Receptacle to the figures which as mathematical are of an ontologically intermediate kind). In both cases, Timaeus moves from a spatially imagistic to a more abstract and mathematical account. In the domain of Reason, *psyche* is constructed by way of numerical proportions; in the domain of Necessity, the elements and eventually the compounds are constructed by way of geometrical figures. The nature of the five Platonic solids is clearly intermediate: they are both spatial and abstract. In Timaeus's account, they link Being and Becoming in their ability to bring Forms into the domain of Becoming via the interior of the Receptacle, e.g., the figures that he says "enter and depart" (*eisionta kai exionta*; 50c6).

Body—both world body as a whole and the proliferation of particular bodies within it—is the outcome in this section of the operation of the intermediate Receptacle (portrayed largely as passive, but nonethess having an effective shaking motion) and the intermediate mathematicals. What follows in this middle section of Timaeus's presentation is talk of the many features of body: its movement and its rest, its heaviness and lightness, its forms as liquid and solid, and its numerous compounds, such as wax, stone, and glass. The section closes with mention of pleasure and pain and qualities humans perceive, such as colors and tastes. Within this section, however, Timaeus's account of body is yet to be enlivened and made human.

Marrow, Eros, *and* Epithumia

We have now identified the four major intermediates that function generatively in the first two sections of Timaeus's presentation. The pattern of establishing intermediates to link polarities continues in the closing section of his talk, where the generation of the mortal human being is under consideration. The polarities expand in this final section from one to two major sets. The first is the body and soul of mortal human creatures; the second is male and female. Let us consider each.

Plato's Late Ontology, pp. 86–88; Julia Annas, "On the 'Intermediates,'" *Archiv fuer Geschichte der Philosophie* 57 (1975): 146–66, 1975; Anders Wedberg, *Plato's Philosophy of Mathematics* (Stockholm: Almquist & Wiksell, 1955).

Regarding the superior intelligibility of triangles and numbers as elements, in contrast to Democritus's atomism, see G. Morrow, "Plato's Theory of the Primary Bodies," p. 23.

Timaeus begins the final section of his talk by asserting a correlation of some of our abdominal organs with two aspects of the soul (the heart and lungs with the *thumos* or "spiritedness," and the liver and spleen with *epithumia*, "appetite"). This matching of organs and psychic aspects appears fairly simple as Timaeus first tells it, giving the initial impression that the interaction of body and soul is unproblematic.[34] But the interrelation of the body even with the lower aspects of *psyche* is, of course, not so obvious, and furthermore, the most superior and immortal aspect of *psyche*, *nous*, remains to be integrated with the mortal body. So, after the preliminary and somewhat unsatisfying start in relating the body and *psyche*,[35] Timaeus makes what amounts to a new beginning. According to Timaeus, bones, flesh, and all such substances in the body—and, as it turns out, the primary organs already named:

> All these had their origin in the generation of the marrow. For it was in this that the bonds [*desmoi*] of life by which the soul is bound to the body were fastened and implanted the roots of the mortal kind." (73b)

The marrow, Timaeus explains, is composed of elementary triangles specially arranged by the god to create a *panspermia*, a universal "seed-stuff" for the generation of all the mortal kinds of entities. Marrow has an intermediate nature as an animate material (91b). The god fashions it directly from the primary triangles (73b), that is, from abstract geometrical figures, dividing and shaping the portions both into different sorts of soul and different parts of the body to be receptive of soul. The marrow, then, accomplishes what a mere matching up of bodily organs and functions cannot: it provides some explanation for how separate and opposed natures might be joined. As a third that partakes of both, it links body and soul. And in its role in the generation of offspring marrow links by making continuous one generation and the next.[36]

34. We might note, by the way, that the hierarchy of soul over body, stated in the first part of his talk, is again emphasized: the bodily organs serve the *psyche*'s needs, and within the *psyche thumos* is superior to *epithumia*. Ontological hierarchies and the principle of the primacy of the *psyche* are never abandoned. See Seth Benardete, "On Plato's *Timaeus* and Timaeus' Science Fiction."

35. This start parallels the preliminary sketch of the proportionate organization of the world body in the first section of Timaeus's talk which, while told first, was incomplete and could not exist first in reality.

36. The marrow is, in a sense, the "offspring" of the two earlier sections of Timaeus's presentation: the god mixes and separates in proportion as the Demiourgos did in Section II, using a medium clearly derived from the discussion of the Receptacle in Section III. But, then, the marrow is not the direct "descendent" of those sections: the fashioning god is not the Demiourgos but apparently one of his own offspring, since at 73a the plural is used to refer to "those who were constructing our kind" and, while he molds the triangles, nothing is said of the Receptacle.

Timaeus presents the second set of generative dualities, male and female, at the end. In fulfillment of his task to speak of "the coming to be of the world up to the generation of humankind" (27a, 90e), he has one more step to provide, namely, that step needed for the generation of a human individual. There are, as before, two intermediates that link male and female: *eros* and *epithumia* of a special sort, the desire of begetting (for the male, the *eros* of generating [91b]; for the female, the *epithumia* of producing offspring [91c]). Spurred on by their desire, Timaeus says, the male and the female are joined.[37] By means of the marrow-seed that derives ultimately from the head, together they sow infinitesimal animalcules in the womb and nurture them.[38] And so they complete the generation of living creatures; here generation amounts to "bringing them forth into the light" (91d). In this way, then, Timaeus has completed his assignment to tell of the generation of the universe up to the generation of human beings.

The male and female pair, familiar from Pythagoras's Table of Opposites, are contraries that permit neither an intermediate continuous with both nor one that partakes of both (i.e., there is no third generative sex). The options for intermediates Timaues availed himself of earlier, therefore, are not appropriate for the male/female pair. Timaeus posits a new kind of intermediate. *Eros* and *epithumia* are strong forces of desire and attraction that join (*sunagagontes*; 91c10) male and female. The joining of the two is a means to satisfy a further desire held by both, namely, for generating or childbearing (91b–c). The prerequisite for the satisfaction of this desire is that the male and female be drawn into close contact.

At all of the major junctures in Timaeus's talk on the generation of the world and humankind we see the linkages develop between two domains or causes or entities, presumed by Timaeus to be separate. At the beginning of each section these pairs are defined at their extremes, sometimes as polarities apparently distantly separated from one another. Immediately in the course of the presentation, however, modifications are underway. Timaeus reduces the radical separation of the initial pairs and introduces a new proximity in their relations by way of a series of intermediates.[39]

37. Their desire appears to be for release of their marrow, for begetting and for each other.

38. Note the use of the plural in this passage, 91c–e: both male and female sow animalcules, both "mold [them] into shape and nourish [them] to a great size."

39. The question of how the several intermediates that figure in the *Timaeus* are interrelated will not be taken up here, but two observations can be made: (1) they appear to stand in relation to one another, and perhaps in a braided way that echoes the "forward–back," "progression–regression" pattern to be found within the dialogue (e.g., when the construction of the world-body is described before that of the world-soul, even though

V. INTERPRETING INTERMEDIATES AS A SOLUTION TO THE PROBLEM OF RELATING FORMS AND PARTICULAR THINGS

The major intermediate kinds we have listed, the Demiourgos, *psyche*, Receptacle, mathematicals, marrow, *eros*, and *epithumia*, occupy positions between Being and Becoming, Forms and particular things. Each in its own way is situated in the interval and by its mediation ameliorates the separation posited at first between the dualities. The proximity or joining allows for interaction so that generation can take place. The pattern of intermediates in the *Timaeus* indicates that mediation is proposed as the key to explaining the relation of Forms and particular things. But can intermediates serve as a solution to the problem of the interrelation and interaction of the two ontological domains, Being and Becoming? Can they help to solve the problem of generation within a Platonic ontology?

There are peculiarities about the intermediates posited in this dialogue. These become perhaps especially manifest in the last section of Timaeus's talk. For example, he proposes "marrow" as the bond linking soul to body, but marrow with its origins in the elementary triangles, is basically unsouled material. How, then, is it capable of bonding with soul? Moreover, his discussion of the final polarity of male and female illuminates very little about how a human child is sexually generated, apart from murky references to the intermediates *eros* and *epithumia*, suggestive at best of certain natural urges.[40] Human sexual generation is simply not treated as a philosophically significant subject at this point. Timaeus gives what ancient commentators and modern scholars generally agree to be a noticeably unsatisfactory account of how human beings come to be. Not only is it metaphoric (relying on familiar Greek agricultural metaphors) and mythic (the genitals themselves are depicted as creatures), but it concludes with an allegory having comic overtones in which birds, wild beasts, reptiles, and fish are the fallen forms of men who had led superficial or evil lives. All of this follows a lofty talk about the care of the soul, and the contrast is striking.[41] Timaeus's treatment, then, of

---

the soul is first; 34b–c); and (2) as mentioned above (in note 21), each of the parts of Timaeus's presentation fulfills the conditions met by the whole.

40. *Eros* and *epithumia*, a love of generating and a desire for discharge, are apparently both possessed by male and female (91b–d).

41. See A. E. Taylor, in *A Commentary on Plato's "Timaeus"* (Oxford: Clarendon Press 1928), p. 635, on the close of the dialogue as playful. Taylor quotes Proclus (pp. 635–36), who thought great difficulties arose from taking the passage seriously. Colin Murray Turbayne believes the closing passages, along with others in the dialogue, point to Plato's use of the cosmology to investigate the diseases and health of the body. See *Metaphors for the Mind* (Columbia: University of South Carolina Press, 1991), pp. 24–25.

these matters is noticeably incomplete, so much so in fact that the entire section seems to be in decline and to call attention to itself.

Not only is there considerable obscurity in the final section, but the intermediates throughout display a bipolar nature and are internally complicated. The divine Demiourgos exhibits a dyadic nature as both "maker and father" of the cosmos. His making and fathering represent two different kinds of capacities brought to bear on a single object, raising questions about reconciling the two (i.e., Is the world made or is it generated?).[42] The *psyche* displays internal duality with its double circles of Same and Different, revolving in different planes in different directions, which serve as the basis for different kinds of knowing. But the Same and the Different in the *psyche*, while they seem to be harmonized by their mathematical proportionality, must still be joined by force (35b). The Receptacle has a double nature: both spatial and material, motionless and moving.[43] And the elementary triangles are irreducibly of two kinds, the scalene and the isoceles; these two do not combine together (54c).

These dualities are not incidental to the intermediates, but, as we saw earlier, are the basis for their ability to function as intermediates, sharing in the natures of both domains or causes or factors that they join together. And their internal duality is a reminder that there is no collapse of difference within the intermediates, that is, no full unification. But the particular dual natures of some of these intermediates present problems, such as reconciling the god's making and fathering of the world and the Receptacle's motionlessness and shaking motions. And insofar as all of them display internal duality a more general difficulty arises: How are their internal dualities to be reconciled? Do each of the intermediates require an internal intermediate as a bond? If they do, then those inner intermediates will themselves display a double nature—since the duality is basic to the functioning of the intermediate—and their own duality will have to be bonded with an intermediate, and so on. In such a regress a true meeting and interaction of Being and Becoming would never occur. Their greater proximity would be at best a promise of interrelation, never to be completed.

According to Aristotle, too, intermediates do not solve the problem of the relation of Being and Becoming. Aristotle makes strenuous criticisms in *Metaphysics A, M,* and *N* of the notion of mathematical intermediates, which he attributes to Platonic philosophy.[44] In his view, mathematical

42. For the *demiourgou kai patros,* see also *Statesman* 273b.

43. These two descriptions of the Receptacle are varied enough that they are sometimes referred to as "primary" and "secondary." See Edward Lee, "On the Metaphysics of the Image in Plato's *Timaeus,*" *Monist* 50 (1966): 341–68.

44. E.g., see *Metaphysics* 991b27–31, 997b13–98a19, 1076a37–77a14, 1090a15–91a22.

intermediates merely multiply the difficulties of a domain of separate Forms, adding an unnecessary third ontological level that can neither function as a link nor be explained on its own terms.[45] In short, the concept of mathematical intermediates is so flawed, in Aristotle's view, that they demonstrate the untenability of a Platonic ontology of separate Forms.

We are left, then, with several alternatives. Either the intermediates are Plato's failed way to answer the question of the relation between Being and Becoming and the working of generation. We would then have to conclude, along with Owen and others, that after all Forms and things are separated, even radically separated in the *Timaeus*, with the many problems that separation entails. Or, giving Plato greater credit at least for cleverness, perhaps Timaeus does not speak for Plato at all and *his* flawed theory in this dialogue is a Platonic critique or spoof of other cosmological ideas in circulation at the time, as Taylor's interpretation holds. Or, as I propose, the very peculiarity and apparent unsatisfactoriness of the intermediates is an *aporia* that Plato uses as an invitation to reflect back on what they now reveal about the limits of the first distinction (*prōton diaireteon*, 27d) of *ousia* and *genesis*, and of the polarities of the causes and other factors in the following sections.[46] We are led, as I suggest, to rethink those polarized relations, to begin again, as Timaeus says, at the natural beginning of the thing (29b). But how might we find some resolution to the *aporia*?

Looking to Being for a model of a solution makes a good deal of sense, both in general in Platonic philosophy and in the present *aporia* over the relation of Being, Becoming, and the intermediates. Timaeus says early on that the world of Becoming is a likeness, a copy of Being (although, he explains, an inferior and distorted version of it; 43a–44c). A much longer study would, at this point, inquire into the nature of Being in other Plato dialogues such as the *Parmenides*, the *Sophist*, and the *Republic*, the echoes of whose proposals on the regulation of generation begin the *Timaeus*. But more briefly, let us make the following two observations about Being: First, Being itself is pervaded not only by the "Same" but by "Otherness," and the perfect and complete manner in which these are structured within Being accounts for its perfect and stable nature;[47]

45. Julia Annas, "On the 'Intermediates,'" pp. 155–56.

46. The challenge in the format is a feature of Plato's pedagogy. See Mitchell Miller, "Platonic Provocations: Reflections on the Soul and the Good in the *Republic*," in *Platonic Investigations*, ed. Dominic J. O'Meara (Washington, D.C.: The Catholic University of America Press, 1985), and Miller, *Plato's "Parmenides."*

47. *Sophist* on *megiste gene* (254b–55e); and Klein, *Greek Mathematical Thought*, pp. 93–94.

Becoming is modeled after Being and is like it in being pervaded by otherness, but not in so stable a structure. In addition, Becoming can be regarded as the external "other" to Being. Second, Being's character, once it is fully appreciated as profoundly different in nature from the material, generated, and decaying world of Becoming, is permitted, precisely because it lacks the limitations of space and time, to be present to, indeed to be intimate with, what is other than it.[48] It can be present anywhere, everywhere because it is not limited by the usual spatial specifications of "where." It can be present to Becoming as readily as it accommodates otherness in itself.

Thus, it is evident why Timaeus's presentation *must* begin with a distinction between Being and Becoming: Being's nature as profoundly different from material Becoming must be recognized first. At the same time, however, the implication of this initial and massive distinction is incomplete. Because once the difference is appreciated in its full significance, the radical separation of Being and Becoming is mitigated by virtue of their very difference. While Being and Becoming, Forms and particulars differ from one another and are always distinguishable (note that they are forever different and never blend; there is no "coincidence of opposites" for Plato),[49] a relation need not be superadded as a third thing, by means of a third item, after their given independence; they are already relatable. Thus, Being and Becoming are capable of coexistence, are conjoinable "both together" from the start. Becoming is a *sunousia,* literally "with Being," as Timaeus's remark in the opening lines of the dialogue perhaps hints (17a).

What no doubt permits the mistake in the first place in regarding Being and Becoming as separate or even radically separate is the tendency, understandable given the human situation in Becoming described in the *Timaeus,* of viewing "distinction" in terms of *spatial* separation or distance. This is, in effect, an *image* of distinctness. The intermediates as they are presented in the *Timaeus* function like images. They are signs, *eikones,* providing images of the relationality of Being and Becoming. The *Timaeus* is, in part, about the inevitability of images in our world and their usefulness, but it offers a warning about them as well. Images are

48. That Being is not subject to the various limits of Becoming is expressed at 38a: "but it belongs not to that which is ever changeless in its uniformity to become either older or younger through time, nor ever to have become so, nor to be so now, nor to be about to be so hereafter, *nor in general to be subject to any of the conditions which Becoming has attached to the things which move in the world of Sense*" (my emphasis). See also *Parmenides,* and Miller, *Plato's "Parmenides."*

49. Klein, *Greek Mathematical Thought,* pp. 94–96.

inadequate, never quite right. Ontologically they occupy a middle position, having some identity but lacking the stability of an original. They may be helpful as indicators, as they are here in the *Timaeus*, pointing out the requirement of the relatability of Being and Becoming. But by their portrayal as "thing-like," along the lines of spatial objects occupying a third place or realm of reality, they are at least vaguely inaccurate, "defective" (e.g., 43a–44c), as images are. Earlier we noted Timaeus's comment on the need for a third thing to bind two things together (31b–c); he makes this telling comment, however, in the context of talk about the formation of the world *body*.[50] The requirement for a third thing is appropriate to the material world of Becoming and to our images of it. The use of such images in philosophical inquiry is an initial and perhaps inevitable capitulation to the weakness of words and of the human condition (29c–d).[51] The intermediates, then, are an "intermediate step" in the process of coming to understand the natures of Being and Becoming.

Thus, the intermediate entities pictured in the *Timaeus* are not the final Platonic answer to the puzzles of the interrelation of Being and Becoming, nor are they to be dismissed as useless because they fail as a solution. Rather, they have both pedagogical and philosophical roles to fill. They show—in a measured way that is initially less paradoxical and therefore less startling—that Being can reside outside a strictly delimited "domain" of Being. They bring us eventually to see the further inquiry into and development of the first conceptions that are necessary in order to understand Being and Becoming.[52] And the intermediates each picture partial aspects of the relation of Being and Becoming: its goodness (Demiourgos), its indestructibility (Receptacle); its precision (mathematicals), and so forth. They also illustrate—again, less than perfectly—the generative proliferation of Becoming in its contact with Being. And by their internally dual nature suggestive of a series of yet further and further divisions and complexities, they picture the deep analyzability of reality. The depth dimension of the world and the *psyche* and the whole of reality—of repeated concern from the start of Timaeus's presentation—is the basis and justification for the ongoing investigation of the world that the dialogue encourages.

50. As Timaeus says at 32b: "for it behoved it to be *solid* of shape, and what brings *solids* into unison is never one middle term alone but always two" (my emphasis).

51. Klein, *Greek Mathematical Thought*, p. 95.

52. There is, then, a pedagogical process underway in the dialogue of refining the motions of the knowing *psyche*, making them more orderly and the *psyche* more accurate in recognizing the Same and the Other (37a–c). Plato accomplishes this teaching in the *Timaeus* partly through the challenge of the incompleteness of the account Timaeus is presenting.

VI. CONCLUSIONS

We have noted the process that is underway in the *Timaeus*, the process of transforming *our* initial characterization of the relation between Being and Becoming. The distinction between them must initiate the account, but the rigidity of the distinction must be modified in order to explain the nature of Becoming and its generation. This modification is made, first, by means of the intermediary Demiourgos and the intermediates we have identified in each of the three sections of Timaeus's talk. However, the intermediates discovered in the fourth section of the dialogue are rather dubious and expose a deterioration in the pattern.[53] Even the more plausible-seeming ones of the second and third sections, the mathematicals, for example, are vulnerable to serious objections. My proposal is that the intermediates raise the issue of the relation between basic dualities, and their problematic nature returns Plato's careful and philosophically critical listeners to a reexamination of the initial distinction between Being and Becoming. That distinction as Timaeus first posits it is inert, so that a relation between Being and Becoming would have to be constructed as a separate third thing in addition to the two. The intermediates in this case and elsewhere in the dialogue provide this, but they do not relate the pairs completely or successfully and thus the difficulties of interaction and hence generation remain unresolved.[54] The grounds for motion and the generation of life by means of the contact of Being and Becoming has to be established—and can be, to some extent, but not ultimately by intermediates but rather by what they point to: a deeper and thus more adequate understanding of the natures of Being and Becoming and their fundamental, intrinsic relatability.

Not long after Timaeus begins his talk, he cautions:

> Socrates, if in our treatment of a great host of matters regarding the gods and the generation of the universe we prove unable to give accounts that are always in all respects self-consistent and perfectly exact, do not be surprised; rather we should be content if we can furnish accounts that are inferior to none in likelihood, remembering that both I who speak and you who judge are but human creatures. (29c–d)

53. That is, the pattern evident in the earlier two sections where an intermediate is introduced between a basic pair (Being and Becoming, Reason and Necessity) and a product is generated, doubles now in the final section of Timaeus's presentation in his discussion of *two* basic pairs, the second of which has two intermediates.

54. Following Mitchell Miller's notion of "Platonic provocation," we might suppose that Being and Becoming, Reason and Necessity, soul and body, female and male are all polarized as a pedagogical means of provoking their philosophical resolution. See Miller, "Platonic Provocations." Miller's analysis of the *Parmenides,* should also be consulted, esp. pp. 88ff.

In response to Timaeus's reminder about the necessary limits of such talk about these matters, Socrates exclaims, "Excellent, Timaeus! We must by all means accept it, as you suggest" (29d). This is Socrates' only intervention in Timaeus's presentation. It is, in effect, an acknowledgment that our early expectations for a brilliant and complete account must be adjusted. Not a perfect account about perfect being but rather one directed by this and touched by it will be satisfying. To these revised expectations, then, with the promise they hold of further thought and dialogue, Socrates replies, "Excellent!"[55]

55. I am grateful to The School of Philosophy at The Catholic University of America for the invitation to present this essay as part of the Matchette Lecture Series on Plato and Platonism in October 1993. I also would like to thank several friends and colleagues from whose insight I benefitted in writing on the *Timaeus:* Harvey Burstein, Drew Hyland, Helen Lang, and Mitchell Miller. John Max van Ophuijsen's astute comments on an earlier version were also helpful.

7 The *Timaeus* Revisited

THÉRÈSE-ANNE DRUART

In the *Theaetetus* (176b) Socrates tells us that those who are philosophically inclined should aim at "becoming as like God as possible." I shall argue that this statement offers a key to understanding some of the puzzling features of the *Timaeus* since, I think, the Demiurge is the God that Plato would like the auxiliaries of the perfect state and all would-be philosophers to emulate as much as they can.

What exactly the Demiurge *does* is disputed, but it is no accident that discussions focus less on what he *does* and more on what he *is* since Plato remains silent about his ontological status.[1] This silence leaves much room for commentators to display their ingenuity, but Plato's own focus on his doing should make us pause. The Demiurge is essentially a "doer," a "man of action." Timaeus's speech gives an account of the three ultimate ontological principles, namely, that which always is, or the realm of Forms; that which becomes, or the sensible realm; and the Receptacle, or *chora* (χώρα). For each ontological level, there is a specific mode of apprehension that provides access to it. Yet what the Demiurge is and how he comes to be known are issues that are not even raised, though he does not seem to belong in any of the three ontological realms. All we are told is that he is the *"aitios"* (αἴτιος) or agent responsible for ordering the realm of Becoming in such a way that it will mirror the realm of Forms.

On the one hand, the model or *"paradeigma"* (παράδειγμα) the ordered Universe imitates is the realm of Forms, or more exactly the Form of the Living Being, but, on the other hand, 29e states that the overarching principle for the ordering of the Universe is none other than the Demiurge's generous desire that all things should come as near as possible to being like himself. Therefore, the ordering of the Universe re-

1. One of the few scholars interested in what the Demiurge does is Richard D. Mohr. See his "Plato's Theology Reconsidered: What the Demiurge Does," in *Essays in Ancient Greek Philosophy*, vol. 3, ed. John Anton and Anthony Preuss (New York: State University of New York Press, 1989, pp. 293–307 (this is reprinted from *History of Philosophy Quarterly* 2 [1985]: 131–44). See also his *The Platonic Cosmology* (Leiden: Brill, 1985).

quires two models: the realm of the Forms for the end result of this ordering, and the Demiurge's activity for the process leading to this end result. Since the model that always is is also the best, the eternal realm of Forms may be the true model for philosophers, whereas the Demiurgic activity that subordinates itself to this realm but is embroiled in Becoming and temporality may be the model suitable for those who though philosophically minded are primarily focused on running and defending the city, or their own soul, that is, the auxiliaries and the philosophers in the making.

The great hero of Timaeus's cosmic epos is not the realm of Forms but rather the Demiurge, and its intended audience is not the philosopher-king so conspicuously absent from the summary of the *Republic* that introduces the dialogue but the auxiliaries who are the very focus of this highly selective summary. If such is the case, G. E. L. Owen's famous view that the *Timaeus* cannot be a late dialogue since it speaks of imitating the Forms instead of using the more sophisticated language of the *Parmenides* and of the other Eleatic dialogues[2] needs not be accepted, and this not only on account of more recent stylometric research.[3] As the *Timaeus* is not intended for a highly sophisticated audience, Plato thought it wiser not to include therein greater and eventually more recent ontological complexities.

The Demiurge's cosmic labors and their motivation, a lack of jealousy, give rise to a cascade of imitations. The secondary gods imitate his very "demiurgy" in providing the human being with the two lower kinds of soul and with a body. Athena, too, imitated the Demiurge when she founded Athens, and later on Egyptian Sais, and provided them both with a constitution (διακόσμησις) or ordering which embodies some striking features of the perfect constitution laid down in the *Republic*. Such a constitution allowed the Athenians of the past to repel Atlantis's barbaric invasion. Now that current Athens has broken away from its glorious past and has stooped to becoming an invader itself, only a foreigner, Timaeus of Locri, who is both a philosopher and a statesman, will be worthy of telling the tale of the great hero who provided the model followed by the Athenians of the past and by Plato's Egyptians. In so doing Timaeus offers a model for the actions of the auxiliaries of the perfect city as well as for all human beings in need of ordering their souls.

2. G. E. L. Owen, "The Place of the *Timaeus* in Plato's Dialogues," in *Studies in Plato's Metaphysics*, ed. R. E. Allen (London: Routledge & Kegan Paul, 1965), pp. 313–38. (Article originally published in 1953.)

3. See, e.g., G. R. Ledger, *Re-Counting Plato* (Oxford: Clarendon Press, 1989), and Leonard Brandwood, *The Chronology of Plato's Dialogues* (Cambridge: Cambridge University Press, 1990), and "Stylometry and Chronology," in *The Cambridge Companion to Plato*, ed. Richard Kraut (Cambridge: Cambridge University Press, 1992), pp. 90–120.

This function of the Demiurge as essentially a model for human action explains the strikingly anthropomorphic characterization of the Demiurge. He is endowed not only with reason but also with deliberation, choice, and reasoning processes that lead him to a progressive determination of the means necessary to reaching his goal, the best possible world. He even exhibits some emotion, and far from being all powerful he must coax Necessity without ever fully overcoming it.

If indeed the Demiurge is a model of rational action[4] for those who have not yet reached the level of perfect philosopher, and so for the auxiliaries in particular, one may wonder why Plato called him a *Demiurge* or "craftsman" since, as the introductory part of the dialogue reminds us, craftsmen are the lower class in the ideal city and should be sharply separated from the auxiliaries. Brisson solves this problem by pointing out that the word *demiourgos* (δημιουργός) has more than one meaning: it also refers to a magistrate or public officer, and so can be applied to members of the ruling classes.[5]

The Demiurge's action of *diakosmesis*, the orderly organization of the chaotic precosmos, prefigures the laying down of a perfect constitution and the proper ordering of the human being overcoming the chaos afflicting his rational soul while an infant, as well as the proper constitution of the tongue for teleological purpose (75d7), is of course guided by reason and contemplation of the Forms. Its means are two "weapons" that constrain willingly or unwillingly, that is, persuasion and violence. The Demiurge persuades a willing Errant Cause or Necessity, but when preparing the mix for the World's Soul violently forces Difference to mingle with Sameness. Persuasion and violence are the very weapons that the auxiliaries use in the perfect city and that each one of us should employ in our dealings with the two lower kinds of soul and the external influences affecting them.

My essay, therefore, shows that one of the crafts "of the demiurge is

4. Among those who emphasize the ethical aspect of the *Timaeus* are Robert H. Whitaker, "The *Timaeus* as a Basis for Plato's Ethics," *Philosophical Forum* 1 (1943): 19–23; and Joan Kung, "Tetrahedra, Motion, and Virtue," *Nous* 19 (1985): 17–27, and "Mathematics and Virtue in Plato's *Timaeus*," in *Essays in Ancient Greek Philosophy*, vol. 3, ed. John Anton and Anthony Preuss (New York: State University of New York Press, 1989), pp. 309–39. This essay was completed before I could consult *Interpreting the Timaeus—Critias*. Proceedings of the Symposium Platonicum (International Plato Studies 9), ed. Tomés Calvo and Luc Brisson (Sankt Augustin: Academia Verlag, 1997). The volume includes four articles on ethics, pp. 327–74.

5. See, Luc Brisson, *Le même et l'autre dans la structure ontologique du Timée de Platon: Un commentaire systématique du Timée de Platon* (Paris: Klincksieck, 1974), pp. 30–55 (2d ed. Sankt Augustin: Academia Verlag Richarz, 1994), and Platon, *Timée/Critias*, trans. with introduction and notes by Luc Brisson (Paris: Flammarion, 1992), pp. 20–27.

the art of psychagogy"[6] or the way to lead souls. Section 1 explains how the introductory part of the dialogue sets the stage to offer a model for rational action and why the *Timaeus* must precede the *Critias*. Section 2 briefly examines some relevant aspects of the Demiurge's cosmic action. The third and last section demonstrates how the ethics advocated in Timaeus's speech, particularly in its third part, is modeled after the Demiurge's action.

I. THE INTRODUCTORY DIALOGUE; OR, THREE IMITATIONS IN QUEST OF A MODEL

The text begins with Socrates' own idiosyncratic summary of the *Republic* which centers on the auxiliaries' function.[7] They are to fight attacks from within or from without and to deal justice to their subordinates fairly gently while resolutely repelling outside enemies. To do so they need to be both spirited and philosophic (18a5). Take note of the order of these two adjectives: "spirited" first and "philosophic" second. The text provides a model for a spiritedness informed by philosophic persuasion but does not require that the reader be a dialectician.

Socrates then complains that this presentation of the perfect city is if not lifeless at least motionless. He now wishes to hear an account of how the ideal city goes to war in a manner worthy of her and in that war achieves results befitting her training and education in deeds as well as in words (*logoi*; 19c4–8). I take it that the "deeds" refer to physical overcoming of resistance and the "logoi" to persuasion (88a speaks of providing teachings and battles in words both publicly and privately).

Needless to say, Socrates claims that he is unable to provide such an account. As for the poets of the past and of today, they too are discarded. They are imitators, and therefore can only reproduce well the surroundings in which they were brought up. As none was brought up in a perfect city, none can fittingly imitate such a city's exploits. The Sophists also get eliminated on the ground that they are wanderers roaming from one city to another,[8] and therefore would not hit upon what men who are both philosophers and statesmen would do and say while warring in deeds and

6. Modifying slightly the conclusion of Glenn R. Morrow's "Necessity and Persuasion in Plato's *Timaeus*," *Philosophical Review* 59 (1950):163.

7. Generally, commentators have paid very little attention to this introduction, and therefore have trouble giving an account of the *Timaeus* as a whole. See, e.g., Francis Macdonald Cornford, trans. and ed., *Plato's Cosmology: The "Timaeus" of Plato* (London: Kegan Paul, 1937), and Brisson, *Le même et l'autre.*

8. They are in fact assimilated to the "wandering" planets, before their wanderings could be predicted by more accurate astronomical knowledge which finds a pattern in their "wanderings," and to the Errant Cause before the Demiurge persuades it into order.

words. Only people such as Socrates' interlocutors, that is, Timaeus, Critias, and Hermocrates, could do so because they are equipped by nature and education for both philosophy and statesmanship.

As Timaeus belongs to an admirably governed state, Locri, where he has enjoyed the highest offices and has reached the highest eminence in philosophy, we should not be surprised that, later on, he should be entrusted with the grandest project. He alone comes from a well-governed city and he alone has reached the highest level in both philosophy and statesmanship. What he will imitate in his speech is no less than the cosmic exploits of the Demiurge who himself is a maker as well as a true poet (ποιητής; 28c3) par excellence since he brings order to the world on the model of the Forms, and for no other reason than that being without jealousy he desired that all things come as near as possible to being like himself (29e).

But I am getting ahead of myself and of the dialogue. Having simply asserted why Critias, Timaeus, and Hermocrates could give an account of the perfect city in action, that is, at war, Socrates lets his interlocutors take the lead as they please. Critias then recalls what Solon told his (Critias's) great-grandfather, Dropides, who told it to his own son, another Critias, who in turn passed on the tale to the current Critias while the latter was still a child. During a trip to Egypt, Solon met a very old priest from Sais who warned him that the traditional Greek genealogies were mere trifles compared to the truth contained in the written records safely kept in Egyptian temples. Such records attest that just before being destroyed by earthquake and flood the Athens of the past was the best at war and the best governed in every respect and beyond comparison. Solon, of course, begs the priest to share the whole story with him. In no way jealous (φθόνος οὐδείς; 23d4), and therefore anticipating the Demiurge's motivation, the old priest recalls for Solon's and Athens's sake, as well as for the honor of Athena, foundress of both Sais and Athens, the basic institutions of these two cities. He then relates the bare bones of the story of Atlantis's invasion of Egypt and Greece and its eventual expulsion thanks to Athens' courage. In both Sais and Athens there are three separate classes, and one of these, the military class, has no other concern than war. So Athena taught the Egyptians how to use spear and shield and in matters of wisdom Sais's law bestows great care both as concerns the order of the world, deriving from those divine things the discovery of all arts applied to human affairs, down to the practice of divination and medicine with a view to health. This program in fact is realized in Timaeus's speech which begins with the ordering of the universe and ends with divination and medicine. All this ordering (διακόσμησις) and system (σύνταξις) the goddess had bestowed earlier on Athens.

Since Athena is "a lover of war and wisdom" (φιλοπόλεμός τε καὶ φιλόσοφος; 24c7–24d1; note again that the love for war precedes the love for wisdom), "[she] chose out the region that would bear men most closely resembling herself."[9] In this she follows the Demiurge's example since he too wanted all things to resemble himself.

The greatest exploit of the Athens of that past was its act of repelling the hubris or insolence of Atlantis, whose corrupt institutions led her to attempt to enslave Egypt and Greece. The Athens of that time was foremost of all in courage and in the arts of war. Left on her own, she singlehandedly vanquished the invaders and then, being like the Demiurge free from jealousy (ἀφθόνως; 25c6), she liberated all who had been enslaved, but then earthquakes and floods sunk Atlantis and wiped away Athens's soldiers and elite.

After this sketch of the glorious defensive campaign that Athens, thanks to its excellent constitution, waged against Atlantis, the reader naturally expects that the full story will now be told. Yet such epos is postponed to give precedence to the speech of Timaeus since he is the best astronomer and has made knowledge of the universe his chief object. He will begin with the genesis of the world and end with the nature of the human being. Then only will it be possible to tell the full story of the war against Atlantis since it will imitate the Demiurge's war against the disorder and lack of proportion typical of the precosmic chaos. The implication is clear: the latter cannot be understood without the former since the former provides the model. In 47a Timaeus explains that astronomy is the gate to philosophy. "Sight is the cause of the highest benefits to us" since contemplation of the revolution of stars and planets "has caused the invention of number and bestowed on us the notion of time, and the study of the nature of the world; whence we have derived all philosophy, than which no greater boon has ever come or shall come to mortal man as a gift from heaven" (47a6–b2). Let us not forget that auxiliaries need to be both spirited and philosophic.

II. A VERY HUMAN DEMIURGE AND THE AMBIGUITIES OF THE MODEL

Timaeus's speech is a very long monologue with only one interruption.[10] Socrates intervenes at 29d4–6 to distinguish what he calls the

9. All the translations come from Cornford's translation of the *Timaeus*, cited in Note 7.

10. Rémi Brague argues that this speech parallels the structure of the body as explained in its second part; see his "The Body of the Speech: A New Hypothesis on the Compositional Structure of Timaeus' Monologue," in *Platonic Investigations*, ed. Dominic J. O'Meara (Washington, D.C.: The Catholic University of America Press, 1985), pp. 53–83.

prelude from the main theme and to give assent to the principles laid down in this prelude. Respecting this division will help us to understand the quasi humanity of the Demiurge as well as to realize that the Forms, though they constitute the official model, play a very limited role.

The prelude provides general metaphysical principles that are applied to the specific case of the Universe. The principles are the following:

1. We must first distinguish that which always is from that which becomes.
2. Thinking along with an account grasps the former, whereas the latter is an object of opinion along with sensation of which no account can be given.
3. All that becomes necessarily becomes thanks to someone who is responsible (αἴτιος) for it.
4. If that which the craftsman looked at and used as his model is eternal and immutable, then the product must be beautiful, whereas if that which he looked at and used as his model is something that became, then the product will not be beautiful.

These principles are taken as self-evident. Principle 3 asserts that someone (that the masculine singular is intended and not the neuter is made clear by the next sentence) is responsible for that which became and this someone is identified as a craftsman. Notice that the entrance of the craftsman precedes the introduction of his model in Principle 4 and that all that is said would apply to any ordinary productive activity.

Applying these principles to the case of the Universe, Timaeus establishes that, since the Universe became, someone must be responsible for it. This person is immediately identified as a maker or poet (ποιητής; 28c3) and as a father. This same pairing of the terms "maker" and "father" applied to the Demiurge is repeated in 41a. It indicates that the Demiurge's activities include both productive and educative skills, since his fatherhood cannot be construed as a begetting. After all, what the Demiurge does is to bring order (*diakosmesis*) into the precosmic chaos affecting the Receptacle and to provide human beings with the means for ordering their three kinds of soul. This fatherhood, therefore, does not refer to conception or generation but rather to education. The Demiurge adopts a very mixed-up child in whom he will instill a discipline to help him literally to "shape up," since he gives shape to the chaos of the Receptacle. This focus on the educational, long-term aspect of raising children broadens considerably his "craftsmanship." So it is no surprise that the organization of the precosmic chaos, the realm of the Errant Cause (so called because its behavior is totally erratic), will not only be a feat of craftsmanship—thanks to the introduction of measures and proportions—but also a form of education. The Demiurge will persuade Necessity (48c)—other name for the Errant Cause—which—or should I say who?—will *willingly* comply with such persuasion.

Since both the Universe and the Demiurge are not only respectively beautiful and good but even the most beautiful thing that ever became and the best of those responsible for any becoming, Timaeus concludes that the model that was used is that which is eternal and immutable, and therefore the Universe is only a likeness thereof. It follows that its account can only be likely (Plato cleverly puns on the terms 'likeness' and 'likely', ὄντος δὲ εἰκόνος εἰκότας ἀνὰ λόγον τε ἐκείνων ὄντας; 29c2). This implies that the principles laid down are true, as Vlastos contended, but that most of their applications, that is, what follows from them, are only likely.[11]

In this prelude and the main theme, terms used to refer to the Demiurge are words indicating human activity and responsibility. The term *aitios* (αἴτιος), which is used to introduce the Demiurge, applies to a person or moral agent responsible for some act. Timaeus then without further ado substitutes "craftsman" for it and, later on, as we saw, the terms "maker" and "father." The moral connotations of some of these terms and of all the Demiurge's actions are of prime importance. In 42d the Demiurge, in order not to be responsible (ἀναίτιος; 42d4) in any way for the evil human beings will commit, addresses their reason before their incarnation into a body and their being joined to the two lower kinds of soul. His address offers them norms of behavior and warns them of rewards and punishments. To escape moral responsibility for evil the Demiurge must not only provide sound moral education but also entrust to his own "children," that is, the secondary gods, the responsibility of fabricating the mortal and lower parts of the soul as well as the body since the spirit and desire along with bodily makeup not only may overpower reason but in fact necessarily oppose it. At the very end of the text Timaeus picks up that theme in claiming that if children have become evil the responsibility rests (αἰτιατέον; 87b) more on their progenitors and educators than on the children themselves since no one is willingly evil. So the term *aitios* (masculine singular) used to introduce the Demiurge rather than the neuter *aition* is significant. Michael Frede holds that in the *Phaedo* Plato carefully distinguishes *aitios*, which refers to a moral agent, from *aitia*, the abstract noun referring to

11. Gregory Vlastos, "Creation in the *Timaeus:* Is It a Fiction," in *Studies in Plato's Metaphysics*, ed. R. E. Allen (London: Routledge & Kegan Paul, 1965), pp. 401–19. (Article originally published in 1964.)

what accounts for the action or event and the agent's motivation in particular.[12] The *Timaeus* follows suit, as the transition from the prelude to the main theme shows.

Since the prelude concludes that the model the Demiurge used is that which always is, one expects the main theme to open with a consideration of this model. Yet it begins with a determination of the motivation (*aitian;* 29d7) that incited the Demiurge to organize the universe. The Demiurge "was good; and in the good no jealousy in any matter can ever arise [ἀλαθὸς ἦν, ἀλαθῷ δὲ οὐδεὶς περὶ οὐδενὸς οὐδέποτε ἐγγίγνεται φθόνος; 29e1–2]. So, being without jealousy, he desired that all things should come as near as possible to being like himself." The focus here is on motivation, and the model has shifted from that which always is to the Demiurge himself. In fact contemplation of the Forms is far from being the starting point of the Demiurge's actions. His desire that all things be like himself, and therefore good, is called the overarching principle of Becoming and of the Universe. So the Demiurge takes over all that is visible and moves discordantly (πλημμελῶς [30a4], linked to harmony and the importance of the sense of hearing) and disorderly (ἀτάκτως; 30a5), and brings it from disorder to order not by considering the model but rather because he thinks that order is in every way better.

Besides, since the best agent can only do what is best, the Demiurge takes thought (λογισάμενος; 30b1) and discovers (ηὕρισκεν [30b1], as if he had never known this) that a whole (the universe is often called τὸ πᾶν, the whole, and so cannot have errant, wandering, or roaming parts) with reason (*nous;* 30b4) is a better product than one without it and that reason cannot happen to anything that does not have a soul.

The Demiurge may be the best agent, but like anyone else he needs to think things through before acting and to reason carefully before determining what will lead to the best result. He must exercise forethought (πρόνοια; 30c1), just like the secondary gods who are in charge of constituting the mortal kinds of soul and earthly bodies (44c7) do. Human beings, too, need to exercise forethought (45b1), and for this reason they were given specific organs: the eyes by means of which they can observe the heavenly revolutions and may discover numbers, and the ears by means of which they may discover harmonic proportions.

The Demiurge's forethought and reasoning determine him to frame the Universe in fitting reason within soul and soul within body. In accord

12. Michael Frede, "The Original Notion of Cause," in *Doubt and Dogmatism: Studies in Hellenistic Epistemology,* ed. Malcolm Schofield, Myles Burnyeat, and Jonathan Barnes (Oxford: Clarendon Press, 1980), pp. 222–23.

with this decision, the Demiurge finally picks out a model, the intelligible living being that encompasses all kinds of living beings.[13] He will first imitate its uniqueness (μόνωσις; 31b1) and oneness.[14] Yet the determination of the means necessary to reach this second goal will not be based on a contemplation of this Form, but rather on mathematical considerations. The Soul of the Universe will be constituted according to harmonic, geometric, and arithmetic proportions. As for its body, its unity will be ensured by inserting the best bond, that is, a geometric proportion, between the necessary two extremes, earth which provides for its being a solid and fire which provides for its visibility. So between fire and earth there will be two means, air and water. These are the four so-called primary bodies whose ultimate constitution will be explained later on.[15] This bond will offer so much agreement and friendship that the Universe's body will be indissoluble, save by the one who bound it together, the Demiurge himself.

Then the soul/reason is fitted to the body suffusing it. When the Demiurge sees the Universe set in motion and alive, (recall that Socrates wanted to see the perfect city in motion and alive), he admires it and delights in it (εὐφρανθεὶς; 37c7), that is, he is moved by the emotion of εὐφροσύνη or delight which in 80b is carefully distinguished from pleasure (ἡδονή), the strongest lure to evil (69d). Being so moved, this father (πατήρ; 37c7) again takes thought to make it yet more like its model, the intelligible living being, by imitating its everlastingness in producing time measures, that is, regular celestial motions, as well as its "all-encompassingness" in providing the four kinds of living beings since this Form too is a whole encompassing parts.

Just like a human being, once the Demiurge is pleased with his own realization he decides to upgrade it. He too proceeds by stages and does not seem able to design at once the perfect product that can no longer be improved. Surprisingly, contemplation and observation of the product rather than of the model provides the incentive for the next stage. The Demiurge needs to tinker to reach his final goal.

He will persuade Necessity in providing the proper basic constituents for the so-called primary bodies, two types of elementary triangles that will give rise to the surfaces of the four regular solids that can be inscribed

13. See Richard D. Parry, "The Intelligible World-Animal in Plato's *Timaeus*," *Journal of the History of Philosophy* 29 (1991): 13–32.

14. See Richard D. Parry, "The Unique World of the *Timaeus*," *Journal of the History of Philosophy* 17 (1979): 1–10.

15. On this topic, see Gregory Vlastos, *Plato's Universe* (Seattle: University of Washington Press, 1975), pp. 66–97, and Thérèse-Anne Druart, "La stoicheïologie de Platon," *Revue philosophique de Louvain* 73 (1975): 243–62.

in a sphere (the fifth one gets equated somehow with the whole, that is, the sphere itself since the Universe is spherical), each one of them being matched with one of the so-called primary bodies. For each its shape and the number of triangles determine its basic properties and the possibilities of interaction. All these in turn will determine the particular constitution of all compound bodies be they animate or inanimate and the types of interactions they can have with other bodies as well as their manner of affecting the human soul.

The order of narration presents the construction of these so-called primary bodies out of their basic constituents as the last step in the Demiurge's action, but we are told that in fact it was his very first *diakosmesis* (69b-c) and the first step on the way to putting the Universe together. The narrative order roughly matches the Demiurge's order of reasoning from end to means. Since the Universe must have reason, it needs a soul that itself requires a body. Such a body is made out of the so-called four primary bodies that themselves are constituted by means of two basic constituents. The order of realization is, of course, exactly the reverse, as one would expect for any well-thought-through complex human action.

The least one can say is that contemplation of the Forms or of the model is not the Demiurge's sole activity or even the main guidance for his actions. The official model does not play the anticipated major role for the Demiurgic activity and the imitators of this activity will not even bother looking at it. The secondary gods imitate the Demiurge's own demiurgy as well as obey his instructions. As for the human beings, Timaeus offers them as a model his own poem whose hero is the Demiurge. What the *Timaeus* asks us to look at is the heavenly revolutions in order that we discover the mathematical and harmonic proportions underlying them and so become able to transfer and apply them for the governance of the circuits of our own reason since our reason is a close image of the Soul of the Universe. This explains why the end of the text describes the various stages down the scale of reincarnations as determined by the degree of inability to contemplate the heavens or its superficiality, which does not allow the human being to discover numbers, which are the condition for access to true philosophy and morality.[16] What Forms are to the Demiurge the heavens are to human beings, at least to those who are not yet ready for dialectic. Therefore, it is no accident that one of the most important properties of the Form of

16. Joan Kung cleverly argued for the necessary connection between mathematics and virtue in "Tetrahedra, Motion, and Virtue," and also in "Plato on Mind and Morality in Nature," *University of Dayton Review* 16 (1982–1983): 57–65.

the Intelligible Living Being, its all-encompassingness, is also exhibited in the Demiurge as model for action. Brisson has pointed out that in the *Timaeus* Plato uses the language of numerous and varied crafts to describe the activities of the Demiurge. The perfect Craftsman encompasses all aspects of "craftsmanship" including technical and educative skills.[17]

The first two sections of Timaeus's speech end with the statement that we need to distinguish between two kinds of causes, the necessary or mechanical, and the divine. "The divine," which is rational causation as exemplified in the Demiurge, "we should search out in all things for the sake of a life of such happiness as our nature admits; the necessary for the sake of the divine," reasoning (λογιζόμενον; 69a2) that "apart from the necessary" we cannot study the divine (68e6–69a5). We can only grasp the divine through the necessary, that is, through a study of the Universe. This study leads to the discovery of measures and proportions which are the gateway to philosophy (see also 47b), since as 87c tells us "the good is always beautiful, and the beautiful never" lacks proportion. Establishing proportions in the Universe as well as in our souls cures all evils and is true virtue.

This section manifests some kind of ambiguity about the model. Only that which always is is called a paradigm or official model but it shares with the Demiurge the title of father (that which always is is compared to a father in 50d). This is not surprising since the official model's role in the demiurgic activity is rather limited. The Demiurge is the real hero and he provides an "unofficial" but powerful model for every type of human activity, and education in particular. After all, the Demiurge reserved for himself the responsibility of fabricating human reason and providing reason with moral guidelines in a prenatal speech, but he entrusted to the secondary gods the task of fabricating humans' mortal souls and bodies. His motivation, manner of deliberation, and realization of his project are very akin to those of ordinary but rational human beings who seriously pursue the good. The Demiurge by introducing regularity can persuade Necessity or the Errant Cause along with its erratic behavior, in order to transform it into secondary and helping causes which are allies (συναιτίων) and servants (ὑπηρετοῦσιν; 46c–d) and provide the means to bring about not only the best possible Universe but also the best for each being. The Demiurge's "humanness" is highlighted by the fact that he is far from omnipotent and cannot completely overcome the resistance Necessity itself cannot help but offer.

17. Brisson, *Le même et l'autre,* pp. 35–54.

III. HUMAN BEINGS' SORRY STATE AND THEIR SALVATION THROUGH DEMIURGIC IMITATION

The Demiurge's basic task was to overcome the erratic behavior of the Errant Cause, source of the precosmic chaos. When the Demiurge persuaded Necessity to accept willingly the ordering and harmonizing process, and this as far as it could, he transformed the roaming and uncoordinated motions of and in the Receptacle into allies, that is, means at the service of his own end. Timaeus's account shows the Demiurge as organizing an external chaos. Yet such an account did not satisfy Cornford, who did not know what to do with a Demiurge dangling as a bad modifier in the ontological scheme, and who therefore simply wiped out the problem in conflating the Demiurge with the Universe's reason and in introducing in the Receptacle an irrational soul foreign to the text.[18] Vlastos put paid to this ingenious interpretation,[19] but Cornford's view is interesting because it highlights the parallel between the cosmic demiurgic action of ordering the Errant Cause and the human beings' task of allowing their reason to organize the microcosm of their own person, comprising body and both the immortal and mortal kinds of soul. Their reason must put order in the chaos originated at birth by the excessive and erratic bodily and psychic activities induced by frequent and lengthy feedings and the intrusion of numerous sensory objects. Most sensations, at least those preceded by pain, be it perceived or not, and therefore causing or arising from unnatural bodily conditions, are always presented as a kind of violence or assault violating the inner bodily motions, which in turn upset the inner motions of the three kinds of soul.

Infants are in a sorry state since everything concurs to upset not only the regular orderly motions of the circles of their reason designed on the pattern of the circuits of the Universe but even their very shape since they are buffeted from both inside and outside, just as the auxiliaries of a city badly in need of reform are compelled to put an end to civil war as well as external attacks. For the infants, the innermost enemy are the excesses of the two mortal kinds of soul, the next enemy the bodily erratic motions caused by diseases,[20] and the outer enemy violation of bodily and psychic motions resulting from sensation and bad education.

18. Cornford, *Plato's Cosmology*, pp. 197–210.

19. Gregory Vlastos, "The Disorderly Motion in the *Timaeus*," in *Studies in Plato's Metaphysics*, ed. R. E. Allen (London: Routledge, 1965), pp. 379–99 (originally published in 1939) and "Creation in the *Timaeus*" (originally published in 1964).

20. On the constitution of the body, its diseases, its relation to the various kinds of soul, as well as both bodily and spiritual medicine in the *Timaeus*, see Catherine Joubaud, *Le corps humain dans la philosophie platonicienne: Etude à partir du "Timée,"* with Introduction by Luc Brisson (Paris: J. Vrin, 1991).

The external influences compound the inner problems. From birth human beings are in a state of perpetual confusion and war. The end of the *Timaeus* provides remedies for this civil and external warfare that afflicts human beings against their will since no one willingly is evil. Those who are evil *become* so unwillingly (86e) because of a poor habit or condition of the body (ἕξιν) and because of an "uneducational" upbringing (ἀπαίδευτον), and these are enemies that attack every human being against his will.

The gentle remedy for the poor habit of the body is proper diet and exercise, both of which regulate the erratic inner motions by inner persuasion. Drugs on the contrary are violent remedies and therefore dangerous and should be reserved for imminent and unavoidable perils since they upset the normal course of diseases. Timaeus does not hesitate to call upbringing (παιδαγωγεῖν; 89c7–8) the treatment by proper diet and exercises.

As for poor education, it results from bad discourses (*logoi*)[21], be they private or public (87b1–2), which presumably instill false moral beliefs, and from bad government (πολιτεῖαι). This is another form of disease of the soul or *anoia* (ἄνοια), lack of control by reason. There are two kinds of lack of control by reason. One is madness (μανία) caused by "roaming" affections of the soul originating in its mortal parts, and the other is ignorance (ἀμαθία; 86b3–4).

When left to their own devices, the mortal parts of the soul suffer necessary but dangerous affections since they are erratic (88c4), and therefore misleading. The first of them is "pleasure, the strongest lure to evil; next, pains that take flight from good; temerity, moreover, and fear, a pair of [senseless] counselors; passion [θυμός] hard to [convince], and hope too easily led astray." These are "combined with irrational" sensations and desires (69c8–d6). Besides, when corruption affects bodily humors, these in turn attack the various kinds of soul and produce "ill temper and despondency" (δυσκολίας καὶ δυσθυμίας) in the appetites, "rashness and cowardice" in the *"thumos,"* and, finally, both forgetfulness (λήθης) and learning disabilities (δυσμαθίας) in reason (86e5–87a7). All the *"dus"* (δυς) prefixes emphasize the difficulties that result from these illnesses.

The secondary gods who wanted to kill two birds with one stone have designed hearing and sight for a double purpose. The main one aims at reason's control and forethought and provides sight and hearing for

21. Johannes M. Van Ophuijsen, who was kind enough to comment on an early version of this essay, made the very interesting suggestion that *"logoi"* here may mean both false discourses and bad proportions.

discovering the heavenly regular motions and their harmonious proportions necessary for the acquisition of virtue. The other ensures pleasure in beautiful sights and sounds as a means of survival. This double purpose confuses human beings, who find it easier to focus on the pleasure of beautiful sights than on the hard task of discovering the numbers embodied in the heavenly revolutions—even though they should imitate their proportions (47b) to regulate the circuits of their own rational soul. They also naturally prefer to pursue the irrational pleasure of beautiful sounds to the study of their harmonic proportions. Yet, if human beings could focus on their main purpose, these senses would no longer be misleading and the source of inner erratic, violent, and unnatural motions but rather would become peaceful allies (σύμμαχος) and auxiliaries (ἐπίκουρος) "against . . . inward discord" (47d and 80b).

Proper education can cure the soul from its most serious disease, ignorance (88b), and therefore offers to human beings the chance to rid themselves of moral evil. Though no one willingly becomes evil, one must earnestly desire (προθυμητέον; 87b) as much as possible to flee moral badness by education (διὰ τροφῆς) as well as activities and studies. Proper moral education will gently cure ignorance in persuading the soul to take proper care of itself, and therefore provide the learning necessary to overcome bodily problems, which affect the proper functioning of the soul, and to ensure reason's control over the lower and mortal parts of the soul which from being enemies will become allies. This will be an epic battle worthy of Athens's own defense against Atlantis. Reason being our guardian genius (δαίμονα), if we keep it in control and well organized (εὖ κεκοσμημένον), then we will be most happy (εὐδαίμονα); an atrocious pun Plato could not resist [90c4–6]). Before worrying about Athens's glory we need to worry about our own soul and the war it must wage to restore its natural and original state as the Demiurge's goodness designed it.

The *Timaeus*, therefore, presents a self-help manual for the budding philosophers who have just realized the sorry state of their own soul and body, eroded and besieged as they are by erratic motions and roaming affections resulting from the roaming Sophists' bad education and from a bad civil constitution such as the one current in Athens. For them a tale will be more helpful than a dialogue. It gives them the elementary teaching necessary to free themselves from ignorance and to treat their various diseases, be they bodily or psychic. The Demiurge will be their model and hero who provides for them the ability to discover the curative harmonic, geometric, and arithmetic proportions exhibited by the heavenly revolutions which they should implant in their own soul and body by means of gentle remedies or persuasion and even when necessary by force. The "Thumos" in particular so typical of the auxiliaries must listen to reason and join with it in restraining by force the desires, when these should not willingly let themselves be persuaded (70a). Then, having developed healthy souls and bodies, they will no longer be at the level of mere craftsmen in the ordinary sense of the word but will be promoted and become auxiliaries and educators. They may even rise still further and turn to dialectic and philosophy proper which require both virtue and the contemplation of the Forms, and therefore an understanding of the ontological and epistemological issues raised by the Eleatic Stranger in the *Sophist* and the *Statesman* but left aside by the *Timaeus*.

8 Forms and Predication in the Later Dialogues

ANNE M. WILES

To a readership acquainted with the *philosophia perennis*, one cannot expect to say anything really new about the essential components of Plato's thought. What follows is intended in part as an aid to recollection of certain central theses of the theory of Forms and of the role of predication in the discovery and articulation of truth. One of the interesting results of considering Plato's later comments on predication in light of his views concerning the forms is that his account of predication, allowing for differences in style and terminology, turns out to be not very different from that of Aristotle, and shows that the Renaissance contrast, immortalized by Raphael, between the "rationalist" Plato and the "empiricist" Aristotle is perhaps too sharply drawn.

The essay is divided into three parts. In section 1, I discuss two approaches to the interpretation of Plato, and set out the principles of interpretation that I follow here. In section 2, I give a brief synopsis of the theory of Forms. In section 3, I discuss Plato's account of predication in the *Parmenides* and the *Sophist*.

1. APPROACHES TO INTERPRETATION

Twentieth-century discussions of Plato's metaphysics, especially in Anglo-American academic circles, have been permeated by two general, and interrelated, issues. The first is the philosophical issue of whether the theory of Forms is true, false, or simply irrelevant. The second is the historical issue of whether Plato ever abandoned or drastically modified the theory of Forms. Writing in 1954, in an article that both spurred and, to a large extent, set the terms of the ensuing debate, Gregory Vlastos noted, "Hardly a text in Plato has been discussed as much in the last 40 years as the two passages in the *Parmenides* purporting to prove that the theory of forms involves an infinite regress."[1]

The general approach under which the work of Vlastos falls is characterized by meticulous attention to the internal structure of the dialogues, careful analyses of the arguments, and philological considerations. For ease of reference, this may be called *the analytic approach* to Plato's metaphysics.

The analytic approach is not monolithic, but generally those who work in this tradition, insofar as they recognize the systematic nature of Plato's work, tend toward a genetic-historical interpretation of the theory of Forms. They assume, for example, that the "separable" Forms are not present in the early dialogues, and that the theory of Forms in the middle dialogues is quite distinct from the "later" theory, somewhat on the model that one speaks of an "earlier" and "later" Wittgenstein. This assumption is sometimes coupled with the claim that Plato abandoned "earlier" versions of the theory because he came to recognize that they were logically flawed. The so-called flaws usually mentioned are those against which the criticisms in the first part of the *Parmenides* are directed. The inherent danger of the analytic approach is that the very narrowing of the focus that gives sharpness and clarity to the arguments at the same time may blur the connections between the individual arguments and the wider context of Plato's thought. Yet, it is this wider context, containing myth, irony, and indirection, that provides the resonance needed for a full understanding of the individual argument.

In the last two decades there has been developing on the continent a different approach to Plato's metaphysics which, for ease of reference, may be called *the synoptic approach.* This approach is represented in the Platonic school of Tübigen by H.-J. Krämer and Konrad Gaiser, and in Milan by Giovanni Reale. Reale, who has carried this work to a full expression in his book *Per una nuova interpretazione di Platone*,[2] began his scholarly work with Aristotle. He describes his work as beginning with that of the disciple to reach that of the master.[3] He finds a much closer connection between the metaphysics of Plato and that of Aristotle than is usually recognized: "Aristotle, read without preconceptions is, in the essential nucleus of his thought, not the antithesis, but the truthfulness, of Plato."[4]

1. Gregory Vlastos, "The Third Man Argument in the *Parmenides*," *Philosophical Review* (1954); reprinted in *Studies in Plato's Metaphysics*, ed. R. E. Allen (London: Routledge and Kegan Paul, 1965), p. 231.

2. Giovanni Reale, *Per una nuova interpretazione di Platone*, 10th ed. (Milan: Universita Cattolica del Sacro Cuore, 1991).

3. Giovanni Reale, *A History of Ancient Philosophy: Plato and Aristotle*, ed. and trans. John R. Catan (Albany: State University of New York Press, 1990), p. xix.

4. Ibid., p. xvi.

The synoptic approach to Plato's metaphysics is based on a model developed primarily by the collaborative efforts of Krämer, Gaiser, and Reale.[5] The basic hermeneutic principle of this model is its denial of the autonomy of the Platonic writings. It takes seriously Plato's claim in the *Phaedrus*[6] that writing, compared to oral discourse, is deficient, and his testimony in the *Seventh Letter*[7] that his thoughts about the primary and supreme principles of reality are not contained in his writing. It insists that Plato the writer is quite distinct from Plato the thinker, and argues that "Plato, when he composed the dialogues, moved in a conceptual area of interest much wider than his piecemeal writings of them."[8]

This model provides reason to doubt both the genetic-historical assumption that the theory of Forms underwent a development in the dialogues and the assumption that Plato's metaphysics can be recovered solely from the explicit arguments found within the dialogues.

Another principle of the synoptic model is that since Plato is writing dialogues, not essays, and the dialogue is primarily a literary construction designed merely to "remind" one of what can only be adequately discovered in oral dialectic,[9] there will be different levels of doctrinal treatment in various dialogues. These will be adapted both to what is to be achieved and to which historical persons are included in the dialogue, so it is not possible to assume from the absence of any doctrine in a given dialogue that Plato has "abandoned" the doctrine.

A third principle is that myth and metaphor in the dialogues must be taken quite seriously. Reale argues that myth, as Plato uses it, is essentially different from prephilosophical myth. Plato's use of myth "does not subordinate the logos to itself, but tries to stimulate logos and fecundate it. . . . [I]t is a myth that, in a certain sense, enriches logos."[10] The relationship between myth and logos is complicated, but Reale captures the essence of the relationship in his claim that for Plato, "to speak through

5. Reale (*A History of Ancient Philosophy*, p. 395) mentions the following writings of Krämer and Gaiser as instrumental in developing the new interpretation: H.-J. Krämer, *Arete bei Platon und Aristoteles: Zum Wesen und zur Geschichte der platonischen Ontologie* (Heidelberg, 1959; reprint, Amsterdam, 1967); Konrad Gaiser, *Platons Ungeschriebene Lehre: Studien zur systematischen und geschichtlichen. Begründung der Wissenschaften in der Platonischen Schule. With the addition of Testimonia Platonica. Quellentexte zur schule und mündlichen Lehre Platons* (Stuttgart, 1963, 1968); H. Krämer, *Platone e i fondamenti della metafisica: Saggio sulla teoria dei principi e sulle dottrine non scritte di Platone con una raccolta dei documenti fondamentali in edizione bilingue e bibliografia. Introduzione e traduzione di G. Reale* (Milan, 1982, 1989) [Published by State University of New York Press with the title *Plato and the Foundations of Metaphysics* (Albany, 1990)]; and K. Gaiser, *Platone come scrittore filosofico: Saggio sull'ermeneutica dei dialoghi platonici* (Naples, 1984).

6. *Phaedrus* 274b–75e.

7. *Seventh Letter* 340b–45c.

8. Reale, *History of Ancient Philosophy*, p. 29.

9. This point is made in the *Phaedrus* 275c–d.

10. Reale, *History of Ancient Philosophy*, p. 31.

myth (μυθολογεῖν) is to express oneself through images, that at various levels remain valid, insofar as we think, besides through concepts, also through images."[11]

The fourth principle is that in interpreting the dialogues, one must be sensitive to irony. In the early dialogues there is both situational and verbal irony in the character of Socrates, but in the later dialogues, such as the *Parmenides*, the irony is more subtle and therefore more difficult to detect.

The fifth and final interpretative principle is that since there are several essential components of Plato's thought, including the metaphysical-epistemological, the mystical-religious, and the ethical, political, and educative themes, an adequate interpretation must do justice to all these dimensions in their complex interrelationships.[12]

The synoptic approach thus provides a wider and richer context for the consideration of the theory of Forms and predication in the later dialogues. It allows what is said in one dialogue to supplement and shed light on what is said in another, and it permits the assumption that Plato could have worked out the main lines of the theory of Forms before he wrote even the first dialogue.

II. SYNOPSIS OF THE THEORY OF FORMS

If the term 'system' is not taken too narrowly, it is evident that Plato has a systematic philosophy of which the theory of Forms is the lynchpin. The central theses that unify the dialogues are: (1) that intelligible objects are ontologically and epistemologically distinct from sensible objects; (2) that knowledge is distinct from belief; (3) that the soul is improved by knowledge and destroyed by ignorance; (4) that intellect guides and directs all; (5) that good intelligence directs well, and bad intelligence does so poorly; and (6) that the human intellect is both cognitive and conative, from which arises the necessity for both dialectic and rhetoric.

To provide a framework for discussion of Plato's account of predication, a brief reminder of the essential characteristics of the Forms and some of their more important attributes will suffice. Plato uses the terms 'Form' (εἶδος) and 'Idea' (ἰδέα) interchangeably. In this essay, I generally use the word 'Form' for either expression, and sometimes also for 'kind' or 'class' in the *Sophist*. Forms are intelligible, incorporeal, and unchangeable in essence; each Form is objective, single, and self-identical.

11. Ibid., p. 32.
12. Ibid., p. 33.

These essential characteristics are mentioned throughout the dialogues, even in the late ones, and are presupposed in the definitions sought in the early dialogues. Forms are contrasted with particular things, which are sensible, corporeal, and subject to generation and corruption. Forms are "present in" particulars; particulars "participate" in Forms.

The Forms are both transcendent and immanent. They function as standards in two ways: first, they provide the basis on which a particular may be classified as a kind or type; second, they are prescriptive standards for the embodiment of a Form in particulars. As prescriptive standards, they are essential for the activity of the philosopher-king, or for ordinary mortals, who try to bring about justice in a historical state, and for the Demiurgos who *looks to,* but does not *create,* the transcendent Forms in order to create the cosmos.

While it is true that the "separation" of the Forms is discussed in the *Phaedo,* exactly what the separation amounts to is much debated.[13] The reference to "separate" existence is explicit in the *Phaedo* (103b), the *Republic* (501b), the *Philebus* (15a–b), and the *Timaeus* (51d–52c). None of the passages in which separation is mentioned commits Plato to the view that the Ideas are eternal sensibles since he consistently maintains throughout the dialogues, even in the *Phaedo,* that the Ideas are intelligible; neither does it commit him to the view that the Ideas are eternal if "eternal" is understood as a never-ending duration since the Forms are not subject to generation and corruption.

At *Republic* 506, Socrates states the general principle that there is a single Form or Real Essence for each set of things called by the same name, with the restriction that the name must indicate a real class and not merely a part. On this basis, the following classification may be made of the Forms discussed in the dialogues: Forms or kinds of very wide application, such as Sameness, Difference, Existence, Motion, Rest, One, and Many, identified in the *Sophist* and the *Parmenides*; moral Forms such as Courage, Temperance, Justice, Piety, and Friendship; mathematical Forms such as Circle, Triangle, Equal, Odd and Even; Forms of nonmoral qualities such as Quickness and Tallness; Forms of arts such as Medicine,

13. At *Metaphysics* 1086b2 Aristotle says of "those who believe in the Ideas," that "they at the same time make the ideas universal and again treat them as separable and as individuals." Cherniss points out that although Aristotle is correct in his claim that Plato (in some way) separated the Forms from particulars, he is mistaken about the consequences of that separation. Of Aristotle's criticism he says: "It is obvious that he tends to press upon it the grossest possible interpretation as when he insists that the ideas are merely 'eternal sensibles' (*Metaphysics* 997b12) or when he argues that the ideas must be spatial if there is 'participation' of them (*Physics* 209b33–35), even though he is well aware that Plato did not believe the separate existence of the ideas to be existence in time and place (*Physics* 203a8–9)."

Rhetoric, and Education; and Forms of artifacts and physical things such as shuttle, bed, clay, and finger.[14]

Two Forms, the Good and the Beautiful, do not fit into this classification. In the *Republic*, Plato says that the form, Good, exceeds all other forms in beauty and power. This might lead one to think that the Form of the Good is God, an assumption that is understandable but totally inconsistent with the role that the Good plays in Plato's theory of Forms. For Plato, neither the Good nor any other Form is an efficient cause.

Instead of being a genus of which all other ideas are species, the Idea of the Good really is a species under the genus Idea. It shares with other Ideas the essential characteristics of being, unity, stability, and intelligibility, while at the same time having a distinctive function that closely associates it with the Idea of the Beautiful. At *Republic* 508E–9a, the Form of the Good is explicitly distinguished from other objects of knowledge:

> This, then, which gives to the objects of knowledge their truth and to him who knows them his power of knowing, is the Form or essential nature of Goodness. It is the cause of knowledge and truth; and so, while you may think of it as an object of knowledge, you will do well to regard it as something beyond truth and knowledge and, precious as these both are, of still higher worth.

Every Form marks some natural division of reality; so too, does the Good, but the Good is also connected with every Form as a kind of regulative principle. If we know the good of something, we know its function, nature, or essential structure. Nettleship, in *Lectures on "The Republic,"* states the point succinctly: "The good or end of any thing is the immanent principle which we have to suppose in it in order to explain it, and which is involved in calling it a whole at all."[15]

The Idea of the Good is an ontological good that does not necessarily correspond with the moral or personal good for anyone. The ontological good is that which, as formal cause, makes a thing "that which it is and not another thing." Every Idea is good in the sense that every Idea is definite, limited, structured, and therefore intelligible. Though it be a privation, even the Idea of Evil partakes of the Good because each kind of evil, as Dante has so clearly shown, has its own essential structure—for example, Greed is essentially different from Gluttony. To know the ontological good of anything is simply to know the thing in its tendencies.

14. This list differs from that given by Anders Wedberg, in *Plato's Philosophy of Mathematics* (Stockholm: Almquist and Wiksell, 1955), pp. 32–33, in that his list does not include forms of nonmoral qualities and forms of arts. Also, Wedberg lists the ideas of Good, Just, and Beautiful under a classification titled "Ethical and Esthetical Ideas."

15. Richard Lewis Nettleship, *Lectures on the "Republic" of Plato* (London: Macmillan, 1961), pp. 222–23.

The Beautiful has a regulative function similar to that of the Good. In the *Greater Hippias* (290d–91b) Socrates says that a ladle made of fig-wood is more beautiful in a pot of soup than one made of gold, because the wooden ladle is more appropriate for dipping soup. The clear implication is that beauty follows function; thus the Beautiful is necessarily connected with the Good.

Throughout the dialogues, knowledge of the Forms is, for Plato, the sine qua non of any other type of knowledge. Knowledge of the Forms may be attained by various methods—definition, hypothetical reasoning, argument by analogy and example, division by genus and species—underlying all of which is the double process of collection and division, described by Socrates in the *Phaedrus*:

> The first [procedure] is that in which we bring a dispersed plurality under a single form, seeing it all together: the purpose being to define so-and-so, and thus to make plain whatever may be chosen as the topic for exposition . . . [the second procedure is] the reverse of the other, whereby we are enabled to divide into forms, following the objective articulation [i.e., dividing reality at the "natural joints" and not hacking off parts like a clumsy butcher]. (265d)

Socrates says, "I am myself a lover of these divisions and collections, that I may gain the power to speak and to think."

III. PREDICATION

Predication is a central issue in both the *Parmenides* and the *Sophist*. In the following account I will use the term 'predication' to refer to any combination of predicate term and subject term that makes a statement. It encompasses what in the contemporary literature is referred to as the 'is,' of identity, the 'is' of predication, and the existential 'is,' as well as real definition; it also includes what Plato refers to as 'participation' and what he describes in the *Sophist* as the "communion" or "weaving together" of kinds.

Participation as Predication

Plato uses several expressions for the relationship of participation. In the early dialogues, he speaks of particulars "having" certain qualities, or of qualities being "present in" particular things. In the *Symposium* (211b), the multitude of beautiful things are said to "partake" of absolute Beauty. In the *Phaedo* (74d), a particular equal is said to be an inferior *copy* of the Form Equality. From the earliest dialogues, Plato argues that there are good reasons for distinguishing common natures from particulars, yet even in the dialogues in which he is said to have "separated" the Forms from particulars, he consistently maintains that there is a strong connection between common natures and particulars that have the same name. Plato holds that the exact description of this relation is less important than the realization that it is because of the Forms that particular things are what they are.[16] This "because" is the cause we have been taught by Aristotle to call the formal cause.

In the *Parmenides* and thereafter, the connection between particular things and Forms is treated as nothing spectacular. In the *Sophist,* the Eleatic Stranger makes fun of those "late learners" who deny that one particular thing can be many, and "delight in forbidding us to speak of a man as 'good'; and say we must only speak of a good as good, and of the man as man."[17]

The short response to the late learners is that predication does not imply *identity* of subject and predicate, although it *may* do so:

> [W]hen we speak of a man we give him many additional names; we attribute to him colors and shapes and sizes and defects and good qualities; and in all these and countless other statements we say he is not merely a "man" but also "good" and any number of other things. And so with everything else; we take any given thing as one and yet speak of it as many and by many names. (*Sophist* 251b)

Although Plato does not here give a complete classification of the different ways a man can be or, linguistically, all the different things that can be said of one, Plato's statement shows he is aware of the distinctions that underlie Aristotle's ten categories, or possible predicates. This passage from the *Sophist* introduces Plato's discussion of the combination of Forms and clearly indicates that a *Form,* being also a one, may also be spoken of as many and by many names.

A passage in the *Lysis* suggests that even in the early dialogues Plato is already distinguishing different kinds of predicates. In this passage, Socrates discusses how whiteness could be said to be "present in" the now golden locks of Lysis. He mentions two possibilities. Lysis's hair could be dyed with white lead, or it could grow white with age. The color of the dyed hair would not differ *in color* from the naturally white hair, yet the *manner* in which the color is present in the hair, or the cause of its presence, is not the same in the two cases.[18] The distinction is easier to make in Aristotelian terminology: natural whiteness is a *property* of the hair when one grows old, but an *accident* of the hair if the color is set there by dye.

16. *Phaedo* 100c–101c.

17. *Sophist* 251c.

18. *Lysis* 217e. Plato stresses the point by asking Lysis: "If a thing be present in a substance, will the substance be such as that which is present with it, or will it be such, if the thing is present under certain conditions, under certain conditions not?"

Definition as Predication

In a real definition, the subject term is a Form and the predicate term is a combination of Forms. Such definitions are sought by Socrates even in the early dialogues, for example, in the *Euthyphro,* where he is attempting to define piety. In fact, since the dramatic setting of the *Parmenides* shows a young Socrates already accepting that there are Forms and being brought along by Parmenides and Zeno, it is reasonable to conclude that Socrates, early in his search for definitions, presupposed the existence of Forms.

Plato assumes that it is possible to give a real definition of *any* Form. Definitions are called for, however, only when the sense impressions arouse reflection. When someone utters the word "iron" or "silver," we all have the same object before our minds and no definition is called for, but of such things as justice, goodness, and love, which have no sensible image, it is difficult, yet important, to give a definition.[19]

Predication in the Parmenides *and the* Sophist

That Forms can be in a subject–predicate relation to each other is nothing new: this relation is presupposed in the attempt to construct adequate definitions. It is sometimes held that Plato did not discuss the combination of Forms in dialogues earlier than the *Sophist.* There are, however, two passages in the *Republic* that explicitly treat the topic. At *Republic* 476a Socrates says,

> in respect of the just and the unjust, the good and the bad, and all the ideas or forms, the same statement holds, that in itself each is one, but that by virtue of their communion with actions and bodies and with one another they present themselves everywhere, each as a multiplicity of aspects.

At *Republic* 511b the activity of the dialectician is described as

> making no use whatever of any object of sense but only of pure ideas moving on through ideas to ideas and ending with ideas,

a statement that certainly presupposes the connection of Ideas. The formal account of Justice in the *Republic* is, in fact, an extended exemplification of the claim that Forms do combine. Other examples of such predication are plentiful in the dialogues, for example, the theoretical account of friendship in the *Lysis,* of rhetoric in the *Phaedrus,* and of the good life in the *Philebus.*

19. *Phaedrus* 263a–c.

The *Parmenides* is a rich source for Plato's views on predication, yet the difficulty of interpreting this dialogue is such that one can well appreciate the comment of Richard Robinson on the concluding page of his book *Plato's Earlier Dialectic*: "The methodological aspect of the *Parmenides* thus seems to be, like its other aspects, bewildering, sceptical, and depressing."[20] Plato's use of irony is one factor that makes interpretation difficult. Plato thought the proper function of rhetoric is to make attractive what dialectic determines is true, and that one of the most effective rhetorical devices is irony. In the early dialogues, the irony is exhibited in the character of Socrates, in his pretense that he does not know or has forgotten some point, or in his denial that he is conducting an *elenchus*. The *Meno* ends with the strong suggestion that virtue cannot be acquired by teaching, and within the dialogue Socrates claims that he is not *teaching* Meno's slave geometry. Here the purpose of the verbal irony is to puzzle the reader so that the strangeness of these claims will provoke his thought. Someone who thinks through the puzzle and understands that in the *Meno* both "teaching" and "learning" are being used in two distinct senses learns something important about what virtue is and how one may become virtuous. Socrates frequently pretends to accept the ideas and methods of those whose views he opposes in order to expose their weaknesses. As the doctrinal content of the dialogues increases, the ironic tactic becomes more subtle, which makes the dialogues more difficult to interpret.[21]

The ironic play, particularly in the *Parmenides*, presupposes considerable skill in logic and dialectic. It is precisely because Plato knows the area so well that he is able to argue from within the positions in order to show their shortcomings and at the same time indirectly suggest various distinctions that need to be made. The *Parmenides* ends in an apparently inconclusive manner, but the conclusion is ironic since Plato within the dialogue has made a number of important points about the various senses in which something can be, or the possible kinds of predicates, which provides, in effect, elements of a systematic metaphysics.

While Cornford's commentary does not explain everything, it is consonant with what is known concerning Plato's use of irony in the earlier dialogues and with the view of Reale and the Tübingen School concerning the unwritten doctrine of Plato vis-à-vis the written dialogues; it takes into account the context in which Plato is writing and by using ancient

20. Richard Robinson, *Plato's Earlier Dialectic*, 2d ed. (Oxford: Clarendon Press, 1953), p. 280.

21. See Reale's discussion of this point, "The Problem of Irony and Its Function in Platonic Dialogues," in *A History of Ancient Philosophy*, pp. 24–26.

sources, including Aristotle, attempts to identify each view being discussed; and, finally, it assumes that there are to be found in Plato's writings, even in the *Parmenides* itself, indications of how the *Parmenides* is to be read. In the second half of the *Parmenides,* Parmenides is clearly tracing out the consequences of various positions concerning being, unity, sameness, and otherness. Although there are many hints given in the *Parmenides,* the positive, explicit account of how these Forms may be predicated of each other does not occur until the *Sophist.*

The technique illustrated by Parmenides is not quite the same as that of Zeno. Zeno constructed paradoxes against the critics of Parmenides, that is, on one side of the question only. The technique illustrated in the *Parmenides* of tracing out the consequences of what can be said on *both* sides of the question[22] is a technique more suited to the discovery of truth than to mere refutation. The two techniques also differ in purpose. In the *Parmenides,* Plato does not try to reduce the hypotheses to absurdity, but only indicates indirectly that predicates that appear contradictory are really compatible if careful distinctions are made between various aspects of being, unity, sameness, difference, motion, and rest.[23]

There are eight hypotheses in the second half of the *Parmenides.* In addition to the substantive claims about predication, there is a list of characters or predicates to be considered for each hypothesis. For each hypothesis considered, Plato goes through the same list of predicates.

For the first hypothesis, which assumes that nothing is real except the One, a series of predicates is considered, although no actual predication is possible. Predicates considered are whether the One has limit, extension, shape, place, motion, rest, sameness, and difference (like-unlike, and equal-unequal), and whether the One is in time. For the second hypothesis, which assumes an *existing* One, in addition to the predicates of unity, being, and plurality, if extension is added as a predicate, the One will also have shape, position, and the contrary predicates of being both at rest and in motion. The One will have various *relations* to itself and to others, including the relations of sameness/difference, like/unlike, in contact/not in contact, and equal/unequal. At 149d–51b the point made is that an extended thing will have the predicate of quantity, and will stand to other extended ones in a quantitative relation of being smaller than, greater than, or equal to each, and at 151e–55c that it will be in time and will stand in certain temporal relations to itself and others.

22. For an explicit formulation of this program, see Aristotle, *Topics* 1.2.101a.34–36.

23. For a discussion of the similarities and differences between the technique of Zeno and that of Parmenides, see F. M. Cornford, *Plato and Parmenides* (New York: Harcourt, Brace and Company, 1939), pp. 105–15. In the following discussion of the hypotheses in the *Parmenides,* I have relied heavily on Cornford's commentary.

In the remaining six hypotheses, which need not here be considered in detail, Plato uses the same list of predicates to trace out the consequences of each view. This list of possible predicates distinguishes various ways of being. In fact, it includes the same predicates given in Aristotle's *Categories*. This is interesting because it shows that Plato had already made the distinctions that Aristotle later systematized.

In the first hypothesis, which assumes that nothing is real except the One and denies the reality even of predicates attributable to the One, the consequence is that no knowledge of the One is possible; nothing can be said about it. *Indirectly*, Hypothesis 1 shows that although a Form may be described as "just by itself," this does not imply that a Form is completely and in every way isolated from all other Forms; if it were, one could not have knowledge of it. Moreover, Hypothesis 1 shows that nothing can be an object of knowledge *unless* the contraries, the One and the Many, are in some sense predicable of it.[24] A Form is *one* in essence, but is *many* in that many names may be predicated of it, for example, "being," "unity," "incorporeal," and so on.

In the first part of the *Parmenides*, Zeno suggested that a Form cannot have contrary predicates, and Socrates agreed that he would be "surprised" to find that it could. In the second half of the *Parmenides*, it is demonstrated that any One that has being *must* have some contrary attributes. However, this does not lead to a contradication so long as the aspects in which the terms are predicated are carefully distinguished.
One way to avoid ambiguity is to specify what the predicates mean, or under what conditions they may be applied. In the *Parmenides*, Plato offers several useful specifications. At 161e, being is said to be predicable of anything of which a true statement may be made. At 139e–40b, the terms 'like' and 'unlike' are defined with reference to predication. Two things are said to be 'like' when the same statement can be truly made about both, and 'unlike' when a statement true of one is not true of the other. At 146d, Parmenides says about difference,

> Now, all things which are "not One" must be different from the One, and the One also must be different from them.

This passage has been interpreted as applying both to numerical difference and conceptual difference. It anticipates the demonstration in the *Sophist* that 'is not' can mean merely 'is different from.' At 155e–56b, various kinds of change are distinguished, including becoming and perishing, locomotion, and alteration in quality and quantity.

Hypothesis 2 shows that if anything has being, it must necessarily have

24. Cornford, *Plato and Parmenides*, p. 134.

both Unity and Plurality, since "One and its being are different from each other" (143b). At 144b, the parts of being are said to be "not more numerous than those into which unity is distributed, but equal in number; for nothing that *is* lacks unity, and nothing that is *one* lacks being." This is essentially the same claim found in Aristotle's proof (*Met.* 1003b.22) that there are as many species of being as there are of unity.[25] The Forms are not mentioned in this hypothesis, but the attributes of being, unity, and plurality are predicable of anything that has being, and a fortiori are applicable to Forms.

The hypothesis bearing most directly on what can be said of the Forms is Hypothesis 5, in which Plato shows that a nonexistent entity may yet have being and can be distinguished from other nonexistent entities. A nonexistent entity has being since if anyone makes two statements such as 'smallness does not exist' and 'largeness does not exist', it is plain that he is speaking of two different things and can distinguish them from each other. This argument opposes the view attributed to the historical Parmenides that anything that *is not* is unknowable and cannot be thought, spoken of, or named,[26] but its importance goes beyond this. The argument shows that statements about what does not exist can nonetheless be meaningful; that something that does not exist can have being as the subject of a sentence; that such nonexistent entities can be known and distinguished from each other; and that nonexistent entities may have various other predicates: "this non-existent One has the characters of being 'that' and 'something,' and of being related '*to* this' or '*to* these,' and all other such characters."[27]

One of the most surprising, and important, points developed in Hypothesis 5 is that a nonexistent one can have the contrary predicates of being both at rest and in motion. This is surprising because one does not ordinarily think of nonphysical or nonexistent things as moving, probably because locomotion and the double process of generation and corruption are the most familiar sorts of motion. However, at 162b–c, after having argued that a nonexistent one has the *being* of nonexistence and the *nonbeing* of existence, Parmenides makes the following statement: "Now a thing which is in a certain condition can not-be in that condition only by passing out of it. So anything that both is, and is not, in

25. Ibid., p. 142.

26. Ibid., p. 220.

27. Cornford says of the passages 161e–62b, "Plato's demonstration here is very remarkable. In conjunction with the preceding sections it clearly distinguishes 'is' meaning 'exists' from the 'is' represented by Plato's (*metexei*), and asserts that any subject of a true statement containing this latter 'is' must have a sort of 'being', distinct from existence. Otherwise any statement of the form 'x does not exist' would be meaningless, being about nothing at all" (pp. 226–27).

such and such a condition implies transition; and transition is motion. . . . Therefore the non-existent One has been shown to be a thing that moves, since it admits transition from being to not-being."[28] Immediately following this passage, other kinds of motion—locomotion, alteration, or internal change of character—are all ruled out as possible kinds of motion for nonexistent entities, so the only kind of motion of which a nonexistent entity is capable is the transition from one condition to another.

Cornford interprets this transition as a movement from (the being of) nonexistence to (the nonbeing of) existence, claiming that since the other types of change have been denied of a nonexistent entity, this is the only possible type of motion left. There are two difficulties with Cornford's interpretation of this point. First, it is clear from the passage just quoted from the *Parmenides* that the sort of movement described is held to be possible for *any* nonexistent entity, and while *some* nonexistent entities could become existent—the friendship that one would like to exist comes to exist—other nonexistent entities, such as a round square, could not move from nonexistence to existence *simpliciter*. *If* a Form is a nonexistent entity, as Cornford says it is, his interpretation also presents difficulties for the theory of Forms, for if a Form per se were to move from nonexistence to existence, it would no longer be a Form.

The second point to be made against Cornford's interpretation is that there *is* another sort of movement from condition to condition that Plato does not rule out and this *is* a transition that would apply to *every* nonexistent entity, and that would not have these unfortunate consequences for the theory of Forms. In fact, it is a transition that will turn out to be necessary if knowledge of Forms is possible. Any nonexistent entity may move from not being the subject of a statement to being a subject, from not being distinguished from others to being distinguished from others, from not being known to being known. All these movements are transitions from one kind of nonbeing to the corresponding kind of being, and so fit Plato's description for transition from one condition to another.

In the *Sophist*, many of the distinctions developed in the *Parmenides* are presupposed, used, and sometimes explicitly mentioned; for instance, the distinction between the One and the Many developed in Hypothesis 5 is used extensively. The predicates (time, place, quantity, etc.) used in the second part of the *Parmenides* are also used in the *Sophist*. These predicates perform essentially the same function as the Categories of Aristotle, marking ways in which something can be, or kinds of being.

28. See Cornford, *Plato and Parmenides*, pp. 226–28, for a discussion of the difficulties in translating 162b–63b.

The really new point about predication introduced in the *Sophist* is that there are certain Forms, namely, Existence, Sameness, and Difference,[29] that do not mark divisions *within* being, but are predicable of each and every being, including themselves. This new element directs attention to the ontology and logic of the Forms; to delineate the connections and distinctions among the Forms at this level is to engage in metaphysics.

Some of the topics treated in the *Sophist* are less controversial now than in fifth and early-fourth-century B.C. Greece, for example, whether nonbeing can be said to exist.[30] Other metaphysical questions discussed in the *Sophist* are of continuing interest, among which may be mentioned the following: Of what may the term 'real' be appropriately predicated? Which Forms are predicable of which others? What is the philosophical importance of predication?

The first question is discussed in the context of a battle between the giants who think only physical things are real and the gods who think only Forms are real. At 247e, the Eleatic Stranger proposes, as a sufficient mark of real things "the presence in a thing of the power of being acted upon or of acting in relation to [another thing]." The giants (materialists) might go so far as to admit that the soul is real, but when it comes to wisdom or other such things they are not willing to say either that these are not real or that they are all bodies. The gods ("friends of the Forms") would have to deny the possibility of knowledge since what is known would be changed by being acted upon and they hold that a Form must be changeless. The philosopher, on the other hand, realizing that the knowing mind and the object known both change in the act of knowing, although they are (in some way) still the same, will accept neither the doctrine that all reality is changing or the doctrine that all reality is changeless, but "Like a child begging for 'both,' he must declare that reality or the sum of things is both at once—all that is unchangeable and all that is in change"(249d).[31]

Discussion of the second question, Which Forms are predicable of which?, begins at 251d with the consideration of whether Existence,

29. *Sophist* 254d–55c.

30. The solution of this problem was itself a result of Plato's treatment of predication in the *Sophist.* At 241d, the Eleatic Stranger urges that "what is not, in some respect has being, and conversely that what is, in a way is not." The demonstration of this claim concludes at 257b in the Eleatic Stranger's statement that "[w]hen we speak of that which is not, it seems that we do not mean something contrary to what exists but only something that is different." The general point is that any statement of the type 'x is not y' merely means 'x is different from y'. This statement, together with the corresponding discussion from the *Parmenides*, resolves the problem of how statements about nonexistent entities can yet be meaningful.

31. The account of the battle between the gods and the giants occurs at *Sophist* 246a–49d.

Motion, and Rest can combine with any other Form. Plato offers three possibilities: (1) no Form combines with any other; (2) every Form combines with every other; (3) some pairs of Forms will combine while other pairs will not. The first alternative is ruled out since it is self-refuting and would make all predication and knowledge impossible. The second alternative is rejected by Theaetetus on the ground that some Forms such as Rest and Motion could not combine, presumably because the combination would result in a statement that is self-contradictory.[32] The philosopher must accept the third alternative.

Not all kinds are considered in the ensuing demonstration of the dialectical method, but only five of the most important kinds: Existence, Rest, Motion, Sameness, and Difference. Each of the five is shown to be a distinct Form, and Existence, Sameness, and Difference are shown to be "all-pervading," that is, each can be predicated of every Form, including each other, and each one is self-predicable. In a careful analysis of this passage, Ackrill has argued that Plato not only recognized the ambiguity of 'is' (ἐστί), but that he clearly distinguishes statements of identity and statements of attribution from the existential (ἔστι).[33]

There is some basis for the claim that Plato not only does distinguish these various senses of 'is', but also distinguishes between ordinary predicates and relative predicates. At 255e, the Eleatic Stranger says that among things which exist, "some are always spoken of as being what they are just in themselves, others as being what they are with reference to other things." In the context of the *Sophist*, Existence, Sameness, Motion, and Rest are predicates of the first sort, but Difference is a relative predicate for whatever is "different" is different only with reference to something else.

It is clear why Plato would choose to consider Existence, Sameness, and Difference as important kinds, but why did he also choose Rest and Motion? A possible answer is that they were the natural choices given the two views of reality being considered, but another possibility suggests itself: Rest and Motion are important because knowledge depends both upon the stability (rest) of the Form and the knower's apprehension of

32. The more obvious point is not mentioned, namely, that if every Form combined with every Form, true statements could not be distinguished from false ones, or alternatively, there would be neither true nor false statements, and therefore no knowledge. The view of the philosopher, which the Eleatic Stranger sets out at 264e, is that "some of the kinds will combine with one another and some will not, and that some combine to a small extent, others with a large number, while some pervade all."

33. J. L. Ackrill, "Plato and the Copula: '*Sophist*' 251–259," in, *Studies in Plato's Metaphysics* ed. R. E. Allen (London: Routledge and Kegan Paul, 1965), pp. 207–18. But see L. M. de Rijk, *Plato's "Sophist": A Philosophical Commentary* (Amsterdam: North Holland, 1986), p. 114, for criticism of Ackrill's view.

the Form, which act *moves* the Form from the condition of being unknown to being known. The point is developed in Hypothesis 5 in the *Parmenides* that even a nonexistent entity can move from one condition to another, and this point is explicitly related to knowledge in the Eleatic Stranger's statement at 248e: "If knowing is to be acting on something, it follows that what is known must be acted upon by it, and so, on this showing, reality when it is being known by the act of knowledge must, in so far as it is known, be changed owing to being so acted upon." The consequence is that every Form, including Motion and Rest, both changes and does not change. It does not change in its essence, but it does change in relation to a knower.

This brings us to the third question: What is the philosophical importance of predication? On the most obvious level, as the Eleatic Stranger points out, discourse itself depends upon the possibility of predicating one form of another. In the *Sophist* (262b–d), Plato says that a statement (λόγος) refers to things past, present, or future and connects a noun (ὄνομα) with a verb (ῥῆμα). Both nouns and verbs name or designate something, but some combinations of these words make sense (yield a *logos*) while others do not.

Examples of combinations that do not make sense are: "Walks, runs, sleeps," and "Lion, stag, horse." Neither of these strings of words make a statement because they do not "signify any action performed or not performed or nature of anything that exists or does not exist" (262c). The Eleatic Stranger points out that even a simple statement such as "'a man understands' . . . gives information about facts or events in the present or past or future . . . and gets you somewhere [states something] by weaving together verbs with names" (262d).[34]

Concerning predication, the Eleatic Stranger sets out some of the now familiar elements of Aristotelian logic: Certain combinations of verbs and nouns make a true statement, for example, "Theaetetus sits," while other combinations make a false statement, for example, "Theaetetus flies." Since any statement is about something, it must be either true or false—true if it states things that are (or the facts as they are), false if it states things that are not as if they were. Judgment is said to be a conclusion of thinking that asserts or denies one thing of another, that is, it is predicative.

Plato constructs this account of predication to show that the sophist deals in false statements that are deceptive semblances of true ones. At the same time, he is also showing that some combinations of forms make

34. See Gabriel Nuchelmans, *Theories of the Proposition* (Amsterdam: North Holland Linguistic Series, 1973), pp. 14–21, for a clear and useful discussion of these passages.

a true statement, while others do not, and that the test of truth in both cases is whether the statement reflects the structure of the reality to which it refers.

Because there are necessary connections and divisions among concepts, the statement 'Existence is different from Sameness' is true, but the statement 'Existence is the same as Difference' is false; 'Justice is a species of virtue' is true, but the statement 'Virtue is a species of justice' is false. Every science, including metaphysics, is possible only because there are discernible conceptual connections and divisions in the nature of the subject itself. The scientific intelligence of the philosopher, using due measure, connects the connectible, and predicates the predicable. The *ostensible* purpose of the *Sophist* is to define the sophist. Of equal or more importance is the task of defining the philosopher, a task that is actually completed before the sophist is captured. The Eleatic Stranger and Theaetetus, having settled that forms do combine, are about to embark on the task of determining which forms combine. The Eleatic Stranger has been pointing out that only one skilled in grammar will know which letters will blend with which, and that only a musician will know which sounds can blend with which, and then Theaetetus suggests that there must be some special science, "perhaps the most important of all," needed to determine which forms "blend with" [can be predicated of] which. At this point, in a passage too well marked to be missed, the Eleatic Stranger exclaims, "Good gracious, Theaetetus, have we stumbled unawares upon the free man's knowledge and, in seeking for the Sophist, chanced to find the philosopher first?" (253c). The evident answer is "Yes" since the Eleatic Stranger immediately gives the description of the dialectian familiar from the *Republic*, the *Phaedrus*, and the *Philebus:*

> Dividing according to kinds, not taking the same form for a different one or a different one for the same—is not that the business of the science of dialectic? . . . that means knowing how to distinguish, kind by kind, in what ways the several kinds can or cannot combine. . . . And the only person, I imagine, to whom you would allow this mastery of dialectic is the pure and rightful lover of wisdom. (*Sophist* 253d–e)

Plato did not write a dialogue titled *The Philosopher* which he said, perhaps ironically, that he intended to write; however, the portrait of the philosopher is drawn in every dialogue, and especially in the *Sophist.* The philosopher is the negation of the sophist. The philosopher is a scientist and a lover of wisdom, dealing not in images, but in realities, a dialectician adept at using the processes of collection and division to discover truth.

The philosopher resembles the sophist in the ability to refute others by discovering contradictions, except that the philosopher discovers real, not pseudocontradictions. The philosopher uses refutation to get rid of false opinions and to purify the soul so it can begin the positive activity of dialectic.

IV. AN AFTERTHOUGHT

Whitehead said "all philosophy is but a footnote to Plato." Aristotle provided the first full footnote by systematizing many of the theories and positions clearly already present in Plato. Justin Martyr thought Plato was the philosopher who could best lead him to wisdom. Clement of Alexandria, Origen, Gregory of Nyssa, and Plotinus drew deeply from Plato. The Platonic philosophy is everywhere evident in the work of Saint Augustine, and even makes an appearance in Saint Thomas.

We write footnotes to Plato because of the depth and breadth of his understanding. Plato understood that science is of the universal, that order and intelligence is present in the universe and can be apprehended by the human mind, that there is a need for truth and a natural human desire to know; and that wisdom is both a joy in itself and of use in living a good life.

9 The Clash of Methodologies in Plato's *Statesman*

KENNETH DORTER

I. THE METHOD OF HYPOTHESIS AND THE METHOD OF DIVISION

In the "middle period" dialogues, especially the *Phaedo* and *Republic*, Plato puts forward the method of hypothesis as an indirect way (δεύτερος πλοῦς) to discern the highest truth when we cannot apprehend it directly. According to the *Phaedo*, the method has three steps: (1) When we accept something as true we accept whatever agrees with it and reject whatever conflicts (100a). (2) But when the initial hypothesis itself comes into question we must examine its consequences to see whether they lead to disharmonious results (101d3-5). (3) And (regardless of whether the consequences were harmonious[1]) when we must give an account of it we do so in terms of a higher hypothesis that is satisfactory (ἱκανόν; 101d5-e1). According to the *Republic*, this point is not attained until we reach the *un*hypothetical principle, the Idea of the Good.

In the *Phaedrus* Plato speaks of another kind of method, one that he does not deploy until the *Sophist* and the *Statesman*: the method of division. According to it, we search for the essence of something by beginning with the highest form or essence, then continue by progressively bisecting this into ever smaller species, until we discover what we are looking for as a part in relation to the whole.

What is the relationship between these two methods? Most interpreters who approach Plato from the direction of analytic philosophy naturally prefer the second, which, in a manner that anticipates features of their own procedure, analyzes the nature and structure of class relationships. The method of hypothesis, on the other hand, operates synthetically and speculatively, and from the point of view of analytic philosophy "speculation" is a departure from logical rigor. Analytic interpreters who

1. See my discussion in *Plato's Phaedo: An Interpretation* (Toronto: University of Toronto Press, 1982), pp. 132–38.

read Plato in a spirit of charity credit him with being astute enough to recognize the superiority of the analytic method of division over the synthetic method of hypothesis; and the fact that the method of division was promulgated after that of hypothesis provides some justification for their view. However, if we read Plato as much as possible on his own terms, leaving aside any prior expectations as to what we would hope to find in his writings—in other words, if we read him as a teacher and not as the object of a custody battle—the relationship between the two methods turns out to be more complicated.

I would like to consider this problem in reference to the *Statesman* because it is there that the relationship between the two types of methodology is most clearly visible. The *Sophist* is the first dialogue that makes overt use of the method of division, and that dialogue is, indeed, almost entirely analytic. The Eleatic Stranger, who conducts the investigation, makes no attempt to search for "higher truths." Terms like "higher" and "lower" are admittedly ambiguous, for both methods may be said to go in both directions. The first part of the method of hypothesis, the deductive moment, goes from higher to lower, while the second moment, the speculative search for a higher hypothesis, goes in the opposite direction. In the case of the method of division, the division itself is preceded by a collection, in which individuals and species are brought together under a higher genus, so it too proceeds in both directions. There are two important differences between the two methods, however. First, in the method of hypothesis the lower is for the sake of the higher: the downward analytic path leads to the upward speculative one, for the goal is the unhypothetical principle from which everything else follows. In the method of division, by contrast, the higher is for the sake of the lower: synthetic collection leads to analytic division, and the goal is the definition of a lowest species. Second, because the unhypothetical principle is the Idea of the Good, the method of hypothesis is ultimately teleological: it seeks the ultimate "why" and is rooted in the ground of value. The method of division, on the other hand, not only refrains from inquiring into the nature of the Good, the highest principle, but the Eleatic Stranger expressly warns that his method makes no distinction between greater and lesser value:

> [T]he method of definitions [λόγων] does not care more or less about sponging than about taking medicine, nor whether one provides us with greater or smaller benefits than the other. It aims at acquiring an understanding of what is akin and what is not akin in all the arts, and, with this intention, it honors all of them equally. (227a–b)

The method of division, then, is very amenable to analytic philosophy, not only because its emphasis is on analysis rather than synthesis, but also because its abstraction from questions of value shares with analytic philosophy a denial that it is possible to derive values from facts, the "ought" from the "is."

In the *Statesman*, however, Plato once again engages in philosophical speculation about the highest principle of value. As a consequence, the dialogue is almost always ignored by analytical Platonists, even though it is the explicit sequel to the *Sophist*. This tendency to attach great weight to the *Sophist*, without paying careful attention to its sequel, has led to a one-sided perception of the method of division.

The *Statesman*, as if in accordance with the methodology of division itself, is bisected down the middle. The first half superficially resembles the *Sophist* with its elaborate bisective divisions, and at 266d the Eleatic Stranger even repeats his earlier injunction against paying attention to distinctions of value. The second half, however, not only explicitly avoids the technique of bisective division but makes constant reference to value distinctions; in fact, the statesman is *defined* as the one who knows what is the best thing to do in any particular situation (304a–5d).

Since the first part of the dialogue defines statesmanship as the nourishing of human beings analogous to the way shepherds take care of their flocks, we might expect the concept of value to enter into the notion of "nourishing." However, the Eleatic Stranger never inquires into the meaning of "nourishing" but only into that of "human being." Later he calls attention to this failure, saying that their investigation did not specify in sufficient detail how the statesman rules (275a). The myth will redress this reticence about nourishment—as will the final part of the dialogue (310a ff.)—by explicitly discussing the nourishment of the human herd, both corporeal and otherwise (271e–72c). A more important mistake, the Eleatic Stranger says, was that by comparing the statesman to a shepherd we confused someone who rules other members of his own species with someone who rules over a lower species; in other words, we confused the statesman with the divine shepherd or god (274e, 275c). As a result of this confusion, the Eleatic Stranger undertakes a new beginning, in which the statesman is compared to a weaver who operates in accordance with what he calls "the science of the mean."

Two points are worth noting here. The first is that the Eleatic Stranger has been making use of the method of hypothesis. He discards the hypothesis that the statesman should be conceived on analogy with a shepherd, because it leads to disharmonious consequences, and he replaces it with the higher hypothesis that the statesman should be conceived on analogy with a weaver. The second point is that in introducing the concept of the mean, the Eleatic Stranger emphasizes the importance of value at the same time that he deemphasizes the value-free technique of bisective division that he had endorsed in the *Sophist* and in the first half of the *Statesman.* The method of hypothesis is back, and with it the concern with value. How are we to understand the schizophrenic nature of this dialogue? We shall approach that question by looking first at a different conflict of methodologies within the *Statesman,* not that between the methods of hypothesis and division, but one within the method of division itself.

II. THE SHORTER WAY

Near the beginning of the dialogue, during the initial diaeresis of the statesman, Socrates' namesake, Young Socrates, proposes that they divide the class of "herds of living things" into herds of humans and herds of beasts. He is rebuked by the Eleatic Stranger for impatiently cutting off a small part (herds of humans) of the whole (herds) rather than gradually narrowing the field by employing progressive symmetrical divisions (262a–b). However, the Eleatic Stranger has not closed the door on shortcuts altogether, for he soon offers Young Socrates the choice of a longer or shorter route by which to track down the statesman (see Figure 1). The longer is methodologically more correct, he repeats, but "it is possible to go by whichever of these ways we wish" (265a). Young Socrates understandably would like to see both, so they take first the longer, then the shorter way. The two ways both start from the assumption that the statesman is a herdsman of human beings, but differ in how a human being is conceived. According to the more famous shorter way, the final division is within the genus of two-footed herd animals, in which human beings are distinguished from birds by virtue of being featherless. According to the longer way, the final division is within the genus of tame, hornless, noninterbreeding, herd animals, in which we are distinguished from pigs by virtue of having only two feet.[2] Which way is better? It is hard to believe that Plato is endorsing either the one that makes us into a bald bird or the one that makes us into a handicapped pig.

In fact the Eleatic Stranger has played a trick on Young Socrates. The common point of departure for the two ways is Step 7 of the diaeresis, that is, the genus of land herd animals that are walkers rather than feathered (πτηνός). This means that birds have already been excluded before the shorter way even begins, and it is therefore redundant for the Eleatic Stranger to distinguish us from them again at the end. Properly

2. It is not explicit that the other species is the pig, but most readers accept Paul Shorey's suggestion that ὕστατα, 'last', is an allusion to ὗς, 'pig' (see "A Lost Platonic Joke [*Politicus* 266 D]," *Classical Philology* 12 [1917]: 308).

FIGURE 1

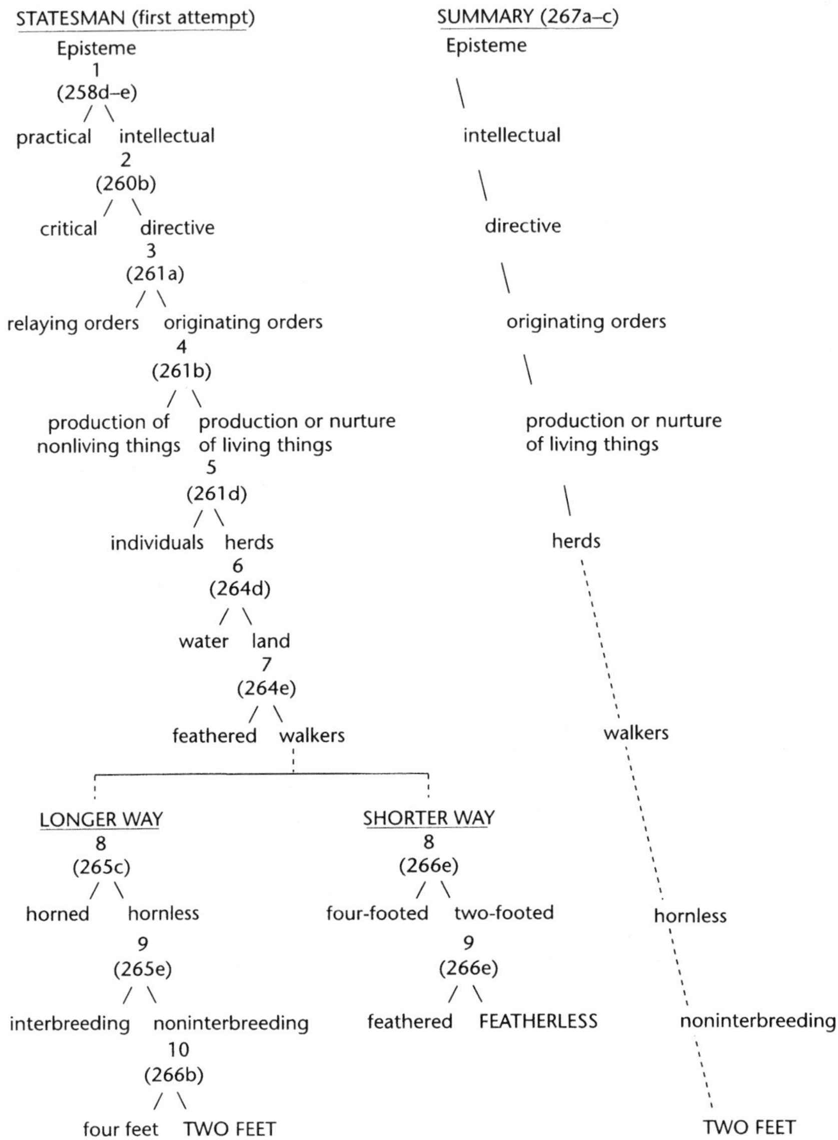
STATESMAN (first attempt)
Episteme
1
(258d–e)
practical
intellectual
2
(260b)
critical
directive
3
(261a)
relaying orders
originating orders
4
(261b)
production of nonliving things
production or nurture of living things
5
(261d)
individuals
herds
6
(264d)
water
land
7
(264e)
feathered
walkers
LONGER WAY
8
(265c)
horned
hornless
9
(265e)
interbreeding
noninterbreeding
10
(266b)
four feet
TWO FEET
SHORTER WAY
8
(266e)
four-footed
two-footed
9
(266e)
feathered
FEATHERLESS
SUMMARY (267a–c)
Episteme
intellectual
directive
originating orders
production or nurture of living things
herds
walkers
hornless
noninterbreeding
TWO FEET

speaking, the shorter way is only a single step, the division of "walkers" into "four-footed" and "two-footed"; the Eleatic Stranger's addition of the feathered/featherless (πτεροφυός/ψιλός) differentia is a pointless redundancy that Young Socrates fails to catch. Understood in this way, the procedure accords better with the Eleatic Stranger's previous description of the shorter way as "to distinguish what is sought from everything else immediately"—which implies a single step. It also leads to a respectable definition of human beings as "two-footed walking herd animals," one that is much more plausible than the longer way's definition of "two-footed noninterbreeding hornless herd animals." It is the definition of the shorter way that serves as the model for Aristotle, who commonly defines "human beings" as the "two-footed animal" (and describes us as "by nature a political [i.e., 'herd'] animal"; *Nicomachean Ethics* 1.7.1097b12, *Politics* 1.1.1253a3). The longer way, on the other hand, remains intractable in its bizarre depiction of us as leg-challenged pigs.

The shorter way turns out to be more convincing than the longer one not only in its one-step definition ("two-footed walker"), but also in its procedure. Since the genus from which both ways begin was "walking," it is more natural to use "number of feet" as the differentia, rather than "presence of horns." Nor do the differentiae "horned/hornless" and "interbreeding/noninterbreeding" tell us anything significant about human nature. Even though they proceed by more symmetrical cuts, they are artificially devised and distract from, rather than focus on, the subject to be defined—as Socrates points out in the *Philebus* (17a), it is possible to go from the one to the many too slowly as well as too quickly. Perhaps it is an implicit criticism of their artificiality that, when this division is later recalled, the order of these two unilluminating differentia is reversed (276a).

If we think of the shorter way in terms of the definition to which it really leads, rather than the redundancy that the Eleatic Stranger tacks onto the end in order to discredit it, then there is a very pointed difference between the results of the two methods. Both take "two-footed" to be the final differentia of human beings, but the shorter way uses this characteristic to distinguish human beings from all walking animals, whereas the longer way uses it to distinguish us only from pigs. Which of these reflects more accurately the distinctive nature of humanity? By dividing walking animals immediately into two-footed and four-footed, we produce a seemingly unbalanced division—humans on one side, all four-footed animals on the other—whereas by the longer way the divisions are more evenly balanced at each step, in accordance with the principle the Eleatic Stranger had articulated at 262a–b. But, on the other hand, the longer way ignores the distinctive nature of human beings. A rigid insistence on balanced divisions may conform to the principle of relative measure, but violate that of the mean (to anticipate a distinction the Eleatic Stranger will make later on). It may be that human beings are so distinctive that it makes more sense to speak of humans as one side and all "other animals" as the other, as Young Socrates was inclined to do.[3] In a later remark the Eleatic Stranger shows that it does in fact make sense to set human beings apart from all other animals as long as we can discern the true differentia: "human beings, who are different and more divine animals, govern the lower species of them" (271e). Later still we are told that the human soul comprises a divine part as well as an animal one (309c), which once again distinguishes us immediately from all other animals.[4]

If the shorter way is superior, why did the Eleatic Stranger rebuke Young Socrates for taking a shortcut when he divided "animals" into "humans" and "beasts" (262a ff.)? The problem with Young Socrates' immediate division of animals into human and not-human is not that it is asymmetrical, but that it does not identify the differentia, the essential *nature* of humanity. "Humanity" itself becomes the differentia for Young Socrates, and so the definition, in its impatience to arrive at the *infimae species*, bypasses the all-important step of specifying the essence. Because it dispenses with an identification of the distinguishing feature of "human being," it fails to give us the very thing that the process of division is supposed to accomplish. Young Socrates—and corresponding members of Plato's own audience—need to learn what it means to give a definition, to see the parts in relation to a whole that is articulated by statable differentiae.

The Eleatic Stranger makes this point as clearly as possible by insisting at first on the simplest model of genus–species relationship, that of symmetrical bisection—a concept that will be familiar to Theaetetus and Young Socrates from their studies with their teacher, the mathematician Theodorus. But this insistence was always in a sense provisional. When he rebuked Young Socrates for his thoughtless division of "animal" into "human" and "beast," the Eleatic Stranger added:

It is finest [κάλλιστον] to distinguish what is sought from everything else immediately, if that correctly reflects how the things really are. . . . [But] it is safer to

3. J. B. Skemp points out that "Aristotle argues very thoroughly against any attempt to reach any of the *infimae species* of the animal world by a process of division by dichotomy [*De Partibus animalium*, 1, 2–4; 642b5–44b20]" (*Plato's Statesman* [London: Routledge, 1952], p. 70).

4. Harvey Scodel, too, notes that "Plato himself continues to invoke the distinction between man and beast despite the Stranger's stricture [at 262a–b] (cf. *Phil.* 16a and *Laws* 653e)" (*Diaresis and Myth in Plato's Statesman* [Gottingen: Vandenhoeck & Ruprecht, 1987], p. 57).

make one's cuts by going down the middle, and one would more likely hit upon the boundaries between the forms. (262b)

It is for reasons of "safety" that the Eleatic Stranger takes such pains to make the shorter way look more problematic than it really is. Once the point has been hammered home, and only then, does the Eleatic Stranger relax this artificial rigidity and demonstrate the "finest" way, that is, that there is another way of dividing genera than by symmetrical bisection. In the first diaeresis of the second half of the dialogue, when the Eleatic Stranger divides the genus of possessions that are contributory causes of statesmanship, he does not bisect the class as a whole; rather, he immediately divides it into its seven ultimate species: tools, receptacles, supports, defenses, playthings, raw materials, and nourishment (287c–89c). The Eleatic Stranger is now employing the shorter way, the immediate articulation of the genus into its ultimate species without intermediate bisections, and he will continue to do so.

As is often the case in Plato, the explanation is one that he wants us to discover for ourselves, so that we will understand the subject itself and not merely a verbal formulation. When the Eleatic Stranger moves from the "safe" longer way of the first half of the dialogue to the "finest" shorter way of the second half, therefore, he makes it seem that he is

FIGURE 2

POSSESSIONS (287c–89c)
1
/ \
raw materials complete thing
6. RAW MATERIALS (288d) 2
/ \
not serious serious
5. PLAYTHINGS (288c) 3
/ \
necessities of life adjuncts to life
7. NOURISHMENT (288e–89a) 4
/ \
to make changes to preserve
1. INSTRUMENTS (287d) 5
/ \
by defending by supporting
4. DEFENSES (288b) 6
/ \
supporting things with integrity of shape — supporting things without integrity of shape
3. SUPPORTS (288a) **2. CONTAINERS** (287e)

forced to do so by the nature of the subject, rather than making a free choice of methodology, but we will see that this claim is disingenuous. It is a stratagem complementary to the one he used in the first half in regard to the superiority of the shorter way. There he tacked a redundant step onto the end of the definition to make the approach seem absurd; now he claims that he is proceeding immediately to the final species only because these genera do not admit of bisection. Both are attempts to

FIGURE 3

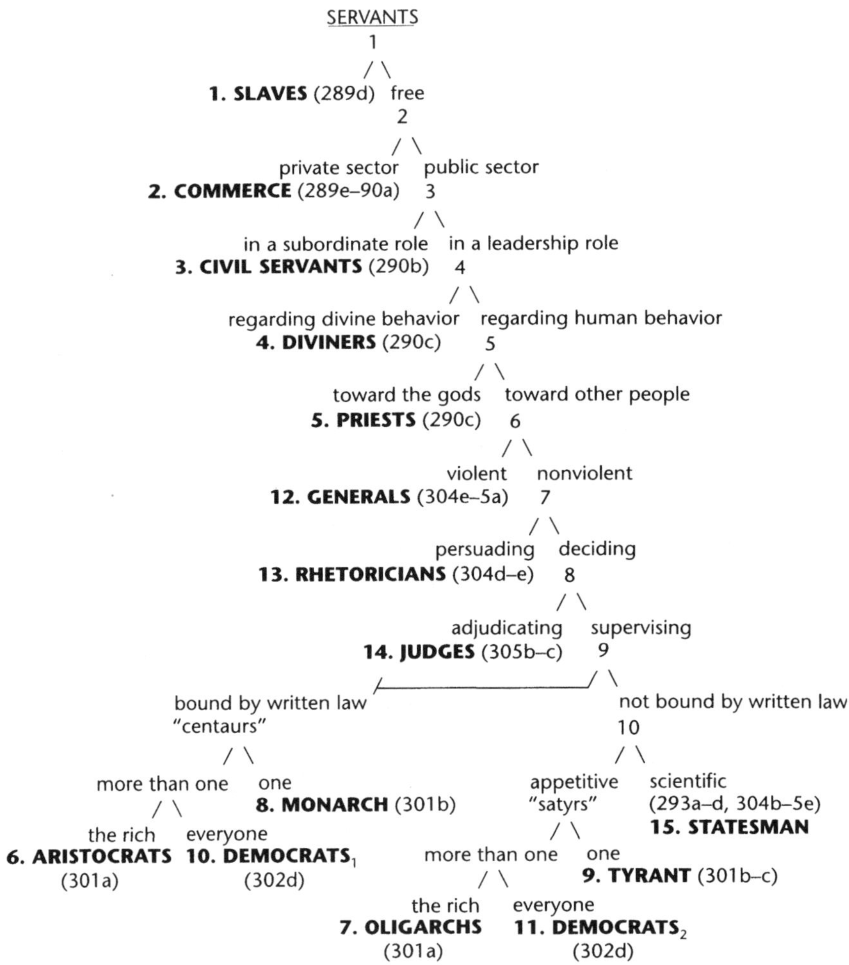

minimize the temptations, to impatient natures, of the shorter way; but both pretexts fall away under scrutiny.

The Eleatic Stranger began the present division with the words "Let us then divide them, like sacrificial animals, by their limbs, since we cannot cut them into two" (287c). He thus suggests that he is dividing them by the limbs only because division by bisection does not happen to be possible in these cases. But in the *Phaedrus* Socrates had introduced the method of division as "the ability to divide according to forms, at the natural joints" (265e). The object of the method of division is not, then, to divide down the middle but to divide correctly into the forms. So the reason that the Eleatic Stranger wants to divide at the natural joints is because this is what the method of division *aims* to do; and not, as he makes it seem, because symmetrical bisection, although inherently superior, happens not to be possible in this case. He never explains why bisection won't work here, but only says that "[T]he reason, I think, will be no less evident as we proceed." In fact these species could as easily be arrived at by progressive bisection as all the previous cases. Had the Eleatic Stranger wished, he could certainly have derived them by a bisective division like that of Figure 2; and as Figure 3 shows, the entire remainder of the dialogue could have been conducted in the same manner if the Eleatic Stranger had wished to do so.[5]

III. THE LONGER WAY

If the second half of the dialogue is an implicit recommendation of the shorter way, the first half seems in retrospect to be an implicit criticism of the longer way, indeed, virtually a satirical treatment of it. Whereas in the *Sophist* all the bisective diaereses were rigorous, those of the *Statesman* are full of extraordinary methodological blunders and inconsistencies. We have already seen two examples of this: (1) the absurd conclusion of the longer way, that the distinctive feature of a human

5. The Eleatic Stranger's reason for avoiding bisection here cannot be that this subject in particular lends itself more naturally to division into seven, for even without the constraint of bifurcation the Eleatic Stranger mentions that certain classes have been left out and can only be included by force:

> Whatever we have left out, if we have forgotten anything not very important, can be fit into one of these. Thus with the class [ἰδέα] of coins, seals, and every other kind of engraved dies. These do not constitute among themselves a large genus with a common name, but some can be made to fit under "playthings," and others under "instruments," although the amalgamation is very forced. With regard to the possession of tame animals, except slaves, the previously partitioned art of herd-nurturing will show itself to include them all. (289b–c)

being is that it has fewer legs than a pig; and (2) the introduction of the class of "feathered" in Step 9 of the shorter way after it had been excluded in Step 7.[6]

The diaeresis began with the same flagrant violation of methodology with which it ended. Just as Step 9 of the longer way used a differentia already excluded by Step 7, Step 2 uses one already excluded by Step 1. Step 1 distinguishes practical from intellectual arts on the grounds that the former eventuates in products (γιγνόμενα; 258e). But when the *latter* (which *ex hypothesi* now *excludes* the producing of products) is divided into "critical" and "directive," the distinction is that the directive art is for the sake of producing (γενέσεώς τινος ἕνεκα; 261a–b) and necessarily has products (γιγνόμενα; 261b). Here too a characteristic supposedly excluded by the previous division reappears and needs to be excluded again in the subsequent one.[7]

The other diaeresis of the first half of the dialogue is that of the weaver, which is introduced as a paradigm of all that a diaeretic search should be. That description must surely be ironic, however, for the weaver division degenerates into an astonishing jumble, as can be seen from Figures 4 and 5. The first two divisions are both nonnormal, but in opposite ways. The *Sophist* divisions began by distinguishing production from acquisition, but this one, on the contrary, begins by lumping them together: "All things whatever that we make or acquire" (279c). Whereas in Step 1 the starting point was not divided when it should have been, Step 2 is divided on *both* sides, for no apparent reason since the progressive definition takes place only in the right-hand divisions and further articulations of the left-hand side do nothing to further it. And in the case of the summary, which in all the other divisions of the *Sophist* and the

6. Step 7 is already problematic on other grounds. Step 6 had divided herd animals into land and water species, and Step 7 now divides the land species into feathered creatures and walkers. This makes birds a species of land animals. In the *Sophist,* however, the Eleatic Stranger had made birds a species of *water* animals *rather than* land animals (220b). The discrepancy is not unimportant, for the method of division was heralded as a way to discover the real essence of things (*Statesman* 285a–b), and what has now happened is that the species of birds has been destroyed. We can find water birds as a species of water animal, and land birds as a species of land animal, but not birds per se. For that, the Eleatic Stranger would have had to divide animals into feathered and featherless *before* dividing them into land and water animals. Perhaps as an indication that this is no accident, the division between land and water animals is the only step that is omitted from the Eleatic Stranger's summary at 267a–c. The summary, in other words, corrects this lapse in the division itself, as if the Eleatic Stranger were aware of it all along.

7. All this seems too confusing even for the Eleatic Stranger. He locates kingship within the directive sciences that are *distinguished* from the critical, but later he will say that kingship was differentiated from other sciences as being *both* directive *and* critical (292b). See Seth Benardete, *The Being of the Beautiful* (Chicago: University of Chicago Press, 1984, 1986), p. III.126.

FIGURE 4

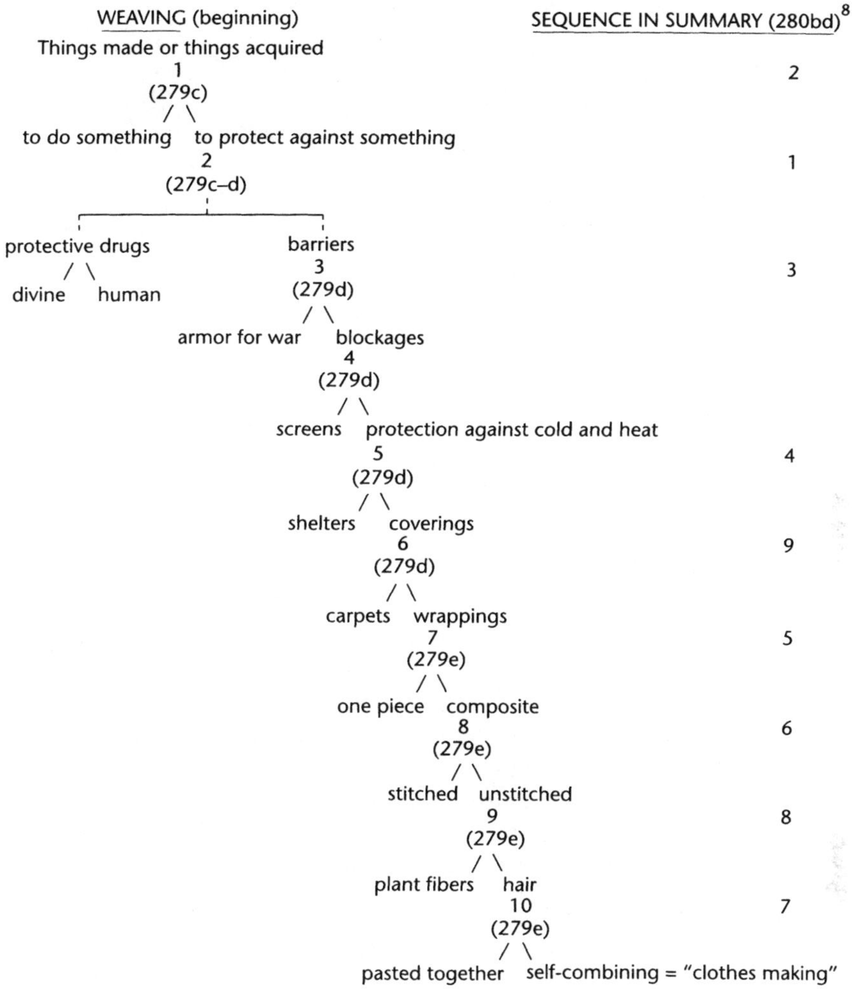

Statesman is either completely accurate or misrepresents only a single step, here the original order is misrepresented at almost every step. Not even the first and last steps are correctly recalled. The order in which it recalls the steps is: 2, 1, 3, 4, 9, 5, 6, 8, 7. The most serious deficiency is the conclusion, which is *acknowledged* to be both too broad *and* too narrow.

8. The list adjusts for the fact that the summary is presented in reverse order.

FIGURE 5

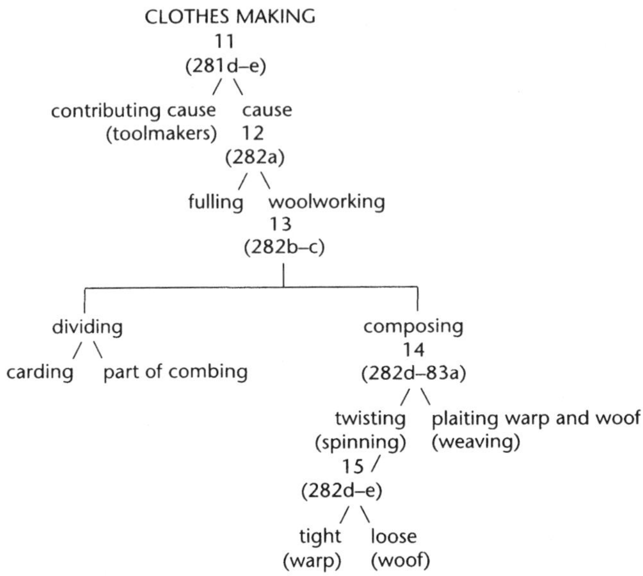

Too narrow because weaving is identified with the art of clothes making even though the Eleatic Stranger acknowledges that only "the *greatest part of it* deals with the making of clothing."[9] Too broad because not only are not all weavers clothes makers, but, as we are reminded, not all clothes makers are weavers (280e–81a).

The conclusion of the diaeresis (Figure 5) is even more chaotic. For example, in Step 13 the Eleatic Stranger says: "Of woolworking there are two divisions, and each of them is by nature a part of two arts" (282b). We would have expected him to say that each *has* two arts as its parts. To say that a species is part of two genera means that the species—like that of birds earlier—is not unified, not wholly subsumed within either genus; in other words, that the division is incorrect, not made at the natural joints between genera. The more closely we look at this supposedly paradigmatic diaeresis, the more the genera fall apart and the species collapse into one another.

9. 280a. The false note was struck with Step 6 (which, perhaps significantly, is treated as the ultimate step by the summary), when the Eleatic Stranger divided carpets from wrappings and seeks the weaver in the latter class. After all, carpets too can be woven. Without this step the Eleatic Stranger would not have had to weaken his conclusion with the unscientific qualification of "for the most part."

What I am suggesting is that the method of bisective division was exhibited in the *Sophist* not as a final recommendation but only as a first step in the development of dialectical competence. In the *Statesman* the shorter way is introduced alongside it, although in a dismissive manner lest it short-circuit in impatient natures the discipline of the longer way. However, in the first half of the dialogue the Eleatic Stranger, while appearing to defend the longer way, actually undermines it by misapplying its principles (in all the ways we have seen above)—something that he had nowhere done in the *Sophist*; and in the second half he chooses to employ the shorter way, on the demonstrably false pretext that bisection simply cannot be applied to these cases.

But what did the Eleatic Stranger mean when he said that the reason why bifurcation is no longer possible will become "no less evident" as we proceed (287c)? No reason becomes evident in any explicit way, but if we follow the lines of the argument carefully something does become evident that may be what the Eleatic Stranger alludes to.

The final diaeresis of the statesman begins as a continuation of the shepherd division (287b) and ends by subsuming the latter within itself, which means that the dialogue as a whole is circular. The eventual delineation of statesmanship, as a science that supervises rather than acts directly, is the same as the opening distinctions of the shepherd division where the science of statesmanship was differentiated from other sciences as being intellectual rather than practical (258d–e), directive rather than critical (260b), and originary rather than transmissive (258d–61a). Some of the same language is even used. Statesmanship was distinguished from the productive or practical arts (πράξεων, πρακτικήν; 258d–e) in Step 1 of the shepherd diaeresis, and is now distinguished from arts like those of the general, rhetorician, and judge in the same terms (πράττειν, πρᾶξιν, πράξεων; 305d)—even though such arts should not be able to appear within the region that remained after Step 1. In Step 2, where the statesman was classified as directive, the word used (ἐπιτακτικόν; 260b) is a form of the term for "to order" (τάσσω); here another form of the same word is used when the Eleatic Stranger says that the practical arts must follow the orders (προσταχθέντα; 305d) of the statesman.

How is this circularity to be explained? We saw that the beginning and end of the shepherd division (Step 2, and Step 9 of the shorter way) were characterised by the reappearance of earlier differentia within later species that ought to exclude them. Those manifestations now seem to be foreshadowings of the circularity of the dialogue as a whole. At 283b the Eleatic Stranger speaks of "going around in a circle" (περιήλθομεν ἐν κύκλῳ) with reference to the weaver division. It is a hyperbole for "taking a roundabout route," but it can be taken quite literally as a foreshadowing of the fate of the statesman diaeresis, of which the weaver diaeresis was said to be a paradigm.

The circularity of the *Statesman*'s overall argument, like the tangles of the longer way, illustrates that for Plato there is no possibility of a definitive mapping of reality. The problems arise because the Eleatic Stranger abandons the artificial tidiness of the *Sophist* divisions and exhibits the multifariousness of relationships by introducing more than one line of derivation at a time. Since things are related to one another in a multiplicity of ways, any attempt at creating a definitive map leads to arbitrariness, inconsistency, or both.[10] Even in the *Sophist*, where the method is displayed to its best advantage, the sophist is defined in many different and not always compatible ways, depending on our starting point and how we divide up the territory. And the *Phaedrus*, where the method of the longer way is first introduced (265e–66b), is also the dialogue that most strongly warns of the impossibility of adequately capturing reality in writings (275c, 276d). There is no single hierarchy of precedence and subordination, and the overarching circle of the *Statesman* illustrates that any place that we begin can lead us to any other place—once we know what we are doing.

Plato was never one-sided: he always recognized the importance of methodological rigor, but he also always recognized its limitations. Methodical rigor is important for leading us out of the cave, up from *eikasia*, the lowest level of the Divided Line, through *pistis*, to mastery of deductive thinking, dianoia. But in order to pass from dianoia to noesis we must pass from the rigidity of deductive rigor to something more flexible. Just as the law-free rule of the statesman supersedes the rule of law because laws are too rigid to apply in a nonarbitrary way to the realities of life (293b–94c), so too the fluidity of the shorter way of thinking, guided by the mean, supersedes the rigidity of the longer way, guided by the artificial rigor of relative measure. The relationships within reality are too intricate to be captured in a formal way.

10. Joseph Novak (in "Plato and the Irrational," *Apeiron* 17 [1983]: 14–27) makes a similar point about the *Theaetetus:*

> Plato is using the operations with irrationals as a model for establishing divisions which are to terminate in definitions. . . . [J]ust as the exact numerical value of an irrational quantity and the non-terminating algorithm, so a Form can never be definitively articulated on account of enormously complex relationships revealed by a division. . . . [A]t 266A the Stranger asks Theaetetus and young Socrates to make a division . . . "by the diagonal and again by the diagonal of the diagonal." . . . This reference to division by irrationals, beyond the obvious pun, probably makes reference to the way irrationals function as a model in division. (pp. 21–22)

IV. RELATIVE MEASURE AND THE MEAN

The Eleatic Stranger's distinction between the two kinds of measurement turns out to be the principle of division that bifurcates the dialogue itself into its two halves, in more ways than one. Not only does the distinction occur precisely in the middle of the dialogue, and function as the boundary that separates the Eleatic Stranger's use of the longer way in the first half from the shorter way in the second; but, more important, it provides the differentia by which the difference between the longer and the shorter ways can be identified.

Beginning at 283d, the Eleatic Stranger distinguishes between one kind of measurement that is made only relative to something else (e.g., something is called big or small only in relation to some other thing), and another kind of measure that is made according to an independent standard of rightness called the "mean" (τὸ μέτριον):

> It is clear that we should divide the art of measurement by cutting it into two, in accordance with what has been said. One section includes all those arts which measure number, length, depth, breadth, or thickness in relation to their opposites. The other includes all those that measure in accordance with what is due, fitting, timely, required, and everything else that dwells at the mean and away from the extremes. (284e)

The "mean" is not a mathematical mean (average), any more than it is in Aristotle's *Nicomachean Ethics*,[11] but refers to the correct degree between two *indeterminate* extremes such as "too long" and "too short." For Plato, as later for Aristotle, we can speak of good and bad, excess and deficiency, only in relation to such a mean. The nature of the mean is in fact inseparable from that of value: as the Eleatic Stranger says about all who employ any techne, "[I]n this way, when they preserve the mean, all of their works are good and beautiful" (284b). No such connection is possible in the case of relative measure.

The distinction between the two measures is precisely parallel to the Eleatic Stranger's earlier distinction between the longer and the shorter ways:

> It is finest to distinguish what is sought from everything else immediately, if that correctly reflects how the things really are. . . . [But] it is safer to make one's cuts

11. Aristotle's distinction between the intermediate τὸ μέσον in relation to the thing itself and in relation to us (*Nicomachean Ethics* 2.6.1106a26–b16) parallels Plato's between relative measure and the mean. Virtue is a mean because it is able to hit the intermediate (1106b27–8; the term translated as 'mean' in Plato is τὸ μέτριον, whereas Aristotle uses ἡ μεσότης, derived from τὸ μέσον, which Plato uses at 284e).

by going down the middle, and one would more likely hit upon the boundaries between the forms. (262b)

"Going down the middle" means comparing the two species to make sure that they are of approximately equal size, that is, dividing according to relative measure. The true mean, however, would be the precise boundary that one is seeking, that is, the shorter way.

After making this distinction between the mean and relative measure, Plato will neither make use again of the longer way, the relative measure of bisective division, nor reiterate the ban on making distinctions based on value. On the contrary, the primacy of value permeates the *Statesman* and all the subsequent dialogues (*Philebus, Timaeus, Critias, Laws*) from now on. Thus the Eleatic Stranger rejects the division of governments in terms of such symmetrical technical differentia as whether they follow written laws or not. The only criterion that matters now is that of goodness:

As long as they employ science and justice and preserve [the city], changing it from worse to better as far as possible; this must, at that time and by those measures, be for us the only right regime. All the others, we say, must be said to be not genuine nor really existent (in their own right), but as imitating this one. Those which we speak of as having good laws imitate it more nobly, and the others more basely. (293d–e)

The science of the mean can be interpreted as a demythologization of Socrates' "divine sign" (δαιμόνιον) that warns him when he strays from the right course. Since a mean can only be defined in relation to its extremes, the science of the mean can no more furnish positive content than does the divine sign. Instead, both the science of the mean and the divine sign enable the subject to feel when a proposed course of action goes too far or not far enough. Each of them seems to reflect a kind of inner equilibrium, in the light of the Good, that allows one to feel any erroneous judgment as a kind of imbalance.

V. THE METHOD OF HYPOTHESIS IN THE ELEATIC DIALOGUES

What is Plato trying to achieve through the elaborate indirection and even misdirection that we have witnessed in the *Statesman*? It may be true that he wants us to discover the connections for ourselves so that we will understand the reality and not just memorize external formulizations. But at least the *Statesman* eventually gives us the antidote to the value-sterile longer way, in the doctrine of the mean. What about the *Sophist*, where no alternative to the longer way is ever introduced? To understand

Plato's overall strategy we must look at the Eleatic tetralogy as a whole, comprising the *Parmenides, Theaetetus, Sophist,* and *Statesman.*[12] In the first of these dialogues Parmenides raises serious questions about the theory of Forms, although it is clear that his attack is not intended as an outright refutation since he stipulates in conclusion that unless one *does* accept some such theory, "he will not have anything on which to fix his thought . . . and in this way he will utterly destroy the power of discourse" (135b–c). Nevertheless, Parmenides' arguments show that the theory of Forms is problematic because it must constantly fall back on metaphor and analogy: the limitations of human conceptualization make this inevitable. In that case, how can the theory of Forms be justified in the face of conceptual aporiae such as those pointed out by Parmenides? The only means available is the method of hypothesis, and in fact the trilogy that follows the *Parmenides* can be read as an extended application of the method of hypothesis in defense of the theory of Forms.[13] F. M. Cornford attributed a function of this kind to the *Theaetetus* (which never brings in the theory of Forms at all), when he wrote: "The Forms are excluded in order that we may see how we can get on without them; and the negative conclusion of the whole discussion means that, as Plato had taught ever since the discovery of the Forms, without them there is no knowledge at all."[14]

The theory of Forms comprises two fundamental claims. First, Forms are universals: it is by virtue of the prior reality of a Form that a multitude of individuals may be identified by the same name.[15] Second, Forms are values: they are articulations of the *goodness* of reality, and therefore

12. I have developed in detail this interpretation of the *Statesman* and the tetralogy as a whole in *Form and Good in Plato's Eleatic Dialogues: The "Parmenides," "Theatetus," "Sophist," and "Statesman"* (Berkeley and Los Angeles: University of California Press, 1994). I employ the description "eleatic" rather than the more usual "critical" because the latter term does not apply to the *Statesman,* and is employed on the assumption, which I do not share, that the dialogues are to some extent repudiations of Plato's earlier views. "Eleatic" is not easily applied to the *Theaetetus,* however, which has neither an Eleatic speaker nor subject matter. On the other hand, Parmenides is mentioned at an important juncture as someone whose views ought to be considered as an alternative to the philosophy of becoming that Theaetetus defends without success (180d–81a), and the failure to discuss the Eleatic philosopher is ascribed only to the fact that he is too important to be considered in the available time (183c–84a). He is thus the only alternative indicated to the theories that founder in the *Theaetetus,* and their collapse may amount to an indirect endorsement of the Eleatic philosophy.

13. The *Statesman* also counters the more radical consequences of the *Parmenides* demonstration of the limitations of metaphorical and analogical thinking, by defending the importance of metaphorical and analogical "paradigms" (277d ff.).

14. F. M. Cornford, *Plato's Theory of Knowledge* (London: Routledge and Kegan Paul, 1935), p. 28.

15. Cf. *Republic* 10.596a: "We are in the habit of positing one Form with regard to each group of things to which we apply the same name."

the most fundamental Forms are the Good, the Beautiful, the Just, and so on.[16] What Plato does after the *Theaetetus* is to reintroduce each of these two aspects sequentially. In the *Sophist* he shows that by reintroducing the concept of universal kinds, we can solve the fundamental aporiae of the *Theaetetus.*[17] However, the *Sophist,* although not explicitly aporetic like the *Theaetetus,* ends in an unsatisfying and unconvincing way. The sophist and the philosopher are not distinguished from each other in terms of their goals or their defining values, as had been the case in previous dialogues, but in value-free technical terms: the philosopher is a maker of accurate images, the sophist a maker of inaccurate ones. The distinction is transparently inadequate, for it reduces the difference between philosophy and sophistry to a difference between truth and falsity, and it is just as little the defining character of philosophers that everything they say is true, as it is the defining character of sophists that everything they say is false. Moreover, in the case of the philosopher, the definition fails to distinguish *love* of wisdom from wisdom itself, a distinction that Plato elsewhere treats as fundamental,[18] and so a philosopher who in a moment of ignorance produces an inaccurate image would be by definition a sophist. On that definition there is no lover of wisdom—there is either a wise person or a sophist, and nothing in between since there is no middle term between "accurate" and "inaccurate." In the case of the sophists, too, the definition fails to distinguish between their products and their intentions, so that if sophists happen to get the facts right about something, that is, to produce an accurate image of it, they will be philosophers by definition, regardless of the purpose to which they put that image. Sophists cannot be distinguished adequately from philosophers without reference to their goals, that is, to the concept of value.

The next dialogue, the *Statesman,* responds to these disharmonious consequences with a higher hypothesis, that not only are there universals, but that underlying everything is the good, the mean. In the light of that concept the Eleatic Stranger explicitly dismisses the importance of

16. Cf. *Republic* 6.509b: "To the things known [i.e., the Forms] not only their knowability, you must say, is provided by the Good, but even their being and essence comes to them from it."

17. The *Theaetetus* foundered in an attempt to give an account of the nature of knowledge, stymied in the end by its inability to find a satisfactory definition of *logos,* in particular with reference to opinion, *doxa.* In the *Sophist,* however, the Eleatic Stranger (who calls his method the method of *logoi;* 227a) does give a definition of *logos,* and in relation to *doxa* (261d–63e).

18. Socrates frequently denies that he (or any human being) has attained wisdom, but he has no compunction about calling himself or others "lovers of wisdom." Also see the *Symposium*'s argument that lovers of something cannot be in possession of what they love (199d ff.).

the distinction between accurate images and inaccurate ones that he had made so much of in the *Sophist*: anyone who produces images at all, rather than directly embodying the mean, he calls "the sophists of sophists" (303b–c). The real difference between the sophistic pretender to wisdom, and the genuine possessor of wisdom, is that the latter alone possesses the science of the mean, that is, of applied *goodness.* Subsequently, in the *Philebus* and the *Timaeus,* the theory of Forms will reappear with renewed vigor, and very much in the service of the question of value. The underlying problems, to which the criticisms of the *Parmenides* had pointed, remain intact, but the limitations of our ability to eliminate them become more evident.

The method of hypothesis has not been superseded by the method of division. On the contrary, the method of division is itself a hypothesis that has been posited as a way of solving the problems of the *Theaetetus.* Or rather, it is a series of at least three hypotheses, each of which supersedes its precedessor. Not only does the shorter way supersede the longer, but it in turn will evidently be superseded by a mysterious higher version about which the Eleatic Stranger says only that "in the present circumstances it is not possible to make it clearly evident" (262c). Whether it turns out to be this third version, or one even higher, the ultimate form of the method of division would seem to be the downward path that follows upon the consummation of the method of hypothesis in the unhypothetical first principle:

> hanging onto the things that hang on this beginning, it thus descends again to a conclusion, making use of nothing perceived by the senses, but moving from forms themselves, through forms, to forms, it concludes in forms. (*Republic* 6.511b–c)

10 Dialectical Education and Unwritten Teachings in Plato's *Statesman*

MITCHELL MILLER

In these reflections† we will be at work on two projects, letting each provide the occasion for the other. One of these projects is relatively narrow in focus; the other is wide ranging.[1]

The narrow project is to interpret the strange passages near the end of the *Statesman* (287b–91a, 303d–5e) in which the Eleatic Stranger completes the work of distinguishing the statesman by enumerating fifteen kinds of art necessary to the polis. First he names the seven "contributive arts":

1. arts that produce raw materials
2. arts that produce tools
3. arts that produce containers
4. arts that produce vehicles
5. arts that produce defenses
6. arts that produce amusements
7. arts that produce nourishments.

Then he names the seven "directly responsible arts":

8. the art proper to slavery
9. the arts of merchants and traders

† This essay was originally prepared for inclusion in *The Sovereignty of Construction: Studies in the Thought of David Lachterman*, edited by D. Conway and P. Kerszberg (Amsterdam: Rodopi, forthcoming), and was then presented as a lecture in the series on Plato and Platonism sponsored by the Franklin J. Matchette Foundation and held at The Catholic University of America in the fall of 1993. The author thanks the editors and publishers of *The Sovereignty of Construction* for their kind permission to republish this essay here.

1. David Lachterman was a midwife for this λόγος. He was a master of generous and searching conversation, and it was his open-spirited questions that first encouraged me to pursue the web of connections between Aristotle's report of Plato's teachings regarding the One and the Dyad and my readings of the *Statesman* and the *Parmenides* (see notes 2 and 6 below). It is a terrible loss not to be able to go on talking with him.

10. the arts of heralds and clerks
11. the arts of priests and diviners
12. rhetoric
13. generalship
14. the art of justice.

Finally he names the art directing all these:

15. statesmanship

Why, in offering this enumeration, does the Eleatic Stranger suddenly abandon bifurcatory division, the mode of diairesis he has practiced in all of the definitional attempts of the *Sophist* and, up until now, the *Statesman*?[2] He does not explain, saying only that "it is difficult to cut [the arts] into two" and that "the reason, I think, will become clear as we proceed" (287b10–c1). Thus Plato leaves it up to his readers to ponder the nonbifurcatory distinctions that the Eleatic Stranger presents. What, we must ask, is the new mode of diairesis he is practicing? What, if any, is the ontological structure this new mode reveals in its object field? And what is the point of presenting such structure only in the closing phase of the dialogue and with such reticence about its significance?

The wide-ranging project is to open up a much larger web of texts and teachings to which the *Statesman* passages belong and which, once we have seen how they fit together, will provide a context within which we can discover compelling answers to the questions those passages raise. I will argue that the Eleatic Stranger's list of fifteen kinds exhibits the ontological structure envisioned by the "unwritten teachings" Aristotle ascribes to Plato in *Metaphysics* A6. To bring this out, however, I must first interpret Aristotle's very compressed and schematic report in A6, and to do this, I must begin by identifying and interpreting the several partial

2. The Eleatic Stranger has stressed the importance of bifurcatory diairesis in at least three ways. (i) Every cut he has made, from the beginning of the *Sophist* up until *Statesman* 287b, has been bifurcatory. (ii) His two paradigms of diairesis—the divisions that isolate the angler in the *Sophist* (218e–21c) and the weaver in the *Statesman* (279b–83b)—are bifurcatory. (iii) When Young Socrates makes the lopsided cut of human from beast at *Statesman* 262a, the Eleatic Stranger objects, arguing that "by cutting down the middle [διὰ μέσων . . . τέμνοντας] . . . one is more likely to hit upon forms" and telling Young Socrates that "it is this that makes all the difference in inquiries" (262b). As models of cutting down the middle, the Eleatic Stranger cites odd/even and male/female. Each of these cuts exhausts the class it divides by sorting its members according to contrary forms into mutually exclusive subclasses. (For a simple diagram, useful for purposes of contrasting the two modes of diairesis, see Figure 1.) At the same time, the Eleatic Stranger has also intimated the limitations of bifurcatory diairesis in the strange passage at 264b–66e in which, with a series of pointedly ironic jokes, he completes the initial series of distinctions in a way that misses fundamentally the essence of statesmanship. For discussion, see my *The Philosopher in Plato's "Statesman"* (The Hague: Martinus Nijhoff, 1980), pp. 16–33.

displays of the "unwritten teachings" that can be found in the *Parmenides* and in the *Philebus.* The path of the essay therefore leads from the *Statesman,* to Aristotle's reports, to passages in the *Parmenides* and the *Philebus,* then back to Aristotle's reports in light of the *Parmenides* and *Philebus* passages, then back to the *Statesman* in light of Aristotle's reports. The result will be a comprehensive reading of the whole web. In the course of this reading, the "unwritten teachings" will emerge with fresh content and by way of, rather than in place of, Plato's indirect communication in the dialogues.

I. AN ORIENTING INTERPRETIVE THESIS: THE *Statesman* AS A MICROCOSMIC EXHIBITION OF THE LONG-TERM PROCESS OF PHILOSOPHICAL EDUCATION

In the *Statesman,* Plato puts the Academicians on stage before themselves in the *dramatis persona* of "Young Socrates," and he shows them the limitations they must overcome in their future education. Thus he provides them an occasion for self-knowledge and self-transcendence. Young Socrates, all too ready to defer to the Eleatic Stranger's authority (see 258c, together with 267a–c, 276e–77a, and 283a–b), shows himself to be unwittingly under the sway of uncritical opinion (262b–e). Chief among the resources the Eleatic Stranger offers him in order to free himself are the technique of bifurcatory diairesis, the use of paradigms, and the notion of due measure. Beyond these, he offers the course of inquiry in the *Statesman* itself as an exemplary exhibition of the stages through which the educational process should lead.[3] We might distill the force of this exhibition into the following set of recommendations: (a) to put a check on the power of uncritical opinion, one should subject oneself to the discipline of the procedure of bifurcatory diairesis; (b) but to learn the use of this method, one should begin with easy, directly perceptible subjects like the weaver, checking the results of one's diairesis against one's direct observation of the subject; (c) only when one has achieved competence in the easy cases, should one turn to the hard ones where no perceptual check is possible; (d) but with mastery of bifurcation comes freedom from uncritical opinion and, with this freedom, the capacity to let the subject matter present itself, so to speak, in its own terms, and when it does, one will want to set bifurcation aside and let the structure of the subject matter itself be the guide for the distinctions one makes.

3. On the mimetic irony of the *Statesman* and the *persona* "Young Socrates," see my *The Philosopher in Plato's "Statesman,"* pp. xiv–xvii, 5–8. On Young Socrates's mistakes, see 20–22, 24–26, 54–57, 59, 64–65. On the exemplary character of the course of inquiry in the *Statesman* for the Academicians, see pp. 69–70, 79–82, 115–17.

Now, my interpretive thesis is that when the Eleatic Stranger turns from the case of weaving to that of statesmanship at 287b ff. and suddenly abandons bifurcation, Plato is projecting for his reader such a future moment, a time when, having achieved mastery of bifurcation, he needs to be ready to set it aside in order to let the subject itself, in its own proper being, determine the form of analysis. If this thesis is correct, then the Eleatic Stranger's reticence is both prudential and pedagogical. Plato has the Eleatic Stranger speak on the basis of an insight for which Young Socrates has shown himself not yet ready. For readers who have recognized Young Socrates' limitations in themselves, the task at hand is to practice bifurcatory diairesis; by his reticence the Eleatic Stranger avoids undermining his recommendation of such practice. For readers, on the other hand, who have gone further, readers who have recognized the way bifurcation, even when it "hits upon forms" (262b), can conceal the essential character of the subject matter, the Eleatic Stranger's reticence is provocative; it challenges them to step in and try to recognize for themselves the way in which that essential character reveals itself in the nonbifurcatory distinctions he presents. For us, this focuses the key interpretive questions: if the Eleatic Stranger's distinction of the fifteen kinds traces the structure of reality itself, what is this structure, and what is the new mode of dialectic that is fit to seek it?

II. FIVE "UNWRITTEN TEACHINGS"[4]

As a point of departure for interpreting the *Statesman* passage, I want to take Aristotle's "concise and summary" (988a18) report of Plato's teachings in *Metaphysics* A6. The teachings Aristotle reports present an account of the structure of the whole of things. We will concentrate on these five theses:

1. Forms and the Dyad of the Great and the Small are conjointly the

4. The phrase is Aristotle's at *Physics* 209b14–15. I should say at the outset what is obvious in any case: I am not attempting to canvass all the "unwritten teachings." Indeed, I have not even exhausted Aristotle's report in *Metaphysics* A6; I have omitted his report of Plato's derivation of number from the One and the Dyad of the Great and the Small. Though I think there is indirect evidence in the *Parmenides* attesting this as a genuine Platonic teaching, it is not relevant to the present project. Nor do I mean to suggest that the only exhibition of "unwritten teachings" in the *Statesman* comes at 287b–91a and 303d–5e. On the contrary, I find generally persuasive H. J. Kraemer's view (see *Arete bei Platon und Aristoteles: Zum Wesen und zur Geschichte der Platonischen Ontologie*, in *Abhandlungen der Heidelberger Akademie der Wissenschaften, philosophisch-historische Klasse, Jahrgang 1959*, 6 [Heidelberg, 1959], pp. 148–77, esp. p. 163) that the "unwritten teachings" are on display in the Eleatic Stranger's account of the mean at 284a–e and in his use of it in the final phase of the dialogue (305e–311c) to locate the virtues on a continuum of vigor and gentleness. But it is necessary to reserve discussion of that for another occasion.

"causes" of "sensibles." Forms are "cause of what [a sensible thing] is," and the Great and the Small are "the underlying matter of which [the Forms] are predicated."

2. The One and the Dyad of the Great and the Small are conjointly the causes of the Forms. The One is "cause of what [a Form] is," and the Great and the Small are "the underlying matter of which [the One] is predicated."

3. the One is cause of "good" (τὸ εὖ); the Great and the Small, of "ill" (τὸ κακῶς).

4. "Intermediate" (μεταξύ) between the timeless, unchanging, unique Forms and the perishable, changing, many sensibles, there are "the mathematicals" (τὰ μαθηματικά); these are intermediate because they are eternal and unchanging like Forms but many like sensibles (987b14–18).

5. The Forms *are*, but only in some limited sense, numbers. (My inclusion of this thesis and, too, its qualified character require immediate comment before we step back to look at the whole assemblage of teachings. First, by contrast with theses #1–4, nowhere in A6 does Aristotle expressly assert that Forms are numbers. Only later, e.g., at 991b9–20, 1073a13 ff., and 1080a11 ff., do we find him explicitly, albeit with varying degrees of certainty and clarity, crediting Plato with this claim. Nonetheless, it is strongly implied in A6 when Aristotle uses virtually identical language to say, first, that the Forms are "causes of everything else" [αἴτια . . . τοῖς ἄλλοις; 987b18–19] and then, only two sentences later, that numbers are "causes of the being of everything else" [αἰτίους . . . τοῖς ἄλλοις τῆς οὐσίας; 987b24–25]. At the same time, the identity needs to be qualified, for Aristotle has also just credited Plato, in thesis #4, with the *distinction* of Forms from mathematicals. Hence my open-ended "in some limited sense." Even as we wonder if there are any traces of this teaching in the dialogues, we must also hope that such traces, should we find them, will show us how to understand just what the teaching means.[5])

Needless to say, Aristotle's reports are anything but self-explaining. For us, there are two levels of question to pursue. First, on the assumption

5. I do not think that the reported distinction between mathematical and eidetic or ideal numbers can be used to interpretively resolve the tension in #5. I cannot go into the obscure issue of the nature of eidetic number here. I hope it is sufficient for the moment to note that Aristotle makes no allusion to the distinction in A6; quite the contrary, he claims that Plato "agreed" with the Pythagoreans "in making the numbers the cause of the being of other things" (987b24–25), and it seems evident that the Pythagoreans—who, Aristotle says, did not separate numbers from sensibles and who had no notion of forms (987b29–33)—had numbers in a mathematical sense in mind.

that Aristotle is reporting, however summarily and in his own terms, genuine Platonic teachings, what is the structure of the whole that Plato articulates in them? Second, how do the closing distinctions in the *Statesman* relate to this structure? To the interpretive claim offered at the close of Part I above, I want to add a second claim: in the closing distinctions in the *Statesman* we have a *specific* exhibition of the *general* structure that Plato articulates in the "unwritten teachings." The main task of this essay is to make good on this second claim.

III. RELATED PASSAGES IN THE *Parmenides* AND THE *Philebus*[6]

There are two sets of texts that can help us interpret Aristotle's reports and, eventually, see the *Statesman*'s closing distinctions as an exhibition of them. These are the account of participation offered in the third (with support in the second and the fifth) of the eight hypotheses on "the One" in the *Parmenides* and the accounts of dialectic and of the four kinds at 16c–18d and 23c–27c, respectively, in the *Philebus*. Here I shall try to distill what each, on my reading, provides.

A. *The Account of Participation in the* Parmenides, *Hypothesis III*[7]

Each Form is a simple and unique one that bestows composite unity on each of the many sensibles that participate in it. The Form does this

6. A key study for anyone interested in the problem of the "unwritten teachings" is Kenneth Sayre's *Plato's Late Ontology: A Riddle Resolved* (Princeton, N.J.: Princeton University Press, 1983). That I have major disagreements with his interpretations of the *Parmenides* (see my *Plato's "Parmenides": The Conversion of the Soul* [Princeton, N.J.: Princeton University Press, 1986; paperback reprint, State College, Pa.: Pennsylvania State University Press, 1991], Preface, note 6) and of the "unwritten teachings" themselves (see [i] and [ii] in note 15 below) does not diminish my appreciation of the effect of his work. By arguing forcefully for readings of the *Parmenides* and the *Philebus* that let the "unwritten teachings" appear *in* the dialogues, he has altered the *status quaestionis*, freeing us from having to choose between affirming an esoteric doctrine not presented by the dialogues (the position, in essence, of the early works by Kraemer, cited in note 4 above, and Gaiser) and rejecting Aristotle's reports as a basic misinterpretation (the position argued by Harold Cherniss in his *The Riddle of the Early Academy* [Berkeley and Los Angeles: University of California Press, 1945]). Another recent work that also tends to undermine this choice, in this case by arguing for the compatibility of affirming the "unwritten teachings" with Schleiermacherian hermeneutics, is T. A. Szlezak's *Platon und die Schriftlichkleit der Philosophie: Interpretationen zu den fruhen und mittleren Dialogen* (Berlin: Walter de Gruyter, 1985).

7. The following paragraph summarizes the interpretation I have worked out at length and within the context of an interpretation of the *Parmenides* as a whole in my *Plato's "Parmenides"* (cited in note 6 above). On the constitution of sensibles, see especially the discussion of 157b–58d in Hypothesis III on pp. 126–36, together with the discussions of 149d–51b in II on pp. 105–11 and of 161a–e in V on pp. 143–46. For the way this exhibits

by imposing πέρας—that is, the internal and external "boundaries"[8] that divide and relate parts and so constitute a whole—upon a sensible substrate. That substrate is the in itself indeterminate magnitude, no more great than small, that only first gains existence when πέρας is imposed upon it. This imposition is thus a metaphysical, not a physical, act: it is the Form's exacting the requirement, of any sensible embodiment of it, that this latter be structured in a determinate way as the whole of a determinate set of parts. Now, in this formation of unformed magnitude we can glimpse the first of the teachings that Aristotle reports. The indeterminate magnitude is the instantiation of the Forms of size, Greatness and Smallness. Hence Forms—that is, in each case the πέρας-providing form—and the Great and the Small are conjointly responsible for sensibles. We can also glimpse the first part of the second teaching Aristotle reports. Each Form, as a simple and unique one that bestows a lower grade of unity on what participates in it, is itself an instantiation of the One itself, or Unity, in its causal power. But this raises the question of how, as Aristotle reports in thesis #2, the Great and Small are involved in the being of the Forms. And of course we have not yet addressed the third, fourth, and fifth theses at all.

On these issues the two *Philebus* passages are helpful.[9]

B. The "Gift from the Gods": Philebus *16c–18d*

In the first, Plato has Socrates introduce as a "gift from the gods" (16c) a new account of dialectical procedure. We begin, Socrates says, by locating whatever we are studying within a "single form" (μία ἰδέα; 16d1), and we then go on to make a series of distinctions, first of the "single form" into "two, if the case admits of there being two, otherwise [into] three or some other number [of forms]" (16d), then of each of these, and so on. We conclude only once we have come to recognize that "the unity we started with" is not only "a one and an unlimited many" but also, between these extremes, "a limited many" (16d). These obscure and schematic

"unwritten teaching" #l and the first part of #2, see chap. 5, n. 29 (but note my revision of point (5) there in Part III.E(ii) below). For a more expansive treatment, especially of the implicit presence of teachings #3–5 in the *Parmenides,* see my "'Unwritten Teachings' in the *Parmenides,*" *Review of Metaphysics* 48, no. 3 (March, 1995), pp. 591–633.

8. The concrete meaning of πέρας is "boundary" or "delimiting extremity," and it is in just this sense that Parmenides uses the word throughout the hypotheses (see 137d6, 145a1, 165a5). This sets the usages of the *Parmenides* and the *Philebus,* where πέρας has a mathematical sense (see section C below), into contrast. For the reconciliation of these usages, see section D(i) below.

9. The following sections B and C are compressed rethinkings of analyses made at length in my "The God-Given Way," *Proceedings of the Boston Area Colloquium in Ancient Philosophy* 6 (1990): pp. 323–59, esp. pp. 325–40.

words are partly clarified by the two exemplary analyses Socrates offers, of musical sound at 17c ff. and of the letter sounds that make up the alphabet at 18b–d. These analyses make clear, first of all, that the "unlimited many" are arrayed as a continuum[10] framed by relative contraries and a midpoint. The midpoint, which represents an equal balance of the contraries, reveals that the other points on the continuum all mark out unequal balances.[11] (See, for illustrations, Figures 2 and 4 in the Appendix.) Second, the "limited many" between the "single form" and the continuum are a set (or sets) of forms that are fit for interplay and comprise a whole that, when they are all well instantiated, yields a good instantiation of the "single form." In the music example, the "limited many" are the forms of the notes that fit together to make up the various "modes" or scales.[12] (Socrates does not work this out in any detail; for an illustration of the kind of structure he appears to envisage, see Figure 3 in the Appendix, a sketch of the Greater Perfect System in Greek harmonic theory.[13]) In the letter sounds example, they are the forms of sounds that, because each can combine with certain of the others to make the syllables of speech, are the members of the alphabet. (Again, Socrates offers no detail; see Figure 5.)

10. J. C. B. Gosling's reflections on the presence of the notion of the continuum both in 16c–18d and in 23c–27c in his *Plato: Philebus* (Oxford: Clarendon Press, 1975), pp. 165–81, 196–206, are seminal for my reading.

11. Thus, on my reading, the "unlimited many" are not the many sensibles that instantiate some form. As places on the continuum, they are the full range of possible proportions of the opposites that sensible instantiations may have.

12. Isobel Henderson, in "Ancient Greek Music," in *The New Oxford History of Music, Vol. 1: Ancient and Oriental Music,* ed. Egon Wellesz (London: Oxford University Press, 1957), pp. 336–403, points out that the identification of "modes" (ἁρμονίαι) with "species of the octave" and so, for us, with scales is made not by "classical composers and . . . musically intelligent prose-writers" but only by "musically ignorant theorists" (p. 347). I accept the judgment of most translators (e.g. Hackforth, Gosling, Waterfield) in taking ἁρμονίαι at 17d4 to mean "scales" because it is mathematicizing harmonic theorists—the phrase οἱ πρόσθεν ("the men of old") at 17d2 presumably refers to the Pythagoreans—whom Socrates cites as his authorities at *Philebus* 17c–d.

13. Fourth-century harmonic theory mapped out the matrix of possible intervals and notes implied by the various tunings in three systems: the Greater Perfect System, the Lesser Perfect System, and the Perfect Immutable System. See Giovanni Comotti, *Music in Greek and Roman Culture,* trans. R. Munson (Baltimore: The Johns Hopkins University Press, 1989), chap. 5; and Henderson, "Ancient Greek Music," pp. 344–46. The Greater Perfect System covers a double octave, structuring it as two conjunct tetrachords with a detached note added on. Each conjunct tetrachord picks out seven notes, with the first and the seventh and the shared fourth in fixed positions and the two inner notes within each tetrachord movable in a variety of ways. The central position of the first note of the second conjunct tetrachord is made explicit by its name, the μέση ("middle"). For a diagrammatic representation, see Figure 3 in the Appendix. I have singled out the Greater Perfect System as a display of the sort of harmonic structure Socrates suggests at 17c–d because, as the analysis in Part IV below will put us in position to see, it is strikingly isomorphic with the Eleatic Stranger's structuring of the continuum of the arts in *Statesman* 287b–91a and

C. πέρας and ἄπειρον in Philebus 23c–27c

In the second passage, we are given an occasion to deepen our understanding of the continuum structure and the relation of the limitedly many forms to it. Socrates turns from dialectic and the eidetic order that it discloses, his focus at 16c–18d, to an account of the structure of "what now exists in the universe" (τὰ νῦν ὄντα ἐν τῷ πάντι; 23c4). He analyzes things as mixtures of two factors, πέρας and ἄπειρον. The ἄπειρον factor, he explains, is in each case a flux and contest between relative contraries; by itself it is unregulated and unstable, with each opposite tending to exceed the other. The πέρας factor, in turn, is a ratio, a "relation of number to number or measure to measure" (25a8–b1). Applied to the ἄπειρον it has a twofold function. First, it fixes the relative quantity (τὸ ποσὸν; 24c6) of the opposites, putting an end to their flux by determining in what proportion they shall be present together. In doing this, second, it realizes "due measure" (τὸ μέτριον; 24c7); the structure it establishes is therefore normative, a good apportionment and harmony (cf. σύμμετρα . . . καὶ σύμφωνα; 25e1) of the opposites. Socrates goes on to give a series of examples of the combination of πέρας and ἄπειρον, including good health, seasonable weather, and virtues of character. Of particular interest for us, at 26a he once again cites musical order: "And as regards high and low, fast and slow, which are ἄπειρα, doesn't the introduction of these same things [namely, ratios that realize due measure] realize πέρας and constitute all of music in its perfection?" The implication is that the array of notes that make for beautiful sound, sound that is on pitch, are a set of means, of normative apportionments of high and low.

This dovetails precisely with what Socrates taught at 16c–18d. There we considered music from the perspective of the dialectician working out a "diairesis" of "forms" (20c), and we saw how the "single form," musical sound or pitch, implicates that definite set of forms that, making up a "mode" or scale, each pick out some definite place on the continuum of possible balances of high and low. Now, looking at the structure of musical notes as mixtures of πέρας and ἄπειρον, we have learned to understand these notes as a normative set of good apportionments of high and low. Putting these thoughts together, we can see that these good

---

303d–5e. This isomorphism may be mere coincidence. On the other hand, *if* it is the new mode of dialectic introduced by Socrates at *Philebus* 16c–18d that the Eleatic Stranger puts into practice at *Statesman* 287b–91a and 303d–5e, *then,* since Plato has Socrates offer harmonic structure as a paradigm for the order disclosed by the new mode of dialectic, it may be that he actually looked to the Greater Perfect System as a model in composing the Eleatic Stranger's structuring of the continuum of the arts in the *Statesman.*

apportionments just *are* the places on the continuum that the definite set of forms picks out. The whole structure that is emerging can be spelled out in three progressively expansive steps. Consider first *each one* of the limited number of forms: for each such form to pick out a place on the continuum of high and low is for it to exact, as a normative schema for its instantiation in actual sound, a definite ratio of the opposites. But no note is musical in isolation; each requires those others that go together with it to make up a "mode" or scale. Hence we can expand the first point: for *each whole set* of forms that defines a "mode" or scale to pick out a correlative set of places on the continuum is for it to exact, as a normative schema for *its* instantiation in actual sound, a definite set of ratios of the opposites. But, finally, each "mode" instantiates the "single form," musical sound or pitch; that no single note can be musical in isolation reflects the prior point that genuinely musical sound exists only in and as the interplay of notes that make up a "mode." Thus we can trace the causal necessity for the mixture of πέρας and ἄπειρον back to "the one" that the new mode of dialectic explores, and we can rearticulate the whole structure with this in mind as follows: for the "single form" to be well instantiated in actual sound requires that the limited number of forms it implicates themselves be instantiated by sounds that conform to the correlative set of ratios of opposites that these forms pick out on the continuum. (For a diagrammatic representation of this multileveled structure, see Figure 6 in the Appendix.)

D. *Implications of the* Philebus *Passages for the Account of Participation in the Parmenides*

The two *Philebus* passages bear on the *Parmenides* passage in two important ways.

(i) Forms of Parts and the Mathematical Sense of πέρας In the *Parmenides*, as we saw, a thing's form constitutes it as a whole of parts by imposing a set of πέρατα, "boundaries," on its otherwise indeterminate and unstructured magnitude. The *Philebus* permits us to make explicit two aspects of this that are left implicit in the *Parmenides*. First, for a form to give rise to whole-part structure in its participant requires that it implicate a plurality of forms of parts. This is the "limited many," the determinate set of forms between the "single form" and the unlimited many, in *Philebus* 16c ff. Second, the sense of πέρας that Plato has Parmenides invoke in the *Parmenides*, that of boundary, bears within it the sense that he will have Socrates invoke in the *Philebus*, that of a ratio that realizes due measure. Boundaries establish both the relative places and the relative sizes of the

parts that they bound. And boundaries that answer to a form will place and apportion these parts in a way that will make the whole they make up a well-structured and well-proportioned instantiation of that form. This implies, to put the point in the language of *Philebus* 23c–27c, that the form puts an end to the flux and contest between the possibilities of being greater and smaller. In implicating a set of forms of parts, it fixes just how great and just how small each of the parts should be, both in relation to one another and in relation to the whole they comprise.

(*ii*) *The Great and Small and the ἄπειρον* These last reflections expand our earlier recognition of the way the πέρας-providing form collaborates with the Great and the Small. This stress on the Great and the Small in the *Parmenides* stands in striking contrast with the way Plato has Socrates treat them in the *Philebus*. There "greater and smaller" is but one pair of relative contraries among a number of others, all of which are said to be governed by more-and-less and to be members of the class of the ἄπειρον. In the several lists of examples Socrates offers, he also includes hotter and colder, drier and wetter, more and fewer, quicker and slower, and the musical contraries of high and low. In his synoptic remarks at 26a–b, moreover, he expands the range of possible continua to cover not only the physical (e.g., weather, strength, health) but also "a host of beautiful features found in our souls." Thus, magnitude, privileged in the *Parmenides*, emerges in the *Philebus* as but one case among others of a more general structure that is to be found in the spiritual as well as the material dimension of reality.

E. The Five "Unwritten Teachings" in the Parmenides *and the* Philebus

These two observations give us occasion to recognize the presence in both the *Parmenides* and the *Philebus* of all five of the teachings Aristotle reports in *Metaphysics* A6.

(*i*) *The Great and the Small as a Case of the Broader ἄπειρον* The first thing we must do is to take explicit note of the privileged status of the Great and the Small in Aristotle's reports. One possibility is that Aristotle, speaking "concisely and summarily" (συντόμως . . . καὶ κεφαλαιωδῶς; A7.988a18), honors a particularly important member of the ἄπειρον class by giving its name to the class as a whole. The *Parmenides*, with the prominence it gives Greatness and Smallness, could be read as possible evidence that in doing this, Aristotle is following Plato's own lead. It may also be that Aristotle focuses on the Great and the Small because in this part of *Metaphysics* A his project is to identify precursors to his own conception of the types of causality, in this case, of matter. However we sort this out, the important point for us is this: Aristotle, when he speaks of the Great and the Small, focuses narrowly what for Plato is ultimately a broader notion; the partner principle with the One is the ἄπειρον, and while the Great and the Small provides a clear exhibition of its dyadic form, the ἄπειρον includes, as well, all the other pairs that are named or even suggested in the *Philebus* passage.

(*ii*) *The Five "Unwritten Teachings" in Interplay* This said, we can now point to the presence of each of the five teachings. *#4: "Mathematicals."* The *Philebus* passages have brought us to recognize the continuum and the select set of ratios that, in each case, the limited plurality of forms picks out on it. Continuum and ratio are essentially mathematical structures, and they are "intermediate" between sensibles and Forms. If, on the one hand, we consider the continuum in its relation to sensibles, it presents itself as abstract and different in kind from them. As the full range of ratios between opposites, the continuum is the totality of structures possible for sensibles; as pure possibilities, these ratios are not located in place and time. Hence they are not subject to the flux that characterizes sensibles; as Aristotle says in A6, they are "eternal and unchanging" (987b16–17). On the other hand, they also lack the uniqueness of the Forms and so are different in kind from them as well. Each continuum is an instantiation of some dyad of Forms, and it bears, as an "unlimited many," an infinite number of abstract instances of each of these Forms. The continuum presents, again in Aristotle's words, "many like cases" (πόλλ' ἄττα ὅμοια), whereas the forms are "each of them just one" (ἓν ἕκαστον μόνον; 987b17). *#5: The identity of Forms and numbers.* We can now recognize a nonreductionist way to interpret teaching #5. The select set of ratios are, of course, "relation[s] of number to number." And it is, first, the limited plurality of Forms that picks these out and, second, the "single Form" that calls for this limited plurality of Forms. If we make a distinction between the nature of a Form and its causal power,[14] we can say that in the first respect Forms are not, and in the second respect they are, identical with numbers. Even while Forms and the ratios they call for are (as #4 asserts) ontologically different in kind, nonetheless, in their causal power Forms are functionally equivalent to these ratios. In picking them out on the continuum, Forms *express them-*

14. For evidence and argument that Plato makes this distinction in the *Parmenides*, see my *Plato's "Parmenides"* (cited in note 6 above), chaps. IV.C.I and V.B.2.b, especially pp. 154–55.

selves as numbers. *#1: Forms and the ἄπειρον*. We saw from the *Parmenides* that a Form provides the boundaries that structure the indeterminate magnitude—itself the concrete instantiation of the Great and the Small—as a composite sensible thing. And we've seen that the Great and the Small is but one member of the class of the ἄπειρον. So we can also see that (now to restate Aristotle's report of #1 with the general notion of the ἄπειρον in place of the specific case of it, the Great and the Small) Forms and the ἄπειρον are conjointly causes of sensibles. *#2: The One and the ἄπειρον*. We can also see what the Forms presuppose in order to accomplish this causal work. To provide boundaries is to make a whole of parts, and this is to bestow unity. But, as we noted, to bestow unity is to instantiate the One or Unity itself in its causal power. These boundaries, in turn, apportion the parts to one another; but this is to fix the proportions of the opposites that pertain to these parts by the selection of a set of ratios on the continuum framed by those opposites. In our three examples, these select sets are ratios of greater and smaller on the continuum of possible magnitude, ratios of high and low on the continuum of possible pitch (see Figure 2), and ratios of voiced and muted on the continuum of speech sound (see Figure 4). Each of these continua is an abstract instantiation of the ἄπειρον. Thus, for the Form to be a cause of sensibles requires both the instantiation of the One (this instantiation is the "single form" in its bestowal of unity on its sensible participants) and the instantiation of the ἄπειρον (this is the continuum); hence, the One and the ἄπειρον are conjointly causes of the Forms *in their being as causes* of sensibles.[15] *#3: The normative status of the select set of ratios*. The task of bringing to focus how the One is responsible for good and the ἄπειρον for ill gives us an occasion to articulate as a whole the causal hierarchy we

15. This is an appropriate point to note two distinctive features of this reconstruction of the sense of the "unwritten teachings." (i) On my reading, what Aristotle reports is not an account of how forms are themselves derived from the One and the Dyad. What a form gains from its participation in the One is its simplicity and uniqueness and—in a repetition, on the level of the form, of the One's bestowal of simplicity and uniqueness on it—its causal power to bestow unity on the sensibles that participate in it; what it gains from its collaboration with the ἄπειρον is the continuum on which, in accomplishing its bestowal of unity on its participants, the forms of parts that it implicates pick out the select set of ratios. What stands logically (not, of course, temporally) prior to all this is the determinate nature itself that the Form essentially is. In this sense, what the One and the ἄπειρον are conjointly responsible for is not the nature that the Form essentially is but only the causal power that it has. (Note that this reading saves the "unwritten teachings" from a damaging obscurity. If one derives the Forms themselves from the One and the ἄπειρον, then one must find the basis for the determinateness of each of the Forms *in these principles*. But the One and the ἄπειρον are general in character. To bring out the problem in an exemplary way: though we can find in the uniqueness of each Form a respect in which it instantiates the One itself, we cannot appeal to the One itself to explain the determinate nature itself that each Form, in its uniqueness, *is*.) (ii) The distinction between the nature that the Form essentially is and

have been retracing. The One is instantiated in a "single form's" bestowal of unity on the in itself indeterminate nature that its participant otherwise would be. A "single form" bestows unity by implicating a set of forms of parts, each of which marks out a ratio on the relevant continuum of opposites. These ratios establish the proportion of the opposites that is appropriate to each part of the whole in its relations to the other parts and to the whole. But "the appropriate" (τὸ πρέπον, one of the names for the mean at *Statesman* 284e6) is a normative notion; a sensible whose parts conform to these ratios will be good, that is, a good embodiment of the "single form." Hence the One, insofar as it is responsible for the "single form's" bestowal of unity, is also responsible for the good.[16] The ἄπειρον, on the other hand, is the counterprinciple to the One. In its abstract instantiation as the continuum, it is in itself indifferent to the priority of one possibility over another that is implied by the selection of a normative set of ratios. And in its concrete instantiation as the indeterminate substrate that the boundaries first structure, it is an unchecked flux and contest between the opposites. Hence, when the parts of a thing exceed or fall short of the ratios set by the forms of the parts, it is the ἄπειρον factor in the thing that is expressed and that is in this sense the ultimate cause.

IV. THE EXHIBITION OF THE "UNWRITTEN TEACHINGS" IN THE DIAIRESIS OF THE FIFTEEN KINDS OF ART IN THE *Statesman*

In the context created by these reflections, we can begin to see what Plato is doing in having the Eleatic Stranger lay out his distinction of the fifteen kinds of art at the close of the *Statesman.* The Eleatic Stranger practices the new mode of dialectic that Socrates introduces at *Philebus* 16c–18d. The fifteen kinds are anything but a mere list. On the contrary,

the causal power that it has frees us, in what I take to be a genuinely Platonic way, from the customary choice between taking the Form to be separate and taking it to be immanent. The nature is underived and transcendent, but its causal power gives it, in its expression as the ratios that structure the sensible, immanence. Traditional two-world readings and the more recent efforts to deny the separateness of the Forms (see, for a powerful articulation of the latter position, Sayre, *Plato's Late Ontology*, esp. chap. 3, part 5) each capture only one of these two aspects of the Forms.

16. In this way the formal causal force of the One coincides with that of the Good. Is this the basis for, and so a key to the interpretation of, the identification of the Good with the One that Aristoxenus appears to report in his famous comment on Plato's lecture on the Good? For seminal discussions, see Kraemer, *Arete bei Platon*; Sayre, *Plato's Late Ontology*; and Rafael Ferber, *Platos Idee des Guten*, 2d ed. (Sankt Augustin: Academia Verlag Richarz, 1989). See also my "'Unwritten Teachings' in the *Parmenides*" (cited in note 7 above), pp. 360–63.

they constitute a specimen case of the ultimate ontological order that Aristotle reports Plato to have articulated in the "unwritten teachings." We can now bring this order into view by three related sets of observations. (For a diagrammatic representation of the field of relations laid bare by the Eleatic Stranger's distinctions, see Figure 8 in the Appendix. It is by reflection on this field that, in the next three sections, we shall try to bring to view the order articulated in the "unwritten teachings.")

A. The One and Its Instantiation in the "Single Form": "Care"

Is there, present and at work in the Eleatic Stranger's distinction of the fifteen kinds, that "single form" that Socrates in the *Philebus* says we must find as the first step in the new mode of dialectic? And does it, a simple and unique one, instantiate the One in bestowing unity of a lower grade on what otherwise would lack it? There is indeed a "single form"; it is ἐπιμέλεια (276b7), that "care" for itself that the Eleatic Stranger finds, in light of his myth of the ages, each human community must take up as its fundamental task. If the overt claim of the myth is that no god or daimon is at hand to "care" for the needs of human beings, its implicit point is that this is a task not for any despotic shepherd of the people but for the community as a whole, to be shared and accomplished by the coordinated practices of the arts. But this is to say, to recast the Eleatic Stranger's anthropological point in terms of the ontology of the *Philebus*, that the "single form" "care" requires, for its instantiation, the instantiation of a limited plurality of forms, the fifteen kinds of art. These fifteen are the analogues to the forms of notes that make up the musical "modes" and, again, to the forms of the letter sounds that make up syllables and words. The Eleatic Stranger implies this from the beginning when, first alerting Young Socrates to the need to abandon bifurcatory diairesis, he says that they must divide the kinds of art *κατὰ μέλη* . . . οἷον ἱερεῖον, "*limb by limb* . . . like a sacrificial animal" (287c3). The analysis of "care" involves recognizing which are the kinds that, like "limbs," are fit for interplay, fit to make up, in their 'organic' relations, a cooperative whole.

B. The ἄπειρον and Its Instantiation in the Continuum Traced by the Series of Fifteen Kinds

On our interpretation of #2 of the five teachings, however, the One exercises its causal responsibility conjointly with the ἄπειρον; the One's instantiation in a "single form" that bestows unity presupposes a continuum on which the forms of parts pick out ratios. Do we find in the Eleatic

Stranger's final distinctions the abstract instantiation of the ἄπειρον in a continuum between opposites? The more closely we study the fifteen kinds, the more evident the underlying continuum becomes.

(*i*) *The list as a series.* The Eleatic Stranger makes the *serial* or *gradual* character of his distinctions explicit; at each step he marks the distance of the kind he is distinguishing from the sought-for form of statesmanship, and by the specificity of his negations, as well as by his pointed revision of the order of the arts in his synopsis of the first seven kinds at 289a, he makes clear that he is moving stepwise and gradually from the arts most remote from statesmanship through those that are closer to it toward statesmanship itself.[17]

(*ii*) *The opposites and midpoint.* The series he traces, moreover, has the genuine *bipolarity* and *midpoint* that characterize the sample continua Socrates cites in the *Philebus.* At the one extreme stands the kind of art that provides the raw materials, the physical stuff, for the subsequent shaping of it into things by the next kinds of art. At the other extreme stands statesmanship proper with its preeminent concern, made explicit in the final pages of the dialogue (305e–311c), for the formation of good character. Thus the opposites that frame the continuum are the material and the spiritual aspects of the life of the community. At the midpoint, in turn, stands the eighth kind, the art of the slave. Slaves are both "possessions" (cf. κτητούς; 289d10) and agents. As agents, they belong to the second set of seven arts, the arts of service, in contrast with the first set of seven, the arts that produce things. But as "possessions" they are like things and stand as "the opposite" (τοὐναντίον; 289d7) to the statesman. In this double status, the art of slaves is analogous to the middle kinds that Socrates picked out in his diaireses of music and letter sounds in the *Philebus,* "even toned" pitch and sounds "not voiced but having a certain noise." Each of the three marks an equal proportion of the relevant opposites.

(*iii*) *The continuum of proportions of material and spiritual.* Finally, once we recognize the poles and midpoint, the continuum traced by the remaining kinds becomes fully evident. Each of the fifteen kinds strikes a distinctive balance of the material and the spiritual in the specific way that it "cares" for the life of the community.[18] In the first seven (the

17. This use of the negatives to indicate the serial character of the list is detailed in my "The God-Given Way" (cited in note 9 above), p. 348, n29.

18. With this vision of the continuum, central to the *Statesman,* in mind, it is striking to read the following passage at *Timaeus* 87c–e: "Everything which is good is beautiful [καλόν],

"contributive arts"), the material dominates the spiritual—but in decreasing proportion as we approach the midpoint. In the final seven (the "directly responsible arts"), the spiritual dominates the material—and in increasing proportion as we approach statesmanship. It goes beyond the limits of this discussion to attempt a detailed commentary, but it is possible to indicate in a titular way how the proportions of material and spiritual shift as we move from each kind of art to the next. Notice, first, how the series moves from arts that produce physical stuff (no. 1 on Figure 7 in the Appendix) to arts that transform this into determinate things designed to produce (no. 2), then to preserve (no. 3), then to bear and transport (no. 4) other things. The vehicles made by the fourth kind of arts, however, can also transport persons; hence this kind is transitional to the next three kinds, which produce things not for other things but for persons, albeit in their physical being. These are the arts that produce physical protections (no. 5), ornaments and sensory diversions (no. 6), and nourishment of all sorts (no. 7). Notice, next, how this last series moves from what is relatively external to persons in their physical being (e.g., in no. 4, ships and wagons, and in no. 5, walls and armor and clothes) to what actually makes up their physical being (in no. 7, food as it becomes part of the body [288e] and exercise, which is itself the body's own activity). Hence, the series leads gradually into the midpoint kind, the art of the slave (no. 8), for a slave produces his own body's activity in order to serve. The next three kinds of art, those of merchants and traders (no. 9), of clerks and heralds (no. 10), and of priests and diviners (no. 11), trace the continuum from the economic deeds of distributing material goods through the administrative deeds of recording and regulating such distribution to the conventionally religious deeds of directing the city's public ritual practices and, so, cultivating traditional piety. From this (after the lengthy interruption by the Eleatic Stranger's reflections on types of factional rule and the function of law) the series moves into the arts that care most fully for the spiritual—that is, the good character of the citizens. Now the Eleatic Stranger leads from the rhetoric

---

and the beautiful is not without proportion [οὐκ ἄμετρον], and the animal which is to be beautiful must have due proportion [σύμμετρον]. Now we perceive lesser symmetries or proportions and reason about them, but of the most basic and greatest [κυριώτατα καὶ μέ γιστα] we take no heed, for with regard to health and disease, virtue and vice, there is no proportion or lack of it [συμμετρία καὶ ἀμετρία] that is greater than that between soul and body themselves. But we do not perceive this, nor do we reflect that when a weak or inferior frame is the vehicle of a soul that is strong and in all ways great or, conversely, when an inferior soul is fit together with a strong body, then the animal as a whole is not beautiful, for it lacks the most important of all symmetries. The animal, on the other hand, that is in the opposite condition [that is, that has due proportion of mind and body] is the most beautiful and loveliest of all sights to him who has eyes to see." (My translation, with the help of those of Benjamin Jowett and R. G. Bury.)

(no. 12) that sustains the citizens' acceptance of the statesman's wise rule (i.e., to recall the moral psychology of the *Republic,* their temperance) through the generalship (no. 13) that, deferring to the statesman's decision whether or not to go to war (and so, again, cultivating temperance), sustains the citizens' readiness to fight (and so their courage) and, next, through the judge's ability (no. 14) to preserve the law and the harmony it aims for between the different groups of citizens (i.e., their justice) to, finally, statesmanship itself (no. 15), which consists in the wisdom that directs the cultivation of temperance, courage, and justice in the citizenry.

C. The Normative Status of the Ratios on the Continuum— The City with the Fifteen Kinds of Art as Sacred

If the reflections in sections A and B are well taken, then the One is instantiated in the way the "single form" "care" bestows unity on actual cities that participate in and embody it. This bestowal involves a complex set of relations: "care" implies a limited plurality of forms of parts, the fifteen kinds of art, each of which marks off, on the continuum between the material and the spiritual, some definite proportion (or range of proportions) of these opposites to one another. But as we have seen, the continuum is, as a series of possible proportions, an abstract instantiation of the dyadic ἄπειρον. Hence the One and the ἄπειρον are conjointly responsible for the "single form's" being the cause of sensibles, that is, for "care's" causal role for actual cities. The one step remaining for us is to mark the normative force of the select set of ratios—and thereby of the limited number of forms, and thereby of the "single form"—for actual cities. For in this we bring to focus the way in which, ultimately, the One is responsible for "good." The Eleatic Stranger indicates that he intends his series of fifteen to express a normative order with his allusion to the sacred at 287c3: as cited in section A (but with a different stress), he introduces his distinctions by telling Young Socrates that they must divide the kinds of art κατὰ μέλη . . . οἷον ἱερεῖον, "limb by limb . . . like a *sacrificial animal.*" Sacrifice was made both to please the gods and to entreat their good will. To be worthy of them and win their favor, the ἱερεῖον must be perfectly formed, and the ritual dismemberment must respect and reveal this perfection.[19] The Eleatic Stranger's simile therefore suggests that in his diairesis he will lay out the "limbs" or

19. Walter Burkert, *Greek Religion,* trans. John Raffan (Cambridge, Mass.: Harvard University Press, 1985), describes how "the bones are laid on the pyre prepared on the altar in just order. In Homer, beginnings from all limbs of the animal, small pieces of meat, are also placed on the pyre: the dismembered creature is to be reconstituted symbolically" (p. 57).

parts that, in their capacity for interplay, make for the perfectly formed city.[20]

To see the normative status of the Eleatic Stranger's diairesis more specifically, we would need to reflect on each of the fifteen kinds in concrete detail. In this limited space I can only sketch the character of such a reflection.[21] The key questions to pursue would be the same in kind as in the cases of the exemplary diaireses of musical notes and of letter sounds in the *Philebus*. First, focusing on any one of the fifteen kinds, we should ask what other kinds it requires in order to fulfill its function. And second, as the possible combinations (the analogues to the modal sets in all their variants in the case of music and to the various possible syllables in the case of the letter sounds) begin to emerge, we should ask whether a city *without* the full web of physical and spiritual activities that these combinations enable would be "caring" for itself as well as it can and should. What we will find is that even while some of the kinds, viewed in isolation, seem unimportant (does a well-formed city really need, e.g., the container-making arts?), in fact each of the kinds both requires and is required by various of the others. Thus, for example, the distribution of material goods presupposes the work of preserving and of moving them, and all of these tasks require raw materials and tools; again, defending the city requires not only good generalship but also strong walls and a healthy citizenry; still again, the basic cooperation involved both in distribution and in defense presupposes the shared values that are cultivated in public rites and sourced in the education for which, in different respects, the arts of the rhetor, the judge, and the law-making statesman are responsible; and so on. The more we probe, the more compelling becomes the Eleatic Stranger's implicit claim that it is the presence and absence of such combinations—and, so, of the full set of "limbs" that are variously at work in them—that make the difference between good and bad cities, that is, between good and bad political instantiations of "care."

V. IMPLICATIONS

In closing, it is worth making explicit several different sorts of implications. (i) I began by observing that the *Statesman* offers itself to its Academic readers, in particular, as an exemplary exhibition of the stages through which the process of philosophical education should lead. We

20. Notice, too, the characterizations of the city as united by the "divine" (θεῖον) bond of "divine" (θείαν) true opinion and, so, as itself "daimonic" (δαιμονίῳ), at 309c3, 309c7, and 309c8, respectively.

21. For an example of such a reflection, see my "The God-Given Way" (cited in note 9 above), pp. 354–56.

have now found, in its closing nonbifurcatory dialectic, a specific exhibition of the ontological order that Plato articulates (according to Aristotle's report) in the "unwritten teachings." This implies that, for the Plato who wrote the *Statesman,* coming to see this ontological order is a long-term goal of the process of philosophical education. To say this is to acknowledge emphatically the importance of the "unwritten teachings." (ii) Notice, however, that this should underscore, not diminish, the importance of the dialogues. Not only have we found the "unwritten teachings" in three Platonic writings—the passages in the *Parmenides, Philebus,* and *Statesman*—but it has been by exploring their presence in these passages that we have been able to work out the first outlines of an interpretation of those teachings.[22] (iii) This brings to the fore a question and, with it, a crucial choice. What do we make of the fact that the "unwritten teachings" are, on our reading, *written*? What is the status of the writings in which we have found them suggested? The options facing us range between two extremes. On the one hand, there is the possibility of taking the texts to operate on two very different levels at once, corresponding to

22. Needless to say, the account we have arrived at so far must be expanded and deepened in key respects. Interpretation of the dialogues will, I hope, continue to prove to be the key. As an indication of the sorts of conceptual issues that we need to think through as we interpret, consider just these four questions. (*i*) *The Good and the One.* What relation between the One and the Good is implied by the normative status of the Forms and the ratios that have the One as their ultimate source? Does it run counter to the nature that the One itself is for it to coincide in its causal power with the Good, or counter to the nature that the Good itself is for it to coincide in its causal power with the One? (See note 16 above.) (*ii*) *The Unity of the Forms.* Is it consistent with the simplicity of the Form that when it does the work of the "single form" (*Philebus* 16c), it implicates a limited plurality of Forms that, in interplay like "limbs" (*Statesman* 287c), comprise a whole? (I have argued for the necessity of both simplicity and whole-part structure in related contexts in my *Plato's "Parmenides"* [cited in note 6 above], pp. 179–83, and in "Unity and Logos: A Reading of *Theaetetus* 201c–10a," *Ancient Philosophy* 12 [1992: 87–111.) (*iii*) *The nature of the mathematicals.* How are we to interpret the notions of ratio and number that the relation of the Forms and the continuum requires? The continuum can be reconstructed in different ways, depending, for example, on whether we key from the relative sizes of parts (the starting point suggested by some of the language of the *Parmenides*) or from the notion that the equality of the opposites defines a midpoint (the starting point suggested by the music example in the *Philebus* and by other language of the *Parmenides*). Of seminal value for the sorts of questions to be investigated here are D. H. Fowler, *The Mathematics of Plato's Academy: A New Reconstruction* (Oxford: Clarendon Press, 1987), and David Lachterman, *The Ethics of Geometry: A Genealogy of Modernity* (New York: Routledge, 1989). (*iv*) *The heterogeneity of the opposites.* The preceding question is complicated by the different kinds of opposites that we include as cases of the Dyad. The four kinds passage in the *Philebus* complicates matters in an initial way when, after establishing that the pairs of opposites that belong to the Apeiron are governed by more-and-less, it goes on to include those opposites whose determination establishes the beautiful features of souls (26b). Our *Statesman* passages complicate matters even further when, on our reading, they pair material and spiritual themselves as opposites. (This is not unique to the *Statesman.* Recall *Timaeus* 87c–e, quoted in note 18 above.) How does it bear on our notion of ratio that the terms apportioned to each other can be (roughly speaking) material, spiritual, or material and spiritual?

the two very different audiences, those outside and those inside the Academy, which they simultaneously address. On this view, Plato's inexplicitness—indeed, his extreme compression—functions in different ways for each of these audiences. With those outside the Academy, who have not been introduced to the teachings, Plato's main concern is to protect against misunderstanding; by his reticence he in effect conceals the teachings from those not prepared to grasp them. But for those inside the Academy, to whom Plato has introduced the teachings in face-to-face conversation, his inexplicitness functions positively: his brief remarks provide ὑπομνήματα, allusive "reminders," of what they have heard and must now go on to understand for themselves. This first possibility might be developed on the basis of a straightforward reading of the famous criticism of the limits of writing in the *Phaedrus*. On the other hand, there is also the possibility of an interpretation of the situation that takes seriously the evidence that the *Statesman* (and, in fact, a number of the later dialogues) mirrors with mimetic irony the teaching situation in the Academy.[23] Does the failure to think philosophically that is represented in the dramatic action of the dialogue by Young Socrates' authoritarian agreements and unquestioning leaps reflect problems of communication and understanding in the Academy itself? Is it, indeed, in response to such problems that Plato writes the *Statesman*? If so, if, that is, Plato felt the need to communicate indirectly *even within the Academy*, then the privileging of face-to-face conversation and the projection of the "unwritten teachings" as its straightforward content become problematic.[24] Instead, the dialogues and the conversation in the Academy will be, in effect, embedded in one another, and our hermeneutics will have to be thoroughly dialectical.[25]

23. I have developed this view in *The Philosopher in Plato's "Statesman,"* cited in note 2 above.

24. For discussion of the problems involved, see Stanley Rosen's Introduction to *Plato's "Symposium,"* 2d ed. (New Haven, Conn.: Yale University Press, 1987), pp. xxxix–lvii.

25. Earlier versions of this essay were presented at the Third Plato Symposium, sponsored by the International Plato Society, in Bristol, England, in August 1992; in colloquia at Vassar College and Boston University in April 1993; and as a Franklin J. Matchette Lecture at The Catholic University of America in November 1993. I owe special thanks to Rachel Kitzinger for valuable discussion and to John Van Ophuijsen for a number of helpful editorial suggestions.

FIGURE 1 *Schema for bifurcatory diairesis ("halving")*

```
    A
   / \
  B   C
     / \
    F   G
```

FIGURE 2 *Initial distinctions in the first example of nonbifurcatory diairesis in the* Philebus*—musical sounds*

```
"the original one":     "sound as treated by music," that is, pitch
                            /              |              \
                         "high"      "even-toned"       "low"

                         h>1 -------- h=1 -------- h<1
```

FIGURE 3 *The Greater Perfect System*

the seven species of the octave (i.e. scales formed by notes selected from the double octave laid out as two conjunct tetrachords plus a completing note):

```
*    * * *   * * *   *
     * * *   * * *   *   *
       * *   * * *   *   * *
         *   * * *   *   * * *
             * * *   *   * * *   *
               * *   *   * * *   * *
                 *   *   * * *   * * *
┌───┬─┬─┐───┬─┬─┐    ┌───┬─┬─┐───┬─┬─┐    |
                 middle note              added note
                   [μέση]           [προσλαμβανόμενος]
-----------------------------------------------------------
HIGH                    EVEN                       LOW
(high>low)            (high=low)               (high<low)
```

(Note: Each of the baseline tetrachords is in the enharmonic genus: the intervals are two tones, quarter tone, quarter tone. The species of the octave differ from each other by virtue of the different sequences of these intervals that each has.)

FIGURE 4 *Initial distinctions in the second example of nonbifurcatory diairesis in the* Philebus*—letter sounds*

```
                           "the        vs.    "others           vs.    "the
                           voiced"            not voiced               not voiced
                                              but having               and noiseless"
                                              a certain noise"

the unlimited plurality    (maximal ------------------------------- (maximal
of uttered sound:          release of breath)                       cutting off of breath)
```

FIGURE 5 *Possible reconstruction of the full diairesis of letter sounds in the* Philebus:

```
the "single form":              "letter" [στοιχεῖον]
                          /             |             \
                       "the      vs.  "others     vs.  "the
                       voiced"         not voiced       not voiced
                                       but having       and noiseless"
                                       a certain noise"

                       /|\ ...         /|\ ...          /|\ ...
the limited number
of "ones":                  [the various letter sounds]

the continuum of uttered sound:
        L_J__L_J__L_J__L_J__L_J__L_J__L_J__L_J__L_J__L_J__L_J__L_J__L_J
(maximal release of breath)                (maximal cutting off of breath)
```

FIGURE 6 *General schema for nonbifurcatory diairesis in the* Philebus:

```
the "single form":                                    X
                                     /      /         |        \       \
the limited plurality of forms:      A  &   B    &    C   &    D   &   E

the "unlimited many," i.e., the
continuum between opposites, and
the set of normative balances (that
is, the set of limits) that the forms
A & B & C & D & E pick out:          |--------|--------|--------|--------|
                                 Opposite                              Opposite

                                 the particulars in place and time that, to instantiate
                                 the "single form" well, must embody the various
                                 normative balances picked out by A & B & C & D & E
```

FIGURE 7 *The continuum of the fifteen kinds of art in the* Statesman:

```
  1,        2, 3, 4,      5, 6, 7,        8,       9, 10,11,     12,13,14,        15,
 rm,        t, c, v,      d, a, n,        sl,      m, c, p,       r, g, j,        st
  |-------|--|--|-------|--|--|---------|------|--|--|-------|--|--|----------|
(concerned with the                                              (concerned with the
material life of the city)                                        spiritual life of the city)
```

FIGURE 8 *The distinction of the fifteen kinds of art in the* Statesman, *represented as a case of the new mode of nonbifurcatory diairesis introduced in the* Philebus *at 16c ff.:*

```
the "single form":          "care" of the whole human community
                                          /|\
                                         / | \
                 "contributive           slave's          "directly responsible
                      arts"       /        art      \            arts"
                                 /                   \
the "limbs":   1,    2, 3, 4,   5, 6, 7,    8,    9, 10,11,   12,13,14,   15,
               rm,   t, c, v,   d, a, n,    sl,   m, c, p,    r, g, j,    st
```

the continuum between opposites and the balances upon it picked out by "the limbs":

```
|------|--|--|-------|--|--|------|------|--|--|-------|--|--|----------|
```

(concerned with the material life of the city) — (concerned with the spiritual life of the city)

particulars in place and time:

the arts in any actual city that—to instantiate well the "single form," "care," and so constitute a good city—must embody the various normative balances picked out by the fifteen kinds

11 The Problem of Sense Perception in Plato's *Philebus*

STANLEY ROSEN

The main part of this essay consists of a detailed analysis of a short but dense and puzzling passage in Plato's *Philebus* that extends from 38c5 to 39c6 in the Stephanus pagination. As a supplement to my discussion of the *Philebus* text, I shall also have to refer, although much more briefly, to a passage in the *Theaetetus*. Stated with introductory concision, the problem raised by these texts is that of how we distinguish between true and false perceptual judgments. In order to bring out the fundamental importance of this problem, I need to say a word about the Kantian doctrine of sense perception, and finally also something about how the difference between Plato and Kant is present, albeit in a confusing way, in the contemporary discussion that takes its bearings by psychology and physiology.

In the *Theaetetus* (185c4 ff., 186e1 ff.), Socrates contends, with the assistance of the eponymous young mathematician, that perception does not share in (*metestin*) truth because it does not share in being (*ousia*) or not-being (*to mē einai*). It is the soul, as Theaetetus puts it, *autē di hautēs* "itself by itself," that arrives at the truth about perceived entities (185d7 ff.). As Socrates clarifies the process, the soul speaks to itself or engages in discursive thinking (*dianoeisthai*) about the *ousia* it has apprehended by itself, and so arrives at a judgment (*doxazein*) about the perceived entity (189e6 ff.).

I interject a philological remark. The Greek words *doxa* and *doxazein* may be translated variously by the appropriate English expressions of "belief," "opinion," or "judgment." The opinion with which we are concerned in both the *Theaetetus* and *Philebus* arises from the choice between opposing or distinct identifications of a perceptual entity. In the *Philebus* (38c6), Socrates uses the verb *krinein*, 'to decide', 'to choose', or to 'judge', to express the first step in this process. To form an opinion is thus to come to a judgment. It should be kept in mind that the terms *doxa* and *doxazein* refer to the result or process of coming to a judgment, and not to the scientific or philosophical certitude of that judgment. Even a true *doxa* lacks the veridical status of *epistēmē* or a true *logos*. With these qualifications in mind, I shall translate *doxa* and *doxazein* throughout as "judgment" and "to judge."

For my present purposes, the upshot of the passage in the *Theaetetus* is as follows: Since the soul arrives at truth about the perceived object entirely apart from perception, it is unclear what role the act of perception plays in the process by which we arrive at true judgments about that object. But furthermore, it is unclear why the communion of the soul with itself concerning the *ousia* and other common properties of the perceived object should license a true judgment about the particular properties of that object. One might assume that the *ousia* in question is the Platonic Idea corresponding to the object, but in fact there is no reference to the doctrine of Ideas anywhere in the *Theaetetus*. And there is no apparent reason why the apprehension of the general property of being should cast any light on the identity of the particular existing object of perception.

At first glance, then, it looks as though Socrates in the *Theaetetus* accounts for true perceptual judgments by way neither of sense perception nor of noetic apprehension of pure Forms or Ideas. The most likely inference from his quite tentative and generally aporetic analysis is that the soul somehow constitutes the object of perception in thought by uniting the particulars of sensation through the agency of a direct inspection of the common properties like being, likeness, sameness, unity, and so on. If this is right, then the result is rather surprising. Socrates turns out in this passage to be a Kantian, or at least a proto-Kantian.

Let me spell out this inference a bit further. Throughout the section of the *Theaetetus* to which I have just alluded, the problem is to explain the connection (*sunapsis*) between the pure apprehension of the being of an entity by the soul and the perception of that entity (195c6 ff.). It is easy to see that this problem has two parts. First, how does the soul "share in" or apprehend the being of the perceived entity? Second, how does the soul connect its apprehension of that being with what we can call the sense data of perception? No answers to these questions are provided in the *Theaetetus*.

It is striking that the first question is not even posed; Socrates and Theaetetus both take it for granted that we do apprehend the unified entity that underlies its perceived properties. As Socrates says, it would be strange if we contained within ourselves many separate senses, which did not unite in *mia idea*, "one idea" or "form," "whether we call it 'soul' or something else," by which we perceive through the instruments (*organa*) of the senses (184d1 ff.). To this we may add, not only would it be strange, but there would be no ordinary experience to analyze. Note that the word 'idea' refers to the soul or unifying intellectual faculty, not to the Form of the unified entity. This is also a proto-Kantian touch.

The second question, namely, the "how" of the connection of thought and perception, is central to the *Theaetetus* but receives no answer. Do I perceive the sensory properties, let us say, of a horse, and then unify these impressions by means of my separate apprehension of the being of the horse? Or do I apprehend the being of the horse within my unification of the separate sensations constituting my perception of the horse? If the first alternative is correct, then obviously perception of individual horses is superfluous to the formulation of true judgments about horses. This would be compatible with the doctrine of separate Platonic Ideas. On the second alternative, the perception of a horse is a consequence of synthetic thought. This would be equivalent to Kantianism.

Let us restate in expanded form the first alternative by assuming that when the soul converses with itself about the *ousia* of the horse, it is referring to the Idea of the horse. *Either* the Idea of the horse is present within each individual horse, and so the act of unifying our separate perceptions of it is also the act of apprehending its Idea; let us call this Aristotelianism. *Or* the Idea of the horse is somehow imposed onto the separate perceptions by the psychic activity of unification; let us call this Platonism. In the first case, it has to be explained how the same Idea can be present within a multiplicity of individual horses without itself being multiplied, or, in other words, how the perception of a particular physical horse can also be the apprehension of a nonphysical form that is common to all horses. In the second case, since the unification of form and perception is effected by pure thought, Platonism seems to be indistinguishable from Kantianism, as Hegel, for example, seems to have held.

I will now summarize and restate the preceding reflections. Let us call Platonism the doctrine of Platonic Ideas and Kantianism the doctrine of the constitution of the form as a joint process of perception and judgment, or, in other words, as a synthetic unification in thought of concepts and sensations. If Platonism is defensible, it must be the case that we have access to the form, and hence to the unified perceptible entity, in the act of perception. Otherwise, Platonism is reduced to the nonsense that Aristotle makes of it, or it succumbs to Kantianism. But further, the form cannot be the same as the *morphē* or shape of the perceptible entity; if it were, there would be no difference between perception and eidetic apprehension, and the form would be a construction of the sensory apparatus (I will not even mention the difficulties arising from the Darwinian doctrine of the evolution of species forms). This distinction between the form as Idea and the *morphē* or physical Gestalt will take on considerable importance later when we turn to the *Philebus.*

The motivation underlying my study of the cited Platonic texts is that I wish to ascertain if the conventionally formulated difference between Plato and Kant in fact holds. But the deeper philosophical motivation of this essay is my conviction that unless Platonism can be sustained against Kantianism, the result is disastrous for philosophy, and hence for the coherence and value of science as well.

The next step of my argument requires me to state as concisely as possible what I regard as the fatal weakness of the Kantian doctrine of perception. Kant is no more able than Plato to explain the synthesis between the common properties or (as he calls them) categories and the perceptible identity of the individual perceived object. The transcendental ego is no less mythical and far more hypothetical an explanation for the synthesis of categories and sensations than Socrates' reference to the soul or discursive thought. No additional evidence is required to ascertain that we engage in discursive thinking when we formulate perceptual judgments, whereas the hypothesis of the transcendental ego rests upon an inference from the fact of discursive thinking.

The "as if" aspect of the transcendental ego is justified by the need to explain the objective unity of thought and perception. This explanation is in turn satisfactory only if it can account for the identity of a perceived object, which in turn serves as the foundation for predicative judgments. In this essay, I shall therefore limit my criticism of Kant to the issue of objective identification. Please remember that the ostensibly "transcendental" status of the Kantian doctrine does not excuse it from the requirement of actually functioning to explain the conditions for the possibility of empirical knowledge. In contemporary terminology, a model is defective if it renders impossible the phenomena it is designed to explain.

Here is a sketch of my argument to the effect that Kant fails to explain perceptual identification, and that he has no basis for the distinction he makes between true and false perceptual judgments.

For Kant, perception is already a combination of sensation and conceptual thinking. The perceived object must not be confused with the subjective or sensed ostensible object, which Kant attributes to British empiricism and its doctrine of psychological association. Kant asserts that this associational or pseudo-object cannot be known or distinguished from dreams and fantasies. The act of perceiving a dog (Kant's own example) is therefore identical with the act by which we constitute the formal unity of the dog by conceptualization. But if to perceive is to constitute or conceive the being and formal structure of the dog, then obviously there can be no false perceptual judgment about dogs.

It is also impossible to explain on Kantian grounds how we perceive a dog rather than a wolf or a cat, since perceptual identification includes in its conceptual apparatus a general rule or schema that lacks the precision to discriminate in this way. This is obvious from Kant's own example: "[T]he concept 'dog' signifies a rule according to which my imagination can delineate the figure of a four-footed animal in a general manner without limitation to any single determinate figure such as experience, or any image that I can represent *in concreto*, actually presents."

Kant goes on to derive the image of the dog from empirical or reproductive imagination and the schema of sensible concepts from the pure a priori imagination.[1] But this must mean that the perceived identity of this dog in particular, say my own beagle, Rex, is imaginary; the image comes from experience, but experience apart from conceptual structure is subjective and useless for objective judgment. Unfortunately, the addition of the structure to the image constitutes the object, and makes all judgments about it true. I have no space to explore the Kantian doctrine of imagination, but this much is evident: once we cease to believe in the transcendental ego, our concepts become linguistic creations of the empirical individual, and our perceptions are reduced to the status of products of the empirical imagination.

As I see it, in other words, the triumph of Kantianism over Platonism is the proximate cause of today's standard depreciation of the given, and so of the accelerated dissolution of ordinary experience. Stated with maximum simplicity, Platonism depends upon our being in direct contact with the entity of perception in exactly the way that is suggested to us by ordinary experience. From this standpoint, Platonism is not a metaphysics of detached forms but a phenomenology of the *Lebenswelt.* This remark would have to be refined, but it is sufficient for our present purposes.

My point here is not that Platonism explains ordinary experience, but that it tries to save the phenomena. Kantianism leads eventually to the degradation of the phenomena to the level of a sort of warehouse for the detritus of repudiated theories, and finally to the status of an unsatisfactory theory in its own right. But if ordinary experience is merely a theory, what is the basis for distinguishing between true and false, or even between better and worse, theories? Why should we take seriously the very popular thesis of the myth of the given? Surely science begins from the given; if the given is a myth, then so is science. Nor is there any coherent inference from the variety of scientific theories to the conclusion that there is nothing but a variety of givens.

Contemporary psychology and neurophysiology have no more ex-

1. *Critique of Pure Reason*, Kemp Smith translation, B180–81.

plained the unification and identification of the perceived object, and more generally of the perceptual field, than did Plato or Kant. I am, of course, not referring here to the extraordinary progress that has been made recently in explaining the neurophysiological substructure of perception. But there remains a disjunction between the analysis of the substructure and the coherence of the given. In my opinion, what in fact happens is this: The working scientist explicitly begins from the givenness of ordinary experience, which he or she proceeds as it were to dismantle. All efforts to reassemble the results of analysis into a model of the coherent world of everyday perceptual identification and judgment proceed with an eye to what is given. Yet many scientists, and many more philosophers of science, resolutely deny that the given is anything more than a myth, or insist that it is a linguistic artifact or a Nietzschean perspective.

This is not the place for an exhaustive documentation of what I take in any case to be obvious. No one, not even proponents of the possible-worlds school of philosophy of science, begins from hypothetical conditions on Mars or in another universe, or with some imagined possibility with respect to nonhuman perceptual faculties and organs. The recourse to logically possible alternatives is always motivated by the need to explain the nature of our own given experience. If the givenness of this experience were so heterogeneous as to preclude a common starting point, then obviously there would be no experience, and certainly no science or rational explanation.

I will nevertheless allude to the fact that scientific students of perception, whether these be Gestalt psychologists, Gibsonian phenomenologists, specialists in Fourier analysis, or relatively unphilosophical psychologists of perception, "take the world's reality as a given and work from there, asking how well the human senses actually describe that world."[2] The quotation is from a textbook by Sekuler and Blake on visual perception, but similar passages could be cited from sources as diverse as Wolfgang Kohler, James J. Gibson, or David Marr.

As I would express the general situation, modern science begins with Kantian assumptions concerning the constructive status of the object of perception, assumptions themselves rooted in the distinction between primary and secondary attributes, but detaches these assumptions from the Kantian doctrine of the synthetic unity of pure thought, which is replaced by various inadequate hypothetical instruments of unification, for example, currently popular parallel distributed processing. The inadequacy of these hypotheses is compensated for, and perhaps even masked, by a Platonic assumption, just noted in the reference to contemporary

2. R. Sekuler and R. Blake, *Perception* (New York: Knopf, 1985), p. 9.

psychology, that the unity of the perceptual field as well as the unity and identity of perceived objects are given initially by everyday experience. We first perceive a dog or a cat, and then attempt to explain how this perception occurs. But the analysis of the perception into light or sound waves, the firing of neurons, or sinusoidal gratings composed of light and dark bars, cannot be reintegrated into the original perception of the cat or dog.

True judgments about perceived objects are thus in fact grounded in the initial apprehensions of ordinary or prescientific experience, which serve ironically as Platonic paradigms for the attempt to unify the scientific data. Science functions thanks to a noble lie, in which the scientist uses ordinary experience as the basis for the denial of the veridical status of ordinary experience. According to anti-Platonist scientific analysis, perception is a case of one computer responding to another, or of the interaction of two distributions of energy. But this is contradicted by the ordinary experience that gives rise to the scientific analysis.

Otherwise put, the phenomena cannot be inferred from the theoretical entities that ostensibly produce them. The domain of everyday consciousness may be a myth in scientific terms, but the myth is indispensable for the scientific enterprise. In sum, whether one turns to neurophysiology or to quantum mechanics in order to explain the deep structure of human experience, what the philosopher requires is essentially the same as what is required by every thoughtful human being: a plausible account of the given. As I am now about to argue, by way of an analysis of a passage in Plato's *Philebus*, there is no satisfactory noncircular explanation or (in the Platonic expression) *logos* of the unity of consciousness and the synthesis of thought and perception. Of course, this is no reason to abandon the attempt to discover such an explanation. But it is also no reason to abandon the very givenness of the phenomenon that we have set out to explain.

I turn now to the passage in the *Philebus*. Socrates introduces his analysis of perception with an animated portrait; we are invited to imagine a man who is attempting to identify things seen at a distance and not very clearly. He wishes to distinguish between and so judge about (*krinein*) what he sees (38c5–7). An identification of some visible (or partly visible) thing is a judgment of the form "that is an *X*" where "*X*" stands for the name of the family or perhaps (without the indefinite article) a proper name.

Our imaginary man, whom we cannot ourselves actually see, now asks himself, in a voice that we cannot actually hear: "Whatever is that thing that appears to be standing next to the rock beneath some kind of tree?" (38c12–d1). The expression translated as "appears" is the participial phrase *to phantazomenon.* As the particle *pote* and the indefinite *tini* convey, the situation is a mixture of clarity and ambiguity, but not of total obscurity. *Phantazomenon* has two senses here: (1) something shows itself or is a *phainomenon;* and (2), as a psychological event, the thing showing is a "fantasm" because I cannot see it accurately or correctly. We therefore have to distinguish between the psychological event and the entity; to misidentify the entity is not to change its nature. Furthermore, even as a misidentification or ambiguous representation, the fantasm exists: it shows itself.

In sum: the participle *phantazomenon* is used by Socrates to refer both to the entity and to the mode of its perception prior to correct identification. The term does not imply that the two, event and entity, are one and the same in the sense that the entity is itself a subjective event or intrinsically lacking in identity until such time as we come to a judgment about it. The entity to which the fantasm corresponds is framed by the rock and some type of tree. The same cannot be said of the fantasm. So long as we keep this distinction in mind, it is both permissible and convenient to refer to the entity that we have not yet identified as a fantasm.

Furthermore, if his perceptions of the rock and of the tree were also fantasms, then our hero could not focus his attention on the fantasm next to the rock. Differently stated, trying to identify something in the everyday environment is not the same as staring at images projected against a dark background in a laboratory. But it is also not the same as trying to constitute or actualize some object, say, a dog or a man. We perceive dogs and men as elements of an articulated visual field; not all of that field is the object about which we are attempting to make a judgment, but neither is it a fantasy or subjective confusion. We are aware that we are standing outside, at some distance from a tree and a rock, and so on, and this awareness is part of the information we require in order to engage in perceptual judgment.

I come now to what will be for us the crucial sentence in the *Philebus* passage. In response to his own question about the fantasm, the hero in Socrates' story could say to himself that it is a man, "thereby hitting the mark" (*epituchōs eipōn*). Alternatively, he could be "carried past" (*parenechtheis*), that is, miss the mark, and take the fantasm to be an image (*agalma*) made by some shepherds, perhaps as a scarecrow (38d5–10). I call your attention to the fact that the speaker is referring directly to the fantasm he attempts to identify; at this stage there is no reference to true or false judgment. These are introduced only later, when the speaker is separated from the fantasm by an interval of time and space, and is attempting to recall it.

I find suggestive the distinction between hitting and missing the mark, on the one hand, and true and false judgment, on the other. What it suggests to me is that if Platonism is to be preserved, the perceived entity must be given to the perceiver independently of the constructive activity of judgment. As I pointed out initially with respect to the Theaetetus, Socrates' analysis of the activity of judgment is very similar to the Kantian analysis (taking "Kantian" in a very broad sense). Nor will the *Philebus* provide us with an unambiguous confirmation of the distinction between perception and judgment. It is therefore not at all clear that Plato is a Platonist.

To make matters worse, there is a parallel passage in the *Theaetetus* in which Socrates employs the same metaphor to describe false judgment. He speaks of the case in which a man knows both Theaetetus and Theodorus and is also perceiving them both, but fails to connect his memory of their identities with the corresponding perception. "But like a bad archer, he shoots beyond the target and errs [*parallaksai tou skopou kai hamartein*], and this is called 'false,'" that is, false *doxa* arising from his transposition (*parallaksai*) of the two perceptions (193e6–94a4).

The cases in the two dialogues are not identical. In the *Philebus*, the problem is not to distinguish between two identities of recognized entities (i.e., two men) but to establish the nature of the entity. Furthermore, the distinction in the *Theaetetus* between true and false perceptual judgment depends upon the memory (195c6 ff.), just as in the case of the *Philebus*. Nevertheless, it would be plausible to argue, contrary to my initial inference, that the passage in the *Theaetetus* supports the interpretation of the *Philebus* passage that "hitting the mark" is synonymous with "forming a true judgment."

There is one other point about the *Philebus* text that adds to the confusion because it seems to cut in two different ways. Socrates introduces the story about the fantasm in order to illustrate his contention that opinion or judgment (*doxa*) and the act of forming a judgment (*diadoxazein*), and so the distinction between true and false judgment, "arise in each case from memory and perception" (38b12–c1). Memory is not introduced in our story until after the perceiver has departed from the scene of the fantasm. This gives some support to the distinction between hitting or missing the mark and forming true or false judgments.

On the other hand, immediately after describing the isolated perceiver's reaction to the fantasm, Socrates asks whether, and Protarchus confirms that, "if someone were with him, he might speak aloud, thereby repeating to his companion what he had initially said to himself; and so arises a *logos* from what we had previously called *doxa*" (38e1–5). By "previously," Socrates presumably refers to the immediate antecedent, in which the perceiver speaks to himself and thereby hits or misses the mark. In this case, "hitting or missing" must be synonymous with "making a true or a false judgment."

I do not think that the Platonic text is sufficiently detailed or lucid to permit us to resolve these questions simply by citing passages. One reason for my close analysis of the relevant passages is precisely to bring out their inconclusiveness. But that does not invalidate their suggestiveness with respect to the underlying philosophical problem, which is, after all, our primary concern. So let it be clearly understood: I am not attempting to read into an ambiguous text a solution to the problem of perception. On the contrary, I am eliciting that problem from the text, but in addition suggesting how a Platonist would have to solve it. Needless to say, this is not the same as solving the problem.

In order to distinguish between a true and a false judgment, or in other words to move from interpretation to *episteme*, we must have access to the entity under consideration in a way that is prior to the act of judgment, and so which allows the confirmation or denial of the judgment that we make, whether by ourselves or by others. If the act of judgment is an immediate product of the act of cognition, by which the entity of perception is transformed into the object of the perceiving subject, then every judgment is necessarily true. But this does not conform to our ordinary experience. On the other hand, there seems to be no way to certify to ourselves that we have immediate access to the certification of judgment. Thus it is circular to certify the basis of certification. And as I shall argue in a moment, recourse to the doctrine of Platonic Ideas does not provide us with the desired certification.

Let me emphasize that all questions about alternative sensory equipment, the transworld identity of the perceived item, and the neurophysiological substructure of perceptual experience are quite separate from our problem today. So too is the attack mounted against Platonism by Darwinian biologists and their philosophical interpreters. I want to make two brief remarks about this attack. So far as I can determine, contemporary taxonomists share the view, expressed in a recent collection of studies on the biological study of species, that whereas "phenetics is an imperfect reflection of interfertility between organisms," phenetic resemblance is the main basis for inferring interfertility.[3]

The second remark concerns a widespread criticism of Platonistic doctrines, which I represent here with a reference from Michael Ruse concerning Aristotelian species. Ruse mistakenly believes that the doc-

3. Robert Sokol and Theodore Crevello, "The Biological Species Concept: A Critical Evaluation," in *The Units of Evolution*, ed. Marc Ereshefsky (Cambridge, Mass.: MIT Press, 1992), pp. 33, 45. See also the essay by Ehrlich and Raven in the same volume.

trine of evolution establishes the failure of the Aristotelian essence inasmuch as, for any property, some ancestor of a given species does not possess it.[4] But this is irrelevant to the Aristotelian doctrine. If the property is accidental, its absence in an ancestor can be explained on the grounds of the variability of matter. If the property is essential, then its presence defines some other species than the one that lacks it.

Let me express this point in Platonic terminology. The *morphe*, or physical shape, of the item is distinct from what Plato means by its Idea or Aristotle by the *to ti ēn einai*; the former can be relative to local sensory apparatus or to other variations in possible worlds, but the Idea or species form cannot be, since if it is, then what is a piece of fruit in this world could be a refrigerator in another world. And in this case, that is, absent all identity, there can be no science, but also no commonsense understanding of everyday experience. By the same token, the gradual and continuous evolution of species is a process of the continuous modification of *morphai*, not of essences or of Platonic Ideas. It should furthermore not be assumed that a Platonic Idea must correspond to every morphological transformation. The same Idea of the horse could underlie an indefinite number of species of horses.

On the other hand, I certainly agree that the question of when a given phenotype ceases to belong to the biological genotype of horses is a scientific or biological question, not one to be settled, or even clarified, by recourse to Platonic forms. The problem that concerns me is a different one. Granted that the perception of any phenotype whatsoever is the starting point for philosophical as well as for scientific analysis, must it not be the case that the phenotype is not a theoretical construction? More precisely, in order to be able to distinguish between true and false judgments about the phenotypical or genotypical properties of an object of perception, must that object not be given to cognition independently of, and antecedent to, the reflexive analysis of cognition?

More relevant to my concerns than neurophysiology or biology is Husserlian phenomenology, and in particular the doctrine of pre-predicative perception as discussed in *Erfahrung und Urteil*.[5] I mention this work only as the closest approximation known to me in contemporary philosophy of the Platonic problematic. It would require a separate study to determine the satisfactoriness of Husserl's analysis. Now we have more than enough to do with Plato. On the other hand, it was incumbent upon me to say something about psychology and biology, in order to

4. Michael Ruse, "Biological Species: Natural Kinds, Individuals, or What?," in *The Units of Evolution*, ed. Ereshefsky, p. 351n3.

5. Hamburg: Claassen Verlag, 1964.

explain the enduring philosophical importance of the attempt to defend Platonism against Kantianism.

Neither in the *Theaetetus* nor in the *Philebus* does Socrates "analyze" the process of perception. Instead, he alludes to perception as the preamble to the formation of true and false judgments via the conjunction of perception and memory. To continue with the *Philebus*, in the first stage of Socrates' story, the perceiver is in the immediate presence of the fantasm, either by himself or with a companion. In the second stage, we regard him as alone and retaining for some time his account to himself (*dianooumenos*) of the appearance, in other words, as having been separated from the fantasm but retaining it in his memory (38e6–8).

As the participles *rethenta* (38c1) and *dianooumenos* show, discursive thinking is associated with perception at both stages. The difference between the two stages is that during direct perception, there is no reference to the memory. We hit or miss the mark through the medium of speech; the discourse in question is identifying rather than predicating. The division here is not between two properties, for example, "tall" and "short," but between two identities, "man" and "image." The division, in other words, is like the selection or reception of an essence; perhaps one could say that it is an existential judgment that serves as the basis for predicational judgments.

The first stage of the drama in the *Philebus* shows that there is no analysis of perception because it is like *noēsis,* a simple or unstructured apprehension of a form. Analysis occurs only later, where "later" can be understood temporally or logically, namely, when the perception serves as the basis for predicative judgments, either directly or through the mediation of memory. If this stage does not occur, and so if existential judgments are logical rather than real predications, to use the Kantian terminology, then there is no way in which to establish contact with the *on* or *res* as given to perception and thereby to thinking. "Essence" and "existence" are then the names of concepts: to be is to be constituted in discursive or conceptual thinking. We are on the way toward the peculiar but widely successful thesis that to be is to be spoken or referred to.

The text in the *Philebus* provides us with a very slight but nevertheless discernible basis for making the kind of distinction that a defense of Platonism requires. But not only do the texts not carry out in detail such a defense, they actually obscure the very possibility of that defense. This is especially obvious in the continuation of the story we have been examining about perception and judgment. We are now discussing the soul of the original perceiver as it functions some time after perceiving the original fantasm. The first thing to notice is that we have not been told whether the fantasm, understood here as a psychological event, was transformed into a genuine phenomenon, that is to say, whether the perceiver did or did not hit the mark, and so, whether the being under the tree and next to the rock showed its identity to him.

Please note also that Socrates does not say that the act of identification is the same as the assertion launched toward the target of perception, for example, "this is a man." We do not identify things by speaking to or about them; in order to utter a true essential or existential judgment, we must first apprehend the essence or existence in question. In stage one the speech follows the appearance (*phantasthenta*) of the fantasm; it does not produce that appearance.

On the other hand, a fantasm is not a complete perception; it is a partial perception that requires something further to be completed, namely, a correct identification. I suggest that something has been omitted in Socrates' account: the step subsequent to the apprehension of the fantasm or veiled appearance but prior to the launching of the judgment "this is a man." If the psychological shift from obscure or veiled fantasm to manifest and identifiable perception is made by the assertion of the identifying judgment, then we have shifted from Platonism to Kantianism. Platonism requires perceptual contact with a being whose identity is intrinsic to it, and not a consequence of our seeing it or speaking about it. But Socrates says next to nothing, and perhaps less than nothing, about how this can occur.

We now consider the soul of the original perceiver as it functions some time after the apprehension of the fantasm. In an oddly Derridean idiom, Socrates says: "I think that the soul is at this time like a kind of book" (38el2–13). To this he adds: "Memory, coinciding with our sense perceptions into the same thing [i.e., the combination produces a memory of the fantasm] and the affections [*pathēmata*] centering around these, appear to me at that time almost as if to write accounts [*logoi*] within our souls" (38e–39a3).

This is a striking metaphor but an unusually obscure one. In the first place, what is written into the book is a memory of the initial sensory phenomenon, not the perceiver's identification of it. He is therefore about to be required to judge the identity of the fantasm, or to transform it (considered as a psychological event) into an icon or veridical image, not by looking at the thing under the tree, but instead by "looking" at his memory of it. Second, this memory is visual, not discursive; but it affects the soul in such a way as to produce a writing: a speech or a *logos* rather than a picture.

To continue: "When this affection [*pathēma*] writes the truth, both true opinion [*doxa*] and statements [*logoi*] arise in us from [that writing]; but when the writer in us writes falsely, the opposite of true statements occurs"

(39a3–7). Socrates' language is far from transparent; he may simply be referring to the process of formulating discursive judgments, or he may be distinguishing between the process of writing and the formulation of discursive judgments. In the first case, the identifying judgment, as just noted, is made on the basis of a memory, not a perception; in the second case, the judgments are made on the basis of a mysterious process of writing about the memory rather than on the basis of direct access to the memory itself.

In either case, the process of judgment is compared by Socrates to demiurgy or the production of psychic artifacts. "Accept the fact that another demiurge comes into existence in our souls at that time" (39b3–4). The second demiurge is a painter "who draws in our souls icons of what the writer has recorded" (39b3–7). I note in passing that the writer is vaguely reminiscent of what the neurophysiologist Michael Gazzaniga calls the interpreter in the left brain–based system, who monitors the effects of the modules of brain organization. "The interpreter considers all the outputs of the functional modules as soon as they are made and immediately constructs a hypothesis as to why particular actions occurred."[6]

These hypotheses are integrated by Gazzaniga's interpreter into a comprehensive belief system or interpretation of human experience that he has already constructed. The functional equivalent to the outputs of Gazzaniga's brain modules is for Socrates the remembered perception; his writer also constructs a comprehensive belief system pertaining to external experience. We are not told that the writer also responds to inner or psychic phenomena, but inner experience cannot be unrelated to our judgments about the external world.

To restrict ourselves now to Socrates, before we turn to the painter, I want to make an extended comment about the implications of the metaphor of the writer. As a demiurge, he manufactures artifacts, which are interpretations of memory. I call these "interpretations" for two reasons. First, a writing cannot be an accurate copy or presentation of a visual memory, and hence not of the original vision. But second, and here more important, the visual memory is itself still a fantasm.

What is remembered in Socrates' story is the appearance of a concealed phenomenon, as the participle *phantazomenon* conveys. Prior to the act of writing, the soul does not know, and in fact has neither a true nor a false opinion of, the actual identity of the original fantasm. Without

6. Michael Gazzaniga, "Brain Modularity: Toward a Philosophy of Conscious Experience," in *Consciousness in Contemporary Science*, ed. A. J. Marcel and E. Bisiach (Oxford: Clarendon Press, 1988), p. 219.

access to the original experience, there is no *theoria* or direct apprehension of the thing under the tree. Hence there cannot be a veridical identification of its essence or existence. To say that the writer interprets a memory, which is itself of a fantasm, is to say that Socrates has become a Kantian. What the writer tells us is a true *doxa* or *logos* is, in other words, an interpretation that can never be independently confirmed.

Nor can the doctrine of Ideas be invoked at this point to rescue us from interpretation and to restore *theoria.* The original appearance is for us a fantasm or concealed presentation. Beneath what I will call the cloak of concealment, that which appears may possess the eidetic structure of a man, but we will not know this until the cloak is removed, and it is certainly not the Idea that itself removes the cloak. Thus I do not transform the fantasm into a perception of a man by looking away from the fantasm up to the heavenly Idea of man. Nor can I see the Idea of man within the fantasm, since the Idea is *ex hypothesi* concealed by the cloak.

In ordinary language, we establish the identity of a disputed or obscure appearance by changing our physical location, improving our view, obtaining better illumination, employing other senses to regulate the obscure vision, checking with other perceivers, and so on. None of these steps changes the eidetic identity of the thing that appears, but that is not what we want to change. We want instead to clarify the appearance, that is, to replace the fantasm with an icon or accurate image. Only after we have succeeded in doing this can we apprehend the Idea of man as the eidetic structure of the thing under the tree.

I would therefore deny that the apprehension of an Idea can transform a fantasm into an icon. The transformation must precede the apprehension, at the very least if that apprehension is to do any work. The Idea explains the unity and identity of the entity as present to and within perception. But we do not identify things by looking at Ideas. We do so by perceiving the thing, and so by clarifying inadequate perceptions. The most one could say is that in this act of clarification, we are assisted by a view of the Idea in which we do not see the Idea as such. But what does this amount to, if not that we perceive the thing rather than the Idea?

This also helps us to understand why Plato associates the apprehension of Ideas with recollection. We recollect or remember the Idea *after* we have identified the perception, and on the basis of this identification. If the identification was itself the apprehension of the Idea, then in the case of fantasms, that is, initially unclear perceptions, we would have to perform two visual acts, one that results in the fantasm and the other that results in its removal through the sight of the Idea.

But how could we see the Idea in the first place, since it is being concealed by the cloak of the fantasm? If someone replies that we see the

Idea elsewhere than in the fantasm, then we return to the doctrine of separate Ideas, which I regard as absurd.

Please note that I am not at all denying that the Idea is present within the perceived entity. I am instead maintaining that it is indeed there, but that it cannot be perceived. It is accessible to thought, not to sense perception. What we perceive is the *morphē* or physical shape. This shape is relative to the nature of our sensory organs. But what is not relative to sense perception is the fact of an identifiable unity. It is this fact that directs us to, or allows us to "recollect," the Idea.

The Platonist will say that if there were no Idea of man, there would be no men to perceive, and this is correct. But noetic apprehension is not perception. The Platonist will repeat Socrates' contention in the *Theaetetus* that perception does not at all participate in being or truth; but this cannot be correct, and on Socratic grounds. If it were correct, then either there would be no true perceptual judgments, or true perceptual judgments would not be about perceptions but about noetic apprehensions of Ideas. The first alternative is falsified by experience; the second destroys the very distinction between *aisthesis* and *noesis.*

The task for the Platonist is not to transform perception into noetic apprehension; it is to explain perception, and, in the particular case, to explain the distinction between true and false perceptual judgments. To ground this explanation in the doctrine of Ideas would also require us to hold that there are Ideas of all perceptible entities, including artifacts. Even worse, there would have to be Ideas of perceptions, since we make true judgments about them, for example, that they do not participate in truth or being. In this case there must be an Idea of a tree and an Idea of the perception of a tree. A true judgment about the perception of a tree would then not be a true judgment about a tree, in which case it would be false to say that a perception of a tree is a perception of a tree.

So much for this difficulty. I note as a correlative point that perception is not only not the apprehension of Platonic Ideas; it is also not the writing of sentences in the soul, which is instead the formulation of a judgment about my perception, as Socrates claims in the *Philebus.* To perceive a man is not to write down a sentence in one's soul, for example, "This thing I perceive is a man." In order to be able to write that sentence, I must first have perceived a man, not an unidentifiable fantasm; the unidentifiable fantasm arises when perception fails, or in other words when I cannot write anything down in my soul, except perhaps something like "What the devil is that?"

To return one last time to Socrates' story, the discursive demiurge in our hero's soul is in the position of having to write down his sentence on the basis neither of a true perception nor a vision of an Idea. He writes down the sentence on the basis of a memory of a fantasm. If this were indeed how we arrived at perceptual judgments, then surely it would be a matter of mere chance that some of these sentences are true. Nor do I see any way in which we could distinguish the true sentences from those that are false.

As to the second demiurge, the painter, he "draws in our souls icons of what the writer has recorded" (39b3–7). Notice the shift from fantasm to icon; the paintings are accurate copies not of the true identity of what initially appeared as a fantasm, but rather of the interpretation given to the memory of the fantasm by the writer. In answer to Protarchus's question of how and when the painter does this, Socrates replies: "[W]henever someone derives from sight or another perception opinions or assertions at that time, and sees somehow in himself icons of what has been opined or asserted" (39b9–c2).

The icons of true opinions or judgments and speeches are true; those of false opinions or judgments and speeches are false (39b9–c6). They are not images of perceptions but of judgments. The fantasm or original incomplete perception is thus a precognitive image, something like Kant's contingent subjective sensations. This precognitive image is appropriated within a judgment of identity that either hits the mark or does not. In either case, it is imprinted into the memory and serves as the basis for the subsequent transformation into a true or false *doxa* by the writer in the soul. This corresponds roughly to the Kantian synthesis of sensations into genuine objects of perception by the imposition of categorial structure. Finally, the icons or illustrations of the text by the painter may be compared to the work of the reproductive imagination in Kant, which ostensibly supplies the empirical image of the perceived object.

In this entire process, the only point at which there is room to envision a direct contact with the entity of perception is in the initial possibility of "hitting the mark." But the subsequent steps of Socrates' account cover over that possibility, or transform the protojudgment from a true identification of a being in the external world to an interpretation by a discursive demiurge or manufacturer of judgments.

The link between the initial appearance and the subsequent judgment is the memory, which furnishes to the writer a protojudgment or discursive reflection on the identity of the fantasm. At this step, the writer takes the word of the memory in preparing his statement. That word is good if and only if the memory is accurate, that is, if the man initially hits the mark. But this cannot be confirmed without checking the initial appearance. We must, in other words, certify that the man initially hit the mark in his attempt to identify the thing next to the rock under the tree. And this cannot be done without returning, not simply to the original scene of the perceptual event, but to that event itself. We have now come full circle, since obviously the only way by which to return to the event itself is via the memory.

There is, of course, another way in which to read Socrates' account of perception. We can take it to say that the possibility of distinguishing between true and false perceptual judgments rests upon the accessibility of the perceived entity to cognitive analysis. After all, if the man misses the mark in his protojudgment of identification, the writer is condemned to record this misidentification, and a false judgment will be recorded as true. In everyday life, we test perceptual judgments by further acts of perception, not simply by an introspective analysis of the structure of judgment. And this seems to mean that, in order to acquire true perceptual judgments, we must first have veridical perceptions.

As one could also put this, in order to perceive, we must already be perceiving, and so already have perceived. I mean by this the following: in order to perceive anything in particular, we must already be ensconced within the perceptual field. In order to identify, or even to misidentify, any particular perceptible entity, or what Kant calls an "object," we must already have perceived a collocation of identified entities that frame the item in question, that allow us to raise the question of identity at all.

In order for a particular truth to be accessible, the truth of the whole must be manifest, not in the sense that we can construct sentences about it in our souls or give a *logos* or a scientific account of the whole, but in the sense that we can rely upon this truth to illuminate our particular judgments of perception. Such illumination does not emerge from the constitution of a particular object, or from the production of a judgment about that particular object. The illumination within which we conduct our investigations is always antecedent to those investigations themselves.

I have not offered these last remarks as a proposed solution to the problem of perception. My point is that there is no solution, if we mean by that a noncircular analysis of the manner in which we arrive at true perceptual judgments, and so at the basis for identifying false perceptual judgments. But perhaps a better way of looking at the whole matter is to say that there is no problem of perception. The problem is not with the faculty of perception, but with our attempts to explain the connection between perception and judgment. Since these explanations are all judgments, we put ourselves as judges in the position of the writer in the soul who manufactures sentences on the basis of the judgments of memory.

Stated metaphorically, we judge on the basis of someone else's judgments. Judging is constructing, whether the constructions be *logoi*, concepts, discursive interpretations, or mathematical models. More precisely, explanation is second-order judgment. What we are explaining depends upon first-order judgment, or upon whether we have hit the mark. But this cannot be determined by additional acts of the construction of cognitive artifacts. I therefore am prepared to affirm the myth of the given, with the correlative assertion that *logos* is grounded in *muthos.* In nonmythical language, perceptual judgments must be about identities of entities that are given, not constructed. I therefore affirm the noble lie of modern science.

As soon as we leave the security of ordinary experience, including the ordinary ways in which we resolve puzzles of perceptual identification, we have taken the path to Kantianism. Some may wish to avoid that path because of internal inconsistencies in Kantianism, or because of consequences of the acceptance of that doctrine. To such persons I recommend the attempt to clarify and defend what I have called here the Platonist version of Socrates' account of perceptual judgment in the *Philebus.* A failure to do so leads finally to the view that ordinary experience is a theory; by depriving us of any basis for scientific truth, this leads not to science but to nihilism.[7]

7. A revised version of this article appears in my *Metaphysics in Ordinary Language* (New Haven: Yale University Press, 1999).

12 Moral Motivation in Plato, Plotinus, Augustine, and Ourselves

JOHN M. RIST

It is possible to study the history of philosophy in the manner of an antiquarian, trying to find out, as a matter of quaint curiosity, or of learned philology, what the old folks had to say.[1] An enquiry of that sort can be carried out with high standards of technical skill, as it sometimes is by current practitioners of ancient philosophy, who will nevertheless confess, out of their own mouths, that of course if you want to profit from real philosophy, you will be more or less wasting your time studying the ancients, fascinating though they may be. We should devote ourselves instead, if ethics and philosophical psychology are our principal interests, to the writings of Donald Davidson, Rawls, Dworkin, Gauthier, or—for the really adventurous—Derek Parfit. Needless to say, I regard such views as at best perverse, at worst genuinely and seriously mistaken. They assume, if they do not assert, that in philosophy we have never forgotten what we once knew.

Such an approach to the history of philosophy, and to the history of ancient philosophy in particular, is not the only obstacle to progress. Antiquarianism, even in the guise of analytic philosophy, may be less of a threat than what might be dubbed "poisoning the wells." The antiquarian, whether "analytic" or other, may turn up some odd things in the course of an honest search, and the human mind not being wholly corrupted, he may then start to wonder whether what he is finding is true; that is, he will start doing some real philosophy. The more sophisticated critic may take another tack. Recognizing that the greatest thinkers of the past are indeed the giants upon whose shoulders we are standing, however big we may be ourselves, he tries to show not merely that the ancients were real philosophers, though with inevitably simpler logical

1. Versions of this essay have been read in Fribourg, Switzerland, and at an SAGP meeting in Binghamton, N.Y. I should like to thank those who on those occasions, as well as at The Catholic University of America, made formal or informal comments.

techniques, but that they started with assumptions very similar to those of their modern descendents, and that despite appearances they were trying to solve the same philosophical questions. That, of course, is to assume that the modern questions are always the right ones, and furthermore to assume that since the ancients must *really* be asking those same questions, since these are the questions and approaches of true *philosophy*, any other questions that they may appear to have asked, and in fact did ask, can be shrewdly contorted into modern and purportedly superior alternatives.

If you look at modern introductory textbooks in ethics—in English there seem to be four or five new mediocre ones published each year—you will notice that their compilers seem to suggest, especially in their introductions, that there is a rather limited repertoire of moral systems. You have to be a utilitarian (or some other kind of consequentialist), or a Kantian, or a contractarian of either the more gentle (Rawlsian) or the more brutal (Hobbesian) sort. If you are a Catholic or some other sort of "traditionalist," you may be allotted some variety of natural law theory, often in a form attributed to Aristotle, and perhaps with a passing nod at Thomas Aquinas. And thanks to recent valiant efforts, various types of "virtue ethics" are now being gradually restored to favor. If you know a bit of ancient philosophy, you may wonder how Plato fits into all this: unless, despite the mandatory bit of, say, the *Euthyphro* in the selection—marking the conventional bow to Socrates as the supposed "founder" of ethics—Plato be supposed not really to have attained a moral theory at all.[2]

If you pursue that question further in the "literature" on the subject, you will find (unsurprisingly) a number of ingenious attempts to fit Plato into one or another of the standard permissible options. What you will rarely find is the avowal that Plato's theory of moral behavior does not fit into the modern categorizations, but is itself a major, and, perhaps, substantially correct approach to moral behavior and to our moral personalities that we, in contempt of the past, have largely forgotten. Instead of saying anything like that, the well-poisoning school of teachers attempts to make Plato and (even) Platonists do the kind of things, ask the kind of questions, and pose the kind of problems that they did not pose—but which, had they been real (i.e., modern) philosophers, they should have posed.

2. Note the reasons offered by J. Annas for omitting Plato (and the Sophists) from an account of "the form and structure of ancient ethical theory" (p. 3); see *The Morality of Happiness* (Oxford, 1993), pp. 17–19. Is this *Hamlet* without the prince himself?

Suppose someone were to ask us how we could improve the level of our moral behavior—whatever that level is, and whatever sort of account we might wish to give of the foundations of ethics. If we were asked such a question, we in turn might think that we were being asked something rather odd. Why should anyone *want* to get "better," and why should we ever believe that we might be able to get better? Now add a further complication: suppose that we are philosophers concerned with problems of personal identity. Then perhaps we are more precisely puzzled as to the referent of the "I" in the proposition "I want [or do not want] to get better." Certainly we would not be helped out of our difficulties if we had been persuaded by contemporary professionals that personal identity is somewhat of a myth—a misdescription of psychological connectedness through time[3]—or that all moral statements are agent-neutral, being concerned not with (or less with) what the problematic *I* ought to do now but with what long-term result *I* (or someone else) achieve or effect. (So Socrates might have [regretfully, not later remorsefully] arrested Leon of Salamis, protected by the knowledge that if he did not do it, someone else would.[4])

In putting together these various questions I want to draw your attention to Plato's approach to them, and to the approaches of others in the Platonic tradition, and then to develop some features of the peculiarly Platonic account of human behavior that our writers of ethics textbooks today appear to have largely forgotten, and that seem to survive, just occasionally, in odd places: such as in theological wrangling about Augustine, and more specifically about the quality of Augustine's Christianity. I shall not want to suggest that Plato and his followers, such as Plotinus, managed to solve all the problems they raised. To the contrary, I shall suggest that their enquiry, though getting some very important things right, collapsed in a crisis uncovered within its own basic texts, and that even now it still needs much further correction. But I shall also suggest that this correction is philosophically worthwhile, indeed perhaps the only future for a grounded ethical theory—as distinct from systematic lying and deception (or theological fundamentalism) about the "moral" realities lying below outbursts of "moral" sentiment or belief.

Perhaps we want to get better, if and when we do, because we think that getting better will pay off in some way for ourselves. You will already

3. So D. Parfit, *Reasons and Persons* (Oxford, 1986).

4. Socrates might, of course, have been deterred (if an agent-neutralist) by considerations of the bad precedent he had set, by fear that he had diminished the general respect for human life, but not merely by the belief that he just should not (for some reason, of course) do this wrong thing now.

recognize a problem debated by Socrates and some of his interlocutors. Plato (in the persona of Socrates) claims that any attempt to argue that moral improvement can be justified in terms of possible materialist prosperity is both unrealistic and futile. For materialist prosperity it might well be sufficient (when necessary) to *seem* good. To answer Thrasymachus, Socrates appeals to some sort of immaterial advantages, to some sort of life in contact with and informed by what is ultimately more satisfying to us humans than material prosperity. That was no crazy suggestion, even if we assume that there are no Platonic Forms. Consider the person who learns to appreciate music, or poetry, or even happily to listen to lectures about moral philosophy or personal identity: it may seem to him that he has entered a different world. And this world has some striking characteristics, as the *Symposium*, much followed in the Platonic tradition and much revered by genuine Platonists, suggests. It is a world in which one can see and in a sense possess beautiful objects, for example, and not lose anything of one's possession of them by sharing them with others. If I drink my glass of vintage wine—just the right amount to maximize my satisfaction—I cannot share that same drink with someone else; and in sexual love it is still often thought unromantic or "inappropriate" to want to share one's delights with all comers. But if I go into the Louvre I do not react to admiring the *Mona Lisa* by thinking that I must have it for my private and secret collection; on the contrary, I may want to share the experience of viewing the painting with my family and friends, and with a wider public, and I might encourage universities to offer courses in which all sorts of people might be taught to better understand the *Mona Lisa*. Let us, for want of a better phrase, call such satisfactions "satisfactions of the mind," and let us suppose that human beings have the ability to appreciate such things and that they have evolved, or were designed, or whatever, to be such as to appreciate them—and, as Plato would say, to be aroused and inspired by them.

If one is inspired by something, there is a sense in which one desires it, though at best unselfishly—here is a "high-grade" Platonic *eros* (ἔρως)—and there is consequently a sense in which we (as at least semi-Platonists) form a hierarchy of desires, some of which are tagged as "higher" because they seem to speak to the most peculiarly human aspects of ourselves. Plato himself, in fact, probably got the order of his hierarchy wrong (at least in the *Symposium*),[5] but that—comparatively—is a detail. In any case, some of the tools for repairing it exist in other Platonic texts.

I doubt whether a chimpanzee will ever manage to *appreciate* the works

5. One thinks of his attitude to the love of laws and constitutions rather than to the love of persons.

of Shakespeare, even if, by luck or judgment, he manages over time to compose them on a computer. Note, however, how easily I could now slip into dualist ways of speaking, and thereby make a mistake that both Plato and Aristotle were at least tempted to make rather regularly. I may claim that it is *more human* to appreciate a painting by Leonardo than to eat a meal, but by that I mean that while both I myself and an ape can eat a meal, only I can appreciate a Leonardo. What I do not mean to imply is that the chimpanzee and I eat our meals in the same way. I can make social institutions and rituals out of eating—one of which is a polite mode of eating—which, not being human, the ape cannot reproduce (or at best can only ape). Similarly, D. H. Lawrence's notions of "sex-in-the-head," or what others might call "eroticism," are clearly irrelevant to the average cow, incapable as she is of reading or writing erotic poetry (or even pornography).

The temptation should be resisted to suppose that we are composed of a human (or "really human," or perhaps it might be called "divine") part, and an animal part, as distinct from possessing the capacity to make human rather than subhuman choices regarding behavior or lifestyle. (I may behave "like an animal," but that does not make me morally like an animal.) Nevertheless, someone who appreciates that human flourishing has to do with the attainment of immaterial goods and satisfactions might suppose that the way to live this better life would be to separate the real me (let us say the soul) from the body that so distracts it. If only one could be separate (at the right time, of course) from the body, one could live the good life!

There is no need to spend much time on this move, which we can recognize as roughly that of the Socrates of the *Phaedo*. For to say that to separate the soul from the body is to enable the soul to live well is to raise the question of why the soul is so inadequate as to be corrupted whenever it happens to have a body to be corrupted by. For to be corrupted is necessarily to be corruptible. In other words, there must be something wrong with *any* soul that falls into wrongdoing when the going gets tough, that is, let us say, when it falls into a body. And note that it is irrelevant to the problem of the condition of the soul—that is, that it is defective—whether the body, or matter, or whatever, is bad. I am not made bad merely by talking to a murderer, unless I am so weak as to be unable to resist the invitation to kill someone myself. (Admittedly this can happen: witness the case of a probation officer in Ontario who was persuaded by one of his charges to join him in a bank robbery.)

Those who offer as a solution to the mind–body problem a "dual-aspect" theory whereby "physical" objects are supposed to have both "physical" and "nonphysical" properties are apparently committed to saying that the brain is unjust.[6] That is hard to take, but cannot be discussed here: a body may be fat but it is not readily identifiable as unjust. What I might reasonably mean, however, if I were to say that the soul joins the body in crime, is that the body is an occasion, an invitation, a temptation to crime. But why should the soul *ever* have been temptable if it is really good? So do not be surprised that the rather simplistic moral dualism of the *Phaedo* is developed less simplistically in later Platonic texts. Instead we get the so-called tripartite soul, which is much more than a new version of the pearl-in-the-oyster theory. For once the soul was the pearl buried in the body, but that is now an inadequate comment. We need to consider the temptability of the soul itself if Plato is going to make any progress. That indeed is what we find in the *Republic*, about which it is necessary here to be more or less dogmatic.[7]

First, Plato never refers to a tripartite soul. Second, Plato's usual word for the divisions of the soul in the *Republic* is not "parts" but "kinds": we are dealing with *eide* of the soul. But what are kinds of soul? In brief they are primarily lifestyles or potential selves—Plato names three but there could be more—that can be best understood by consideration of the extreme cases. The best life is the life in which reason is at the helm; then, when we wonder what to do, we reason rather than rationalize. When, on the other hand, we live the *epithumetikon* life, the lifestyle of the possessive soul (I suggest Macpherson's notion of possessive individualism deliberately[8]), we are Humeans, and our reason is and ought only to be—so we muse—the slave of the passions; we are passion servers, consumers, exploiters.

Plato in the *Republic* taught that the rational life is within our grasp, or at least within the grasp of some of us. Note that he did not speak of the emotionless life, for the good man desires the good, feels righteous anger, and the like: just check the end of *Republic* 9 (e.g., 586e–88a), where there is no trace of a Cartesian sort of antithesis between reason and the passions. In this claim about the rational life lies his justification for the Ideal State, for where Socrates can become an institution, there can be rulers uncorrupted by power. But note again, in Book 10, that Plato's position still requires the pearl-in-the-oyster theory, though in a more complex form. Our real self seems somehow to be like the sea god

6. See, e.g., T. Nagel, *The View from Nowhere* (Oxford, 1986), pp. 28–32. Of course, if Nagel were right, we should have to reconstruct our notion of the "physical" radically. It could no longer be identified with the material; in that sense the brain would not be a material object.

7. For a more detailed discussion, see J. M. Rist, "Plato Says that We Have Tripartite Souls. If He Is Right, What Can We Do about It?," in *Chercheurs de sagesse: Hommage à Jean Pépin* (Paris, 1992), pp. 103–24.

8. C. B. Macpherson, *The Political Theory of Possessive Individualism: Hobbes to Locke* (Oxford, 1962).

Glaucus (611c–12a), encrusted by the barnacles of the ocean, but able to be cleaned up, and then we shall be good; or at least some of us, the philosopher-kings, will be good in the strict sense.

In the same *Republic*, however, there are deeper shadows, even if in a partly mythological setting. The Ideal State comes to an end, the rulers make a mistake, and the reader of Book 10 who learns that we choose our own destiny and slide down the ramp of reincarnation into beasts may be puzzled as to how, once started down the slippery slope, we ever manage to recover our footing and return from a worse life to a better one. And in any case who is the "we"? Or to put the question differently: Do we have our own various possible lifestyles, and is the real "we" something over and above them: pure and inviolate? Or is one lifestyle a representation of the real "we," somehow already achieved? The latter seems to be the requirement; there must be a "we" incapable of wrongdoing but somehow liable to add another self to itself during this incarnate life, thus appearing to offer "us" (but what does this add up to?) a choice of lives. Plato does not work that out (I am not even sure how far he had thought it through), but Plotinus assumed that this was what was in Plato's mind, and he accordingly distinguished an empirical self (the "us," the ἡμεῖς) from an ideal self that is forever in contact with the intelligible world, whether "we" are aware of it or not.

That leaves all sorts of unanswered questions about our individuality, and about who is really responsible for what evil. But for Plato himself two things at least are already clear in the *Republic*: (1) that most of us are no unified self; and (2) that such a state has only been achieved, and that barely, by people like Socrates and Pythagoras. The second point is that *eros* is the means of achieving such a self, the *eros* that has already been debated in the *Symposium* (though as yet only in the light of the simple "soul–body" psychology of the *Phaedo*), and that in Book 6 of the *Republic* is seen in the person of the philosopher in love with Lady Philosophy herself.[9] So what the shadow to which I alluded in the *Republic* seems to be is that, despite the encrusted sea god of Book 10, there is another and more disturbing thesis: we are not yet identified as ourselves, the self is something to achieve. When attained, or, in Platonic language, when we are unified and thus godlike, we shall be able to live well, like the gods. But the problem of how to get from here to there, perhaps insuperable in the ordinary citizen unassisted by the philosopher-king, is even lurking in the souls of the élite. Hence after reading the *Republic* we may hope that Plato will go further.

In the *Phaedrus* Plato returns to the theory of *eros* in the light of his

9. *Rep.* 6.490b; and for Philosophy's unworthy lovers, 495c.

new "tripartite" psychology. There is a new treatment of how different lifestyles can be recognized in the different sorts of love we pursue, and a new emphasis on the personal experience of "being in love."[10] But I want to limit myself largely to Plato's contrast between exploitative *eros* and "real" *eros*: the exploitative desirer wants to get as much as he can from the beloved (being among other things an ancestor of the Epicurean *sanus amator*[11]); the Socratic lover wants to make the beloved better. Notice that Socratic love for Beauty itself still drives the good man; he is still inspired. And, like the philosopher-kings of the *Republic*, he always wants to better (at least one) human being. If you like, that is what his desire to beget in the beautiful, in the language of the *Symposium*, confirms him in wanting. Insofar as we possess a Socratic sort of *eros*, we cannot be atomized and possessive individuals.

Yet the more basic question of the limits of our capacity for perfection haunts the *Phaedrus* too. We may all, at times, be exploitative desirers. Each human soul is compared to a charioteer and two horses, each of the three representing one of the lifestyles of the *Republic*. But the black horse cannot be entirely suppressed, in any of us. We are never free of the urge to live darkly. And "suppression" is the right word for the rather brutal description Plato gives of our attempts to rein in the black horse.

So now Plato has spelled out his doubts about the possibility of the perfect life in the here and now. The problem is not that we are "tripartite" as such; there are different situations of life apparently even for the gods, and different types of god, whose souls too are tripartite. But whereas the gods are in harmony with themselves, and in that sense single-minded, or like pearls with three facets (their black horse in fact seems to be white), that is not true for us. We are under threat, and hence we may wonder whether our desire for the good will not, at some time, be perverted into a desire for something wholly other, for a form of the seeming good, perhaps even knowingly taken to be the good.[12] That is to say that there is something irretrievably perverse about human life, a something from which we cannot escape. There is a weakness about the

10. See the interesting remarks of A. W. Price, in *Love and Friendship in Plato and Aristotle* (Oxford, 1989), pp. 55–56.

11. For whom see esp. K. Kleve, "Lukrez und Venus (*De rer. nat.* 1.1–49)," *So* 41 (1966): 86–94, and "Lucrèce, l'épicurisme et l'amour," *ACGB* (1969): 376–83. M. Nussbaum's wide-ranging reflections around such subjects, themselves the subject of spectacular "advance praise" (see blurb), ignore Kleve's work; see *The Therapy of Desire* (Princeton, N.J., 1994), esp. 149–91. (For balanced comment on Nussbaum's approach, see the first pages of P. Green's review in the *New Republic*, September 5, 1994, pp. 38–42.)

12. Price (*Love and Friendship*, pp. 83–84) seems to consider this option, but because of his insufficient awareness of the "darker" strand in Plato, rejects it in favor of the black horse becoming "a transformed appetite which is no longer appetite at all."

human soul in company with the body that our innate desire for the good is incapable of eliminating. For it seems that "we" do not want to remove it. Little wonder that in the *Laws* Plato has given up his philosopher-kings along with his belief that human beings can be freed by education from the corruption of power.

The Platonic stage might seem to be set for asking directly what is this evil to which we are so oddly and fearfully attracted, and whether we (as distinct from our bodies) should have any reason to believe that we can master it. If we cannot, the prospects for Platonic improvement seem to have receded. The philosopher (or, as we would say, the would-be philosopher) may be in love with Lady Philosophy, or even wedded to her, but what sort of *eros* is it when the inspiration runs out? Is there need of a marriage counselor, to remind us, among other things, of what Plato seems to have grasped in his alternative theme in the *Republic* and the *Phaedrus*, that we are not yet ourselves, despite the sea god analogy, and that in this life we are not able to be ourselves? For if we are not yet ourselves, how, or through whom, can we motivate ourselves to live better, to escape the inevitably downward path to which Book 10 of the *Republic*, at least if pressed, seems to be pointing us? Aristotle and the Stoics rather neglected such questions. Most (though not all) of Aristotle's discussion of man in the *De anima* neglects Plato's emphasis on the fact that we are moral decision-makers with divided minds, and his apparent insistence that unless the philosopher thinks of man as a moral agent he is not thinking of man as man. Aristotle is concerned with quite other matters when he talks about the soul–body composite, and offers little that might explain to the Socrates of the *Phaedo* why it is that although his body tells him to run off to Thebes, he has decided to remain in prison in Athens. Indeed *acrasia* notwithstanding, Aristotle's account of man, from Plato's standpoint, largely avoids rather than resolves problems of personal identity and the divided self—and we should notice that the only metaphysical comments on evil in the Aristotelian corpus are to be found in *Theta* 6 of the *Metaphysics*: where evil in general seems to be some kind of by-product of potentiality, and where moral evil is not specifically mentioned. Sometimes it seems that Aristotle pays too high a price for his formal distinction between the "sciences." Or is it that the lines of distinction are not always well drawn in the case of the science of man, Aristotle being too concerned with emphasizing our "metaphysical" unity (in terms of form and body) and too little concerned with our "moral"—not to say other—plurality?

Platonist problems with the Stoics are of a different order. The Stoics were certainly interested in moral evil, and in moral good they saw the only true good. In emphasizing a side of Socrates treated in a more nuanced way by Plato, they wanted to claim, in reductionist fashion, that moral evil is just irrationality, or the misuse of the reason that we possess. That approach certainly has its value, and if we want to think about the differences between reasoning and rationalizing—both of which are acts of the human mind—we have much to learn from the Stoics. But though the Stoics did not make the Cynic mistake of supposing that the good man will, qua good, be devoid of emotion, their reduction of the real self to the power to reason rightly meant that emotion, and also of course Platonic *eros*, becomes incidental to goodness. The reason itelf, tending now to be viewed in a more Humean way as *contrasted* with the emotions or passions,[13] has the power to bring us to goodness, and although the Stoics admitted that the wise and good man is as rare as a phoenix, they seem to have paid insufficient attention to why this is so. Saying that almost all humans are fools and criminals, as the Stoics did, may be plausible in itself, but one might at least expect a reasonable explanation of this sorry state of affairs in a world governed, as is that of the Stoics, by the providence of a perfect God.

Stoic attempts to explain the attraction of evil, let alone its nature, are inadequate to solve the problems that Plato had posed. Indeed, they are often little more than controversial assertions. Many evils, they said, are not really evils to the good man—himself conveniently deprived of the capacity to sympathize in order to be impervious to the blows of fortune, though desirous (but by what kind of desire?) to rectify whatever injustices he may be able to handle without losing his equilibrium, and devoid of any shadow of regret if he fails to bring about what he strives for. What appear to be evils are often, as Aristotle might have implied and as Marcus Aurelius said explicitly, like sawdust in a carpenter's shop: messy but unavoidable. Those who worry about them merely show their corruption by so doing. As for sickness, the deaths of friends, and such trials, the good man is no fool. When you kiss your child goodnight, remarks Epictetus, remember to whisper to yourself "You will die tomorrow" (3.24.88ff.). But that is not to solve the problem of evil; indeed, it is hardly to recognize it. Metaphysically, it is to deny the existence of evil in a world of providence; morally, it is to reduce right action to the strict promotion of impersonal justice.

But why should the Stoics even want to promote justice? Are they equating knowing what is right with wanting to do it? Perhaps they are, but if so, only because their account of rationality is more Platonic, or rather contains more of a residue of Platonism, than they were prepared

13. Note that the Hellenistic philosophers are often better compared with thinkers from Descartes to Hume than with Plato and Aristotle.

to admit or than they were fully aware of. Perhaps we may be allowed a modern comparison before we leave them to return to the Platonic tradition. The Stoics do seem to have retained something of the Platonic view of a motivating, *eros*-driven mind, while formally repudiating the Platonic metaphysics with which it is intimately connected—rather in the manner of many current moral and political philosophers who want to retain the notion of inalienable human rights while divesting it of the theistic, indeed specifically Christian, underpinnings with which Locke and others originally endowed it. They want the dogma without the metaphysics, or at least those bits of dogma that happen to take their fancy. Whitehead said that the history of philosophy is a series of footnotes on Plato; it might be nearer the mark to say that much philosophy has consisted in claiming some of Plato's conclusions without claiming the structures with which he had proposed to uphold them.

Plotinus and his Neoplatonic successors, as well as a number of early Christians who had previously been Platonizers, saw some of the problems of identity and moral motivation, ambiguously linked as I have suggested in Plato himself, with a much greater degree of clarity, and came up with different answers. In the remaining part of this essay I want to introduce the topic of how, within a framework of Platonic ethics, a few of them reacted to the Platonic difficulties I have outlined, and then to ask what other way out of the dilemmas there could be if the subject of moral philosophy is to remain in existence. For there are contemporary alternatives to moral philosophy, though those who offer them may still exclaim, and usually believe, that they are practitioners of ethics as it was traditionally studied. In fact, they have changed the subject while retaining the name, though Parfit is more straightforward; one of his subheadings in *Reasons and Persons* is "How Both Human History and the History of Ethics May Be Just Beginning" (p. 453).

I would want to claim that, whether or not he understood that the problems that worried him about human moral capacity are generated within the Platonic text itself, Plotinus grasped at least some of the key issues, and offered characteristically bold advice that he took to be Platonic in spirit. Whether Plato himself would have seen matters in the Plotinian way is a question that interests and puzzles me. Augustine thought he could not have done so; according to the saint, he would have "changed a few words and phrases and become a Christian" (*DVR* 4.7). But how few is "few," or has Augustine got his tongue in his cheek?

As for Plotinus himself, he failed to conceal his irritation with what he took to be an unthinking religious attitude among his contemporaries, but instead of asking whether the religious—almost certainly not the orthodox Christians—had any serious philosophical grounds with which to justify their position, he dismissed their attitude as a mere excuse for laziness, if not for vice. "It is ridiculous for people to do everything else in life according to their own ideas, even if they are not doing it in the way the gods like, and then be merely saved by the gods without even doing the things by which the gods themselves command them to save themselves" (*Enn.* 3.2.8.43ff.; Armstrong trans.); and again, "It is not lawful for those who have become wicked to demand others to be their saviours and to sacrifice themselves in answer to their prayers, nor furthermore to require gods to direct their affairs in detail, laying aside their own life" (3.2.9.10ff.).

Note how alien this would sound to some ancient religious thinkers, Paul, for example, or Augustine. They would immediately contend that religion is precisely the way in which man finds support to live the right kind of life since he is somehow unable to live rightly by his own efforts. But Plotinus knows that it is of the essence of Platonism to insist that we choose our own destiny, and that, if we can retain the pearl-in-the-oyster that is our already existing perfect self, we can fight the Herculean fight for the godlike life. That implies, as we have seen, that we have the means to self-perfection within us. The pearl-in-the-oyster is the security to which we can cling, and *eros* is the means by which we, or some of us, can fight our way "upward," while retaining our hold on our own inner core. And there really is a pearl-in-the-oyster; Plotinus calls it the "soul above," and he is prepared to cling to it "contrary to the opinions of others" (4.8.8.1; cf. 5.1.10.17ff.); that is, I suppose, "other" Platonists who were less clear than himself about the centrality of the theory if the consistency and coherence of the dominant version of Platonic ethics is to be maintained. Furthermore, Plotinus would hold, we can learn from the example of such as Socrates that the desire for and dependence on the Good with which we are endowed by nature will provide us with the necessary strength and endurance to return to the world where we rightly belong.

But Plotinus is no more successful than Plato in maintaining complete consistency: and there is one powerful but only partially integrated thesis in the *Enneads* that—being itself no complete novelty within the Plotinian system but rooted in the thinking of many earlier generations of Platonists and Pythagoreans—might have impressed (and even have dominated) its author as much as it impressed Augustine and others later on: the account of *tolma* (or pride) in *Ennead* 5.1.1. For Plotinus's view of *tolma* (τόλμα) implies a much more serious problem with moral evil, a problem far less easy to explain away in a Stoic manner, than anything else in the *Enneads*: a problem furthermore that oddly reconnects the difficulties that we (or our souls) face over the possibility of moral growth with the fact that we are inadequate unities, or in more modern terms with the problem of that identity and unity that we in the Platonic tradition have long sought to impose on our conflicting lifestyles (our private life, our public life, our sex life, etc.) so that we might become and remain, like Socrates or the philosopher-king, all of a piece.

We start with Plotinus's general view that there is in us, or rather over our empirical self (which Plotinus, in contradistinction from his master, specifically identifies), an upper soul that does not sin; and we shall see that a deepening sense of pessimism about human nature as we now experience it leads Porphyry tentatively and Iamblichus definitively to abandon this sinless inner self. For if we were "once" like that, why are we not like it now? Here is where Plotinus introduces the concept of *tolma*. His question, directly enough posed, is "Why did the souls forget their father?" This is a legitimate question indeed within the Platonic tradition, for although Plato himself is certain enough that we are not gods (for the gods, unlike ourselves—see the *Statesman* and the *Timaeus*—have not fallen), we look in vain in Plato for a nonmythological account of the precise nature of our fall.

There is a serious metaphysical reason why Plato cannot answer questions about the "fall" where Plotinus might reasonably suppose that he can. However closely modern interpreters may want to connect the Form of the Good to God or the Demiurge in the *Timaeus* and the *Laws* —a matter on which I have now passed into what in Anglo-Saxon terms is more or less a heretical position[14]—in Plato's cosmos there still remains the questionably intelligible Receptacle or Matrix or Mother of material objects, the relation of which to the Good and to the Divine Mind seems to be that of sempiternal coequal. But in the *Enneads* the entire world system is unambiguously dependent on the One—though this still leaves Plotinus with a problem that he notoriously failed to solve about the origin of the physicality, the materiality, the sheer bulk of physical objects: Is matter in fact just form run, as it were, to fat?[15]

Thus there is a serious problem of theodicy in Plotinus that Plato can avoid confronting, for in the *Enneads* the existence of everything is in some sense to be attributed to the One. That includes the existence of plurality, and moral evil, and *tolma* itself. In *Ennead* 5.1.1 Plotinus sets out to explain why it is that souls have forgotten their father, and he lists a number of what, for want of a more precise terminology, we can call "factors to be considered." There is "primary otherness," and "coming-to-

14. See J. M. Rist, *The Mind of Aristotle* (Toronto, 1989), pp. 197–205.

15. Cf. J. M. Rist, "Is Plotinus' Body Too Etherialized?," in *Multarum Artium Scientia: Festschrift for Godfrey Tanner. Prudentia Supplementary Number*, ed. K. Lee, C. Mackie, H. Tarrant (Auckland, New Zealand, 1993), pp. 103–17.

be," and "wishing to belong to themselves," for a start. What is this all about? Nothing less serious than a potential contradiction within the heart of the Plotinian system itself, and indeed within the whole of Platonic metaphysics in its Plotinian version. For it is clearly a Platonic principle that an effect of being good is doing good, an effect of seeing the beautiful, as the *Symposium* has it, is production in the beautiful.

Leave aside the difficulty of what kind of products are in question. Concentrate rather on the fact that the Plotinian One is the star exemplar of this metaphysical phenomenon. The One is by nature and not by necessity or any kind of external compulsion productive. But the laws of logic are assumed; the One cannot reproduce itself. Anything other than the One is, in Plotinus's language, "secondary," in some sense a plurality. The multiplicity that we, at our best, would desire to be rid of is present at the highest "created" level: the first product of the One, again in Plotinus's language, is that very primary otherness that is listed among the conditions, or causes, of the souls' forgetfulness of their father. For since the One cannot produce another self, for the two would be indistinguishable and hence identical, its first product must be other than, and less than, itself, itself in its turn incapable of producing even what the One produces. Thus as the goodness of creativity flows outward from the One, the degree of comparative imperfection—"comparative otherness" in Plotinus's words—must increase. It would be odd indeed, to put the matter in more contemporary parlance, if God could generate *another* God.

Thus far we might seem to be within the realm of logic and metaphysics; the One's products must be inferior to itself. There still seems to be no reason why they should be *morally* inferior, or, perhaps more accurately, why the inevitability of a plural world should necessitate the existence of a world containing moral evil. Plotinus is emphatic, even if slightly incoherent, in a few passages that at no level of the cosmos above that of the human soul is there any question of moral guilt. He seems to want to say, however, that at a certain point in the production of plurality plurality itself turns into, or is seen as, moral ambiguity. And he seems to see this moral ambiguity as *tolma*, as pride, as an assertion of the self, as wishing to belong not to one's origin but to oneself. He seems to have thought that a certain degree of plurality, of lack of unity, brings a lack of strength of purpose to living beings, specifically to men. The pull of *eros*, at higher levels unambiguously directed back to one's source, is now insufficient. That may seem reasonable enough, as a metaphysical claim, but it seems almost stipulative to say that this is precisely the nature of moral weakness, and it is certainly hard to find a Plotinian *argument* to that effect.

More to our present point, however, if our *eros* is now so ambiguous, how do we find the strength to do by our own efforts what we no longer seem able to do "naturally"? We may look morally or spiritually lazy, as Plotinus seems to have thought, but out of his own mouth he seems now to be condemning us to be not just morally lazy but lazy in virtue of our metaphysical structure. And if that is so, we could not pull ourselves up by our own bootstraps. Moral evil has turned out to be much more serious, much more damaging to the very intelligibility of the cosmos, than we might have supposed. Of course, one might dismiss moral evil as a manmade convention, a mere function of man's choices in society. That route, popular among our own contemporaries, was unacceptable to the Stoics, who certainly linked it with atheism, and even more so to Plotinus. We are supposed to be not conventionally but "really" just. So perhaps the modern ethicist can mock Plotinus for insisting on absolute justice while giving a metaphysical account that seems to make injustice both inevitable and morally unintelligible: and probably only punished arbitrarily, since inevitable.

Of course the upper soul is supposed to help in this situation; that is why it is retained "contrary to the opinion of others." It is to provide the raft to which we can cling and pull ourselves up from our empirical selves to our real selves, but only at the price of showing that our empirical experiences are ultimately more or less insignificant—though that is much too unnuanced a comment. Plotinus is right to see that for an undiluted Platonic ethics not merely an upper soul but an *untainted* upper soul is an essential part of the structure, but its presence certainly highlights the problem of why we fell in the first place; or it suggests that our fall is of no great significance and that the multiple self that Plato took so much trouble to delineate is merely a superficial covering for something much more important and secure.

Of course, if Plato wanted to say that our fall is more significant than Plotinus (apart from his unintegrated doctrine of *tolma*) wanted to make it, then our historical existence is much more closely tied to our "real" existence than Plotinus wanted to allow. In a Platonic world it would follow that our bundle of potential selves is not yet (though it has been) our real self. That real self has still to be remade; we are not yet single-minded; we do not yet (or we no longer) live an undivided life; in a sense we do not live a single life at all.

Plotinus's account of wrongdoing apparently failed to convince his successors. Whether they thought he had trivialized the nature of immoral acts, or for more personal reasons, such as the sheer inability to live a good life, they lost their nerve. Elsewhere I have attempted to discuss the crisis in Neoplatonic ethics associated with the abandonment (tentatively by Porphyry, more radically by Iamblichus) of the theory of the unfallen upper soul.[16] For now we know where we want to go, but without divine aid, somehow obtained through theurgy, we cannot, according to Iamblichus, do more than merely think about the good life; we cannot raise our philosophical souls to the One. What this means specifically, for a Platonist, is that the power of *eros*, divine though it may be, and a gift of the gods, is insufficient to enable the soul to return to its origin. Iamblichus, however, offers no more help than Plato (or at least than Plotinus) in explaining very specifically why we are in this unhappy state, why we no longer want, or are no longer able to do, what Socrates did (though Plato himself suggested that even that might be *theia moira*) and what the philosopher-kings are supposed to do. He merely invokes further divine aid in seeking our return.

Note how that invocation appeared to Augustine. It seemed an attempt both blasphemous and futile to secure our return by dishonest means where honest ones had manifestly failed. To Augustine, eventually, the answer to the dilemma thus posed is obvious: not to attempt to be God, like the theurgists—a project doomed from the outset—but to recognize, *pace* Plotinus, that if we are (ever) to live the good life, the undivided life, the life that finds not ourself but God within us (see *Conf.* 1.1.1), if we are to be anything other than that bundle of potential selves that Plato in his darker moments had so powerfully described, then the gratuitous help of God himself, through the grace of Christ, must be the only way and the only hope.

Augustine suggested that if Plato were alive in his day he would be a Christian; in saying that he has many things in mind, but one of them is that he thought it obvious that Plato's basic thesis about moral motivation through love of beauty and the inspiration of the good (that is, through *eros*) is correct as far as it goes, but that Plato had failed to recognize that there is a gap between what *eros* was once intended to achieve, and what it actually achieves. And despite Plato's attempts to sort this out, and the Plotinian theory of *eros* that Augustine obviously approves and to which he gives a wider and more full-blooded application, the Platonists, for Augustine, remain in a morass: they must either give up or pervert the truths they have discovered, or they must become Christians. It is easy to see why Augustine, and other Christian Platonist intellectuals, thought that they, and often that their Athenian master, had no real choice.

As for ourselves, we have then an identity only in hope, since we are, as

16. J. M. Rist, "Pseudo-Dionysius, Neoplatonism, and the Weakness of the Soul," in *From Athens to Chartres: Neoplatonism and Medieval Thought: Studies in Honour of Edouard Jeauneau,* ed. H. J. Westra (Leiden, 1992), pp. 135–61, esp. 140–44.

Augustine always puts it, *in via*; hence attempts to determine what "further fact" lies behind our physical or psychological continuity are doomed to failure, not for the reasons urged by Parfit, who would reduce us all to figures in an impersonal universe (thus making goods much easier to quantify), but because what we strive for neither existed in the past, as the Platonists suggested with their accounts of reincarnation and *anamnesis*, nor exists (except in flux) in the present, though it could exist in the future. For the present, we are indeed a set of potential selves, held together by whatever degree of goodness, and hence love of more of it, that we happen to have from time to time: like the charioteer and his horses in Plato's *Phaedrus*.

As for the moral acts that we try to perform, or are inspired to perform, I am not trying to suggest that ethics should be reduced to desire for the good as beautiful, any more than I would want to follow the now largely discredited Kantian line that all moral acts are to be reduced to duties and obligations. Augustine would certainly have to insist—he should insist even if he didn't quite do so—that the story of the relationship between *eros* for the good, moral obligation, and virtue requires much more attention than Plato had given it. But if Augustine is dissatisfied with the Platonic traditions about ethics and moral motivation he inherited, it was not that he thought them quite misguided, but that he thought that they did not go far enough, that, without a certain sort of theism, they were not, and could not be, as stated, fully consistent. His challenge still remains for those of us dissatisfied with ethical nihilism in theory disguised by sentimental self-deception in practice.

13 Neoplatonist Conceptions of the Philosopher-King

DOMINIC J. O'MEARA

In A.D. 524, while awaiting execution in prison in Pavia, Boethius contemplated the ruin of his ambitions, of his distinguished political career, of his life. As he describes the scene at the beginning of his book, *The Consolation of Philosophy*, a personification of philosophy appears to him and he, in his misery, addresses her in these bitter words:

> Was this how I looked, was this my expression, when I used to seek out with you the secrets of Nature? When with your rod you drew for me the paths of the stars? When you shaped my character and the whole manner of my life according to celestial models? Are these our rewards for obedient service to you? It was you who established through the words of Plato the principle that those states would be happy where philosophers were kings or their governors were philosophers. You, through that same Plato, told us that this was why philosophers must involve themselves in political affairs, lest the rule of nations be left to the base and wicked, bringing ruin and destruction on the good. It was in accordance with that teaching that I chose to apply in the practice of public administration what I learned from you in the seclusion of my private leisure. You, and God, who has set you in the minds of philosophers, know me well, and that I undertook office with no other motives than the common purpose of all good men.[1]

Under philosophy's guidance, Boethius had attemped to realize the hope that Plato had once expressed in the *Republic* (473c–d), that philosophers would become kings, or kings philosophers, for only with the union of philosophy and political power would there be respite from evils for mankind.

Without going into the reasons for and the significance of Boethius's failure, we might ask ourselves how *seriously* Boethius took Plato's notion of philosopher-kings. Are we dealing simply with a rhetorical commonplace, to be found throughout the literature of late antiquity? Or was Plato's notion an integral part of Boethius's general philosophical stance? If so, we

1. Boethius, *Consolation of Philosophy*, trans. S. Tester (London and Cambridge, Mass., 1973), 1.4.4–8, p. 147.

must then face another problem. Boethius is in general much inspired by the Neoplatonic philosophy taught in his time in Athens and Alexandria. This philosophy exhorts us to set aside the things of the world, to escape from material occupations, in order to achieve union with a transcendent immaterial absolute, the One. How could there be room, in such a world-renouncing philosophy, for Plato's ideal of the philosopher-king?

This problem extends well beyond the case of Boethius, and can take the form of a paradox, if not a contradiction, in the words and deeds of Neoplatonist philosophers who, on the one hand, preach escape from the world, but, on the other hand, are found to be present and active to varying degrees at the centers of Roman power. Let me sketch rapidly this political presence of Neoplatonists in the late Roman Empire in order to give some idea of the extent of this phenomenon.[2]

We might begin with Plotinus, founder of Neoplatonism, and his circle in Rome in the second half of the third century A.D. In his *Life of Plotinus*, Porphyry portrays his master as so abstracted, so wrapped up in the transcendent, that he is hardly here, in this world, at all. Plotinus, Porphyry tells us, tried to dissuade a pupil from political involvement.[3] Yet we also learn that Plotinus's circle included a good number of senators, among them a consul and a proconsul, and that Plotinus was on friendly terms with the Emperor Gallienus and his wife, attempting to use this contact in order to set up a city to be governed by Plato's laws, Platonopolis. Opposition in the imperial court blocked the project.[4] What was this city to be? A sort of pagan philosopher's monastery? A city to be based on the utopia of Plato's *Republic* or on the more realistic model Plato later proposed in the *Laws*?[5] Why would world-renouncing Plotinus have an interest in such a project? If we move to the second major phase in the history of Neoplatonism, to Iamblichus and his school in Syria at the beginning of the fourth century A.D., we find that Iamblichus himself was a wealthy member of the princely house of Emesa; that, of his many students, one would become a councilor of Constantine, another an ambassador to Persia, and another, Aidesius, the teacher of the future emperor Julian who called to his court several other pupils of Aidesius.[6] Turning finally to the Neoplatonic school of Athens in the fifth century A.D., we

2. On this subject, see G. Fowden's instructive thesis, *Pagan Philosophers in Late Antique Society* (Ph.D. diss., Oxford University, 1979).

3. Porphyry, *Vita Plotini* 7.20–21 (Zethus; see also the case of another pupil, the senator Rogatianus, 7.32–45); cf. L. Brisson et al., *Porphyre: "La vie de Plotin"* (Paris, 1982), vol. 1, p. 109.

4. Porphyry, *Vita Plotini*, chaps. 7 and 12.

5. On this subject, see L. Jerphagnon, "Platonopolis, ou Plotin entre le siècle et le rêve," in *Néoplatonisme: Mélanges . . . J. Trouillard* (Fontenay, 1981), p. 216ff.

6. On Iamblichus and his pupils, see Fowden, *Pagan Philosophers.*

find in the philosopher Proclus a respected teacher and influential personality in the city, who counted many high government officials among those who attended his school, among them senators, consuls, and a future emperor, Anthemius.[7] We know of one case of Proclus encouraging a pupil to go into politics.[8]

Looking over this evidence, we might ask ourselves how it could square with the theoretical requirement to renounce this world that is so prominent in Neoplatonism. Might we, using a sociological approach, compare with this the social and political roles assumed by Christian monks, hermits, and other types of holy men in the world of late antiquity? Peter Brown has discussed the problem posed by the Neoplatonist philosophers in the light of the social and cultural values that they could be seen to embody.[9] Here, however, I would like to approach the problem from the point of view of philosophical theory, using Plato's ideal of the philosopher-king as a key, and asking the question: What place, if any, could Plato's ideal of the philosopher-king have in the theoretical framework of Neoplatonism?

As it turns out, Plato's philosopher-kings make their presence felt quite frequently throughout the writings of Neoplatonists. In order to keep this essay within reasonable limits, I must select from the results of my enquiry and concentrate on one aspect of the notion of philosopher-king. On encountering this notion in Plato's *Republic*, the modern reader is provoked into posing many questions: Is not the ideal of the philosopher-king terribly dangerous, a recipe for technocratic tyranny? Is it not naïve? How in particular could the incorruptibility of Plato's philosopher-rulers be preserved? But is it not also millenia ahead of its time, in calling for women among the philosopher-rulers? Yet is Plato not unfair and unjust to the philosophers themselves, who, having been enabled to escape from the fetters and the cave of ignorance and opinion, to contemplate reality, the Forms, in the truth, in the light of the Form of the Good, are then obliged to return to the cave, to put their knowledge in the service of the state? Does this not mean sacrificing the philosopher's personal happiness, the contemplation of the Forms, to the good of the state? For what reason must philosophers descend from contemplation and assume political office? Why, that is, should philosophers become kings? In what follows, I would like to concentrate on this last question in exploring some Neoplatonic interpretations of Plato's philosopher-kings.

7. On Proclus's school, see *Proclus: Théologie platonicienne*, ed. H.-D. Saffrey and L. G. Westerink (Paris, 1968), vol. 1, pp. xlix–liv.

8. Archiadas; see Marinus, *Vita Procli*, 14.

9. P. Brown, "The Philosopher and Society in Late Antiquity," *Center for Hermeneutical Studies Colloquy* (Berkeley, Calif., 1978), pp. 1–17.

I

I would like to begin with the following passage in Plotinus *Ennead* 6.9.7: Plotinus is describing the escape of the soul from the world and its ascent to contemplative union with the transcendent cause of all things, the One:

> and having been in [the One's] company and had, so to put it, sufficient converse with it, [the soul must] come and announce, if it could, to another that transcendent union. Perhaps also it was because Minos attained this kind of union that he was said in the story to be the familiar friend of Zeus, and it was in remembering this that he laid down laws in its image, being filled full of lawgiving by the divine touch. Or, also, it may think political matters unworthy of it and want to remain always above; this is liable to happen to one who has seen much.[10]

According to Plotinus, then, the soul, having reached union with the One, must announce this experience to another, the announcing taking the form, for example, of an activity of legislation in the image of the divine life, inspired by the contact with the divine. Or, Plotinus adds, one may wish to remain in the transcendent union, judging politics to be unworthy. Plotinus is inspired here in the first instance by the Platonic dialogue *Minos* (319b–20b), or perhaps by a similar text in the *Laws* (624a), where the legendary legislator Minos is represented as receiving instruction from Zeus. However, I would also suggest that an important background to Plotinus's thought here is the ascent of Plato's philosopher-kings to knowledge of the Form of the Good, which Plotinus identifies with the One, and their descent, their return to political office, ruling the city, as Plato says (*Rep.* 500d–e) in the image of the divine.[11]

10. Plotinus, *Ennead* 6.9.7, 20–28 (A. H. Armstong trans., modified). For a different reading of the Greek, see P. Hadot, *Plotin Traité* 9 (Paris, 1994), pp. 98–99, who thinks that the last part of this passage ("Or, also, it may think . . .") refers to Minos and not to the soul who announces to another its union with the One, essentially because it seems difficult to consider that announcing a mystical vision is a "political matter." (See also P. Meijer, *Plotinus on the Good or the One* [Amsterdam, 1992], p. 225.) I attempt, however, in this essay to show that political action is precisely, for the Neoplatonists, the attempt to communicate divine life.

11. The notion of legislation in the *image* of a divine model is formulated neither in the *Minos* nor in *Laws* 624a; it has therefore become part, in Plotinus's mind, of the story of Minos and Zeus through the influence of the passage in the *Republic* (for this notion, see also Plotinus, *Enn.* 1.2.2, 16–26; 5.9.11, 22–24). However, the *Republic* passage concerns an *intelligible* legislative model, whereas our text from *Ennead* 6.9.7 relates to the One, which is beyond intelligible reality. Thus J. F. Balaudé (in "Communauté divine et au-delà: Les fins du dépassement selon Plotin," *Philosophie* 26 [1990]: 90), thinking that "the union . . . with the One can scarcely be considered a pertinent model for law-making," suggests that Plotinus has "slipped" in 6.9.7 from the evocation of ecstatic union to that of an intellective union of a communitarian type. Balaudé also notes that Zeus is usually associated in Plotinus with soul and not with the One. However, we might reply that the use of the figure of

Plotinus's comment that one may wish to remain above in the transcendent also has its counterpart in the reluctance of Plato's philosophers to get involved in politics (519c–20a). But why must the philosopher abandon contemplative bliss and assume political leadership? In Plato, it looks as if some obligation to serve the common good, that of the city, applies to the philosopher.[12] In Plotinus, the grounds of the obligation to communicate the One, to legislate in the image of the divine, are not specified. Assuming nevertheless that there are such grounds, I would like to take a suggestion made by a later Neoplatonist and show that it points to an answer that we can apply in the case of Plotinus.

Proclus, in his book on the existence of evils, talks of pure souls who participate through contemplation in heavenly goods, but who also, imitating the divine, in an activity free of all envy, desire to confer benefit on the inferior, making it like them.[13] This beneficent activity, free of envy, reminds us of the divine Demiurge of Plato's *Timaeus* (29e) and, more generally, of the Neoplatonic metaphysical principle that the Good is self-diffusive, giving of itself as an expression of its intrinsic perfection: *bonum est diffusivum sui*, according to the medieval formulation. This principle was first systematically formulated and applied by Plotinus.[14] It governs his whole view of reality as a cascading series of expressions externalizing the intrinsic perfection of the One, of the Good, as source of reality. Proclus suggests that pure souls, sharing in transcendent goods, in divine life, will, in imitation of the Good, seek to communicate the Good to what is below them. Could this also be the motivation of the legislative soul in our passage in Plotinus *Ennead* 6.9?

Another Plotinian treatise, *Ennead* 3.8, gives us some reasons for thinking so. *Ennead* 3.8 is largely concerned with the question of the generation of the world. Plotinus argues that the world is not produced as the result of some laborious calculation, but emerges as a kind of by-product or secondary activity accompanying the contemplative life of higher realities, soul and intellect. In arguing for the priority of contemplative activity and its fecundity in giving rise to expressions of its perfection, Plotinus appeals to the sphere of human activity as illustrating the same relation between *theoria* (contemplation), *poiesis* (making), and

---

Zeus in our text is guided by the story of Minos. Nor should we forget that intelligible reality, in Plotinus, is itself an image or expression of the power and life of the One.

12. For a recent discussion, see T. Mahoney, "Do Plato's Philosopher-Rulers Sacrifice Self-Interest to Justice?," *Phronesis* 37 (1992): 265–82.

13. Proclus, *De malorum subsistentia* section 23, in *Proclus: Trois études sur la providence*, vol. 3: *De l'existence du mal*, ed. and trans. D. Isaac (Paris 1982), p. 58.

14. See K. Kremer, "Bonum est diffusivum sui," in *Aufstieg und Niedergang der römischen Welt*, ed. W. Haase and H. Temporini (Berlin, 1987), vol. 36, part 2, pp. 994–1032.

praxis (action).[15] Plotinus asserts that when we make or do something, we act thus as a kind of secondary consequence of, or as a substitute for, contemplation (4.31–43). He gives the example of geometers who draw diagrams as they think: the geometrical diagrams are, as it were, "precipitates" of geometrical thought, not its objects (4.7–10). Plato's philosopher-kings also do geometry on their way up to contemplating the Forms, and they produce diagrams as images of their objects of thought (*Rep.* 520d–e). However, Plotinus is mostly concerned here with the creativity of this activity as an example of the creativity of contemplation in general. If, then, a soul that contemplates the One will naturally give expression to this contemplation in action or making, imitating in this the productivity of the Good in which it shares, we may infer, I think, that the action involved may be political such as the legislative action described in *Ennead* 6.9.[16] We can conclude, then, that the motivation of the philosophical legislator, the philosopher-king, in Plotinus does not relate to a political theory of the preeminence of the good of the state as integrating the private good (see *Rep.* 519e). It relates to the metaphysical principle of the self-diffusiveness of the Good which applies throughout reality and, in the case of the philosopher, leads from contemplative union with the One or the Good to communication of the Good that can take the form of political action.[17]

If this is right, we can say that the presence of Plato's philosopher-kings in *Ennead* 6.9, and the reported project of Platonopolis, are not at odds with Plotinus's otherworldly philosophy. This philosophy calls us to escape the world in order to achieve union with the One, which can result in a return to the world, a desire to communicate and express the Good, for example, in the form of legislation. As late as the sixth century the last Neoplatonists at Alexandria were to give a simplified, popularized expression to these ideas. In explaining the goal of philosophy, defined by Plato as assimilation of man to god (*Tht.* 176b), they find in god a twofold activity: knowing all things and providential care for the inferior. Assimilation to god then implies for the philosopher a corresponding twofold life: that of contemplation, and that of the political activity of legislation and jurisdiction.[18]

15. See R. Arnou, *Πρᾶξις ετ Θεωρία* (Rome 1972).

16. See also Proclus, *Sur le premier Alcibiade*, ed. A. Segonds (Paris 1985), vol. 1, p. 78, 17–23.

17. It is possible that a political motivation inspired by the desire of the Good and of the good of others is already present in the *Republic* (see Mahoney, "Do Plato's Philosopher-Rulers," pp. 278–82; also see *Symp.* 206b); a comparison between the cosmic Demiurge of the *Timaeus* and the political demiurges that are the philosopher-kings of the *Republic* also points in this direction.

18. Ammonius *In Porphyrii Isagogen*, ed. A. Busse (Berlin, 1891) (*Commentaria in Aristotelem graeca*, 4.3), p. 3, 8–19; Olympiodorus, *In Platonis Gorgiam*, ed. L. G. Westerink

II

Let us move now to the fourth century and to the phase of Neoplatonism marked by Iamblichus. So little of Iamblichus's own work survives that it cannot take us very far in our inquiry. Certainly in fragments surviving from a letter addressed to Dyscolius, probably a governor of Syria, Iamblichus proposed a conventional-sounding "Mirror of Princes." In a fragment from another letter, he advocates political rule based on divine exemplars, very much along the lines taken by Plato's philosopher-kings (*Rep.* 500e).[19] And if we read one of his few surviving books, *On the Pythagorean Life*, as expressing his own preferences, we can consider its description of the ancient Pythagoreans as contemplative philosophers also engaged in politics not only as pointing to what might have inspired Plato's own notion of the philosopher-king, but also as expressing Iamblichus's ideal for the late antique philosopher.[20] For our purposes, more can be discovered in the works of one of Iamblichus's philosophical heirs, the emperor Julian. I would like to take up two works Julian composed shortly after his accession to power in 361 A.D., both reacting to advice given him as to how he should rule by the Cynic philosopher Heraclius and by the influential professor of philosophy at Constantinople, Themistius.

Julian's response to Heraclius takes strong exception to the impiety expressed by the Cynic philosopher with regard to the gods.[21] The connection Julian sees between piety and political rule is explained by the extraordinary myth that he proceeds to tell and that is a parable of his own life and political mission (227c ff.). The myth starts with Constantine accumulating great wealth, in ignorance of the gods and of the art of managing his possessions, leaving all to heirs who fight over the inheritance, creating an age of impiety, chaos, and slaughter. Considering all this from above and wishing to remedy the situation, Zeus instructs his offspring Helios, the sun god, in collaboration with Athena, to protect and educate in piety an abandoned child among Constantine's heirs, Julian. One day Hermes appears to Julian and leads him up a wonderful path to the mountain where the gods reside. Helios appears to Julian in a vision. Julian

(Leipzig, 1970), pp. 166, 14–16, pp. 116, 29–117, 2. For an example of the standard view that assimilation to god means, for the Neoplatonist, disdain for politics, see M.-P. Edmond, *Le philosophe-roi: Platon et la politique* (Paris 1991), pp. 17–19.

19. On these letters, see my article "Aspects of Political Philosophy in Iamblichus," in *The Divine Iamblichus: Philosopher and Man of Gods*, ed. H. Blumenthal and G. Clark (Bristol, 1993), pp. 67–70, and reprinted in my *The Structure of Being* (Aldershot, 1998).

20. Ibid., pp. 70–71.

21. *Contre Heracleios le cynique*, in *L'empereur Julien: Oeuvres complètes*, ed. and trans. G. Rochefort (Paris, 1963), 204c ff., vol. 2, part 1, p. 44.

pleads with Helios to allow him to stay in the vision of the gods, but he is told that he must return to the murky world below, as ruler of men, sent by Zeus and equipped with divine aid (231d, 232c). He is given instructions on good leadership, among which the importance of piety is stressed, and he is promised as reward a return to the vision of Zeus (234c).

I have given the briefest of summaries of Julian's myth, but perhaps enough to indicate that several philosophical parables structure it: that of the road of Parmenides far from the ways of men that leads to a divine revelation; that of the gift to men by Zeus, through the mediation of Hermes, of political science (Plato, *Prot.* 322c–d); but especially that of an ascent from darkness, political disorder, ignorance, to the light of the sun, the sight of the divine, and then a return, armed with this knowledge, to the darkness to undertake political reform. This is, of course, the parable of the cave of the *Republic*, the ascent and descent of Plato's philosopher-kings.[22] But if we compare Julian's myth with Plato's text, we cannot but notice some striking differences: what is seen by the philosopher in the ascent, the Forms, is personalized, so to speak, as a series of divinities in Julian. This is a characteristic feature of later Neoplatonism, which sought to show how the world of the Forms and transcendent causes corresponds to the pagan pantheon. The motive of Julian's descent in order to rule is also personalized: it is not an obligation to the state, nor is it quite Plotinus's metaphysical principle of the generosity of the Good. This metaphysical principle is personalized in Julian's myth: the Good is Zeus, and Zeus instructs Julian to descend, even if he, like Plato's philosopher-kings and Plotinus's contemplative soul, may feel some reluctance to do so.[23] This personalization expresses also the importance of piety in its relation to rulership: as the desire and sight of the Forms are the foundation of good rulership in Plato, so are love and a vision of the gods indispensable for political reform in Julian.

I turn now to Julian's response to Themistius. Themistius had made a name for himself as an Aristotelian specialist and had achieved considerable political standing and influence in the imperial courts of his time.

22. Numerous relationships between Julian's writings and the central books of the *Republic* are noted by P. Athanassiadi-Fowden, in *Julian and Hellenism: An Intellectual Biography* (Oxford, 1981), pp. 56–57, 92–93 (where she also refers to Plotinus *Enn.* 6.9.7), 149, 170, 217–18. See also P. Huart, "Julien et l'hellénisme: Idées morales et politiques," in *L'Empereur Julien: De l'histoire à la légende*, ed. R. Braun and J. Richer (Paris, 1978), pp. 112–15.

23. *Contre Heracleios*, pp. 56–57. Obedience to the gods in Julian (ἑπόμενος . . . ἡμῖν *Against Heracleius* 234c); harks back to a maxim ἑποῦ θεῷ emphasized as Pythagorean by Iamblichus, in *De vita pythagorica* 86–87, ed. L. Deubner [Stuttgart, 1975], pp. 50, 20–51, 6; 137, pp. 77, 16–78, 4; *Protrepticus*, ed. H. Pistelli (Stuttgart, 1967), p. 112, 11–26. Boethius, *Consolation* 1.4, 38. Iamblichus also insisted on piety as a fundamental Pythagorean virtue (*Vita pyth.* 134).

He was not a member of the Neoplatonic groups to which Julian belonged and indeed recommended that Julian abandon the studious life of a Neoplatonist recluse,[24] citing as paradigms various philosopher-kings of the past and exalting not contemplation life, but the political life of the "architect," in Aristotle's words, of "fine actions."[25] Julian reacted strongly to this anti-Neoplatonic appropriation of Plato's philosopher-kings, this exaltation of the active political life at the expense of the contemplative life. I would single out in particular the following elements of Julian's response to Themistius. Julian emphasizes his own limitations and deficiencies in relation to the function of the philosopher-ruler: not just anybody can aspire to that function, but only those endowed with the appropriate nature and education. The unsuitable are therefore to be discouraged from such an ambition, as Socrates discouraged some, according to Julian (255c). This is a sound point, true to Plato's own views (*Rep.* 412d–14b), and one that allows us to infer that the reported cases of people being turned away from politics by Neoplatonists in no way entail that in *all* cases political involvement was discouraged. Julian then disputes Themistius's subordination of the contemplative life to the active, political life. He notes (with Themistius) that Aristotle himself seems in some places to give priority to the contemplative life. He interprets the Aristotelian text that Themistius cites as applying, not to political executives (such as Julian had become), but to "political philosophers" acting as advisers and legislators (263d), as friends of the ruler, we may suppose, such as Julian would gather around him, drawn from the pupils of his teacher Aidesius. Such advisers, not being involved in the daily exercise of power, can maintain their contemplative existence while guiding the ruler. Under the pressure, then, of Themistius's claim for the unity of power and philosophy as being prior to contemplation, Julian qualifies the unity of power and philosophy proclaimed in Plato's text, distinguishing the executive power from its advisers and legislators, and seeing in these the political philosophers who can guide the state on the basis of transcendent knowledge (cf. 262a–b). Julian also relativizes the importance of political rule, asserting that philosophers can exert a moral and pedagogic influence that has a far more profound impact than the actions of kings (266a).

Summarizing, I would suggest that Julian's concept of the philosopher-king fits broadly into the pattern set by Plotinus: contemplation of transcendent realities may issue at a lower level in political reform inspired by this contemplation. The motive for this action in Plotinus, the

24. Julian, *To Themistius* 262d, ed. Rochefort, p. 24.
25. 263c, p. 25 (Aristotle *Pol.* 7.3.1325b).

metaphysical principle of the generosity of the Good, becomes in Julian's mythic account the command of the highest and ineffable god, Zeus. However, as an experienced leader, aware of his own inadequacies and of the limitations and vagaries of human affairs (255d ff.), Julian tones down these high ideas. Plato's philosopher-kings become councillors to the king, a role that in fact corresponds to the political status held by a number of Neoplatonists. The king himself, Julian, torn between the realities of executive action and the high ideal by which he wishes to live, reforms the state in light of transcendent principles, in the hope of being released one day to the vision of the gods.

III

Some forty years later, in 399, an ambassador from Cyrene in Lybia spoke before the emperor Arcadius in Constantinople. The ambassador was Synesius, an aristocrat, landowner, and devoted pupil of the woman mathematician and philosopher Hypatia of Alexandria. Synesius had come to Constantinople to obtain tax relief for his city. He delivered before the emperor a famous speech on kingship which, if including much conventional advice derived from the rhetorical "Mirror of Princes," also offers some remarkably direct criticism of Arcadius's style of rule.[26] At the end, Synesius holds up before Arcadius Plato's ideal of the philosopher-king, the union of philosophy and political power. The context shows, I would argue, that this is not a rhetorical commonplace, as Synesius uses it, but relates to a theory of the relation between philosophy and politics that is Neoplatonist in character. Synesius calls on the emperor to revive the love of philosophy which is now much neglected and in danger of dying out.[27] He sketches a personification of philosophy who abides in the divine and has no need to descend to this earthly place. However, her presence or absence in human affairs makes the difference between the better and the worse for man, between happiness and unhappiness. It is then for mankind's good that philosophy should be brought to union with political power, as advocated by Plato. If Arcadius would carry this out, Synesius claims, he would become the ideal ruler that Synesius has portrayed. Philosophy, as described then by Synesius, lives essentially in contemplative union with the divine and is not in any way dependent on, or subordinated to, political goals, but may communicate the Good on the lower level of political action, as does

26. *Le Discours sur la royauté de Synésios de Cyrène*, trans. C. Lacombrade (Paris, 1951). On ancient "Mirror of Princes," see P. Hadot, "Fürstenspiegel," in *Realencyclopädie für Antike und Christentum* (Stuttgart, 1972), vol. 7, 556–621.

27. Ibid., section 32, 1105d, p. 75 f.

Plotinus's legislative soul. This is the sense of Plato's call for the union of philosophy and political power, for philosophers to become kings.

IV

About thirty years later, Hierocles, who studied Neoplatonic philosophy at Athens with Proclus's teacher and who himself taught in Alexandria, composed a treatise *On Providence* which he addressed to a certain Olympiodorus whom he describes as a successful diplomat and ambassador, a lover of philosophy possessing "political wisdom." The description fits the Egyptian historian who took part in an embassy to the Huns in 412. Hierocles' treatise is lost, but the patriarch Photius took some notes in reading it and thus provides us with an idea of some of the contents of the work. Of particular interest as regards our enquiry is a passage where Hierocles attempts to explain the distinction he finds in Plato's *Phaedrus* (248a ff.) between the philosopher and the lover (ἐρωτικός). According to Hierocles, the sense of this distinction is the following:[28] The "philosopher" cultivates the contemplative life, avoiding political praxis, purifying himself in seeking union with the divine. The "lover," on the other hand, is the philosopher-king of Plato's *Republic* who communicates intelligible goods to others, modeling cities on the pattern of divine paradigms, the Just, the Beautiful, thus bringing to bear contemplative intellect on political action. In comparing the philosopher and the lover, as he interprets them, Hierocles emphasizes that they are equally valuable, sharing the same philosophy, even if the contemplative life prevails in its individual mode of life (ἰδιοπραγία) whereas the lover prevails in philanthropy (φιλανθρωπία).[29]

If we compare Hierocles' distinction to ideas we have found in Plotinus, we can say that Hierocles somewhat formalizes the distinction Plotinus allows in *Ennead* 6.9.7 between contemplative union with the One and the political expression of this union. The intrinsic superiority of contemplative union is asserted in Hierocles, as it had been by Plotinus and by Julian. However, what is striking here, especially if we compare Hierocles with Julian, is the very positive valuation of the "lover," or philosopher-king. Through giving of the transcendent Good to others, the philosopher-king leads a life whose extrinsic value balances the superior intrinsic value of the purely contemplative life. This quality of the philosopher-king is described as "philanthropy," a term that had

28. Hierocles, *De prov.*, in Photius, *Bibliotheca* 251, 464b, ed. and trans. R. Henry (Paris, 1974), vol. 7, p. 200.
29. Ibid., 465a, p. 202.

been an inevitable feature of theories of kingship since Hellenistic times. In Hierocles, the term is adopted to express the notion of communicating divine goods grasped in contemplation. It relates, then, I would argue, to the metaphysical principle of the absolute Good as diffusive of itself.[30] The philanthropic motive of Hierocles' philosopher-kings is then essentially that of Plotinus's legislative soul in *Ennead* 6.9.7: contemplative sharing in the Good inspires a motion to communicate the Good, to give of it to others. In the political sphere, this means reforming the state on the basis of the knowledge of transcendent principles, a process Hierocles describes in words largely taken from Plato's *Republic* (500e).

V

The last text that I would like to consider brings us to the time of Boethius's execution. It is an anonymous dialogue in Greek "On Political Science" of which some fragments are preserved in a Vatican palimpsest. Its modern editor Carlo Mazzucchi dates the dialogue to between 507 and 535.[31] It seems to be the work of a high government official, a peer of Boethius in Justinian's court. The author is familiar with both Greek and Latin political theory and develops a critical comparison between the theories of Plato, Aristotle, and Cicero. Of interest to us are the fragments surviving from Book 5 of the dialogue, from Chapter 8 in particular, which develops the claim that the true king should govern human affairs in imitation of God and of divine things.[32] One of the interlocutors of the dialogue, Thomasius, describes an ascent of the intellect modeled on that traced in Plato's *Republic* for the future philosopher-kings, from opinion and discursive thought (διάνοια) based on hypotheses to divine light and scientific truths stamped in the resemblance of the Form of the Good.[33] This intellect then inquires, in an interior dialogue, into the first cause of all things, and finds a hierarchical scheme of reality, a structure of causation and rule, going from a transcendent first cause, through intermediary intelligible principles, to the material world and to man. Each level of reality is ordered in the likeness of what is above it, sharing thus in the beneficence of the Good.[34] Among men, the king is the principle of order and resemblance to the transcendent Good. He is Plato's philosopher-

30. On philanthropy in Iamblichus, in Pythagoreanism, and in Pythagorizing Neoplatonism, see my "Aspects of Political Philosophy," pp. 69 and 72n11.

31. *Menae patricii cum Thoma referendario De scientia politica dialogus*, ed. and trans. Ital. C. Mazzucchi (Milan, 1982), p. xiii. See A. Pertusi, *Il pensiero politico bizantino* (Bologna, 1990), first part: "La concezione politica e sociale dell'impero di Giustiniano."

32. Ibid., p. 15, 12–14.

33. Ibid., p. 35, 16–36, 1.

34. Ibid., pp. 36, 2–37, 2.

king, asserts the other speaker in the dialogue, Menodorus, who, on discovering the first cause will wish to govern men in imitation of it.[35]

The anonymous dialogue, one might comment, is very close in conception and terminology to late Neoplatonic theories of the structure of reality, yet what is said about kings imitating the Ruler of All Things hardly departs from conventional theories of rulership to be found throughout late antique literature.[36] In this regard, the mention of Plato's philosopher-kings does not seem to imply necessarily a specifically Neoplatonic interpretation of the philosopher-king such as that which we have traced in Plotinus, Julian, Synesius, and Hierocles. However, a little later in the dialogue, Menodorus brings us nearer to such an interpretation. He suggests that political science such as that which inspires the king derives from God, who, through his great goodness and care for mankind in its exile here below (ἀποικία) devised a divine method, political knowledge, to promote good order and help men return in due course to the heavenly metropolis, to the dignity of the immortal state.[37]

On reading this passage, we should avoid assuming that it expresses a specifically Christian point of view, even if, as seems clear, the author of the dialogue is in fact Christian. For several of the ideas expressed here occur earlier in pagan Neoplatonic literature. Julian, for example, speaks of the exile of mankind, in the sense of a colony set up here below (ἀποικία) away from the heavenly home city. In this earthly city, according to Julian, we strive to harvest virtue with piety in order to return to our heavenly origin.[38] The image of the heavenly homeland from which we are exiled can be traced back further to Plotinus's spiritual interpretation of Odysseus's travels in *Ennead* 1.6.8. Furthermore, the idea of a political science given to men by god to save them from chaos has already been encountered in Julian's autobiographical myth; it derives ultimately from Plato's *Protagoras* (322b–23a). Finally, the notion of a heavenly city is implicit in Plato's call for philosopher-kings to order the city in imitation of a divine pattern, and is made explicit by Neoplatonist interpreters of the *Republic*, in particular by Proclus.[39]

These intellectual filiations argue, in my view, that the ideal of the philosopher-king put forward in the anonymous dialogue derives from a

35. Ibid., pp. 36, 21–37, 16; see p. 53, 1–4.

36. See in particular P. Hadot's "Fürstenspiegel," cited in note 26 above.

37. Ibid., p. 49, 15–22.

38. Julian, *Discours III [II] De la Royauté*, in *Oeuvres complètes*, vol. 1, part 1, ed. and trans. J. Bidez (Paris, 1932), 90b, p. 166; *Discours VIII [V] Sur la mère des dieux*, ed. and trans. G. Rochefort, in *Oeuvres complètes*, vol. 2, part 1 (Paris, 1963), 169bc, pp. 116–17.

39. Proclus, *Comm. in Tim.*, ed. E. Diehl (Leipzig, 1903), vol. 1, p. 32, 1 ff.; trans. A. Festugière (Paris, 1966), vol. 1, p. 64. See also Plato, *Rep.* 592b2–3 where the heavenly city as paradigm is connected with the idea of a moral "colonization" of the soul.

Neoplatonic understanding of Plato's *Republic.* The philosopher-king strives to govern in the light of knowledge of transcendent principles. He does this inspired by the vision of the first cause, described as the Form of the Good, and, in imitating this first cause and in making the state divinelike, he acts as part of a universal metaphysical pattern in which the inferior is ordered and improved by the beneficence of the superior, the Good. The absolute Good takes on, as in Julian, a more personalized aspect, intended this time no doubt to evoke the Christian god.

In conclusion, I believe I have brought together enough evidence to argue that Boethius's ambition to live Plato's ideal of the philosopher-king was no mere literary conceit, but rather an integral part of his general philosophical stance. Nor was the proximity of Neoplatonists to political power at odds with their otherworldly aspirations. The theoretical fit between political action and otherworldliness in Neoplatonism is revealed, I think, by the way in which the Neoplatonists and their pupils interpreted Plato's notion of the philosopher-king. Of course, there are variations, differences of emphasis, diverging elements that indicate that we should speak of a variety of Neoplatonic interpretations of the philosopher-king. However, there are also, I think, some fundamental ideas common to these interpretations which I would now like to recall very briefly. The otherworldly tendencies of Neoplatonism have to do with the need for the intellectual soul to disengage itself, or purify itself, from material preoccupations so as to be able to reach a contemplative union with the transcendent first cause of all things, the One or the Good. This is, we might say, the Neoplatonic version of the escape from the cave in Plato's *Republic.* However, sharing in this union means sharing in the absolute Good whose perfection is such that it is self-diffusive, giving of itself to lower realities. Hence the soul can also desire to communicate the good it possesses, and can do this in the form of a political action that seeks to order human society after the pattern of the transcendent Good. This is, we might say, the Neoplatonic version of the return to the cave in Plato's *Republic.* The philosopher-king's motivation, what inspires the philosopher to become king, and his political action, become a limited and subordinate expression of universal metaphysical principles of the production, ordering, and amelioration of all things. Philosophers become kings not because they are parts of the state or have some obligation to their fellow citizens. They become kings in the way the divine creates the world: as benefactors, as patrons of mankind.[40]

40. A French version of this article has been published in *Images de Platon et lectures de ses oeuvres,* ed. A. Neschke (Louvain, 1997), pp. 35–50. I am much indebted to my colleagues for many helpful questions and suggestions.

14 The Continuity of Plato's Dialectic: An Afterword

JOHANNES M. VAN OPHUIJSEN

for L. M. de Rijk

I. DIALECTIC: PUTTING PLATO IN CONTEXT. *i.* A test case for an evolutionary view of Plato's thought: dialectic, considered as to (1) form, and to (2) ultimate object. The ancient tradition: Monolithic. *ii.* Plato's dialectic as distinct from those of Aristotle and of the Stoa. Danger of adopting Aristotle's perspective. *iii.* A "formal" discipline? Taken to be so in strongly developmental accounts. Wrong question? II. ITS FORMAL ASPECT. *iv.* Later dialectic (division) repudiated by all parties. One defense unconvincing. *v.* Division in its context: Testing (elenchus) of definitions. Value of elenchus. *vi.* Relation of division to hypothesis: Complementary. New method called for by conception of forms as intertwined. III. ITS OBJECT: VALUES, THE GOOD? *vii.* One statement on object-neutrality to be read as bearing on form rather than object. *viii.* The argument from silence. (Form of) the Good vanishes from sight, but is still implied: in larger plan of "trilogy" (*Tht.*, *Soph.*, *Pol.*), in fundamental commitment to rational ordering of world and soul; *ix.* Is confirmed by allegiance to teleology: Good still basic to understanding because basic to being. *x.* Centrality of notion of One does not detract from importance of Good. Revised account bound up with refined formal apparatus: forms intertwining, logos analysed. *xi.* Reference to other "transcendentals" or "forms of perfection" compatible with this interpretation. IV. DISENGAGING PLATO FROM HIS CONTEXT. *xii.* One attempt to counterbalance Aristotelian bias. *xiii.* Exploiting the linguistic resources: Application to one relation between highest forms. *xiv.* Conclusion.[1]

I

i. The term "dialectic" and its cognates occur frequently and conspicuously in Plato's writings and they are ubiquitous in modern discussions

1. It is my pleasure to thank Thérèse-Anne Druart and Daryl Tress for critical comments on a prototype of this essay, and Saleh Agha and Peter Bornedal for going over a more recent version. Its dedication is an acknowledgment of my debt to De Rijk both as the author of the insufficiently publicized book quoted in note 102 below, and as my teacher, together with the late G. Nuchelmans, in philosophy and its history.

of his thought; next to that of a Form or Idea, dialectic is probably the concept that is taken to be the most distinctive of Plato's approach to philosophy. Yet it is far from clear to what extent either his explicit statements, through the speakers of his dialogues, on dialectic and its ultimate object, or his actual practice of dialectic in these dialogues add up to a consistent and constant conception. On this subject various discontinuities have been either explicitly asserted or tacitly assumed. The *form* that dialectic takes in the later dialogues, that is, the method of division and collection, has been described as one radically independent from the form it took in earlier ones, which has opened the way for widely different valuations of this species of dialectic and of what Ryle called Plato's "progress." As to its *object*, it is often assumed that, whereas in the *Republic* dialectic was directed to the Good, in its later form it was no longer so:[2] diaeresis, it is said, as a "neutral" method "must disregard questions of better and worse" or "relations of better and worse";[3] it abstracts from questions of value and denies that it is possible to derive values from facts.[4] So it seems that Plato's expressed view of dialectic could be a testing ground for an approach to Plato in terms of organic growth, of his gradually unfolding and articulating what remains basically one program.

Here as with other features of Plato's philosophical activity the ancient tradition was not aware of any such major changes. Thus in *Republic* 7 we read

> Then don't you think that we have dialectic placed on top of the subjects of learning [μαθήματα] just like a coping-stone [θριγκός], and that it would no longer be possible correctly to put yet another subject above this, but that learning is now complete [ἔχειν τέλος]?[5]

Here *mathêmata* (μαθήματα, the source of our word 'mathematics'), bears a wider sense than its modern English descendent. The Greek word covers all the objects and branches of intellectual instruction and of exact, quantifiable knowledge, including arithmetic, plain and solid geometry, astronomy as a species of geometry written on the face of nature, and harmony as its pendant underlying and manifested in the acoustic realm; in general, the disciplines describing an order that is partly revealed or at least suggested to or through the senses, as distinct from the purely notional order traced in dialectic.[6] In the context, the expression makes dialectic the culmination of the training of the philosopher-king, but still only preparatory to that vision of the Good that is "on the far side even of Being in dignity and power,"[7] which constitutes the

2. Allan xliii.
3. Rosen (1983) 119–20; cf. n. 64 below.
4. Dorter, p. 200 above.
5. *Rep.* 7.534E2–35A1. Translations mine.
6. See *vi*, note 62 below.
7. *Rep.* 6 509 B 9.

summit of intellectual, and generally of human, attainment. This ultimate object of philosophy, the Form of the Good, was earlier in the *Republic* (at 505a) called the *megiston mathêma* (μέγιστον μάθημα), the "greatest object of intellectual instruction," which links this "coping-stone" to philosophy.

Alexander of Aphrodisias actually uses the phrase "coping-stone *of philosophy*," in the context[8] of distinguishing between conceptions of dialectic in the Academy, the Peripatos, and the Stoa:

> Plato, who extols the method of division and declares it the coping-stone of philosophy, also calls it by the name of dialectic. He posits as its function the ability to make one thing into many and reduce the many to one, which seems equivalent to being able to divide genera into their species and what comes under these, and conversely to collect the individual things, reduce them to one genus and bring them under one heading.

Alexander is here freely mixing ingredients from the description of dialectic in earlier and later Platonic dialogues. This is not because, not being a Platonist, he is less scrupulous in reporting on Plato. The same amalgam of the doctrine of Forms from the *Republic* with the method of division from later dialogues is found in Plotinus' treatise on dialectic: in *Ennead* 1.3, he too calls dialectic the most valuable part of philosophy, associates it with the Good[9] and with what is beyond Being,[10] mentions the preparatory role of mathematics,[11] and describes this dialectic as applying division throughout the intelligible.[12]

It may be worth questioning the alleged discontinuities. When dialectic has become, or has come to include, division and collection, is the ultimate object of philosophy still the same? Is its relation to this object still the same? Can we say that the development of dialectic affects the conception of its object, or vice versa? This complex question is bound up with a question of method. Are the views on Plato of such authors as

8. *In Top.* 1.14–19.

9. 1.1–4 (Henry–Schwyzer, general ed.): "What is the art or method or practice which takes us up there where we must go? Where that is, that it is to the Good, the First Principle, we can take as agreed and established by many demonstrations"; 4.6–7: "It discusses [διαλέγεται περὶ + gen.] good and not good, and the things that are classed under good and its opposite." (Translations here and in the next three notes are by A. H. Armstrong, modified.)

10. 5.4–8: "For, Plato says, dialectic is 'the pure part of intelligence and wisdom' [τὸ καθαρὸν νοῦ τε καὶ φρονήσεως; *Philebus* 58 D 6–7]. As the most valuable of our mental abilities, then, it must be concerned with real being and what is most valuable: as wisdom it is concerned with real being, as intelligence with what is on the far side of being." Cf. *Soph.* 248 E 6–49 A 9, cited note 74 below.

11. 3.5–10: "He must be given mathematical studies to train him in philosophical thought (. . . ;) he (. . .) must be (. . .) after his mathematical studies instructed in dialectic [λόγους διαλεκτικῆς δοτέον; 11], and made a complete dialectician."

12. 4.12–15: "using Plato's Division (. . .) till it has traversed the whole intelligible world."

Alexander and Plotinus from their telescopic, conflating perspective admissible as evidence, or simply superseded from what has too easily been taken to be our stylometrically enlightened vantage point?[13] Any answer to this question of method, except a wholesale rejection of such testimony from later antiquity, needs to be supplemented by an answer to the question of substance that recognizes significant continuities.

ii. To recognize Platonic dialectic as "one in species," it may help to contrast it with two forms of dialectic that are different in relevant ways, and liable to being confused with it for historical reasons.

Dialectic as a subject of teaching distinct from formal logic has long disappeared from the curriculum. Before the adoption of the term by Kant, Hegel, Marx, and their various followers, its meaning was defined by a medieval tradition drawing in the main on three conceptions of dialectic descended from competing ancient schools. (1) Socrates' refutations of his partners in Plato's earlier dialogues, deriving from the reduction to impossibility invented by Zeno the Eleatic and adopted by Gorgias and other Sophists, gradually widened and dissolved into the mature Plato's vision of a constructive discipline with positive results. (2) The rules for debate that Aristotle prescribes in his *Topics* have been supposed to reflect the practice of Plato's Academy more directly than do Plato's own dialogues. At the same time, they are often condemned as a debased travesty of Plato's ideal.[14] That they can appear so tallies with Aristotle's explicit degradation of dialectic to a rank below demonstration, as just one preliminary method of inquiry rather than the royal road of science and philosophy. (3) The Stoic conception continues the Aristotelian tendency to conceive of dialectic as a formal discipline without a specified object. To this extent Stoic dialectic competes not with Aristotle's dialectic but with his syllogistic, and Stoic criticism of that, as well as the Stoics' cultivation of propositional rather than predicate logic, carry the tendency toward abstraction and formalization beyond Aristotle. Still, their conception of dialectic is nearer to Plato's in that it restores to it its Platonic title to establishing truth, not mere plausibility.

Alexander mentions all three varieties of dialectic, and Plotinus too was familiar with elements of Stoic as well as of Platonic and Aristotelian dialectic. When we nowadays try to reconstruct Plato's conception of dialectic, we are less likely to be confused by the Stoics, or what little we have of them, than by Aristotle: our view of Plato's dialectic is defined not only by his own enigmatic statements and by the explicit statements

13. For a radical challenge, closely and eloquently argued, to mainstream assumptions about the chronology of Plato's writings, see Howland (1991).

14. E.g., by Guthrie (1981, vol. 6, p. 151).

of Aristotle, more precise[15] but not therefore to be accepted without question, but more fatally by the fact that the valuation of dialectic within Aristotle's division of the sciences and arts is nearer to the one that has since gained currency. It is hard to decide to what extent he detected defects in Plato's dialectic as measured against its Platonic aims, and to what extent he merely projected onto it his own view of dialectic. This is not because Aristotle was either uncharitable or obtuse, but because he too had to draw out what was at most implied in Plato's statements before he could come to terms with them—to terms rooted in his own epistemology.[16]

iii. The juxtaposition with Aristotelian and with Stoic dialectic suggests a question that is crucial to the continuity or discontinuity of Plato's dialectic: To what extent can this dialectic be considered a formal discipline, and does it show any development in this respect? One extreme position is implicit in the nineteenth-century use of the term "Platonic dialectic" as equivalent to the theory of *Republic*-style Forms.[17] The opposite extreme may be exemplified by the deliberately provocative position of Ryle,[18] who extolled dialectic as a method (loosely assimilated to Aristotle's) applied, in "what we now call 'logical' enquiries,"[19] to, for example, "trans-departmental propositional connections"[20]—at the expense of the theory of Forms, played down as a regrettable temporary aberration from the path of *genuine* philosophy. However, these extremes are at one in dismissing or disregarding the possibility of a rectilinear development toward a progressively more formal conception of the discipline.

Landmark efforts to disengage the method of dialectic from its subject matter were made by Julius Stenzel (^{2}1931) and Richard Robinson (^{2}1953).[21] Both of them, like Ryle, proclaim a developmental perspective in their very title.[22] Robinson limited himself to dialogues usually

15. See esp. his statement in *Prior Analytics* 1.31 46 a 32–33 that division is a "syllogism without force" (ἀσθενής) and in *Posterior Analytics* 2.5 91 b 12–13 that "the way through the divisions does not syllogize" (οὐ συλλογίζεται).

16. See IV below.

17. E.g., Zeller or Ritter-Preller.

18. Ryle (1966). Though *Plato's Progress* is not the book on which Ryle's fame will rest, its influence lingers on. The adjective and adverb 'dialectical(ly)' are used lightly and in senses rarely defined but clearly owing less to Plato than to Aristotle. See note 22 below.

19. Ryle (1965, p. 65; or 1966, p. 143). It is worth comparing the two versions of this chapter: in some places the changes seriously affect the argument, as at (1966, p. 144) where 'endoxon' has become 'truism.'

20. Ryle (1965, p. 65, or 1966, p. 142). Cf. "concerned with those 'common' concepts which are . . . trans-departmental" (1965, p. 59; or 1966, p. 132); "topic-neutral premisses," "trans-departmental truths," and "axioms" (1965, p. 59; or 1966, p. 133); "trans-departmental Formal or Logical principles" (1965, p. 60 or 1966, p. 134); "formal or 'common' concepts" (1965, p. 65; or 1966, p. 143).

21. Both books had first been published in wartime, in 1917 and 1941, respectively.

22. *Studien zur Entwicklung der platonischen Dialektik von Sokrates zu Aristoteles* and *Plato's*

regarded as not later than the *Parmenides*, but Stenzel considers the supposedly later dialectic. As to its relation to the ultimate object of philosophy, he assumed a fundamental change of direction. In the words of his translator, Stenzel tries to show "above all, that [dialectic in the *Republic*] differs from the later method in being directed to the Good."[23] Stenzel's own text contains arguments that are indirect and circumstantial, but the claim seems largely to rest on an argument from silence:[24] the observation that the Form of the Good is not singled out from others in later dialogues as it is in the *Republic.*

An evolutionary approach in terms of progressive articulation might argue that a question as to the more or less "formal" nature of Plato's dialectic is anachronistically expressed in terms of a non-Platonic distinction: that both the postulate of "separate" Forms and the analysis of Forms and proposition in the *Sophist* are instruments having what we would now characterize as both logical and ontological functions, whereas Plato did not envisage the possibility of separating these functions.[25]

The following sections (*iv–xi*) do not pretend to offer more than hints toward implementing such an approach in relation to both the internal constitution of dialectic and its orientation toward an object.[26]

II

iv. Plato's method of division[27] has been disparaged both by Aristotle, who objected that it has no demonstrative force, and by moderns; by tra-

Earlier Dialectic, respectively. Dialectic as such has not often been discussed in recent years. There is no Stenzel or Robinson for our time, and there never was a *Plato's Later Dialectic* to supplement Robinson's *Plato's Earlier Dialectic*, even though we had monographs on *Plato's Later Epistemology* from S. Runciman and on *Plato's Later Ontology* from K. Sayre. Philosopher-scholars have apparently expected more illumination from applying the traditional categories of modern philosophy to Plato than from defining a notion central to Plato's explicit program. See note 18 above.

23. The conclusion of D. J. Allan's extensive introduction to his translation of Stenzel (1931), *Plato's Method of Dialectic* (1940, at p. xliii). It is preceded by the disclaimer that Stenzel "of course, makes no special claim for his division of Plato's thought into two phases" and "realizes that all such divisions are artificial." Allan's summary has hardly prepared the reader for the strong claim he ends with.

24. See below, *x.*

25. Plato was not pursuing logical inquiries as distinct from ontological ones. See Hare (1982, p. 34): "[I]t it is simply not profitable to ask Plato the question 'Are you defining words or things?,' because he would not understand what we were asking." Also see notes 47 and 107 below.

26. I hazard committing the fallacies of what Robinson (1953, pp. 1–2) called "mosaic interpretation." The questions at issue require a fuller discussion; still it is in my view essential that they should be treated in one connection.

27. I will use 'division' as shorthand for '[the (theory of the) method of] division and collection'.

ditional friends of the Forms as well as by analytic philosophers. One surprising feature of Ryle's eulogy of dialectic was that division got even lower marks from him[28] than from more traditional Platonists such as Paul Shorey, who from his diametrically opposed valuation of Plato as a logician would "acquit [Plato] of any serious interest in it."[29] Ryle forced himself into such ingenious constructions as these:

> [T]he inferred propaedeutic place of division and definition in the curriculum of Plato's own Academy, together with Plato's own non-production of kind-ladders in his *Parmenides, Part II*, and in the philosophical core of his *Sophist* itself, . . . require us to suppose that in the *Phaedrus* he means but omits to say explicitly that division is only a preparation for dialectic.[30]

In a collection of responses to Ryle, Ackrill came to the defense of division. He explained Plato's use of dichotomous division in the *Sophist* and the *Statesman* by claiming that Plato

> is not here seeking to bring to light the structure of a whole genus, but to achieve a definition of a particular species. For this purpose the important thing is at each stage to hit on the relevant sub-genus of the superior genus; the irrelevant sub-genus can be thrown away—and it doesn't matter if here are some other (irrelevant) sub-genera we have not mentioned.[31]

However, the primary demand on a division, as Ackrill himself acknowledged,[32] is that reality be cut at the joints. This would seem to mean that for any instance of division the limbs cut apart should be all of them, and equally, real. If so, it would seem that Platonic division can be defended only at the price of granting that dichotomous division will not always do, and that it cannot be known a priori when it will do. It is, of course, always possible[33] to reduce divisions to dichotomous form simply by using a pair of contradictories to characterize the parts into which a division is made: for example, by first dividing the genus "primary color" into red and non-red, and by then dividing the non-red into blue and non-blue, thereby yielding a species of "non-blue non-red" coinciding with yellow. The Platonic objection to this method would presumably be that non-red as distinct from blue and yellow is not equally real with red, and that for its non-blue species, though this is equally real with the blue, "non-blue" is a name that reveals less of reality and truth than "yellow" does. To the

28. Ryle (1965, pp. 60–64; or 1966, pp. 135–41).
29. In the words of Allan (1940, p. xliii).
30. Ryle (1966, p. 141); Ryle (1965, p. 64) less cautiously refers to "the actual propaedeutic place of division and definition in the curriculum," and instead of "require us to suppose" has "satisfies me."
31. Ackrill (1970, p. 384).
32. Ackrill (1970, p. 384); similarly Dorter, 207 above.
33. See Dorter, 207 above.

synoptic view that Plato encouraged us to strive for, there is no "irrelevant" subgenus that can be trashed: if we have not correctly marked off the cospecies of the species we are trying to define, we cannot be sure that we have correctly marked off that species itself, so we fall short of knowledge. The precept in the *Statesman* that

> one should cut into the nearest possible number in any instance[34]

is better understood in connection with the complaint in the *Philebus* against those clever people (σοφοί) who

> make one and many, as the case may be, faster and slower than they should: after the one immediately the unlimited number, whereas the things in the middle escape them.[35]

It is meant to prevent our skipping intermediate levels of species, not to encourage us to disregard cospecies at the same level.[36]

v. In an attempt to understand and appreciate division as a stage in the organic development of dialectic, it is not enough to bring together remarks from the later dialogues in which it is explicitly discussed. The traditional disparagement of division seems to rest on the assumption[37] that division is the whole of later dialectic, and that it comes to replace rather than to supplement elenchus and hypothesis. In fact, it is, like elenchus, an instrument for definition;[38] more precisely, it is an instrument in the elenchus or testing of definitions. In the *Sophist*, in a context devoted to division, elenchus is assessed as "greatest and most decisive of purgations."[39] Its practitioners, it is said,[40]

> question what a person thinks he is talking sense[41] about when in fact he is talk-

34. Sc. to two ('seeing we cannot <divide> in two'): *Statesman* 287 C 4–5.

35. *Phil.* 16 E 4–17 A 3.

36. Some more papers have since been devoted to division, none of which seem to settle the question of the "philosophical significance of this method, for Plato and for philosophy in general," as Moravcsik puts it in one of the most helpful ones (1973b, p. 345; cf. his 1973a, p. 177). An older, most perceptive but lapidary discussion is Lloyd (1954; reprint, 1965), where it is pointed out that "[d]ialectic meant always the discovery of the One in the Many, and in the later Dialogues this consisted of Collection and Division" (1965, p. 220).

37. Explicit in Alexander and in Kneale (1962, p. 9). Robinson (1953, p. v) is admirably cautious.

38. See Hare (1965, p. 22) on λόγον τῆς οὐσίας and λόγον διδόναι.

39. *Soph.* 230 D 7–8; cf. 226 D 9–227 C 9, quoted in *vii* below at notes 64–68. The statement, in the context of the dialogue as a whole and of the series of conversations beginning with the *Theaetetus*, seems to seriously qualify Robinson's assumption, however carefully expressed, that "elenchus is prominent in the early and not in the middle or late dialogues" (1953, p. v).

40. *Soph.* 230 B 4–8.

41. τι λέγειν (230 B 5).

ing nonsense, and then easily examine[42] their rambling opinions,[43] collecting[44] and juxtaposing them in their arguments and demonstrating them to be, about and in view of and in relation to the same things, opposed to themselves.

An assessment of division should therefore address the two related questions What does division contribute to elenchus? and What is the point of elenchus itself.[45] To the latter question one answer is that

it is an assumption in dialectical debate that [. . .] we all naturally have the right answers, but are just very confused because of all the false [. . .] beliefs, incompatible with the truth, which we have also acquired. [. . .] On such an assumption it is easy to see how the Socratic elenchus cannot fail to succeed in defeating the respondent as long as we are confused and have false beliefs, but also how it is to lead to knowledge in the long run, if ultimately the only way to be consistent is to retain the true beliefs one has and to jettison the false beliefs one has acquired.[46]

The assumption that "we all naturally have the right answers" was at some stage justified by the doctrine of recollection. This fits in with the devaluation of dialectic in Aristotle's *Topics*: once recollection is abandoned, the natural aptitude that Aristotle grants humans is not enough to guarantee that we arrive at the right answers. Now all that dialectic can achieve is consistency among our beliefs; it cannot decide whether our final set of consistent beliefs corresponds to the true state of things. But—leaving aside the question of whether Plato himself continued to hold a doctrine of recollection—even on the supposition of recollection, isn't the dialectician in danger of actually obscuring his innate true beliefs by hammering out a harness of consistent but false ones?[47] We

42. ἐξετάζειν (B 5): Socrates' usual role.

43. Literally 'the opinions of these as of men rambling' (B 5).

44. A nontechnical but possibly deliberate use of the term (συνάγοντες; B 6).

45. One might object that it cannot be taken for granted that the role of elenchus in the later dialectic is the same as before, and ask what is the use of elenchus—the natural instrument of a Socrates who disclaims any knowledge of his own and plays the midwife to the latent knowledge of others—to a Visitor from Elea who comes on stage in full possession of positive doctrine. I here assume that elenchus continues at least to serve the same *didactic* function, so that it makes no difference at least from Theaetetus's point of view whether he is talking to the Visitor or to Socrates.

46. The "suspicion" of Michael Frede (1992a, 218). It recalls the view of Socrates developed by Vlastos.

47. An attempt to counter this objection is found in Hare (1965, p. 34): "It has often been objected to such a method (substantially similar to the Socratic elenchus) that, relying as it does on the mere failure to refute a proposed view, it does nothing to establish its truth. . . . When what we are trying to establish are definitions, however, it is not clear that this objection is well taken . . . are we not, in practising [the elenchus], looking for possible falsifications of the empirical hypothesis that, in their ordinary discourse, people use a word in a certain way?" Hare himself conceded that this interpretation of the definition-hypothesis as an empirical one, about usage, would not have recommended itself to Plato, since "definitions had in Plato's thought an ontological as well as a logical rôle to play" (1965, p. 29; cf.

should remember that elenchus by reduction has the power to achieve more than mere consistency. To derive a logical impossibility from any proposition can be a purely negative exercise, but within binary oppositions such as motion/rest, limited/unlimited, and mortal/immortal disproving one alternative converts into a positive result. In this way elenchus can lead to the formation of conglomerates of consistent beliefs, the truth of some of which has been established by showing that their contradictory leads to absurdity. By continuing the elenchus, that is, by confronting propositions with each other in various permutations and working out their logical relations, it should be possible to eliminate remaining vices or viruses in the form of false assumptions and fallacies, to find additional and cumulative confirmation of the surviving assumptions, and to incorporate several of these conglomerates into fewer of wider comprehension. Though this would not amount to demonstration in an Aristotelian sense, the ongoing elenchus would in Platonic terms prepare the intellect (νοῦς) for the decisive act that transforms these many partial accounts (λόγοι) into the desired synoptic view of reality, when the intellect has traced their necessary connection to a common foundation in the ultimate source of reality and truth—in the language of the *Republic*, the Form of the Good. Compare the *Seventh Letter*:[48]

> The truth about virtue and vices must necessarily be learnt at the same time as what is true and false in Being [οὐσία] as a whole. This, as I began by saying, requires intensive practice over a long period. As they are laboriously practised each in relation to the other, all these items—names,[49] accounts,[50] visual and other perceptions [ὄψεις τε καὶ αἰσθήσεις][51]—being tested in good-willing, uninvidious tests [ἐλέγχοις][52] by persons engaging in question and answer, all at once there blazes up insight and understanding [φρόνησις . . . καὶ νοῦς] with respect to each of them exerting itself to the utmost of human capability.[53]

vi. The contribution of the method of division to this preparation could perhaps be described as *complementary* to that of the method of hypothesis. Many of the propositions subjected to elenchus were defini-

---

1982, p. 34, quoted above at note 25). Plato, like Aristotle, was after "essential or real definitions," what Hare calls "the archetype of all synthetic a priori propositions." The attribution to Plato of ordinary language philosophy is not entailed by the understanding of elenchus as falsification; but this by itself falls short of what Socrates, Plato, or Aristotle required of an account (λόγος) anyway.

48. Now fairly generally admitted as evidence for Plato's (mature) thought.

49. And nouns: ὀνόματα.

50. And definitions and propositions and arguments: *logoi* (λόγοι).

51. These perceptions correspond to the images (εἴδωλα) of 343 C 7; also see *Symp.* 212 A 4, quoted in note 77 below.

52. Cf. 343 C3: εὐέλεγκτον and D 2: ἐλέγχειν.

53. *Epist.* 7 344 B 1–C 1. See Gadamer (1980, pp. 112, 117, 122).

tions. Hypothesis[54] had considered what one tends to represent as vertical relations:[55] those that Aristotle will represent as the relation between one species and its genus. What distinguishes division is that it takes into account more than one item at each "lower" level. This makes it possible to trace collateral relations between definienda.

Hypothesis is not mentioned in the same contexts as that of division, but this need not imply that it had been superseded.[56] Like division, it has its place *within* an elenchus as delineated in the *Seventh Letter*. We must clear our minds from modern connotations of the term "hypothesis," in particular of the notion that hypotheses are propositions. Whether, or where, or to what extent a Platonic hypothesis is[57] a proposition[58] or a nonpropositional entity, some sort of simple nameable, has often been disputed.[59] The fact that neither interpretation is adequate for all contexts may suggest that we have another anachronistic distinction, one that takes analysis further than Plato allows. Plato does not seem to have elaborated a formal distinction between "virtue as being knowledge" and "that virtue is knowledge": certain hypotheses, while not themselves propositions, "bring certain propositional assumptions with them."[60] Hypothesis is operative in the context of real definition,[61] and Plato seems to envisage a hierarchy of definitions so that we may deduce one from the other with logical necessity.[62] Settling the question "Can virtue be taught?" to Plato's satisfaction requires a definition of virtue that reveals its essential nature as knowledge, and one of knowledge that reveals, by entailing, its essential characteristic of being teachable. The higher, more abstract definition in turn has to be derived, by means of any number of intervening definitions, from an understanding of the first principle or principles: the Good, or whatever Plato came to accept as a more adequate and accurate designation of the principle. Within such a scheme that which in one description is the "foundation" and "presupposition" (ὑπόθεσις) of an object of inquiry might in another one figure as the "higher" Form (εἶδος) or Kind (γένος) to which it bears the relation, revealed by division, of part to whole—not of course

54. Used as shorthand for "[the (theory of the) method of] hypothesis."
55. For strictures on this tendency, see Rosenmeyer (1960).
56. 'replaced' Kahn (1995) 55.
57. More strictly, the act of laying down a proposition.
58. Thus Ryle (1965, p. 59/1966, p. 133).
59. Significantly, a similar question applies to Aristotle's first principles (ἀρχαί).
60. In the phrase of Hare (1965, p. 23), applying to the hypotheses of *Rep.* 510 C 2–D 3.
61. Cf. Hare (1965, pp. 22–23).
62. More precisely with mathematical necessity: it was arithmetic and geometry and mathematical astronomy that suggested to him an ideal of rigorous deductive proof, and from which he derived by extrapolation the formal requirements of his highest branch of intellectual instruction, the study of ideas. See *i* above at note 6.

in terms of material extension. The new method thus would not mark a radical change of purpose; it would serve as a new device to fill in and detail the map of the world of Forms, conceived as a structure of relations defining these Forms, along what might be called the horizontal dimension of collateral relations. The need for this extension of the method is brought into relief by the new conception of a "plaiting together" or "twining together" of forms (συμπλοκὴ εἰδῶν).[63] But the extension would nonetheless function within the ongoing project of building a conglomerate of beliefs of tested consistency: heuristically, by generating a supply of propositions that share terms, invite confrontation, and suggest possible refutations, but ultimately in a more positive way by strengthening the coherence of this conglomerate.

III

vii. If dialectic remains essentially the enterprise both of expressing and of stimulating by verbal means insights into articulations of a structured realm of Forms, then to what extent does the later Plato's conception of dialectic modify its orientation toward the Form of the Good as its ultimate object as indicated in the *Republic*, or more generally its relation to issues of value? Allegedly negative evidence is supplied in the *Sophist* where the visitor from Elea tells Theaetetus that

> it so happens that the method of arguments doesn't care any less, nor any more for the art of making sponges or that of making potions even if the one benefits us by purging lesser, the other by purging greater things.[64]

This statement should be read in its context. The visitor had previously noted that the class of bodily purgations comprises a number having names that "are *thought* [δοκοῦντα] ridiculous,"[65] and Theaetetus had agreed with this qualification. Just after the sentence quoted, the visitor explains that this method

> when for the sake of acquiring understanding [νοῦς] it tries to discern [κατανοεῖν] what, in all the disciplines, is akin and what is not, esteems them all

63. For Plato's dialectic as "opposing the *logos*, as the *koinônia* of the ideas, to the fruitless undertaking of defining things atomistically," see Gadamer (1980, p. 109). Cf. (1980, p. 152): "the logos always requires that one idea be 'there' together with another. Insight into one idea per se does not yet constitute knowledge"—perhaps "insight into one idea" almost amounts to a contradiction in terms?

64. *Soph.* 227 A 7–10, the prime witness adduced by Rosen and Dorter, see notes 3–4 above; cf. *Soph.* 230 D 7–8, quoted in *v* above at note 39. I could not here do justice to the complications addressed by Rosen in this context; see, e.g., p. 121: "the 'neutral' discrimination of like from like . . . is in fact 'better than' the distinction between better and worse."

65. *Soph.* 227 A 5.

equal with reference to this purpose, and does not think one part more ridiculous than the other as far as their similarity is concerned.[66]

Plato thus makes it clear that he is considering the *formal* requirements of a satisfactory division, that is, the rules that the dialectician has to observe in applying the method. He ends by stating that what the method is looking for at this moment is one single name, elegant or not, binding together all bodily purgations in separation from those of the soul,[67] since its present undertaking is separating off the purgation of thought (διάνοια) from all these others. All that Plato has written at any stage of his putative career should dispose us to understand a mention of these objects as implying a ranking in value. The warning to the aspiring dialectician to think no object beneath his attention does not detract from this: it is a warning against intellectual primness and preciosity, against *Schöngeisterei.* One may compare Socrates' reluctance in the *Parmenides* to admit Forms of hair, mud, and dirt, and Parmenides' reply:

Yes, Socrates, you are still young, and philosophy has not taken hold of you as I think it will some day, and then you will not depreciate any of these things; but now, owing to your age, you still care about what people think.[68]

The insistence on an "equal esteem" for more unassuming and more imposing objects of the same discipline (τέχνη) is the same as that found in the presumably earlier *Republic,* in a context explicitly concerned with the realm of what we now call values. Here Socrates submits that we, and our guardians, shall only be what he calls "musical" when we come to recognize the Forms of self-control, of courage, and of several other virtues, and what is "sibling" to them,[69] and also what is opposed to them: when we perceive their presence and that of their images in what they are present in, and when we

do not depreciate them whether they are in little things or in great, but take them to belong to the same discipline and pursuit.[70]

viii. The most operative argument against an orientation of later dialectic toward values may be the argument from silence: dialogues later than the *Republic* do not refer to the Form of the Good, and in general less often refer to value concepts as a prominent or somehow privileged

66. 227 A 10–B 4.

67. χωρὶς τῶν τῆς ψυχῆς καθάρσεων; 227 C 2–3.

68. δόξας; cf. the δοκοῦντα 'judged ridiculous' of *Soph.* 227 A 5.

69. ἀδελφά, from the same parent (*Rep.* 3 402 C 4; cf. 401 A 7–8). See *xiii* at note 103 below.

70. τέχνη and μελετή, respectively—a standard juxtaposition in Greek educational thought, but entirely compatible with a characteristically Platonic stress on the close connection between theory and practice.

subset of Forms. Within the discussion of Being and Not-Being in the *Sophist*, we could account for Plato's silence about the Good precisely on the assumption that the qualification of this as "not being but on the far side even of being in dignity and power"[71] still holds. But the cross-references between the *Theaetetus*, the *Sophist* and the *Statesman* warn against isolating any of these dialogues from the other parts of what has been called a "trilogy."[72] At *Theaetetus* 185a–86a Socrates mentions, and so announces, the great kinds of the *Sophist* and some others: Being, Other and Same, One and Number, Similar and Dissimilar. When Theaetetus gives proof of his understanding by mentioning Even and Odd, Socrates adds to all these the Good, the "Fine" (καλόν), and their contraries. The reader of the *Sophist* has thus been warned that these have yet to receive an adequate discussion.[73]

Moreover, some of the Visitor from Elea's propositions about Being presuppose the recognition of a realm of value. Thus his rejection of the notion that true being could be devoid of life, soul, and understanding[74] is seen in the end to rest not on an argument in any strict sense but on the rejection of any claim that is not grounded in knowledge, understanding, and insight, and so upon a commitment, shared by Theaetetus, to the assumption of a rational and intelligible world order. It is natural to connect this paradoxically unargued commitment to rationality with Plato's utterances about the formative value of understanding for the soul: in the words of the *Timaeus*, about

> making that which discerns similar to that which is discerned, in accordance with its original nature[75]

and about the person who

> having devoted his efforts to the love of learning and to true thoughts [φρονήσεις], and having trained himself in these above all other things that belong to him, now thinks divine and immortal thoughts,[76]

and so with those contexts that associate insight with virtue and extol the

71. *Rep.* 6 509 B 9; cf. *x* below at note 91.

72. For the suspicion that Plato never intended to give us a dialogue entitled *The Philosopher*, see Wiles, above, 196; contra Griswold, above, 118. For the philosopher, see *Soph.* 249 C 10–D 4 and 253 C 8–254 B 2, and cf. the description, recognized at 231 A 1–6 as too generous to suit the Sophist, of the purifier by refutation at *Soph.* 230 B 4–231 B 8 (see *v* above at notes 39–42).

73. See the explicit statement in the *Seventh Letter* that the truth about virtue and vice can only be apprehended together with what is true and false of Being as a whole: 344 A 8–B 2, quoted at the end of *v* above; see Gadamer (1980, pp. 117, 122).

74. 248 E 6–7 (φρόνησιν)–249 A 2, 4, 9 (νοῦν). See note 10 above.

75. *Tim.* 90 D 4–5; cf. 46 C 7–E 4, cited at notes 82–84 below.

76. *Tim.* 90 B 6–C 1.

life devoted to this combination as the closest approach to immortality that humankind is capable of: as that assimilation to God[77] that recommended Plato to Fathers of the Church from Clement of Alexandria to Augustine.

ix. An intimate involvement of dialectic with the category of goodness is also implicit in Plato's continuing commitment to teleological explanation. In the *Phaedo* Socrates required that[78]

> the person who wished to find out about each thing the reason [αἰτίαν] why it comes into being or perishes or is there, has to find out why it is best for this thing to be there or to be subject to or to produce whatever effect.

This requirement seems to be echoed in the *Timaeus*[79] when the cosmos is qualified as "fine" and "finest of things that have come into being," and the Demiurge as "good" and "best of all causes."[80] In the *Phaedo* this true reason, often assimilated to the Aristotelian "final cause," is distinguished from "that without which the cause could never be a cause,"[81] the necessary material conditions. This distinction in turn is reflected in Timaeus's reference to

> the auxiliary causes [συναίτια] that the god uses to serve him in realizing the form of the best to the extent that this is possible.[82]

They are said to be taken by most people to be the actual causes of everything, on account of their physical effects, although they

77. *Tht.* 176 B 1–3: "the escape [from this place of evil] is assimilation [ὁμοίωσις] to God as far as possible, and assimilation is to become just and pious with understanding [φρόνησις]"; *Symp.* 212 A 3–7: "Don't you think that there alone it will befall him, when he sees beauty by that by which it can be seen, to produce not images of virtue—since what he has grasped is not an image—but the genuine thing, and when he has given birth to true virtue and nourished it, it is open to him to become one beloved of the gods, and himself immortal if any human can be so"; *Rep.* 6 500 B 8–D 1: "The person whose thought dwells truly with what Is, (. . .) [will] view and contemplate certain things that are ordered [τεταγμένα] and constant, neither committing injustice nor suffering it from each other but all exhibiting order [κόσμῳ] and proportion [κατὰ λόγον], and [will] imitate and to the utmost possible make himself similar to these (. . .) . Associating with what is divine and orderly, the philosopher becomes divine and orderly as far as possible for a human being"; *Rep.* 10 613 A 8–B 1: "(. . .) the person who is willing to make an effort to become just and, practising virtue, to make himself similar to God as far as possible for a human."

78. *Phaedo* 97 C 6–D 1. The sequel (D 1–3) is "By this account a human ought to consider, both with respect to this and to all other things, nothing but what is best and most preferable."

79. Its date is no longer hotly disputed. For the stylometric probabilities, see Brandwood (1992, esp. pp. 113–14).

80. *Tim.* 29 A 2–3, 5–6. See Wedberg (1971, p. 52).

81. *Phaedo* 99 B 2–4.

82. *Tim.* 46 C 7–D 1.

are incapable of reason [λόγος] and intellect [νοῦς]: for among all things there are, only soul is fit to acquire intellect, and this is invisible, whereas fire, water, earth and air [i.e., these collateral causes] are all visible bodies. The lover of intellect and knowledge [ἐπιστήμη] must necessarily pursue the causes of sentient, intelligent [ἔμφρων] nature first[83] (. . .) those which, accompanied by intellect, produce what is fine and good.[84]

Such a statement is most easily compatible with the assumption that the good still serves or rather rules not only, in the terms of *Republic* 6, as the cause of knowledge and truth, but also as that which provides the objects of knowledge with their very being.

x. The notion that Plato's later dialectic is no longer "directed to the Good" could also come to be accepted as a corollary of the wider claim that, in the formula of Ross, by Plato's latest period

the Idea of One had taken the place formerly occupied by the Idea of Good, as the centre of Plato's system.[85]

To what extent can a basic continuity within Plato's dialectic be maintained in the face of such a claim for change in its original object? The evidence quoted by Ross are Aristotle's two statements in his *Metaphysics*, that Plato had now assigned the cause of good to the One,[86] and that "[o]f those who maintain the existence of the unchangeable substances some" [i.e. the Platonists] "say the One itself is the good itself; but they thought its substance [οὐσίαν . . . αὐτοῦ] lay mainly in its unity." In Ross's paraphrase:

for Plato unity, not goodness, was the fundamental character of the first principle which was in fact both one and good.[87]

In the careful wording of Christopher Stead,

In the *Republic* [Plato] had suggested that [the Forms] all depend (. . .) on a single transcendent Form of the Good; the indirect evidence however suggests that Plato finally came to envisage his ultimate principle under the *aspect* of unity.[88]

It may be attempted to connect this with the discovery[89] in dialectic of the structure of the proposition as it is presented in the *Sophist*, and suppose

83. *Tim.* 46 D 4–E 1.

84. *Tim.* 46 E 4.

85. Ross (1951, p. 243).

86. *Met.* 1.6 988 a 14–15: "he has assigned the cause of good and that of evil [κακῶς] to the elements, one to each of the two," i.e., to the One and to the Dyad of the Great and the Small.

87. Ross (1951, p. 243).

88. Stead (1977, pp. 49–50); italics added.

89. Frede (1992b, p. 423) stresses the "dogmatic and systematic character" of the

that Plato is not satisfied with the name[90] "good" being conferred upon the object at which dialectic is directed as if it could express the correct account of an independent quasi substance. If the Good was "on the far side of Being,"[91] and it was impossible to give an account-in-speech (λόγος) of it within an earlier scheme of dialectic as the road toward Forms, then the new conception of such an account—one on which only a compound of referring expression and predicate can serve as a bearer of truth and falsity, and so as an articulate expression of Being and Not-Being—allows us to see why the old designation by an unanalyzed name (ὄνομα) was inadequate, and at the same time suggests the form that a more adequate account should have. This is compatible with the predicate (ῥῆμα) "good" remaining crucial to Plato's view of reality and criterial for the adequacy of accounts of it, or parts of it: to be good, the most fundamental reality or nature has to be one; if there is to be Good, there has to be Unity.

The later descriptions of ultimate reality could thus be read as attempts to meet increasingly specific demands on the structure of an account of things, incorporating definitions into a system whose internal relations are traced by division and collection. Such an account should from its foundation onward display a map of the world of plurality as transparent as its intelligible aspect could make it to a human intelligence cognate with it. From this point of view, the concept of Unity was recommended by its demonstrated explanatory power as *a*, or indeed *the*, foundation of mathematics, which suggested that it would prove more illuminating to say that prior to everything else there is the One and that the One is Good, than that the Good is One. Part of the gain would be that such complementary principles as the Unlimited or the Great and Small allowed for defectiveness without invoking an actual principle of evil.

In this light Ross's formula[92] that "unity entails goodness" could be said to provide a systematic perspective, roughly corresponding to Aristotelian demonstration, whereas the perspective of heuristics and of Plato's own evolution and enduring motivation is better expressed by saying that "good presupposes unity." Compare Stead's claim that Plato's arithmetical theory, which derived Ideas from the One and the Great and Small

---

Sophist, the attempt made in it "[b]y careful analysis . . . to settle an issue definitively," and Plato's "singular achievement" in bringing this off.

90. Or noun, or referring expression: ὄνομα.

91. *Rep.* 6 509 B 9; see *viii* above at note 71.

92. Ross (1951, p. 244).

did not spring from a mere shift or contraction of Plato's interests to the problem of the origin of number, but from some sort of prophetic glimpse of the possibility that the derivation of the mathematical Ideas from ideal unity might be the formal pattern which would explain the interrelation of all forms of perfection.[93]

xi. The interrelation between a set of such "forms of perfection" including unity and goodness is explored in what seems to be the Platonic Socrates' philosophical swan song, the *Philebus,* where it is proposed that

> if we cannot catch the Good by one form [ἰδέα] let's do so by three: beauty, symmetry and truth, and say that it would be most correct to hold these, as one, responsible for the qualities in the mixture [sc. of lives]: that due to it, as being good, the mixture has come to be so [i.e., good].[94]

Here Ross commented that

> these are not three species of the genus good, but (. . .) three conditions which that which is good must satisfy.[95]

On any description of them the second item, literally 'the symmetrical' (σύμμετρον) but more nearly *proportion* or *commensurability,* suggests the same concern for a (quasi-) mathematical quantification that seems to underlie the hypostatization of the One, and the repeated use of the numeral one in the sentence underlines the connection of Plato's groping for a quantitative account of reality with his concern to establish absolute and irreducible value.[96] Without elaborating a "single system,"[97] Plato does indicate that what became the "forms of perfection" of a later tradition are coextensive and that, insofar as an order obtains among them, this is such that we need the others in order to understand the Good. This seems to confirm that, although the Good may no longer

93. Stead (1977, p. 50). See the conclusion to Ross's book (1951, p. 245): "Plato . . . seems never to have brought his 'highest Ideas' into a single system, but in the Good of the *Republic* and the *Philebus,* the Existence of the *Sophist,* the Truth of the *Philebus,* and the One of the Idea-number theory, we find the sources of the original list of transcendentals."

94. *Phil.* 65 A 1–5.

95. Ross (1951, p. 242).

96. The close link between goodness and "beauty," amounting to a suggestion that they are coextensive, is as old as Diotima's claim at *Symposium* 212 A 3–5 that the initiate who has seen beauty has been in touch with genuine virtue; see *viii,* note 77 above. (To suppose that 'beauty' [τὸ καλόν] is here used in a different sense is breaking the spell of one language only to submit to that of another.) At *Republic* 6 509 A 6 the Form of Good (508 E 2–3) is called a Beauty that is "unmanageable," that is, not to be grasped (ἀμήχανον). On the other hand, the treatment in the *Republic* of both being and truth as resting on the foundation of the Good and so not by themselves fundamental, or in the terms of the *Phaedo* "unfounded" (ἀνυπόθετον), is not contradicted by the treatment of Being and Not-Being in the *Sophist,* which does not present Being as an ultimate foundation either.

97. See note 93 above.

be proposed as ontologically basic, it continues to be the dominant objective of philosophy and of the philosophic life. Plato's elaborations of dialectic as including collection and division in the *Sophist* and the *Philebus* offer no reason to doubt that he still considered it the ultimate task of dialectic to throw light on the order that provides the setting for the Good, or rather to prepare the intellect for discerning that light: for receiving the illumination that proceeds from this very order.[98]

IV

xii. Ross's reference to "*species* of the *genus* good" takes us back to the distorting effect of received Aristotelian notions upon our view of Platonic dialectic. We should remember that such a use of 'species', like that of 'conditions' contrasted with it, is not straightforwardly Platonic. With as much or as little Platonic justification, we might speak of three properties or characteristics of the good, or of predicates coextensive with goodness. It is worth comparing Ross's terminology to the treatment of the relation between the Forms in a slightly older book on the contemplative life of the dialectician.[99] Festugière, after uncontroversially observing that for Plato pure Being is unchangeable and intelligible, and pure knowledge is the product of abstraction in the sense that we arrive at the Form by abstracting from matter and change, specifies that in this process of abstraction, as we encompass a greater number of realities, at the same time we discover a greater number of relations between these realities. Abstraction leads both to universality and to a synoptic view; we should disaccustom ourselves from the assumption that with increasing abstraction a term loses in comprehension what it gains in extension, so that each higher Form, in its aspect of species, qualifies the greater number of subjects falling under it ever more indeterminately, and the highest and most abstract of them constitutes a concept as far as possible void of substance, an almost purely logical denomination. On the contrary, Festugière claims, the degrees of abstraction, as they extend to a greater number of individuals, correspond to steps on the way to a synoptic view: to a more and more synthetic comprehension of a larger number of relations between things. Thus Being can be at once the most abstract and universal concept and yet not the emptiest but on the contrary the fullest and richest, and what is most one is that which includes and unifies the

98. For the *Statesman*, see Dorter and M. Miller above. That Plato chooses a subject obviously related to that of the *Republic* for another demonstration of his more developed method of dialectic by itself tells against a major change in the discipline's motives and objectives.

99. Festugière (1936, pp. 180–83).

greatest amount of plurality (*le plus de multiple*)—in Kantian terms, most of the manifold. Knowledge or science is an analytic deduction a priori making all this "virtual content" explicit, its consummation a synoptic view embracing all species.

Here Festugière invokes a distinction, proposed by the logician Goblot, between *concept* and *idea*, where 'idea' stands for this "rich," Platonic notion, 'concept' for the more familiar, ultimately Aristotelian one in which extension and intension are in inverse proportion.[100] He notes that Goblot was criticized for this proposal by Maritain,[101] and ascribes these criticisms to an Aristotelian bias on Maritain's part.

This dispute provides an occasion for distinguishing between (1) the merits of such constructions as exercises in logic, which were at issue between Goblot and Maritain, (2) their fidelity and validity as a historical reconstruction of Plato's thought, and (3) their hermeneutical usefulness for understanding Plato's position. In Goblot's and Festugière's very opposition to Aristotle it may be that what is explicitly Aristotelian in terminology or what forms part of a tradition deriving from Aristotle outweighs what Plato might recognize as his own. I have been suggesting that in tracing the formation and evolution of the earliest fully accessible author of the Western philosophical tradition, none of the concepts and categories of this tradition can be taken for granted, and that we may derive heuristic light from such accounts as those quoted without prejudging either their logical adequacy or their historical accuracy. To appreciate how the presence of the Good beyond Being is supposed to permeate first the realm of Being and secondarily that of Becoming, and to envisage the relation and process that Plato calls by the name (among others) of participation,[102] we need all the help we can get, and in an attempt to do justice to Plato's objectives (or Democritus's, or Protagoras's) as distinct from those of Aristotle, analytical tools developed or transformed by Aristotle and his followers are necessarily ambivalent assets.

xiii. Thus Aristotle's objection to Plato's method of division as lacking demonstrative force presupposes both that Plato's aims were fundamentally similar to his own, and that he was in a position to supply the authoritative and definitive formulations of these aims. But the very resemblance between Platonic division and Aristotle's more familiar and influential variety can be misleading. To understand Plato, we have to free our

100. Festugière (1936, p. 184, note); Goblot (1922, p. 115, § 72).

101. Maritain (1923, pp. 36–38; or 1937, pp. 25–27).

102. In a phrase of De Rijk (1986, p. 184) applying to the *Sophist*, "Plato has now succeeded in giving a fuller sense to the old notions of 'sharing' and 'presence *in*' without detracting [from] the 'paradigm' function of the Forms."

minds from the convention that, of the two notions, Kind and Form or Species, Kind is always the wider one, and from the restriction that a Species-Form can belong to one Kind only. The latter is ruled out for Plato by the very notion of a plaiting together of Forms at the level of such all-pervasive "Kinds" as Same and Other in the *Sophist*: if all that is, is both Same and Other, then for Plato it does not as for Aristotle destroy the unity of a Species to belong to more than one Kind. As to the extension of each of the two concepts we should not disregard the connotations of the Greek term for Kind (γένος), literally also 'generation, family', outside its Aristotelian technical usage. These include the existence of any number of cogenera on a par with it;[103] their extraction, not from a more comprehensive superclass, but from a comparable, somehow discrete entity, or more standardly pair of entities, as their parent(s); and being involved in "generation" (γένεσις) as an action, that is, in coming to be and becoming. As Plato found them in everyday speech, the concept of a "Kind" has plurality, change, and productivity written over it much more conspicuously than the concept of a "Form" or "Look." Against this background Aristotle is seen to be deliberately downgrading the Platonic Forms—just as he downgrades the dialectic designed to identify them—when he subsumes them under the Kind or genus, and so quite literally incorporates them in generation. In the context of the Form or Idea of the Good in the *Republic*, it would have been unnatural for Plato to refer to the Good itself as the Kind or genus of the Good: the expression "*genos* of the Good" would naturally be understood as denoting its offspring,[104] and Plato actually refers to the offspring (ἔκγονος) of the Good with a transparently related noun.[105]

xiv. Along such lines it can be shown that the articulation of the realm of Forms along carving lines revealed by division and collection affects the description of the highest of these Forms themselves as well as of their relations to each other. The new representation is in terms that to later generations have suggested an Aristotelian genus or even a class,[106] rather than a discrete unit, and it is hard to divest these terms of their Aristotelian associations. If Plato ever held a conception of the Forms as Super-exemplifiers, then it seems clear that he moved away from it. His realist commitment remains unqualified; but it is not simply reaffirmed. Given that he is the first to attempt a characterization and an

103. Cf. the "sibling" virtues of *Rep.* 3 401 A–402 C; see *vii* above at note 69.

104. As the poet Aratus, quoted by Saint Paul (*Acts* 17.28) can say, "For we are also his offspring" (τοῦ γὰρ καὶ γένος εἶμεν).

105. *Rep.* 6 506 E 3.

106. Cf. Kahn (1995) 59 (28).

account of universals, it is to some extent misleading to father upon him the extreme realism traditionally known as Platonism.[107] It is not as if this was his option in the sense of a choice among other options: alternatives had not been developed into articulacy. There is a difference in dialectical status between Plato's asserting and Aristotle's denying that Forms are separate or separable (χωριστά); one can argue that Plato never intended to assert they were separate in the sense in which Aristotle denies that they are,[108] and at the same time give Aristotle credit for focusing and forcing the issue in such a way that it now became necessary to specify just in what sense they might be said to be or not to be separate. Actually, it is hard to decide how much of this credit is due to him and how much of it Plato himself can take.[109] Having offered one answer to his own question about the nature of universals, Plato is his own severest critic and keeps reformulating his answer so as to meet the criticisms of all comers. In function of this quest his method, the verbal and rational method of dialectic, is progressively transformed; it grows more complex and comprehensive even while the dialectician is as much as ever, in the words of the Eleatic Visitor, "dedicated to the Form of Being," an area whose divine splendor makes it hard for the eyes of the soul of the many to catch sight of him.[110] In this way it makes sense to speak, on and in Plato's own terms, of Plato's progress—the progress toward an elusive entelechy that Aristotle was in no position to acknowledge.

107. See Hare (1982, pp. 31–32) on the views attributed to Plato by Aristotle, the Neoplatonists, the Cambridge Platonists, and Hegel and other romantic philosophers: "It is by no means clear that Plato was a 'Platonist' in any of these senses." A similar point is made in a different context by Rosen at 250 above.

108. Plato in his turn was primarily contradicting what seemed to be implied in common ways of speech: a prototheory or protothesis that qualities, and in general universals, are in or bound up with material objects, and in general with particulars, in a way that would put them in danger of varying and perishing together with these.

109. "Greatness in science consists mainly in leaving the subject much more advanced than when you entered it"; Robinson (1953, p. vi). "Science" may be taken to include the philosophy that sets its agenda; advances may be in the questions by which it does so as much as in the answers it suggests.

110. *Soph.* 254 A 8–B 1.

List of Contributors

Reginald E. Allen studied at St. Andrew's University in Scotland and received his Ph.D. at Yale University in 1958. He is a professor of classics at Northwestern University. His seminal contributions to the study of Plato over four decades include *Plato's "Euthyphro" and the Earlier Theory of Forms* (1970), *Plato's "Parmenides"* (1983), and a series, in progress, of highly acclaimed annotated translations of the dialogues.

Ronna Burger received her Ph.D. in philosophy from the New School for Social Research in New York in 1975. She is a professor of philosophy in the Department of Philosophy at Tulane University. She is the author of *Plato's "Phaedrus": A Defense of a Philosophic Art of Writing* (University of Alabama Press, 1980) and *"The Phaedo": A Platonic Labyrinth* (Yale University Press, 1984). She has also published numerous articles on Plato and Aristotle in such journals as *Interpretation, Proceedings of the Boston Area Colloquium in Ancient Philosophy,* and *Review of Metaphysics.* She is currently writing a book on Aristotle's *Ethics.*

Kenneth Dorter received his Ph.D. from Pennsylvania State University in 1967. He has been a member of the Philosophy Department at the University of Guelph in Canada since 1966. He is the author of *Plato's "Phaedo": An Interpretation* (University of Toronto Press, 1982) and *Form and Good in Plato's Eleatic Dialogues: The "Parmenides," "Sophist," and "Statesman"* (University of California Press, 1994). His most recent publications are "Three Disappearing Ladders in Plato" (*Philosophy and Rhetoric,* 1996) and "Wisdom, Virtue, and Knowledge" (*Review of Metaphysics,* 1997).

Thérèse-Anne Druart obtained her Ph.D. in Greek philosophy at the Université Catholique de Louvain and her B.Phil. in oriental studies (with a specialty in medieval Islamic philosophy and theology) at Oxford University. She is a professor in the Philosophy Department at The Catholic University of America. She has published a critical edition of al-Farabi's *Summary of Plato's "Laws,"* edited *Arabic Philosophy and the West: Continuity and Interaction,* and written some thirty-five articles on Arabic philosophy and Plato. She is subeditor of Richard C. Taylor's English translation of Averroes's *Long Commentary on Aristotle's "De anima."*

Charles L. Griswold Jr. is a professor of philosophy and chairman of the Philosophy Department at Boston University. His areas of interest include the history of philosophy and philosophy and political thought. He is author of *Self-Knowledge in Plato's "Phaedrus"* (Yale University Press, 1986; paperback reprint, 1996), which was awarded the Franklin J. Matchette Prize by the American Philosophical Association. Griswold edited *Platonic Writings, Platonic Readings* (Routledge, Chapman, and Hall, 1988), and has published numerous articles. His *Adam Smith and the Virtues of the Enlightenment* is forthcoming (Cambridge University Press). Griswold has been a guest lecturer at universities throughout the United States and Europe, and has received awards and fellowships from the American Council of Learned Societies, the Catholic Philosophical Association, the Earhart Foundation, the National Endowment for the Humanities, the National Humanities Center, the Reason Foundation, and the Woodrow Wilson Center.

Fred D. Miller, Jr. received his Ph.D. from the University of Washington, Seattle. He is a professor of philosophy at Bowling Green State University, where he teaches Greek philosophy and political philosophy. He is also executive director of the Social Philosophy and Policy Center, associate editor of the journal *Social Philosophy & Policy,* and assistant editor of the *Philosopher's Index.* He is the author of *Nature, Justice, and Rights in Aristotle's "Politics"* (Oxford University Press), and coeditor (with David Keyt) of *A Companion to Aristotle's "Politics"* (Blackwell). He has also published numerous articles on Plato, Aristotle, and other Greek philosophers, as well as articles on ancient Greek religion and on modern political philosophy.

Mitchell Miller is a professor of philosophy at Vassar College. His teaching interests range over the history of philosophy, with a special focus on Greek philosophy and cultural history. He is the author of *Plato's "Parmenides": The Conversion of the Soul* (Princeton University Press, 1986; paperback reprint, Pennsylvania State University Press, 1991) and *The Philosopher in Plato's "Statesman"* (Martinus Nijhoff, 1980). He is currently at work on a study of Greek music theory and the later dialogues.

Dominic J. O'Meara received his Ph.D. from the Université de Paris (the Sorbonne). He was a fellow at the Dumbarton Oaks Center for Byzantine

Studies (Washington, D.C.), and then an associate professor of philosophy at The Catholic University of America, before becoming professor and chair of ancient philosophy at the Université de Fribourg (Switzerland). His publications include *Pythagoras Revived: Mathematics and Philosophy in Late Antiquity* (Oxford University Press, 1989), *Plotinus: An Introduction to the "Enneads"* (Oxford University Press, 1993), *Plotin Traité 51* (Université de Paris, 1998), and *The Structure of Being and the Search for the Good* (Aldershot, 1998).

Kurt Pritzl, O.P., received his Ph.D. at the University of Toronto in 1982; his dissertation topic was Aristotle's *De anima.* He received his Master of Divinity degree at the Dominican House of Studies in Washington, D.C., in 1991. He is an associate professor of philosophy at The Catholic University of America. His area of specialization is ancient Greek philosophy, especially the pre-Socratics and Aristotle with respect to the theory of knowledge and philosophical method. He has written a number of journal articles and reviews.

John M. Rist is the author of a number of books on the major philosophers of the period from the fourth century B.C. to the fifth century A.D., including *Plotinus: The Road to Reality, Epicurus: an Introduction, Stoic Philosophy, The Mind of Aristotle: A Study in Philosophical Growth,* and *Augustine: Ancient Thought Baptized.*

Stanley Rosen received his B.A. and Ph.D. from the University of Chicago and is Evan Pugh Professor Emeritus at Penn State University and Borden Parker Bowne Professor of Philosophy at Boston University. He has published twelve books, several of which have been or are being translated into French, Italian, Catalan, Polish, Japanese, and Chinese. He has lectured widely in North America and Europe, is past president of the Metaphysical Society of America, and holds an honorary doctorate from the New University of Lisbon.

Daryl McGowan Tress is an assistant professor of philosophy at Fordham University. Her specialty is ancient philosophy. Her most recent writings are "Aristotle's *Child:* Development through *Genesis, Oikos,* and *Polis*" (*Ancient Philosophy,* 1997) and "The Philosophical Genesis of Ecology and Environmentalism" (*The Greeks and the Environment*).

Johannes M. Van Ophuijsen has taught at The Catholic University of America, the American University of Beirut, and the Universities of Leiden and Amsterdam. He has published on Plato, the school of Aristotle (Theophrastus, Demetrius of Phalerum, Alexander of Aphrodisias), on ancient theories in grammar, logic, and rhetoric, and on Herodotus.

Anne M. Wiles is a professor of philosophy at James Madison University, where she teaches classical philosophy. She specializes in Plato, but has interests that extend from metaphysics to ethics. She is coeditor of *The Continuing Quest*, a textbook on the history of philosophy. She has also published in the *Review of Metaphysics* and the *American Catholic Philosophical Quarterly*. Her most recent work is a study of the political and social philosophy of Rabindranath Tagore, the Indian poet and statesman.

Bibliography

Ackrill, John L. "Plato and the Copula: *Sophist* 251–59." In *Studies in Plato's Metaphysics.* Edited by R. E. Allen, 207–18. London: Routledge and Kegan Paul, 1965.

———. "In Defense of Platonic Division." In *Ryle: A Collection of Critical Essays.* Edited by Oscar P. Wood and George Pitcher. London and New York: 1970.

Adam, J. *The "Republic" of Plato.* Vol. 1. Cambridge: 1902.

Adkins, A. W. H. *Merit and Responsibility: A Study in Greek Values.* Chicago and London: 1960.

Adorno, F. "Appunti su *homologein* e *homologia* nel vocabolario di Platone." *Dialoghi di Archeologia* 2 (1968): 152–72.

Allen, R. E. *Plato's "Euthyphro" and the Earlier Theory of Forms.* London: 1970.

———. "Law and Justice in Plato's *Crito.*" *Journal of Philosophy* 69 (1972): 557–67.

———. *Socrates and Legal Obligation.* Minneapolis: 1980.

———. *Plato's "Parmenides".* Minneapolis: University of Minnesota Press, 1983.

Allen, R. E., ed. *Studies in Plato's Metaphysics.* London: 1965.

Ammonius. *In Porphyrii Isagogen* 4.3. In *Commentaria in Aristotelem graeca.* Edited by A. Busse. Berlin: 1891.

Annas, Julia. "On the 'Intermediates.'" *Archiv für Geschichte der Philosophie* 57 (1975): 146–66.

———. *The Morality of Happiness.* Oxford: 1993.

Anonymous. *Menae patricii cum Thoma referendario: De scientia politica dialogus.* Edited and translated by C. Mazzucchi. Milan: 1982.

Anscombe, Elizabeth. "Modern Moral Philosophy." *Philosophy* 33 (1958): 1–19.

Aristophanes. *Clouds.* Edited by K. J. Dover. Oxford: 1968.

Aristotle. *Metaphysics.*

———. *Topics.*

———. *Politics.* Translated by C. Lord. Chicago: University of Chicago Press, 1984.

———. *The Complete Works of Aristotle: The Revised Oxford Translation.* Edited by J. Barnes. 2 vols. Princeton: 1984.

Arnou, R. *Praxis et Theoria.* Rome: 1972.

Athanassiadi-Fowden, P. *Julian and Hellenism: An Intellectual Biography.* Oxford: 1981.

Averroës. *Averroës on Plato's "Republic."* Translated by R. Lerner. Ithaca: Cornell University Press, 1974.

Balaudé, J. F. "Communauté divine et au-delà: les fins du dépassement selon Plotin." *Philosophie* 26 (1990): 73–94.

Bambrough, R., ed. *New Essays on Plato and Aristotle.* London: 1965.

———, ed. *Plato, Popper, and Politics.* New York: Barnes and Noble, 1967.

Barnes, J. "Aristotle and the Methods of Ethics." *Revue internationale de philosophie* 34 (1980): 490–511.

Benardete, Seth. "On Plato's *Timaeus* and Timaeus' Science Fiction." *Interpretation* 2 (1971): 21–63.

———. "On Wisdom and Philosophy: The First Two Chapters of Aristotle's *Metaphysics* A." *Review of Metaphysics* 32:2 (1978): 205–15.

———. *The Being of the Beautiful: Plato's "Theatetus," "Sophist," and "Statesman."* Chicago: University of Chicago Press, 1984.

———. *The Rhetoric of Morality and Philosophy: Plato's "Gorgias" and "Phaedrus."* Chicago: University of Chicago Press, 1991.

Blits, Jan. "The Holy and the Human: an Interpretation of Plato's *Euthyphro*." *Apeiron* 14 (1980): 20–23.

Blundell, Mary Whitlock. *Helping Friends and Harming Enemies: A Study in Sophocles and Greek Ethics.* Cambridge: 1989.

Boethius. *Consolation of Philosophy.* Translated by S. Tester. London and Cambridge: 1973.

Bornhamm, G. "*Homologia*: Zur Geschichte eines Politischen Begriffs." *Hermes* 71 (1936): 377–93.

Brague, Rémi. "The Body of the Speech: A New Hypothesis on the Compositional Structure of Timaeus' Monologue." In *Platonic Investigations.* Edited by Dominic J. O'Meara, 53–83. Washington: The Catholic University of America Press, 1985.

Brandwood, Leonard. *The Chronology of Plato's Dialogues.* Cambridge: Cambridge University Press, 1990.

———. "Stylometry and Chronology." In *The Cambridge Companion to Plato.* Edited by Richard Kraut, 90–120. Cambridge: Cambridge University Press, 1992.

Brisson, Luc. *Le Même et l'Autre dans la structure ontologique du "Timée" de Platon: Un commentaire systématique du "Timée" de Platon.* Paris: Klincksieck, 1974.

Brisson, Luc, and Tomés Calvo, eds. *Interpreting the* Timaeus-Critias. Vol. 9, *Plato Studies.* Proceedings of the International Symposium Platonicum. Sankt Augustin: Academia Verlag, 1997.

Brisson, Luc et al. *Porphyre: La vie de Plotin.* Vol. 1. Paris: 1982.

Brown, P. "The Philosopher and Society in Late Antiquity." Paper presented at the Center for Hermeneutical Studies Colloquy. Berkeley, 1978.

Brumbaugh, Robert S. *Plato's Mathematical Imagination.* Bloomington: Indiana University Press, 1954.

Burkert, Walter. *Greek Religion.* Translated by John Raffan. Cambridge: Harvard University Press, 1985.

Calogero, Guido. "*Gorgias* and the Socratic Principle *Nemo Sua Sponte Peccat.*" In *Essays in Ancient Greek Philosophy.* Edited by John P. Anton and George L. Kustas. New York: 1971.

Cassirer, Ernst. *Language.* Translated by Ralph Manheim. Vol. 1 of *The Philosophy of Symbolic Forms.* New Haven and London: 1955. Originally *Philosophie der symbolischen Formen: Die Sprache.* Berlin: 1923.

Charles, David. "Perfectionism in Aristotle's Political Theory: Reply to Martha Nussbaum." *Oxford Studies in Ancient Philosophy* suppl. vol. (1988): 185–214.

Cherniss, Harold F. *Aristotle's Criticism of Plato and the Academy.* Baltimore: Johns Hopkins University Press, 1944.

———. *The Riddle of the Early Academy.* Berkeley and Los Angeles: University of California Press, 1945.

———. "The Philosophical Economy of the Theory of Ideas." In *Studies in Plato's Metaphysics.* Edited by R. E. Allen. New York: Routledge and Kegan Paul, 1965.

———. "The Relation of the *Timaeus* to Plato's Later Dialogues." In *Studies in Plato's Metaphysics.* Edited by R. E. Allen. New York: Routledge and Kegan Paul, 1965.

Cicero. *Tusculan Disputations.*

Clay, D. "Reading the *Republic.*" In *Platonic Writings, Platonic Readings.* Edited by C. Griswold, 19–33. New York: Routledge, Chapman, and Hall, 1988.

Comotti, Giovanni. *Music in Greek and Roman Culture.* Translated by R. Munson. Baltimore: Johns Hopkins University Press, 1989.

Cooper, J. "The Psychology of Justice in Plato." *American Philosophical Quarterly* 14 (1977): 151–57.

———. "Plato's Theory of Human Motivation." *History of Philosophy Quarterly* 1 (1984): 3–21.

Cornford, Francis M. *Plato's Theory of Knowledge.* London: Routledge and Kegan Paul, 1935.

———. *Plato and Parmenides.* New York: Harcourt, Brace and Company, 1939.

Cornford, Francis M., trans. and ed. *Plato's Cosmology: The "Timaeus" of Plato.* London: Kegan Paul, 1937.

Crombie, I. M. *An Examination of Plato's Doctrines.* London: Routledge, 1962.

Davis, Michael. *Ancient Tragedy and the Origins of Modern Science.* Carbondale: Southern Illinois University Press, 1988.

de Lattre, A. "La liberté socratique et le dialogue platonicien." *Kant Studien* 61 (1970): 467–95.

de Rijk, L. M. *Plato's "Sophist": A Philosophical Commentary.* Amsterdam: North Holland, 1986.

Den Uyl, D. and D. Rasmussen. *Liberty and Nature: an Aristotelian Defense of Liberal Order.* La Salle: Open Court, 1991.

Descartes, Rene. *Discourse on Method.*

Diogenes Laertes. *Lives.*

Dodds, E. R. *The Greeks and the Irrational.* Berkeley and Los Angeles: University of California Press, 1951.

Donagan, Alan. "The History of Philosophy as a Discipline." In *The Philosophical Papers.* Edited by J. E. Malpas with a foreword by Stephen Toulmin, 1–13. Vol. 1: *Historical Understanding and the History of Philosophy.* Chicago and London: 1994.

Dorter, Kenneth. *Plato's "Phaedo": An Interpretation.* Toronto: University of Toronto Press, 1982.

———. *Form and Good in Plato's Eleatic Dialogues: The "Parmenides," "Theatetus," "Sophist," and "Statesman."* Berkeley and Los Angeles: University of California Press, 1994.

Dover, K. J. *Greek Popular Morality in the Time of Plato and Aristotle.* Berkeley and Los Angeles: University of California Press, 1974.

Dreisbach, D. F. "Agreement and Obligation in the *Crito.*" *New Scholasticism* 52 (1978): 168–86.

Druart, Thérèse-Anne. "La stoicheïologie de Platon." *Revue philosophique de Louvain* 73 (1975): 243–62.

Earp, F. R. *The Way of the Greeks.* Oxford and London: 1929.

Edmond, M.-P. *Le Philosophe-roi: Platon et la politique.* Paris: 1991.

Epictetus. *Discourses.*

Epicurus. *Kuriai Doxai.*

———. *Sententiae Vaticanae.*

———. "Letter to Menoeceus." In *Epicurus: the Extant Remains.* Translated and edited by C. Bailey. Oxford: Clarendon Press, 1926.

Ferber, Rafael. *Plato: Idee des Guten.* 2d ed. Sankt Augustin: Academia Verlag Richarz, 1989.

Festugière, A. J. M. *Contemplation et vie contemplative selon Platon.* Paris: 1936.

Foot, Philippa. *Virtues and Vices.* Berkeley and Los Angeles: University of California Press, 1978.

Fortenbaugh, W. W. "On the Antecedents of Aristotle's Bipartite Psychology." *Greek, Roman, and Byzantine Studies* 11 (1970): 233–50.

Fowden, G. "Pagan Philosophers in Late Antique Society." D. Phil. Thesis, Oxford University, 1979.

Fowler, D. H. *The Mathematics of Plato's Academy: A New Reconstruction.* Oxford: Clarendon Press, 1987.

Frede, Michael. "The Original Notion of Cause." In *Doubt and Dogmatism: Studies in Hellenistic Epistemology.* Edited by Malcolm Schofield, Myles Burnyeat and Jonathan Barnes. Oxford: Clarendon Press, 1980.

———. *Essays in Ancient Philosophy.* Minneapolis: University of Minnesota Press, 1987.

———. "Observations on Perception in Plato's Later Dialogues." *Methods of Interpreting Plato and His Dialogues, OSAP* suppl. vol. (1992).

———. "Plato's *Sophist* on False Statements." In *The Cambridge Companion to Plato.* Edited by R. Kraut, 397–424. Cambridge: Cambridge University Press, 1992.

Friedländer, Paul. *Plato: An Introduction.* New York: Harper, 1958.

Fuks, A. *The Ancestral Constitution: Four Studies in Athenian Party Politics at the End of the Fifth Century BC.* London: 1953.

Gadamer, Hans-Georg. *Dialogue and Dialectic: Eight Hermeneutical Studies on Plato.* Translated with an Introduction by P. Christopher Smith. New Haven: Yale University Press, 1980.

Gaiser, Konrad. *Platons Ungeschriebene Lehre: Studien zur systematischen und geschichtlichen Begründung der Wissenschaften in der Platonischen Schule.* With the addition of *Testimonia Platonica: Quellentexte zur Schule und mündlichen Lehre Platons.* Stuttgart: 1963, 1968.

———. *Platone come scrittore filosofico: Saggio sull'ermeneutica dei dialoghi platonici.* Naples: 1984.

Galston, W. A. *Justice and the Human Good.* Chicago: University of Chicago Press, 1980.

———. "Pluralism and Social Unity." In *Liberal Purposes: Goods, Virtues, and Diversity in the Liberal State.* New York: Cambridge University Press, 1991.

Garrett, J. E. "The Moral Status of 'the Many' in Aristotle." *Journal of the History of Philosophy* 31 (1993): 171–89.

Gazzaniga, Michael. "Brain Modularity: Toward a Philosophy of Conscious Experience." In *Consciousness in Contemporary Science.* Edited by A. J. Marcel and E. Bisiach. Oxford: Clarendon Press, 1988.

Geach, P. T. "Plato's *Euthyphro*: An Analysis and Commentary." *Monist* 50 (1966).

Goblot, Edmond. *Traité de logique.* 3d ed. Paris: 1922.

Goodman, Lenn E. *Avicenna.* London and New York: 1992.

Green, P. Review of *The Therapy of Desire* by Martha C. Nussbaum. *New Republic* (September 5, 1994): 38–42.

Green, T. H. *Lectures on the Principles of Political Obligation.* London: Longmans, Green, and Co., 1895.

Greenberg, N. A. "Socrates' Choice in the *Crito.*" *Harvard Studies in Classical Philology* 70 (1965): 45–82.

Griswold, Charles. *Self-knowledge in Plato's "Phaedrus."* New Haven: Yale University Press, 1986.

———. "*Politike Episteme* in Plato's *Statesman.*" In *Essays in Ancient Greek Philosophy.* Edited by J. Anton and A. Preus. Vol. 3. New York: State University of New York Press, 1989.

———. "Unifying Plato: Charles Kahn on Platonic *Prolepsis.*" *Ancient Philosophy* 10 (1990): 243–62.

———. "Stoning Greek Philosophers: Platonic Political Philosophy and the Trial of Socrates." *Classical Bulletin* 67:1 (1991): 3–15.

———. "The Politics of Self-knowledge: Liberal Variations on the *Phaedrus.*" In the *Understanding the "Phaedrus."* Edited by L. Rossetti, 173–90. Sankt Augustin: Academia Verlag, 1992.

———. "Le libéralisme platonicien: de la perfection individuelle comme fondement d'une théorie politique." In *Contre Platon: le platonisme renversé.* Vol. 2. Edited by M. Dixsaut, 155–95. Paris: Vrin, 1995.

Griswold, C., ed. *Platonic Writings, Platonic Readings.* New York: Routledge, Chapman, and Hall, 1988.

Grote, G. *Plato and the Other Companions of Sokrates.* 3 vols. 2d edition. London: 1867.

Guthrie, W. K. C. *A History of Greek Philosophy.* Vol. 4–6. New York: Cambridge University Press, 1975–81.

Hadot, P. "Fürstenspiegel." In *Realencyclopädie für Antike und Christentum.* Vol. 8. Stuttgart: 1972.

———. *Plotin Traité.* Paris: 1994.

Haksar, Victor. *Equality, Liberty, and Perfectionism.* Oxford: Oxford University Press, 1979.

Hare, R. M. "Plato and the Mathematicians." In *New Essays on Plato and Aristotle.* Edited by R. Bambrough, 21–38. London: 1965.

———. *Plato.* Oxford: Oxford University Press, 1982.

Heath, T. L. *History of Greek Mathematics.* Oxford: 1921.

Henderson, Isobel. "Ancient Greek Music." *In Ancient and Oriental Music.* Vol. 1 of *The New Oxford History of Music.* Edited by Egon Wellesz, 336–403. London: Oxford University Press, 1957.

Hesiod. *Theogony.*

Hierocles. *De providentia.* In *Photius Bibliotheca.* Vol. 7. Edited and translated by R. Henry. Paris: 1974.

Hoernlé, R. F. A. "Would Plato have Approved of the National-Socialist State?" In *Plato, Popper, and Politics.* Edited by R. Bambrough. New York: Barnes and Noble, 1967.

Homer. *Odyssey.*

Howland, Jacob. "Re-reading Plato: the Problem of Platonic Chronology." *Phoenix* 45 (1991): 189–214.

Huart, P. "Julien et l'hellénisme: Idées morales et politiques." In *L'Empereur Julien: De l'histoire à la légende.* Edited by R. Braun and J. Richer, 112–15. Paris: 1978.

Hume, David. *A Treatise of Human Nature.* 2d ed. Edited by L. A. Selby-Bigge and P. H. Nidditch. Oxford: 1978.

———. "Idea of a Perfect Commonwealth." In *Essays Moral, Political, and Literary.* Revised edition. Edited by E. Miller. Indianapolis: Liberty Press, 1987.

Husserl, Edmund. *Erfahrung und Urteil.* Hamburg: Claassen Verlag, 1964.

Hyland, D. "Plato's Three Waves and the Question of Utopia." *Interpretation* 18 (1990): 91–109.

Iamblichus. *Protrepticus.* Edited by H. Pistelli. Stuttgart: 1967.

———. *De vita pythagorica.* Edited by L. Deubner. Stuttgart: 1975.

Irwin, Terence H. *Plato's Moral Theory.* Oxford: 1977.

Jaynes, Julian. *The Origin of Consciousness in the Breakdown of the Bicameral Mind.* Boston: 1976.

Jefferson, Thomas and John Adams. *The Adams-Jefferson Letters.* Edited by L. J. Cappon. Chapel Hill: University of North Carolina Press, 1988.

Jerphagnon, L. "Platonopolis, ou Plotin entre le siècle et le rêve." In *Néoplatonisme: Mélanges J. Trouillard.* Fontenay: 1981.

Joubaud, Catherine. *Le corps humain dans la philosophie platonicienne: Étude à partir du "Timée."* Introduction by Luc Brisson. Paris: J. Vrin, 1991.

Julian, Emperor. *Oeuvres completes.* Vol. 1. Edited and translated by J. Bidez. Paris: 1932.

———. *Le Discours sur la royauté de Synesios de Cyrène.* Translated by C. Lacombrade. Paris: 1951.

———. *Oeuvres complètes.* Vol. 2. Edited and translated by G. Rochefort. Paris: 1963.

Kahn, C. "Plato's Theory of Desire." *The Review of Metaphysics* 41 (1987): 77–103.

———. "Did Plato Write Socratic Dialogues?" *Classical Quarterly* 31 (1981): 305–20.

Kant, Immanuel. *Critique of Pure Reason.*

Kerschensteiner, J. "Zum Gebrauch von *sun* und *xun* bei Platon." *Münchener Studien zur Sprachwissenschaft* 1 (1952): 28–41. Revised 1956.

Kirk, G. S., J. E. Raven and M. Schofield. *The Presocratic Philosophers: A Critical History with a Selection of Texts.* 2d ed. Cambridge: 1983.

Klein, Jacob. *A Commentary on Plato's "Meno."* Chapel Hill: University of North Carolina Press, 1965.

———. *Greek Mathematical Thought and the Origin of Algebra.* Cambridge: MIT Press, 1968.

Kleve, K. "Lukrez und Venus (*De rer. nat.* 1.1–49)." *SO* 41 (1966): 86–94.

———. "Lucrèce, l'épicurisme et l'amour." *ACGB* (1969): 376–83.

Klosko, G. *The Development of Plato's Political Theory.* New York: Methuen, 1986.

Kneale, William and Martha. *The Development of Logic.* London and Oxford: Oxford University Press, 1962.

Knox, B. *The Oldest Dead White European Males.* New York, 1993.

Kosman, A. "Platonic Love." *Phronesis.* Suppl. vol. 2. (1976): 53–69.

Krämer, Hans J. *Arete bei Platon und Aristoteles: Zum Wesen und zur Geschichte der Platonischen Ontologie.* In *Abhandlungen der Heidelberger Akademie der Wissenschaften: philosophisch-historische Klasse* 6: 148–77. Heidelberg: 1959; Amsterdam: 1967.

———. *Plato and the Foundation of Metaphysics.* Albany: State University of New York Press, 1990. Translated with an introducation by Giovanni Reale. Originally *Platone e i fondamenti della metafisica: Saggio sulla teoria dei principi e sulle dottrine non scritte di Platone con una raccolta dei documenti fondamentali in edizione bilingue e bibliografia.* Milan: 1982, 1989.

Kraut, R. "Egoism, Love, and Political Office in Plato." *Philosophical Review* 82 (1973): 330–44.

———. *Socrates and the State.* Princeton: Princeton University Press, 1984.

Kraut, R., ed. *The Cambridge Companion to Plato.* Cambridge: Cambridge University Press, 1992.

Kremer, K. "Bonum est diffusivum sui." In *Aufstieg und Niedergang der römischen Welt.* Vol. 36:2. Edited by W. Haase and H. Temporini, 994–1032. Berlin: 1987.

Kung, Joan. "Plato on Mind and Morality in Nature." *University of Dayton Review* 16 (1982–83): 57–65.

———. "Tetrahedra, Motion, and Virtue." *Nous* 19 (1985): 17–27.

———. "Mathematics and Virtue in Plato's *Timaeus.*" In *Essays in Ancient Greek Philosophy.* Vol. 3. Edited by John Anton and Anthony Preuss, 309–39. New York: State University of New York Press, 1989.

Lachterman, David. *The Ethics of Geometry: A Genealogy of Modernity.* New York: Routledge, 1989.

Ledger, G. R. *Re-Counting Plato.* Oxford: Clarendon Press, 1989.

Lee, E. N. "Plato's Theory of Social Justice in *Republic* II–IV." In *Essays in Ancient Greek Philosophy.* Vol. 3. Edited by John Anton and Anthony Preus, 309–39. New York: State University of New York Press, 1989.

Lee, Edward. "On the Metaphysics of the Image in Plato's *Timaeus.*" *Monist* 50 (1966): 341–68.

Levinson, R. B. *In Defense of Plato.* Cambridge: Harvard University Press, 1953.

Lewis, Marlo. "An Interpretation of Plato's *Euthyphro,*" Part 1. *Interpretation* 12:2–3 (1984).

———. "An Interpretation of Plato's *Euthyphro,*" Part 2. *Interpretation* 13:1 (1985).

Lloyd, A. C. "Plato's Description of Division." Reprinted in *Studies in Plato's Metaphysics.* Edited by R. E. Allen, 219–30. London: 1965.

Lloyd, G. E. R. *Polarity and Analogy.* Cambridge: Cambridge University Press, 1966.

Lloyd-Jones, H. *The Justice of Zeus.* Berkeley and Los Angeles: University of California Press, 1971.

Lyons, John. *Semantic Structures: A Study of Part of the Vocabulary of Plato.* Oxford: Blackwell, 1962.

MacIntyre, A. *Three Rival Versions of Moral Enquiry.* South Bend: University of Notre Dame Press, 1990.

Macpherson, C. B. *The Political Theory of Possessive Individualism: Hobbes to Locke.* Oxford: 1962.

Madison, James. *The Federalist Papers.* Edited by C. Rossiter. New York: New American Library, 1961.

Mahoney, T. "Do Plato's Philosopher-Rulers Sacrifice Self-Interest to Justice?" *Phronesis* 37 (1992): 265–82.

Maimonides. *Guide of the Perplexed.*

Mara, G. M. "Socrates and Liberal Toleration." *Political Theory* 16 (1988): 468–95.

Maritain, Jacques. *Petite logique.* Paris: 1923. Translated as *An Introduction to Logic.* New York: Sheed and Ward, 1937.

McPherran, Mark. "Socratic Piety in the *Euthyphro.*" *Journal of the History of Philosophy* 23:3 (1985): 298–309.

Meijer, P. *Plotinus on the Good or the One* (Enneads VI, 9). Amsterdam: 1992.

Meinwald, Constance C. "Good-bye to the Third Man." In *The Cambridge Compan-*

ion to Plato. Edited by Richard Kraut, 365–96. Cambridge: Cambridge University Press, 1992.

Mill, John S. *On Liberty.* Edited by C. V. Shields. Indianapolis: Bobbs-Merrill, 1976.

———. *Utilitarianism.*

Miller, F. *Nature, Justice, and Rights in Aristotle's "Politics."* Oxford: Clarendon Press, 1995.

Miller, Mitchell. *The Philosopher in Plato's "Statesman."* The Hague: Martinus Nijhoff, 1980.

———. "Platonic Provocations: Reflections on the Soul and the Good in the *Republic.*" In *Platonic Investigations.* Edited by Dominic J. O'Meara. Washington: The Catholic University of America Press, 1985.

———. *Plato's "Parmenides": The Conversion of the Soul.* Princeton: Princeton University Press, 1986. Reprint. State College: Pennsylvania State University Press, 1991.

———. "The God-Given Way." *Proceedings of the Boston Area Colloquium in Ancient Philosophy* 6 (1990): 323–59.

———. "Unity and Logos: A Reading of *Theaetetus* 201c–210a." *Ancient Philosophy* 12 (1992): 87–111.

———. "'Unwritten Teachings' in the *Parmenides.*" *Review of Metaphysics* 48:3 (1995): 591–633.

Mitsis, P. *Epicurus' Ethical Theory.* Ithaca: Cornell University Press, 1988.

Mohr, Richard D. *The Platonic Cosmology.* Leiden: Brill, 1985.

———. "Plato's Theology Reconsidered: What the Demiurge Does." *History of Philosophy Quarterly* 2 (1985): 131–44. Reprint. In *Essays in Ancient Greek Philosophy.* Vol. 3. Edited by John Anton and Anthony Preus, 293–307. New York: State University of New York Press, 1989.

Moline, J. "Plato on the Complexity of the Psyche." *Archiv für Geschichte der Philosophie* 60 (1978): 1–26.

Morrow, Glenn R. "Necessity and Persuasion in Plato's *Timaeus.*" *The Philosophical Review* 59 (1950): 147–63.

———. *Plato's Cretan City: An Historical Interpretation of the "Laws."* Princeton: 1960.

———. "Plato's Theory of the Primary Bodies in the *Timaeus* and the Later Doctrine of Forms." *Archiv für Geschichte der Philosophie* 50 (1968): 12–28.

Mueller, Ian. "Mathematical Method and Philosophical Truth." In *The Cambridge Companion to Plato.* Edited by Richard Kraut, 170–99. Cambridge: Cambridge University Press, 1992.

Nagel, T. *The View from Nowhere.* Oxford: 1986.

Neschke, A., ed. *Images de Platon et lectures de ses oeuvres.* Louvain: 1997.

Nettleship, Richard Lewis. *Lectures on the "Republic" of Plato.* London: Macmillan and Company, 1961.

Nietzsche, F. "Schopenhauer as Educator." In *Untimely Meditations.*

Noussan-Lettry, L. "Das Bedeutete und das Gesagte: Zu *doulos, douleuein* im Platons *Kriton.*" *Wissenschaft und Weltbild* 26 (1973): 147–50.

Novak, Joseph. "Plato and the Irrational." *Apeiron* 17 (1983): 14–27.

Nuchelmans, Gabriel. *Theories of the Proposition.* Amsterdam: North Holland Linguistic Series, 1973.

Nussbaum, Martha C. "Aristotelian Social Democracy." In *Liberalism and the Good.* Edited by R. B. Douglass, G. M. Marey, and H. S. Richardson, 203–52. New York: Routledge, Chapman, and Hall, 1990.

———. *The Fragility of Goodness.* Cambridge: 1986.

———. "Nature, Function, and Capability: Aristotle on Political Distribution." *Oxford Studies in Ancient Philosophy* suppl. vol. (1988): 145–84.

———. *The Therapy of Desire.* Princeton: 1994.

Olympiodorus. *In Platonis Gorgian.* Edited by L.G. Westerink. Leipzig: 1970.

Onians, Robert. *The Origins of European Thought about the Body, the Soul, the World, Time, and Fate.* Cambridge: Cambridge University Press, 1954.

Owen, G. E. L. "The Place of the *Timaeus* in Plato's Dialogues." In *Studies in Plato's Metaphysics.* Edited by R. E. Allen, 313–38. London: Routledge and Kegan Paul, 1965 (originally published 1953).

O'Meara, Dominic J. "Aspects of Political Philosophy in Iamblichus." In *The Divine Iamblichus: Philosopher and Man of God.* Edited by H. Blumenthal and G. Clark, 67–70. Bristol: 1993. Reprint. In Dominic J. O'Meara, *The Structure of Being.* Aldershot: 1998.

Parfit, D. *Reasons and Persons.* Oxford: 1986.

Parry, Richard D. "The Unique World of the *Timaeus.*" *Journal of the History of Philosophy* 17 (1979): 1–10.

———. "The Intelligible World-Animal in Plato's *Timaeus.*" *Journal of the History of Philosophy* 29 (1991): 13–32.

Payne, T. "The *Crito* as a Mythological Mime." *Interpretation* 11 (1983): 1–24.

Pearson, L. *Popular Ethics in Ancient Greece.* Stanford: Stanford University Press, 1962.

Pelikan, Jaroslav. *The Excellent Empire: The Fall of Rome and the Triumph of the Church.* New York: 1987.

Penner, T. "Thought and Desire in Plato." In *Plato: A Collection of Critical Essays.* Vol. 2. Edited by G. Vlastos. Garden City: 1971.

Pertusi, A. *Il pensiero politico bizantino.* Bologna: 1990.

Pistelli, H., ed. *Protrepticus.* Stuttgart: 1967.

Plotinus. *Ennead* 6. Translated and modified by A. H. Armstrong.

Popper, Karl. *The Open Society and Its Enemies.* 2 vols. Princeton: Princeton University Press, 1962.

Porphyry. *Vita Plotini.*

Price, A. W. *Love and Friendship in Plato and Aristotle.* Oxford: 1989.

Pritzl, Kurt. "Ways of Truth and Ways of Opinion in Aristotle." *The Importance of Truth: Proceedings of the American Catholic Philosophical Association* 67 (1993): 241–52.

———. "Opinions as Appearances: *Endoxa* in Aristotle." *Ancient Philosophy* 14 (1994): 41–50.

Proclus. *Comm. in Tim.* Vol. 1. Edited by E. Diehl. Leipzig: 1903.

———. *Comm. in Tim.* Vol. 1. Translated by A. Festugiere. Paris: 1966.

———. *Théologie Platonicienne.* Vol. 1. Edited by H.-D. Saffrey and L. G. Westerink. Paris: 1968.

———. "De malorum subsistentia." *De l'existence du mal.* Edited and translated by D. Isaac. Vol. 3 of *Proclus: Trois études sur la providence.* Paris: 1982.

———. *Sur le premier Alcibiade.* Vol. 1. Edited by A. Segonds. Paris: 1985.

Quandt, K. "Socratic Consolation: Rhetoric and Philosophy in Plato's *Crito.*" *Philosophy and Rhetoric* 15 (1982): 238–56.

Rawls, John. *A Theory of Justice.* Cambridge: Harvard University Press, 1971.

———. "Kantian Constructivism in Moral Theory." *Journal of Philosophy* 77 (1980): 515–72.

———. "Justice as Fairness: Political not Metaphysical." *Philosophy and Public Affairs* 14 (1985): 223–51.

———. "The Priority of Right and Ideas of the Good." *Philosophy and Public Affairs* 17 (1988): 251–76.

Raz, Joseph. "Right-Based Moralities." In *Theories of Rights.* Edited by J. Waldron. Oxford: Oxford University Press, 1984.

Reale, Giovanni. *A History of Ancient Philosophy: Plato and Aristotle.* Edited and translated by John R. Catan. Albany: State University of New York Press, 1990.

———. *Per una nuova interpretazione di Platone.* 10th ed. Milan: Universita Cattolica del Sacro Cuore, 1991.

Rees, D. A. "Bipartition of the Soul in the Early Academy." *Journal of Hellenic Studies* 47 (1957): 112–18.

Reeve, C. D. C. *Philosopher-Kings: the Argument of Plato's "Republic."* Princeton: Princeton University Press, 1988.

Rist, J. M. *The Mind of Aristotle.* Toronto: 1989.

———. "Pseudo-Dionysius, Neoplatonism, and the Weakness of the Soul." In *From Athens to Chartres: Neoplatonism and Medieval Thought: Studies in Honour of Edouard Jeauneau.* Edited by H. J. Westra, 135–161. Leiden: 1992.

———. "Plato Says That We Have Tripartite Souls. If He Is Right, What Can We Do About It?" In *Chercheurs de sagesse: Hommage à Jean Pepin.* Paris: 1992.

———. "Is Plotinus' Body Too Etherialized?" In *Multarum Artium Scientia: Festschrift for Godfrey Tanner: Prudentia Supplementary Number.* Edited by K. Lee, C. Mackie, and H. Tarrant, 103–117. Auckland: 1993.

Robinson, Richard. *Plato's Earlier Dialectic.* 2d edition. Oxford: Clarendon Press, 1953.

———. *Essays in Greek Philosophy.* Oxford: Clarendon Press, 1969.

———. "Plato's Separation of Reason from Desire." *Phronesis* 16 (1971): 38–48.

Robinson, T. M. "Understanding the *Timaeus.*" *Proceedings of the Boston Area Colloquium in Ancient Philosophy.* Edited by John J. Cleary. New York: University Press of America, 1987.

Rosen, Stanley. *Plato's "Sophist": The Drama of Original and Image.* New Haven: Yale University Press, 1983.

———. Introduction to *Plato's "Symposium."* 2d edition. New Haven: Yale University Press, 1987.

———. *Plato's "Statesman": The Web of Politics.* New Haven: Yale University Press, 1995.

Rosenmeyer, T. "Plato's Hypothesis and the Upward Path." *American Journal of Philosophy* 81 (1960): 393–407.

Ross, Sir David. *Plato's Theory of Ideas.* Oxford: Oxford University Press, 1951.

Ruse, Michael. "Biological Species: Natural Kinds, Individuals, or What?" In *The Units of Evolution.* Edited by Marc Ereshefsky. Cambridge: MIT Press, 1992.

Ryle, G. "Dialectic in the Academy." In *New Essays on Plato and Aristotle.* Edited by R. Bambrough, 39–68. London: 1965.

———. *Plato's Progress.* Cambridge: Cambridge University Press, 1966.

Sachs, David. "A Fallacy in Plato's *Republic.*" *Philosophical Review* 72 (1963): 141–58. Reprinted in *Plato,* Vol. II. Edited by G. Vlastos, 35–51. South Bend: University of Notre Dame Press, 1978.

Salkever, S. "'Lopp'd and Bound': How Liberal Theory Obscures the Goods of Liberal Practices." In *Liberalism and the Good.* Edited by R. B. Douglass, G. M. Mara, and H. S. Richardson. New York: Routledge, Chapman, and Hall, 1990.

———. *Finding the Mean: Theory and Practice in Aristotelian Political Philosophy.* Princeton: Princeton University Press, 1990.

Sandel, M. J. *Justice and the Limits of Liberalism.* Cambridge: Harvard University Press, 1982.

Sayre, Kenneth. *Plato's Late Ontology: A Riddle Resolved.* Princeton: Princeton University Press, 1983.

Scodel, Harvey. *Diaresis and Myth in Plato's "Statesman."* Göttingen: Vandenhoeck and Ruprecht, 1987.

Sekuler, R. and R. Blake. *Perception.* New York: Knopf, 1985.

Shorey, Paul. "A Lost Platonic Joke (*Politicus* 266 D)." *Classical Philology* 12 (1917): 308.

Sidgwick, H. *The Methods of Ethics.* 7th ed. Reprint. Indianapolis: Hackett, 1981.

Snell, B. *The Discovery of the Mind: The Greek Origins of European Thought.* 1953. Translated by T. G. Rosenmeyer. New York: 1960.

Sokol, Robert and Theodore Crevello. "The Biological Species Concept: A Critical Evaluation." In *The Units of Evolution.* Edited by Marc Ereshefsky. Cambridge: MIT Press, 1992.

Sophocles. *Ajax.*

Sprague, R. K. *Plato's Use of Fallacy: A Study of the "Euthydemus" and Some Other Dialogues.* New York: 1962.

Stalley, R. F. "Plato's Argument for the Division of the Reasoning and Appetitive Elements within the Soul." *Phronesis* 20 (1975): 110–28.

Stead, G. Christopher. *Divine Substance.* Oxford and London: Oxford University Press, 1977.

———. *Philosophy in Christian Antiquity.* Cambridge: Cambridge University Press, 1994.

Stenzel, Julius. *Plato's Method of Dialectic.* Translated with introduction by D. J. Allan. 1940. Originally *Studien zur Entwicklung der platonischen Dialektik von Sokrates zu Aristoteles.* 2d ed. Leipzig: 1931.

Stone, I. F. *The Trial of Socrates.* Boston: Little, Brown, 1988.

Strauss, Leo. "On Plato's *Apology of Socrates* and *Crito.*" In *Studies in Platonic Political Philosophy.* Edited by T. L. Pangle. Chicago: University of Chicago Press, 1983.

———. "On the *Euthyphron.*" In *The Rebirth of Classical Political Rationalism: Essays and Lectures by Leo Strauss.* Edited by Thomas Pangle. Chicago: University of Chicago Press, 1989.

Szlezak, T. A. *Platon und die Schriftlichleit der Philosophie: Interpretationen zu den frühen und mittleren Dialogen.* Berlin: Walter de Gruyter, 1985.

Taylor, A. E. *A Commentary on Plato's "Timaeus."* Oxford: 1929.

Teloh, Henry. *The Development of Plato's Metaphysics.* University Park: Pennsylvania University Press, 1981.

Thesleff, H. "Looking for Clues: An Interpretation of Some Literary Aspects of Plato's 'Two-Level Model.'" In *Plato's Dialogues: New Studies and Interpretations.* Edited by G. Press, 17–45. Lanham: 1993.

Thorson, T. L., ed. *Plato: Totalitarian or Democrat?* Englewood Cliffs: Prentice-Hall, 1963.

Turbayne, Colin Murray. *Metaphors for the Mind.* Columbia: University of South Carolina Press, 1991.

Van Ophuijsen, Johannes M. "*oun, ara, dê, toinun*: The Linguistic Articulation of Arguments in Plato's *Phaedo.*" In C. M. J. Sicking and J. M. van Ophuijsen, *Two Studies in Attic Particle Usage: Lysias and Plato.* Leiden: E. J. Brill, 1993.

Veatch, H. *Human Rights: Fact or Fancy?* Baton Rouge: Louisiana State University Press, 1985.

Versenyi, Laszlo G. "Plato and His Liberal Opponents." *Philosophy* 46 (1971): 222–37.

———. *Holiness and Justice: An Interpretation of Plato's "Euthyphro."* New York: University Press of America, 1982.

Vlastos, Gregory. "Creation in the *Timaeus*: Is It a Fiction?" In *Studies in Plato's Metaphysics.* Edited by R. E. Allen, 401–19. London: Routledge, 1965.

———. "The Disorderly Motion in the *Timaeus.*" In *Studies in Plato's Metaphysics.* Edited by R. E. Allen, 379–99. London: Routledge, 1965.

———. "The Third Man Argument in the *Parmenides.*" *Philosophical Review* (1954). Reprinted in *Studies in Plato's Metaphysics.* Edited by R. E. Allen. London: Routledge and Kegan Paul, 1965.

———. "Justice and Psychic Harmony in the *Republic.*" *Journal of Philosophy* 66 (1969): 505–21.

———. "Socrates on Political Obedience and Disobedience." *Yale Review* 63 (1973–74): 517–34.

———. *Plato's Universe.* Seattle: University of Washington Press, 1975.

———. "The Theory of Social Justice in the *Polis* in Plato's *Republic.*" In *Interpretations of Plato.* Edited by H. F. North. Leiden: E. J. Brill, 1977.

———. *Platonic Studies.* 2nd ed. Princeton: Princeton University Press, 1981.

Vlastos, Gregory, ed. *Plato: A Collection of Critical Essays. I: Metaphysics and Epistemology.* Garden City: 1971.

Voigtlander, H.-D. *Der Philosoph und die Vielen.* Wiesbaden: 1980.

von Wilamowitz-Moellendorff, U. *Die Heimkehr des Odysseus.* Berlin: 1927.

Webster, T. B. L. "Personification as a Mode of Greek Thought." *Journal of the Warburg und Courtauld Institutes* 17 (1954): 10–21.

Wedberg, Anders. *Plato's Philosophy of Mathematics.* Stockholm: Almquist and Wiksell, 1955.

West, E. J. M. "Socrates in the *Crito:* Patriot or Friend?" In *Essays in Ancient Greek Philosophy.* Vol. 3: *Plato.* Edited by John Anton and Anthony Preus, 71–83. Albany: 1989.

West, Thomas and Grace, trans. *Euthyphro.* In *Four Texts on Socrates.* Ithaca: Cornell University Press, 1984.

Whitaker, Robert H. "The *Timaeus* as a Basis for Plato's Ethics." *Philosophical Forum* 1 (1943): 19–23.

Whitehead, Alfred North. *Process and Reality: An Essay in Cosmology.* Revised edition. Edited by D. R. Griffin and D. W. Sherburne. New York: Free Press, 1978.

Williams, B. "The Analogy of City and Soul in Plato's *Republic.*" In *Phronesis* suppl. vol. 1 (1973): 196–206.

———. *Ethics and the Limits of Philosophy.* Cambridge: Harvard University Press, 1985.

———. *Shame and Necessity.* Berkeley and Los Angeles: University of California Press, 1993.

Woods, M. "Plato's Division of the Soul." *Proceedings of the British Academy* 73 (1987): 23–47.

Wright, Crispin. *Truth and Objectivity.* Cambridge: Harvard University Press, 1992.

Young, G. "Socrates and Obedience." *Phronesis* 19 (1974): 1–29.

Zahn, T. *Zum Wortfeld "Seele-Geist" in der Sprache Homers.* Munich: 1987.

General Index

ABBREVIATIONS

adj.	adjective
def.	defined, definition(s)
dist.	distinguished from, (as) distinct from, distinction
f., ff.	(and) following
n	note
non-t.	non-technical use
opp.	(as) opposed to, opposite of, opposition

Index Locorum